MY LIVES

MY LIVES

EDMUND WHITE

HarperCollins books may be purchased for educational, business, or sales promotional use. For information, please write: Special Markets Department, HarperCollins Publishers, 10 East 53rd Street, New York, NY 10022.

Portions of this book have appeared in different form in *The New Yorker, McSweeney's, Granta, Boulevard,* and *Ontario Review.*

First published in Great Britain in 2005 by Bloomsbury Publishing Plc.

Printed on acid-free paper

Library of Congress Cataloging-in-Publication Data
White, Edmund.
 My lives / Edmund White.—1st U.S. ed.
  p. cm.
 ISBN-10: 0-06-621397-5
 ISBN-13: 978-0-06-621397-2
 1. White, Edmund, 1940– 2. Novelists, American—20th century—Biography.
 3. Biographers—United States—Biography. 4. Gay men—United States—
 Biography. I. Title.

 PS3573.H463Z47 2006
 813'.54—dc22
 [B]   2005049506

06 07 08 09 10 OFF/ RRD 10 9 8 7 6 5 4 3

To J. D. McClatchy

Contents

Edmund at age two

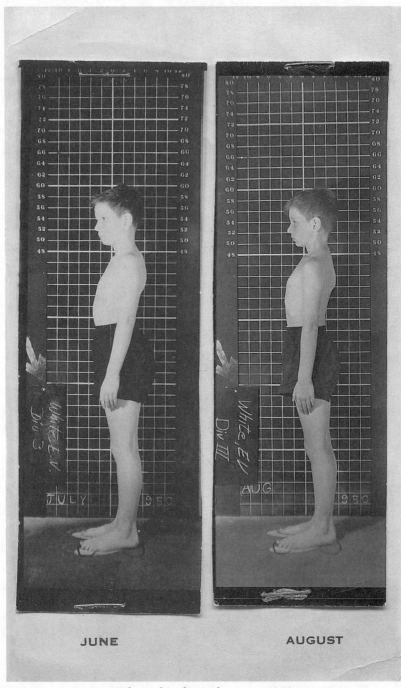

JUNE   AUGUST

Edmund's physical report, 1950

My Shrinks

In the mid-1950s, when I was fourteen or fifteen, I told my mother I was homosexual: that was the word, back then, *homosexual*, in its full satanic majesty, cloaked in ether fumes, a combination of evil and sickness.

Of course I'd learned the word from her. She was a psychologist. Throughout my early childhood, she'd been studying part-time for a master's degree in child psychology. Since I was not only her son but also her best friend, she confided everything she was learning about me – her live-in guinea pig – to me. For instance, I was enrolled in an 'experimental' kindergarten run by Dr. Arlett, my mother's mentor in the department of child psychology at the University of Cincinnati. Dr. Arlett, however, decided after just one semester that I was 'too altruistic' to continue in the school. I was dismissed. I suspect that she meant I was weirdly responsive to the moods of the female teachers-in-training, for whom I manifested a sugary, fake concern, just as I'd learned to do with my mother. No doubt I was judged to be an unhealthy influence on the other kids. But my mother, who chose against all evidence to interpret my vices as virtues, my defeats as victories, decided that what Dr. Arlett really meant was that I was too advanced spiritually, too mature, to hang back in the shallows with my coevals.

My reward was a return to loneliness. We lived at the end of a lane in a small, rented Tudor house. My older sister, who disliked me, was attending Miss Daugherty's School for Girls; she sometimes brought friends home, but she didn't let them play with me. I played alone – or talked to my mother when she wasn't at school or studying.

My mother was intensely spiritual; at least she spoke often of her inner life and said she prayed, though I never saw her pray. She'd been brought up a Baptist in Texas, but she'd converted to Christian Science, initially to please my father but later out of a genuine affinity with the thinking of Mary Baker Eddy. Like Mrs. Eddy, my mother denied the existence of evil (except as it was embodied by my father's mistress) and believed in thinking mightily positive thoughts. She had a pantheistic, nearly Hindu conviction that every living creature was sacred and God a wave cresting out of, then dissolving back into, Universal Mind. When my mother was distraught, which occurred on a daily basis, she found consolation in bourbon and Eddy's *Science and Health* and *Key to the Scriptures*. My mother dismissed Mrs. Eddy's hostility to medicine as an ideal beyond our grasp given our current state of imperfect evolution.

She also detected signs in me of a great soul and highly advanced spirituality.

When I was seven my parents divorced. It was a good thing Mom had taken that degree in psychology because now, at age forty-five, she had to go to work to supplement her meager alimony. She labored long hours for low pay as a state psychologist in Illinois and Texas, and later in Illinois again, administering IQ tests to hundreds of grade-school students and even 'projective' tests (the Rorschach, the House-Tree-Person) to children suspected of being 'disturbed.'

True to my status as guinea pig, I was tested frequently. She who was so often overwrought at home, given to rages or fits of weeping, would become strangely calm and professional when administering a test. Her hands would make smoothing gestures, as though the lamplit table between us were that very sea of mind that needed to be stilled back into universality. Her voice was lowered and given a storytelling sweetness ('Now, Eddie, could you tell me everything you see in this inkblot?'). I, too, was transformed when tested, but toward anxiety, since a psychological test was like an X-ray or a blood test, likely to reveal a lurking disease: hostility, perversion or craziness or, even worse, a low intelligence.

I must have been eight when my mother gave me my first

Rorschach, for it was during our last summer at our big, rambling vacation house on Mullet Lake, Michigan, which our newly imposed poverty made her sell for the disappointing sum of fourteen thousand dollars. I think she wanted to impress me, or herself, with how well she could separate out the scientific precision of administering a professional test from the messy, emotional squalor of our everyday life.

She wrote down everything I saw in each plate and exactly where in each inkblot I detected a tomb or a diamond. She then went off for a few hours and consulted her thick dark-blue-bound manual of interpretation with its burgundy label. I was afraid of the results, as absolute and inarguable in their objectivity as they were mysterious in their encoding and decoding.

My mother was nearly gleeful when she told me I was a 'borderline psychotic' with 'strong schizophrenic tendencies.' Apparently the most telling sign of my insanity was my failure to see anything human in the inkblots. All I saw were jewels and headstones.

What remained unclear was whether I was inevitably sliding over the frontier toward full-blown psychosis or whether the process was reversible. Did the Rorschach lay bare my essence or my becoming? Was I becoming better or worse?

In fourth grade, no matter how mentally ill I might have been, I continued to get good grades in every subject except arithmetic (we moved too often for me to be able to follow a coherent sequence of math courses). Perhaps the only public sign of craziness was my obsession with playing a king on stage. In third grade, in Dallas, I wrote and starred in *The Blue Bird*, a script I'd plagiarized from Maeterlinck (my first piece of writing was a plagiarism). My mother rented a gold, bejeweled crown, a blue velvet doublet and white knee breeches from a costume shop.

When I was eleven, we lived for a year in the Faust Hotel in Rockford, Illinois, a grim industrial town where my mother worked as a state psychologist. For some reason she decided that the local state schools were good enough for my sister but not for me, a decision my sister bitterly resented. I was sent to Keith Country Day, where the classes were small – no more than fourteen students. One of my friends was Arnold Rheingold, perhaps the first Jew I'd ever met. His father was a psychiatrist. When I dined at

Arnold's house I was impressed by the deference paid to their son by his parents just because he was a boy. And I was awed by the father, the first man I'd ever met who read books and sought out new ideas rather than preaching familiar ones. That he had migraines and had to nurse them in his darkened study after dinner struck me as the possible and certainly glamorous price he had to pay for living the life of the mind.

A while later I wrote a play, *The Death of Hector*, in which I starred as the tragic hero; my best friend, a handsome jock, played the nearly silent, sadistic role of Achilles, who killed me and then, in a radical departure from classical tradition, mourned me with noisy, wordless wailing before, rather illogically, setting off to desecrate my corpse by dragging it around the walls of Troy behind his chariot (offstage action seen and reported by a leaden, talentless Chorus, a chubby girl I knew and liked). It was a headily passionate range of emotions to assign to my blond, vacant-eyed Achilles who, in real life, seemed mainly baffled by me to the point of sheepishness. I could make him hang his beautiful, blond head and blush.

When I played with my two girl cousins in Texas or later with friends in Ohio or Illinois, I always had a single game in mind: king and slave. Like Jean Genet's lunatic servants in *The Maids*, I didn't much care which role I played so long as the drama of domination and submission got properly performed. There wasn't much to this pathetically static 'game' beyond procession and coronation for the king and bowing or even kneeling for the slaves. When my cousins Sue and Jean started giggling and became distracted, I redubbed them queens and ordered them to make the solemn entrance. I bowed obsequiously with a grand salaam designed as a silent reproach to their insufficient servitude. I hoped they'd catch on, though they could never quite grasp the grandeur of the ceremony.

In sixth grade in Evanston, Illinois, I played a weak, nearly hysterical King Charles to a tomboyish Saint Joan, acted by my pal Anne Miner who had a thrillingly husky voice and a forthright, big-sister manner that would have served her even better as Wendy in *Peter Pan*.

That summer, at Camp Towering Pines near Racine, Wisconsin, I wrote and starred in my version of *Boris Godunov*; I was imperially robed in the stiff red wool blanket from the Hudson

Bay Company that my mother had bought to keep me warm on chilly northern summer nights. I conflated the coronation scene and the mad scene.

The formula emerges: I wanted to be a king, but I also needed to die, go mad or undergo humiliation for my arrogance, a scenario that resembled the plots of queer novels of the 1950s, though I'd never read one. (The only homosexual narrative I knew of was the life of Nijinsky who, to be sure, had devolved into madness and silence. My mother, who perhaps both feared and hoped for a strange destiny for me, had given me his biography when I was nine or ten.)

Teachers and camp counselors, when I campaigned for yet another royal tragedy starring me, exchanged weary glances over my head – and over my mother's (she was just five feet tall). But Mom was blissfully unaware of any rain on my procession. When one mother said that her son was naturally less talented than I because *he* had never received any professional training as an actor, my mother shouted, 'Neither has Eddie! He is *absolutely* untrained!' As if no better encomium were needed.

That same summer at camp, the summer of *Boris Godunov* (in which I clutched at my blanket and staggered before the ghost of the tsarevich I'd murdered while Kremlin bells tolled and Ivan Kipnis half-sang and half-intoned the Mussorgsky monologue), I had my first sexual experience, or rather tasted the first penis that wasn't my own. I put the matter so precisely because before then I'd wrestled for hours and hours with friends in Evanston, Illinois, where we lived when I was eleven and twelve, and while alone I'd actually managed to lick my own penis by lying nude on my back and throwing my legs over my head in the first stage of a backward somersault. By craning my neck upwards off the mattress and pulling my pelvis down with my hands I could just graze the glans with the tip of my tongue and catch one clear drop of liquid as sticky, if not as sweet, as the nectar I liked to work up the honeysuckle blossom. Once I'd drunk long and hard at a big, smelly, teenage cock there at camp I no longer needed to tread the boards as a suicidal monarch. I stopped conspiring to bend everyone to my need to rule or serve; I discovered that I was happiest while serving, and serving under someone else's scepter.

Happy? That's not the word.

Predestined and agonized. Abject. Bewitched. Perhaps that's closer.

I'd read in one of my mother's psychological manuals a long entry on homosexuality that I could scarcely understand. But I did understand that, whereas adult homosexuality was an entrenched ego disorder caused by an unresolved Oedipus Complex resulting in secondary narcissistic gains that were especially hard to uproot, in every early adolescence the individual, the *boy*, passes through a homosexual *stage* that is perfectly normal, a brief swirl around the Scylla of orality and the Charybdis of anality before surging to the sunny open seas of mature heterosexual genitality. I could only hope that I was just passing through a phase.

I was afire with sexual longing and looked for partners everywhere. The same maniacal energy I'd devoted to playing a succession of dying kings right out of *The Golden Bough* I now consecrated to scoring. I haunted the toilets at the Howard Street elevated station, the one that marked the frontier between Chicago and Evanston. A few men let me touch them and twice a man drove me in a car full of children's toys down to the beach. I wasn't ugly but I was jailbait, and life even for a part-time homosexual was hard enough during the Eisenhower years.

Betraying my partners was something I felt drawn to. At Camp Towering Pines I'd let an older boy 'hypnotize' me and press my mouth down on his penis, but I couldn't resist informing my mother, nominally the camp psychologist, of what he'd 'attempted.' Did I hope to shift the blame for unhealthy desires and practices onto someone else? Or did I merely hope to stir up trouble, create a drama? Or was I trying to draw my mother's attention to behavior I was horrified by the moment after I'd ejaculated? Or was I angry with these young men for not loving me as much as they desired me? If they loved me they would have attempted to run away with me, wouldn't they? Love was what I wanted, though I don't think I could have been loved any more than a porcupine can be embraced.

My mother sent me to a Freudian psychiatrist in Evanston for an evaluation. I had just read Oscar Wilde and was determined to be as brittle and brilliant as his characters. I sat on the edge of my chair, hectic red flowers blowing in my cheeks, and rattled on and on about my condition, my illness, which I was no more able to defend than Wilde. All he or I had to offer was defiance and a dandified insolence. If we were pinned down by a prosecutor or an examining psychiatrist, what could we say – that homosexuality was defensible? Neither of us was *that* clever; no one could escape his particular moment in history, especially since I, as an American living during the tranquilized 1950s, scarcely believed in history at all. For us nature had replaced history. What I was doing was against nature, anti-physical.

The psychiatrist told my mother that I was 'unsalvageable.' That I should be locked up and the key thrown away. My mother promptly reported this harsh, scary judgment to me, and to my father, though I begged her not to. Of course neither she nor I was capable of dismissing this diagnosis as a dangerously narrow-minded prejudice held by a banal little suburbanite in a brown suit. No, it came from a doctor and was as unquestionable as a diagnosis of diabetes or cancer. The man's level of sophistication or humanity was irrelevant.

My mother had a younger friend named Johanna Tabin who had studied with Anna Freud in London and was now practicing as a psychoanalyst in Glencoe. We occasionally spent social evenings with her and her husband and two sons in their big suburban house or at our much smaller apartment beside the lake. They represented everything we aspired toward – wealth and calm intelligence and respectability, social and professional importance and family love. Johanna's husband, Julius, had been a nuclear physicist and had become a patent lawyer for nuclear inventions.

Johanna's sons, a few years younger than my sister and I, were treated with elaborate respect by their mother. Whenever they would ask her a question or say something to her, she would immediately turn her attention to them, even if she was on the phone listening to my mother. This indulgence was very unhealthy, my mother decided, and she resented it as much as she disapproved of it. But Johanna was intractable. The second there was a treble squeak in the background, she'd put the receiver aside and say, 'Yes, darling, I'm listening. What is it, darling?' She analyzed their dreams and games with an equal attentiveness. I remember when

Geoffrey, the younger son, kept singing a song he'd made up about a tumbleweed, she'd decided that he was the little tumbleweed who made the big horse, his father, rear back in fright – a perfectly normal desire to intimidate the patriarch, she said with a happy smile.

Rather mournfully, I thought my mother was too self-absorbed ever to have interpreted my behaviour so ingeniously, and if she'd managed to detect a sign of defiance in me she would have squelched it rather than nourished it. Now I can see that she was all alone in the world, poor and overworked and profoundly wounded by my father's rejection. Even though she called us the Three Musketeers, we were in fact painfully divided each from the other. My sister was convinced that our mother and I were shamefully bizarre. She herself was unpopular and withdrawn. I was obviously a freak. Only when my mother was administering a test or diagnosing a child did she feel calm and whole and professional.

She must have been jealous of Johanna's happy marriage, because she was always picking up hints of its imminent collapse. 'Poor Johanna,' she'd say. 'The poor little thing is terribly neglected by Julius. It's only a matter of days before he abandons her.'

Despite these dire predictions, Johanna's marriage continued to flourish stubbornly, her career to become more and more distinguished, her husband more and more successful, her sons increasingly brilliant. 'Poor Johanna,' Mother crooned. 'She buries herself in her work because she's so unhappy in her marriage.'

The only thing that amazed me was that Johanna remained so attached to my mother. Did my mother possess undetectable attractions? In a similar way I'd been disconcerted when I'd read my mother's thesis on the religious experiences of children and discovered in it so many big words I didn't know and had never heard my mother pronounce.

One evening at Johanna's, I talked to her about my homosexuality. I don't remember how the subject arose. Had my mother already set it up? All I remember was that we were seated briefly on the glassed-in sunporch just two steps down from the more brightly lit living room. Dinner was over. Johanna kept casting sunny smiles back at her boys, who were out of earshot and racing around the couch, but when she returned her attention to me she lowered her big sad eyes behind the pale, blue-rimmed glasses and a delicate frown-line was traced across her pure brow. She wore no makeup beyond a faintly pink lipstick. She didn't really follow fashion and was content to appear neat. My mother, who got herself up as elaborately as an *onnagata* in the Kabuki, thoroughly disapproved. Johanna scrunched forward and rested her chin on her palm. She was as lithe as a girl. She had beautiful teeth (her mother was a dentist).

'I'm very worried,' I said. 'I don't seem to be moving out of the normal homosexual stage of development.' I was fifteen.

'Yes, dear,' she said, 'I can feel you're very concerned.' She had a way of reflecting through restatement what her interlocutor had just said, a technique ascribed to Carl Rogers that my mother found insulting and maddeningly condescending but that I liked because it seemed so focused and nonjudgmental. Johanna's life was so manifestly a success that I was happy to bask for an instant in her attention.

'Do you think I should see a therapist?'

She studied my face with her huge, sympathetic eyes and said nothing.

'Could I see *you?*' I asked. I knew that she received many patients a day in the soundproof office in the basement. My mother had also told me that Johanna had cured a lesbian who was now happily married to a New York writer.

'Have you,' she asked with a tentativeness that suggested a sensitivity in me I was far from enjoying, 'have you, dear, ever actually . . .'

'Had sex?' I asked brightly. 'Oh, yes, many times.' For an instant I was proud of my experience, until I saw my admission shocked and saddened her.

'I had no idea,' she said, shaking her head as if it suddenly weighed much much more, 'that you'd actually gone on to *act out*, to act on your impulses.' She looked mournful. Whereas Christianity had taught me that the thought was as bad as the deed, Johanna seemed to think 'acting out' was worse than merely desiring. By realizing my fantasies I'd – what? Made them harder to root out? Coarsened myself?

'You thought I just had a few fantasies?' I was almost insulted, certainly amused, although I could also see I should downplay the extent of my debauchery if I didn't want to break her heart.

She peered deeply into my eyes, perhaps searching for some reassuring sign of remorse, or the pain I must undoubtedly be feeling. She shook herself free of her thoughts and said, 'I'm afraid I can't see you as a patient, dear, since we're all such friends. But I *can* recommend someone who . . .' Here she put her words together carefully: '. . . who might help you find your way toward a life that would fully express *you*, who you really are.'

With a brilliant flash of lightning over the dark landscape of my personality, I suddenly saw that homosexuality, far from being saturnine or interestingly artistic, was in fact a lack, an emptiness, a deformity preventing a full and happy development.

Already I hoped to be writer but, as I was beginning to realize, successful writing entailed a grasp of universal values and eternal truths, which were necessarily heterosexual. Foolishly I had imagined I could transform the dross of homosexuality into the gold of art, but now I saw I could never be a great artist if I remained ignorant of the classical verities of marriage and child-rearing, adultery and divorce. But if psychoanalysis could convert me into a heterosexual, might it not at the same time ablate the very neurosis that made me want to write? Should I tamper with my neurosis?

I began to read books about psychoanalysis – Freud himself, especially *A General Introduction to Psychoanalysis* and *The Interpretation of Dreams*, but also the softer, less pessimistic American adaptations of his thought by Erich Fromm. I learned that making art was an act of neurotic compensation and sublimation – although Theodor Reik made his unorthodox mark by arguing that art was the highest form of mental health. I couldn't find much about homosexuality in any book, but found enough to know it was sterile, inauthentic, endlessly repetitious and infantile.

Somewhere I came across the theory that homosexuality was caused by an absent father and a suffocating mother. Perhaps my mother had been the one to suggest that my father's absence had queered me, for she was always eager to work out the multiple ways in which his desertion had harmed us all. She was eager to remarry – to bring me the benefits of a suitable father figure – but no man was willing to take on the burden. I was sent to live with my father for one year in Cincinnati, but he ignored me.

When I realized that I wasn't getting any better, that I was just as obsessed with men as ever, I begged my parents to enroll me in a boys' boarding school. My reasoning was that if I was homosexual because I was suffocated by my mother and deprived of male models, then a tough, nearly military school would be sure to shape me up. Reluctantly they complied, but after a year away from home, when I realized I was more besotted with boys than ever, I asked my father to send me to a shrink.

I had one all picked out. Half the students at my school, Cranbrook, outside Detroit, Michigan, were day boys and half were boarders. We boarding students were occasionally allowed to spend a weekend with a day boy's family if we got written permission from our parents. I was invited home by Stephen Schwartz. His family played classical music (the Mozart Clarinet Concerto, Bach's cantatas) on a stereo that was piped into every room of the compact wood house which, to my eyes, looked half-Hopi, half-Japanese. He was a shaggy-haired mouth-breather, arty and intelligent, who was neither scandalized by, nor interested in, my perversion. He liked to write and knew a lot about jazz; he was neither a grade-grubber nor an athlete, the only two admissible types at Cranbrook. He had a crazy sense of humor. All the grim striving of his fellow students and the severity of our anti-intellectual, martinet masters only made him laugh. We worked together on the student literary magazine, to which he contributed satires.

His father was a psychiatrist who recommended me to James Clark Moloney. I made an appointment with Moloney and my mother wrote a note granting me permission to take a taxi to his office in Birmingham, the nearest large suburb.

My father was reluctant to take on the expense of regular psychiatric fees, which amounted to fifty dollars an hour at a time when a good dinner at a restaurant cost five dollars, for instance, and a general practitioner charged only ten dollars a visit. Someone wealthy at that time earned seventy or eighty thousand dollars a year. Dr. Moloney wanted to see me three times a week, which came to six hundred dollars a month, a sum that exceeded my mother's alimony by a hundred dollars.

My father also objected just as strenuously to the notion of psychoanalysis, which he saw as a form of soak-the-rich charlatanism, an ineffectual and dangerously self-indulgent stewing over problems engendered by idleness and entrenched through the principle of the more you scratch the more it itches. As a good businessman he made me put all my arguments for psychoanalysis in clear, terse letters, which he countered in short missives printed in his neat hand on stationery that read 'From the desk of E. V. White.' He addressed me as 'Dear Ed V.' (I was Edmund Valentine White III.) I wrote to him explicitly about my unsuccessful struggle against homosexuality and about the smothering-mother, absent-father etiology, intended as an indirect reproach against him.

My father's conviction that mental problems could be cured through willpower and self-discipline seemed designed to fail before the tenacity of sexual orientation. I *wanted* to be heterosexual. Who could want to be sinful, abnormal, sick, criminal, a prey to blackmailers and a pariah in every area of public life? What writer would want to duck aside from all the crucial rites of passage? But the will felt defenseless when confronted by its own stronger desires. It was as if a plant were asked not to flower. Even the Japanese could succeed only in stunting, not in eradicating, blossoms.

I had no idea what to expect at Dr. Moloney's, but I certainly thought he'd be a small man with a varnished pate and an inky comb-over, many books (some in German) and in his waiting room the smell of old tobacco and grief. I was in no way prepared for the cages of shrieking birds, the Papuan deities and, in the garden as seen through a plate-glass window, a gilt statue of a meditating bodhisattva. I fancied myself a Buddhist but of the austere Theravada sort, and I sniffed at Dr. Moloney's idolatry, even though I'd come here precisely because I sought a compassionate intercessor, a bodhisattva of my own.

He didn't have a secretary. Another patient let me in and we sat uncomfortably staring at each other, rigid with sibling rivalry. At last Moloney stumbled out, escorting a sniffling little woman. He appeared surprised that he'd double-booked his next hour.

'Don't worry,' he said to me. 'There are enough teats to suckle the whole litter.' He chuckled, revealing neatly spaced teeth in a handsome red face. He cocked an eye at me.

He had a leonine mane of white hair, a bulbous nose with a sore on one side, close to the tip, which he kept vaguely clawing at, as an old dog will halfheartedly try to free itself of its collar. He wore sandals on big, yellow-nailed feet, shapeless trousers held up with a rope, a short-sleeved Hawaiian shirt. He licked his lips constantly. He made me feel very prim, especially since I'd put on my favorite Brooks Brothers sack suit with the brown and black twill. I didn't like the idea that he'd already decided I was a famished pup before I'd said even a word.

He decided to see the other patient first, though not for a full hour, he explained, but more for a patch-up. As I sat in the waiting room I could hear the drone of the patient's voice and the grunt of the doctor's. I couldn't hear words, just the rhythm and intonation of their voices, but the mere possibility of eavesdropping frightened and attracted me.

Moloney had but one master theory and he proposed it to everyone as an answer to every ill. He believed in the introjected mother. Every infant has the right to expect and enjoy unconditional love from his mother, at full throttle and all the time. Modern American women, however, are deformed by societal inhibitions and their own deprivations as children, incapable of giving complete, nourishing love. When I told Dr. Moloney that my mother hadn't breast-fed me because she had inverted nipples, he slapped his knees, let out a great cry and leapt to his feet. 'You see!'

The emotionally starved, alienated child decides to mother himself. He incorporates into his inner pantheon the faint, elusive image of his mother's face and warmth. No longer dependent on her vagaries, caprices and eclipses, he can beam her up whenever he needs her. If he sucks his thumb he is nursing himself. He has become a closed circuit – with only one crucial disadvantage: such total independence is virtually synonymous with madness. He has lost all vital connection to the outside world. He's self-sufficient, but at a terrible price. When he thinks he has fallen in love with a real woman, in point of fact all he's done is to project his mother's imago onto a neutral screen. He is enamored of half of his inner cast of characters. Since he's not relating to a real person in all her shifting specificity but instead to the crude, fixed outlines of the introjected mother, he cannot interact with the flesh-and-blood woman. If she should break through his defenses by smiling her real smile, breathing her real breath on his cheek, he will panic and break it off. As an infant he learned how dangerous it was to open up to an actual, autonomous Other.

I was taught all this during my very first hour with Dr. Moloney – or rather my first ninety minutes, since he was eager to prove to me he was not like one of those goddam tight-ass Freudians with their finicky, fucking fifty-minute hours. He also needed to lay out his entire theory during our first encounter so that it could begin to sink in.

As I learned in session after session, Dr. Moloney had served in the Pacific as an army doctor. In Okinawa, he observed that infants were fearless and happy because they never left their mother's side; they were carried everywhere, papoose-style, bound to their mother's back, their heads looking out *above* hers – 'That way they feel united to her but in charge.' Once I saw an elegant young father on the streets of Birmingham, a baby peering out at the world from his back, and I recognized one of Dr. Moloney's Michigan Okinawans.

Moloney gave me his books to read and even one of his manuscripts to improve. 'Don't think I'm a castrating asshole like your father, an anal perfectionist who can't admit that another man can help him. I need all the help I can get.' He loved to insult my parents, whom he'd never met and who were not at all the straw men he'd set up. They were as eccentric as he – impoverished rural Texans unprepared for the world they'd created for themselves by earning money and moving North. Moloney cursed them for being uptight patricians, unfeeling aristocrats, but in fact they were self-made crazy people, all too full of dangerous feelings. I would never sink to the indignity of going into Moloney's backyard and hacking away at the logs he painted with the words 'Mom' and 'Dad.'

Yet Moloney was warm, an easygoing bohemian with ethnographic interests who believed he could give me the unconditional love that he thought I craved and that his version of my mother had denied me. He would often interrupt me to say, 'I love you, goddam it.' His eyes would fill with tears and he'd idly pick at

14

his infected nose, or claw at the sore on his forehead from above, fat fingers stretching down, his elbow cocked to the ceiling. But on some days he had to search for my name.

As best I could figure out, he'd had a more conventional past, reflected in his first, unimpeachably Freudian book, but now he'd become cracked over the introjected mother and the Okinawan papoose cure. He wore heavy turquoise and silver bracelets, black amulets on his hairy chest, and lived surrounded by bobbing, chiming deities from the Pacific, Asia and Africa (Freud himself had inaugurated this taste for carved primitive statues, as photos of his Vienna *cabinet* revealed).

The other Freudian remnant was the couch. After a few intimidating sessions in a chair I was graduated to the couch, while out of sight behind me, at a desk, Moloney took notes (or wrote something, perhaps one of his pamphlets). I could hear him back there coughing or rummaging around for something or scratching with his pen. More than once I caught him dozing. That he was asleep changed his preceding silence in my eyes from a sharp, therapeutic instrument into an obtuse abnegation. I bored him. This man who claimed to love me was zoning out on me. 'I know what you're thinking!' he shouted. 'You're probably mad as hell. And you have a right to be. You have a right to unqualified love. No time limits, no lapses, eternal, unqualified love. But even Homer nods. The baby squalls, and he's completely in his rights. If I were perfect – and you deserve perfection, it's your birthright –' Here he broke off, confused, and began scratching his nose.

When Johanna asked me during Christmas vacation how things were going, I said, 'I'm very disappointed. He's a nice man. But he doesn't remember anything about me and each time I mention a friend I have to situate that person all over again.'

'Surely you're exaggerating—'

'Not at all. He's not really interested in the details of my life. Or my life. I don't think he likes men. Or they don't catch his interest. He constantly accuses me of over-intellectualizing, although he's happy enough to exploit my proofreading skills.'

Over-intellectualizing was considered one of my most serious defenses. If I disagreed with one of Moloney's interpretations he'd laugh, show his small white teeth and say, 'If you go on winning every argument this way you'll soon enough lose every chance at happiness. No one around here doubts your intelligence. It's just that I want you to break out of your closed circuit and touch another living human being, goddam it. Come on, take a chance on life –' He groped for my name before sketching in a feeble gesture that ended in a shrug. I learned to question all my impulses, to second-guess my motives, to ascribe a devious unconscious purpose to my most unobjectionable actions. If I had a dream about making love to Marilyn Monroe, Moloney would interpret it as a 'flight into health,' a ruse I'd invented to throw him off my track by appearing normal, cured. 'In this dream I'm Marilyn Monroe,' he'd say, perfectly seriously. 'Like her I have long hair, a wide mouth, I'm voluptuously put together.'

Now I'd say the worst consequence of my years in psychoanalysis was the way it undermined my instincts. Self-doubt, which is a cousin to self-hatred, became my constant companion. If today I have so few convictions and conceive of myself as merely an anthology of opinions, interchangeable and equally valid, I owe this uncertainty to psychoanalysis. Fiction is my ideal form because a character, even a stand-in for me, occupies a dramatic moment, wants one thing rather than another, serves the master narration. The novel is a story rather than an assertion, a development in time rather than a statement in the eternal present of truth. Fiction suggests that no one is ever disinterested. It does not ask the author to adjudicate among his characters. It is the ultimate arena of situationist ethics.

I saw Moloney three times a week during my last two years at boarding school. I discovered that one of my favorite teachers was also a patient; we met in the waiting room. Though the teacher looked uneasy, as if unmasked, he soon shrugged it off and if one of our appointments happened to coincide with the other he'd drive me in. He was a reserved man, probably not more than six years older than I, twenty-three to my seventeen, but at that age such a gap is unbridgeable. I always wondered what was his 'presenting symptom,' but I never found out about anything beyond his inability to 'commit.' He'd broken off several engagements to marry. Problems such as frigidity, however, were never treated as the thing itself; what needed to be treated was some mysterious, underlying neurosis.

I could never get Moloney to concentrate on my homosexuality, for it, too, was just a symptom. 'You'll see, old boy,' he'd assure me, moving heavily but serenely like a shaggy, friendly St. Bernard padding in for his daily ration of strokes, 'once we clear away the psychic underbrush all that will wither away.' He made my homosexuality sound like the state in the socialist future. He wasn't even very interested in my sexual adventures at school and elsewhere, though he warned me that 'excessive acting out' would make me less sensitive to treatment. Just as the term *over-intellectualizing* called into doubt my mental faculties, so *acting out* suggested that each sexual encounter with another man could be reduced to every other, all of them a childish and annoying, if not very serious, automatism. Nothing could come of acting out beyond a further pointless delay in the treatment process. If I entered into detail about my love for a teacher or my sexual bribery of a football star, he'd wave his hand as if brushing cobwebs out of his face and say, 'Spare me, spare me.' When I asked him if smoking marijuana was dangerous, he assured me it led directly to heroin addiction. He advised me to report a teacher who was 'turning on' the boys (and who also let me suck his cock). I always regretted squealing on that teacher, though no doubt my penchant toward betraying my sex partners would have sufficed even without Moloney's counsel.

The only moment when Moloney would truly pay attention to me was when I reported a dream to him. To remember a dream I had to write it down right away. On Sundays, when we were allowed to sleep in an extra hour, till eight, I had the greatest likelihood of awakening slowly, not to a bell, and of recalling the last episode or two of a dream.

Moloney was Freudian, I suppose, in believing that a dream was 'the royal road to the unconscious,' although he had a different system of interpretation, more Jungian in that it traced the ponderous movements of an endlessly proliferating tribe of archetypes. Now I agree with an Italian doctor friend who ascribes the primacy of dreams in Freud's system to the Viennese habit of eating cheese after dinner, and who says, 'Cheese produces excessive neural transmitters; dreams are the downshifting of the brain's gears.'

Like Freud, Moloney felt that one of the analyst's main tools is picking through the transference. Freud, however, insists that the patient must know nothing concrete about the analyst, so that it will be clear even to him that he has invented everything and *attributed* it to the doctor. In the classic Freudian transference, the *analysand* re-creates with his analyst his damaging relationship with his parents; when he recognizes that the doctor has done nothing at all to justify such wrath, resentment or fear, he is forced to admit (and abandon) his habit of endlessly 'projecting' bad motives and harmful feelings onto everyone around him. With Moloney, however, the experiment was compromised because ours wasn't a laboratory-pure isolate. Because he constantly chattered about himself I did know a lot about him, which I had the right to interpret as I saw fit. He might say, 'Stop projecting!' but only his authority lent credibility to such an objection.

He was my first shrink, I had nothing to compare him to and he was my only chance of becoming a heterosexual, of ending the terrible suffering I was enduring as an outcast. He told me so himself; he was certain he was the only qualified doctor around. I contemplated suicide more than once. Never had I met or read anyone who defended homosexuality, although the Kinsey Report had recently done so (I just didn't happen to know anything about it, since copies were kept out of kids' hands).

But even if someone had tried to refute my horror of homo-sexuality I would have instantly rejected his insinuating proposals, tempting me to settle for second best. I *knew* that only the most insulting pity and condescension could lead someone to recom-mend that I surrender to my disease.

Moloney convinced me that I should not go away for school (I had been accepted to Harvard) but should attend a nearby state university so that I could continue my sessions with him. All other psychoanalysts were frauds – money-grubbing impostors or un-feeling, straitlaced Freudians. Only he could help people – that's why he kept taking on more and more patients. He had close to fifty now and was seeing them from six in the morning till mid-night, seven days a week. To stay awake he was swallowing handfuls of Dexedrine and then coming down in the evening with constant swigs of bourbon.

I'd drive every week the thirty-five miles from Ann Arbor into Detroit in a borrowed car. I'd have the eleven p.m. hour, when Moloney was smiley and drunk, then I'd sleep on the analytic couch and awaken him, with great difficulty, for the six a.m. session. I'd have to blast him out of bed by playing his favorite record, 'There Is Nothing Like a Dame.'

His own life was beginning to come apart, he told me. He'd fallen in love with a patient who was seriously ill and he'd left his wife for her. But then, when his wife was diagnosed with a terminal illness, he'd gone back to her. Now his wife was dead and the patient was in a mental hospital.

Moloney seemed more and more disoriented. He was often confused, and no longer just the overworked, sometimes indifferent, frequently forgetful doctor, but someone who was obviously lost. He'd aged quickly. He forgot to shave and sometimes he smelled of hangover. His hands trembled and he no longer took notes. His old bravado still hung from him in rags, as if he were a scarecrow in a field the farmer had let go fallow.

I was bitter because I saw I had sacrificed my academic career to him, to the forsaken prospect of being cured. And at the same time I felt a deep affection for him, because he was vulnerable and hurt. I discovered that despite his medical training and his years of psychoanalytic experience, he was sure that there was nothing in a male homosexual that couldn't be straightened out by a good woman – or even just a woman. He introduced me to Suzie, another patient, my first anorexic, a tall redhead who wanted to be a model and who, when periodically hospitalized and force-fed, would run up and down the stairs to wear off the disfiguring ounce she might have regained. She had eyes that crossed interestingly and an overlapping incisor always smeared with lipstick. Her teeth were brown from her obsessional vomiting. She wore such high heels, such chic clothes and so much makeup that she appeared years older – a real lady rather than a companionable girl. Wherever I went with her she threw herself at my male friends: a 'nympho.'

During the summer between my freshman and sophomore years at college I saw Johanna again and told her everything. She smiled and said, 'Far be it from me, darling, to criticize someone for being unconventional, so long as . . .' Her voice trailed off strategically.

'As long as he's helping me?' I asked. She bit her lip and nodded sadly, huge eyes trained on mine. 'No, I think it's time I . . . *terminated*.' I'd found the accurate word.

But when I thought of driving into Birmingham to break off with Moloney, my unconscious invented several excuses. My eyes swelled up – 'angio-neurotic edema' was Moloney's diagnosis over the phone: 'skin rage.' He added, 'The baby is swelling up like a poisonous toad in order to scare off the Good Mother: me, in this case.' My foot became swollen and infected; I was hospitalized in the school infirmary. I slept under sheets that were draped over a metal cage placed above my foot in order to keep all pressure off it, but the pain did not prevent me from hopping at night over to the bed of the other patient, a white guy in traction with a very black penis. While I was still there the school psychotherapist visited me. I was flunking chemistry and physics, part of my pre-med pre-paration, since I'd decided over the summer to become a doctor and eventually a psychoanalyst. 'Still nursing yourself, White? Sucking the old thumb?' Moloney asked.

The school therapist wondered why I'd chosen such a demand-ing scientific major for which I was so obviously ill suited – and why I was succumbing to so many psychogenic illnesses. I must have revealed that I was disturbed about my sexual orientation, for he said, 'Well, perhaps things like that can't be changed. And perhaps one can learn to live with them quite successfully.'

'I'd never settle for that!' I said angrily. Obviously this guy was homosexual. I wondered if I should seduce him, denounce him, or both. All the antibiotics I'd swallowed for my foot had destroyed my digestion. I suffered from chronic diarrhea and only the buttermilk a friend sneaked into the infirmary was able to stop it and stopper it.

At last I decided I'd never get well until I broke with Moloney. A fraternity brother, a handsome American Indian with a sleek black brush cut, a square jaw, perfect teeth, brown skin and a big, hairless athletic body, drove me in, smiling and chewing gum all the way. I didn't trust myself behind the wheel – I'd be sure to plow into a semi. I limped into Moloney's office. The sore on his nose had become the size of a quarter and he'd let his brows grow so shaggy they half-covered his eyes. Through this white fringe he looked out at me with huge red eyes. For some reason I thought of a white plant feasting on shadow and decay – a mushroom.

'I'm leaving you,' I said, my voice hard and unsteady. 'I can't go on seeing you. It's not working out.' I had prepared many arguments but I didn't need them. Moloney said, 'You're right. I think you're right.' I was never sure of what became of him. My old teacher, the other patient, said Moloney had given up his practice and moved to Mexico. Suzie said he'd lost his mind and been confined to an asylum.

After Moloney I had an orthodox Freudian from Vienna who'd renamed herself Alice Chester. At least her name didn't really go with her heavy German accent and her Jewishness; I invented a difficult war for her, possibly a concentration camp. In fact I knew nothing about her except that she was a small, heavy-lidded woman who smiled with an irony that seemed at once exhausted and twinkly, if that's possible. She almost never 'offered an interpretation.' I knew from my reading that a strict Freudian, the sort I'd been longing to see, didn't offer interpretations during the first half-year of treatment. I appreciated her taciturn seriousness as well as her merry little lopsided smile when I cracked a joke.

Although I was analyzed by her for two years, she never said much. I longed for a detailed reconstruction of my infancy and childhood, week by week, but she never delivered. Sometimes I feared she didn't really understand English; her constant, ironic smile could just as well have been benign incomprehension or a frightened camouflage of her ignorance. Once, when I was talking about how I 'identified' with Harry Haller, the suicidal hero of Hermann Hesse's *Steppenwolf*, she nodded, exhaling smoke, then suddenly lit up with recognition and eagerly exclaimed, '*Ach! Der Steppenwolf!*' She nodded vigorously and smiled hugely. The air was juicy with the explosive German words.

How she must have missed her Vienna of Karl Kraus, Stefan Zweig and Robert Musil as she sat there in her tidy little house in the Detroit suburb of Royal Oak, a thousand miles from the nearest café. How she must have resented that dim, larval life of Detroit, to which irony or self-consciousness would have seemed as irrelevant and unusable as jalapeños in Krakow. I once saw a film of Karl Kraus in the 1930s haranguing a crowd in his high-pitched voice, his right arm trembling spasmodically with rage, his thin-lipped mouth full of wet black teeth and botched fillings as he denounced the idea of organized tours to World War I battlefields. Detroit had known race riots and labor demonstrations and seismic evangelical awakenings but it was hard to picture them while cruising the cold, twilit suburban streets where no one ever walked and the only human contact was the exchange of hostile glances at a stoplight on Woodward Avenue. Sometimes respectable-looking men even drag-raced each other; it was a car town, after all. I wondered if Dr. Chester knew how to drive.

I sometimes told friends at school that my shrink was a member of 'the original Vienna Circle,' as if she'd worked with Freud himself, which was just possible chronologically if she was as old as the century (I had no idea of her age).

She never showed me any affection, not in Moloney's hearty if impersonal doggy style. At most I'd say she regarded me as an amusing, cultured buffoon since sometimes she'd shake her head and chuckle silently over what I began to think of as my 'antics.' When I spoke of my friends in the music and theater departments at school she offered, with no particular investment in it, the observation that the sexuality of dancers and actors was sometimes quite 'plastic.' Perhaps she meant bisexual? One time she said she thought I was sexually compulsive because I was so secretive about my forbidden acts of john cruising. On another occasion she looked puzzled when I equated art with effeminacy. She laughed and said that as a European she thought of creativity as primarily a male activity.

Once she said she thought my school friends sounded as if they were self-amused and non-relating – which I instantly repeated with whoops of exaggerated laughter to them. I'd discovered a few other gay guys in Ann Arbor and I regaled them with stories about my shrink. They'd hold their sides and shout, '*Ach! Der Steppenwolf!*' We thought we were terminally sophisticated.

The New Yorker had made cartoons about shrinks as popular as their cartoons about vagrants. Roland Barthes, I suppose, would have said that the function of such jokes was to domesticate two bits of American weirdness that embarrassed and scared us – an incipient madness, if that meant the inability to live through a contradiction, and extreme poverty, which we preferred to reassign to a kind of droll and desperate dandyism rather than face as proof of the cruelty of capitalism in a democracy.

Much of the dry-martini gay humor of that period obeyed a similar reflex by laughing at what was most troubling. There was never a gathering that dissolved before one of us felt the other's head for a fever and declared, 'But, my pet, you're not a well woman,' making light of the effeminacy we feared and the mental illness we could not deny. 'We're all sick,' we'd say complacently as we wilted into stylized attitudes of illness. We mocked our low self-esteem without in any way elevating it. If *The New Yorker* never, ever made the slightest allusion to homosexuality, that was because our life was still both invisible and unmentionable or, in any event, too repellant to provide the subject for a cartoon.

When I was graduated and moved to New York in 1962 I was too poor to afford a psychoanalyst. I was no longer on my father's payroll. Besides, I was too immersed in Greenwich Village gay life to want to be cured right away. In college I had dated several women, but now even that therapeutic measure I put aside . . . until later. I wanted to sow my wild tares.

Three years later, however, I was back in psychotherapy, this time with Frances Alexander, a PhD psychologist who conducted groups and practiced something called 'transactional therapy.' At that time, in 1965, even sophisticates had not yet learned to ridicule 'New Age' or 'California Feel-Good' systems. The 1960s was a magma of political explosion and lifestyle creativity and no one felt obliged to cup such expressions inside inverted commas. The words didn't yet feel worn out.

I never read the best-selling book, *Games People Play*, on which that system (now forgotten) was based, but apparently it labeled most exchanges between people according to a fairly limited taxonomy of games or transactions. Therapy, as best I could tell from our group sessions, was aimed at unmasking these strategies in order to force the participants to return to (or invent) a sincere, heartfelt communication of feeling. We learned not to play the martyr ('Poor Me!' another client would cry out triumphantly), nor to invoke authority, nor to induce guilt in others, nor to cloak our healthy anger in humble depression ('Let it out, goddam it!'). Freudian psychoanalysis – with its high fees, its glacial slowness, its obsession with childhood sexuality, incest, dreams, the unconscious, the patriarch, the anus, with its arrogant conviction that the patient should be kept ignorant of its methods and theories – was already foundering, challenged by the more democratic group therapy and its principle of every man as his own shrink.

I was especially good at detecting game-playing ruses in the other group members, who were mostly housewives from New Jersey suffering from Empty Nest Syndrome. Sometimes Frances would point out that I was such a useful group member that no one ever bothered to ask me about my own problems.

And then Stonewall came along, the uprising in Greenwich Village in June 1969, which announced the beginning of gay liberation. The cops raided the bar off Sheridan Square, in the heart of the Village, but for once the gay customers resisted arrest. It was a hot night; Judy Garland had just died and everyone was feeling emotional. With hindsight, I can see that everything was in place for just such a revolution in consciousness. Feminism, the sexual revolution and the Vietnam War protests were in full force. It was just a matter of moments before the cards were reshuffled and someone shouted, 'Gay is good,' to make a grand slam with 'Black is beautiful.' Lesbian feminism provided the first and strongest sign of the new homosexual spirit, maybe because every woman could potentially feel the tug of feminism, maybe because women's sexuality was more responsive than men's to politics, the will and the benediction of simple affection.

Soon enough Freudian psychology went up in flames and became no more powerful or present than the smell of ashes in a cold fireplace the morning after. Most of the problems Freudianism had addressed were no longer experienced as an individual need to adapt to conventions, but as conventions that needed to adapt to individuals. The various movements of women, blacks and gays redefined personal problems into public campaigns. Everyone asserted his or her rights. In the 1950s people had been ashamed to admit they were inadequate; in the 1960s they became proud to announce they were victims. Psychoanalysis had been addressed to a culture of shame; now identity politics addressed a culture of complaint. Rilke had said, 'You must change yourself!' but now people said, 'Everyone else must change.'

Although a few journalists began to speak of the failure of communism, Marx had won out over Freud – history had replaced nature, the economy, not biology, now appeared to be determinative if not exactly determined, and neuroses pointed to divided class loyalties more often than to a blocked psychosexual development.

In the mid-1970s, during another unhappy love affair, I would seek help from Charles Silverstein, a gay psychotherapist. He was one of the psychologists who'd led the so-called 'nomenclature' battle in the American Psychiatric Association. A band of gay therapists had convinced the larger organization to reclassify homosexuality as falling within the normal range of behavior instead of being an ego disorder. Just by going to him I'd already scrambled all the rules of the game – now I wanted to be a happy gay rather than a rehabilitated homosexual.

Charles was as eccentric as Dr. Moloney had been but not at all crazy. Charles was fat and chain-smoked, wore sandals and sloppy clothes – and of course he had the usual carved African deities in his West Side living room. He was pleasant but made no protestations of love. Love was irrelevant, which seemed more honest. I could accept sex for money but not love.

For the first time I'd found a shrink who listened with what I might call a fresh ear. When I complained of low self-esteem, he had me look in a mirror and list all my weak points and strong points; I was shocked to find out the strengths were twice as numerous. Sexual dysfunctions he approached in a straightforward behaviorist fashion – he refused to psychologize them. For the more mysterious regions of the psyche, he traced out surprising new cause-and-effect relationships, tailor-made to my own development. I'd imagine I had ended one subject (my father's death) and begun another (writer's block), but he'd show how the first caused the second. He taught me the subtle ways in which internalized homophobia had left its traces all over me, like a lapdog's muddy footprints on clean sheets. He gave a strong impression that he didn't see himself as an authority, much less as a judge, but rather as a technician, someone who could put his professional training at my disposal. The possibility of transference was never discussed.

He was a Gestalt psychologist. I never figured out what that meant except with regard to dream interpretation. Whereas someone like Alice Chester would interpret the props and personages in a dream as stand-ins for earlier real events and people, Charles Silverstein saw each element in the dream as one part of the personality interacting with every other. He'd invite me to be the sail *and* the compass, the sun *and* the shark, and to speak for them. The dialogue felt more complex and representative – even if in the end it was just as arbitrary.

But Charles's strongest suit was listening and understanding with a mind almost devoid of received ideas. He was also very sensitive to the moods of other people, the moods and buried feelings. I attended a marathon group session that took place over a weekend. I quickly realized that the American manner – joshing, anecdotal, tepidly ironic – was merely a cover-up disguising the most unimaginable differences. Once we began to hear about the lives of various group members – and to re-create them by staging them amongst ourselves – we saw how weird and appalling American family life could be. A tall, sturdy Puerto Rican with clipped black hair that clung to his head like a skullcap, responded to every challenging remark with a shit-eating grin. When Charles re-created the violent childhood scenes during which Ramon's father had beat him for being gay, we learned that the grin was a scaled-down version of the defiant laugh shaken out of him with every last stroke of the belt.

Charles asked me to re-create my childhood game of king and slave. I was able to arrange everyone just as I saw fit, bowing as I made my entrance – and then, nothing. It turned out my fantasy went no further. Once everyone had made an obeisance to me, there was nothing more I required of them. My daydream was incomplete, its gleaming metal cube was empty. Once the combination was entered and the safe opened, there was nothing inside.

Therapy with Charles was terminated when I got the job of writing *The Joy of Gay Sex* with – well, surprise, with Dr. Charles Silverstein. I had been selected after I penned a few sample entries. It was only then that I learned the identity of my future collaborator. Quite rightly he said to me, 'You can either be my patient or my collaborator, but not both.' Since I was broke and was supporting my nephew, I chose to write the book. Freud had said that at the end of therapy the patient should feel he's his doctor's equal. What better way to bring about such a satisfyingly orthodox conclusion to my years of analysis?

Of course I had to confess I missed the fuss, the scrutiny, the accountability of being in therapy. My new shrink-free liberty was as disappointing as the silence and solitude that follows a definitive rupture with a fiendishly jealous lover. I couldn't help but feel that all my juicy dreams were going to waste, that my most recent sidesplitting *lapsus linguae* was just one more neural or vocal blip, devoid of humor or even significance. All the wrong notes my brain struck on the high-strung keyboard of my psyche went unheard. I was alone with the suddenly pointless minutiae of my life.

Two decades later, in the fall of 1993, I started seeing a shrink once again. My young French lover, Hubert Sorin, was dying. I found a gay American therapist, Rik Gitlin, who hailed from San Francisco. Although I had been living in Paris for a decade I didn't want a French psychoanalyst. I despised Lacan, a double-talking charlatan who counted his money while his patients talked and who invented the twenty-minute 'hour' and felt authorized to reduce it to five minutes if the spirit moved him, probably so he could cram in one more lucrative turnover. Lacan had long since been dead, but his influence was felt everywhere for typically chauvinistic reasons – he was France's answer to Freud. No matter that he wrote incomprehensible gibberish when he wasn't spouting dangerous untruths or tricking truisms out in fancy words. (*Entre-deux-morts*, it turns out, is a 'technical term' that refers to the period between someone's death and the extinction of his memory among the living. That's it, folks. *Basta*.)

I wanted to talk to my own kind of funny, disabused American gay man, someone who'd laugh when I laughed and who developed his ideas by moving from anecdote to anecdote, like a long-armed ape brachiating from branch to branch. I knew I'd be going through a lot during and after Hubert's death, and I didn't plan to make the journey alone.

Rik was in his thirties, attractive, bright and respectful (I was nearly twice his age). Like me, he had a French lover, and was willing to compare notes, minor as well as major. He liked to rollerblade through Saint-Germain and had the thighs to prove it. He'd come to Paris because he loved a man, not the city, and was far less of an unconditional Francophile than I. He was a compulsive shopper but had a nearly Zen taste for spareness – a paradox that meant he needed lots of storage space. We sat in good chairs and looked at each other; the couch had been relegated to the Freudian attic. He took notes after each session and kept track of my numerous friends, as complicated as those cast lists that used to appear at the beginning of nineteenth-century Russian novels. He was far more a part of fast-lane gay life than Charles had ever been. I may have been a bit past it, but the gay ghetto had been formative for me (its sexual opportunities, its shrugging wit, its sketchy history, its alternately glorious and scrappy culture), and I was relieved not to have to explain anything.

I'd been living for a decade as someone who was HIV-positive and my lover was dying of AIDS. When I asked Rik if he'd ever nursed anyone with AIDS, he said with understated aplomb, 'Yes, both my parents died of AIDS.'

It turned out he meant that he'd been raised by two gay men and he'd taken care of them when they were terminally ill. As a San Franciscan he'd lived through dozens of deaths. He knew what it was like to put one's own life on hold indefinitely. He forgave the disgraceful little resentments that might tarnish any Florence Nightingale's nobility. He also grasped all the practical reasons for sacrificing oneself entirely to a sick friend.

He was one of the 'What-I'm-hearing-is-a-certain-amount-of-shame' school of therapy, in which the psychologist peers through the client's social smiles and ironic demurrals to discern the stark outlines of his real feelings, often the opposite of those he intends to convey. This method depends on sound instincts and nothing else, a nearly canine perception of signals pitched above the ordinary range of human hearing. Rik was gifted with this sort of sensitivity. He was also very companionable.

When I reflect on my life, which has been touched by psychotherapy in every decade, I realize that during my youth Freudianism was my main form of intellectuality, a severe, engrossing discipline too devoid of comfort to serve as a substitute for religion. Freudianism developed in me an interest in the individual and his or her sexual development and a strong sense that the progression from one stage to another could go in only one direction in someone healthy. The 'residue' of this indoctrination was a narrow, normative view of humanity. But when I came to reject Freudianism in my late twenties and early thirties, I replaced it with its opposite – an interest in groups rather than individuals, a morality that was situationist rather than absolute, and a rejection of every urge to 'totalize,' if that means to submit experience to one master theory. In my biography of Jean Genet, for instance, I sought to show how he was at once a product of a provincial peasant world – and how he transcended it. If anyone ever transformed himself radically and repeatedly it was Genet, who went from being a foster kid in a village to criminal to celebrated novelist, avant-garde playwright and political activist on behalf of the Black Panthers and the Palestinians. This career trajectory was paralleled by a psychological evolution nearly as impressive and unpredictable.

Psychoanalysis did leave me with a few beliefs, including the conviction that everyone is worthy of years and years of intense scrutiny – not a bad credo for a novelist. That's it: as a writer I was always competing with Freudianism, and it was no accident that I revered Proust, the supreme psychologist in fiction, someone who was in no way influenced by Freud. I remember that Nabokov (or one of his characters) argues somewhere that Freud thought we admire a woman's hair because we desire her body, whereas the truth is we want to sleep with her because we're so awestruck by her beautiful hair. A novelist can work with Nabokov's insight because it respects the details, the sensuous surface, of experience, but not with Freud's theory, which is arid and reductive.

I sought out therapy because I was in such terrible pain, driven by desires I wanted to eradicate because I felt they were infantile, grotesque, damaging and isolating. I was never cured, but society changed and redefined homosexuality as an orientation that was acceptable, or nearly so.

Edmund's father

My Father

My father was such an original man – so unpredictable, such an unusual combination of motives and manners and values – that he was hard to grasp. I never met anyone else like him. When I was a child and adolescent I was forced to lead my father's life from time to time, but when that long captivity came to an end I fled to New York and eventually to Paris, far from his world of solitude and night and work.

My father was a chain-smoker of cigars – expensive Cuban cigars made of fragile, wrapped leaves housed in wood boxes decorated with gold and red and green pictures as gaudy as a Ruritanian medal of honor. The edges of the box were sealed with green stamps. Inside each wood box the cigars – pungent, the color of mud – were as shocking as a fetishist's collected feces.

In those days the smoker had full, unquestioned rights to light up wherever and whenever he liked. My father chose to smoke in restaurants, at home and in his closed, air-conditioned Cadillac. We were a bit green around him, steeped in his smoke that seemed to nourish him but poison us. Like many American men in the 1950s he drove five hundred, six hundred or even seven hundred miles a day on our long trips, refusing to stop for weak bladders, and as the big car with its roaring motor lurched around tight corners at seventy miles an hour and at eighty down the open road (in those days usually just a narrow two-lane highway), my father lit one cigar after another from the dashboard lighter, which glowed bright red in the dark.

My father had a prominent nose that a mule had kicked off-center when he was a teenager doing a summer job in construction.

When he was in his fifties he had it operated on – not, he insisted, for cosmetic reasons but to make his breathing easier at night. He had thinning, straight hair that became gray but never white. His face was long and looked pained in a patrician way except when he flashed at rare moments his insincere, salesman's smile – the effect was ghastly, since his small teeth were brown and his lips thin and pale. He took pride in his wrinkle-free face and indeed splashed it daily with witch hazel to firm it up. He stared at his reflection with what I used to think was narcissism but now I recognize as insecurity. But it wasn't that he was unsure of his effect on other people, whom he cared nothing about. He was wondering if he was ugly or handsome in some absolute sense and each time he approached the mirror he expected a surprise, a verdict. He could spend hours manicuring his nails with an expensive twelve-instrument kit bound in ostrich skin. His nails were his hobby, as toy trains might be another man's.

He disapproved of cologne, of facial hair, of long sideburns, of cigarettes, of wristwatches, of rings or any other jewelry, of wearing black and brown together, of colored shirts, of button-down collars, of bold designs or vivid colors, of all sports clothes, of brown in the evening, of white socks at any time, of a man's exposed ankle or calf. He wore knee-high black lisle stockings held up by garters, just as his trousers were held up by dark suspenders, not the clip-on kind but the kind that fitted over buttons sewn into the inner waistband. He wore casual clothes only when he was playing tennis or mowing the lawn. Even then, more often than not his work clothes were the trousers to old business suits and frayed or stained formal white shirts. Once he bought tacky casual clothes – a workman's cap, a pink shirt, a string tie that passed through a holder showing a pink jackass on a black background – all as an elaborate way of 'bringing me down a peg' when he visited me at my boarding school, where he thought I'd become 'too big for my britches.' Yes, for him casual clothes were what poor men wore – and they could be borrowed as a joke, a parody, for a 'hobos' night out.' He liked to tell the story of his foppish dentist, Bill Pifer, who wore faddish shoes with blue suede tops and black patent leather sides to a dinner and the hostess asked him if he'd like to remove his galoshes. How Dad laughed over that one.

He was a Texan who'd gone to engineering school at Boulder, Colorado, and moved on to Gary, Indiana, for his first job building bridges and eventually to Cincinnati, Ohio, where he switched over to the chemical business and where he lived for many years. He'd lost his Texas accent and gave a Southern twist only to a very few words. He pronounced 'greasy' as 'greezy' and said 'dawmitory' instead of 'dormitory.' And he placed the emphasis on the first syllable of 'insurance.' He made the usual Southern substitution of 'i' for 'e' (he said 'fountain pin,' an improvement on *his* father's 'founting pin'). But otherwise he spoke clearly and grammatically and with the fussiness of a generation of Texans who'd studied elocution in grade school and could all recite patriotic poems and historic speeches by heart. The only word he mispronounced was 'statistic,' which he turned into 'stastistic.' Of course he'd let out a deafening rebel yell when it suited him.

His father, my grandfather, was a math prof and eventually dean of students at Texas State College for Women in Denton, Texas. My grandfather liked to say he'd become a professor to avoid manual labor; as a boy he'd driven a plow behind a mule and hated it. He said all the boys he knew 'wanted to work in the shade.' Their motto: 'Less sunshine, more shade.'

My grandfather was named Edmund Valentine White, the first name after his grandfather, Edmund Woodard, the second for his other grandfather, Joseph Valentine White, Jr., whose father had married into the Valentines and was also related to the Culpeppers and the Thurmonds (Strom Thurmond, the oldest American senator in history, was his cousin). My grandfather White was born on August 11, 1879 in Ringgold, Louisiana, in Bienville Parish. When he was just two (and his brother Wirt just a few months old) they traveled in a covered wagon west some four hundred miles to the region near Abilene. The Whites bought land outside what would soon be Merkel, Texas. They planted corn and cotton and raised cattle. And my great-grandfather White was the first teacher in the Merkel one-man school.

My father became Edmund Valentine White II and I the third, in typical Southern fashion, though when I began to write fiction and drama about angry blacks and troubled gays my father came to regret he'd passed his name on to me. He had a highly abstract notion of honor – he was a recluse and had no friends – but he wanted to be above reproach in some official way I never understood. He believed in God but only in an absentminded, ceremonial fashion. He'd been raised by his mother to be a Christian Scientist but he never attended church and seemed quite vague about its bewilderingly kooky tenets. Yet if queried he'd say that religion – that is, Protestantism with its many offshoots – was a good thing, almost as if it were good for the uninstructed masses if not exactly for him. Strangely enough, he considered his divorce from my mother to be the only 'blot on his record' (he would never have said 'sin,' which sounded too Papist, and in the form of the Lord's Prayer we learned we asked God to forgive us our 'trespasses'). The divorce had been a mistake because it was a blemish, a demerit, a public and legal shortcoming, not because he still loved my mother, if he'd ever loved her.

As a child my father (at least according to my melodramatizing mother) had been severely mistreated by his mother in the one-story bleak house in dusty Denton. Grandma Ollie White had made her son E.V. (always known by his initials, as was his father) do the whole family wash once a week in the bathtub. The poor little tike stood on a three-step ladder and bent over the steam and lye for hours before feeding the heavy hot linens into the mangle on the back porch. Grandma was apparently off in her shaded bedroom lying on a white chenille bedspread, surrounded by milk-glass bowls reflected in a tabletop of blue mirror.

She was deeply depressed. My mother always told me that 'Mother White' had committed suicide, though if true her cause of death was hushed up in the family and community. Mother White had told my father when he was still a boy that she hadn't wanted him. She'd beaten her stomach with her fists during her pregnancy, hoping to abort. After my father was born she went on to have another boy, Uncle Bill, and a little girl, who became my Aunt Jody. I don't know if she abused them as well. My father rather thought that Bill had been 'spoiled,' which led to his being weak-willed and shiftless and eventually mad.

Grandma White (who'd been born Olive Martin) had converted to Christian Science after reading some of its 'literature.' She practiced her exalted, highly spiritual and somehow 'modern' religion all by herself in Denton. Today people scorn Christian Science for its unconscionable rejection of modern medicine, but when I was a boy attending Sunday School it was a religion for the rich and 'progressive' – all those who didn't want to be troubled by virgin births and an improbable trinity and who liked the up-to-date idea of combining Christianity and science, who thought of Jesus as someone like Plato, and who enjoyed visits at home when they were ill from other perfumed, mono-bosomed ladies, the Christian Science 'healers' reading to them in cultured tones from Mary Baker Eddy's *Science and Health* and *Key to the Scriptures*. It was a murmuring, matronly religion that published a top-notch national newspaper and opened a Reading Room in every major city (run by more matronly volunteers). Now Eddy is treated as a dangerous charlatan whose doctrine brought brain damage to countless children denied antibiotics and even aspirin, and gripped by high fevers that caused encephalitis. We all knew at least one woman who'd been eaten alive by a horridly painful and smelly breast cancer and whose friends would murmur over her closed coffin that now, at last, she was 'healed.' Back then Mrs. Eddy was perceived (at least by us) as advanced, intellectual, classy, Bostonian. Nonetheless my mother would always break down and call a doctor if we were seriously ill, but only then. To this day I tend to forget to take prescribed pills and, as Mrs. Eddy would have liked, I am blind to evil. If forced to stare it in the eye I dismiss it as she did as a manifestation of ignorance.

If my father regretted sharing his name with me, I was always worried about being confused with my grandfather, the author of three books of 'nigger jokes.' More respectably, he'd written *Mental Arithmetic*, hints about how to do sums in the head. But his real life's work, or rather the ornament to his life, was composing his joke books, which he published at his own expense. He'd also written his memoirs. Even in his formal writings he enjoyed peppering his sentences with bits of Negro humor: 'I have tried to keep in mind the philosophy of Uncle Solomon: "De littler de ideas a man have de louder he talks!"' Or, in dismissing his own modest academic career and its shared duties, he would recollect, 'The responsibility in the main lay jointly with the President and a loyal, capable faculty. As the Negro said about his duties as "Supreme Potentate" of the lodge, "Dat am one of the littlest offices in de whole unscrupulous lodge!" No, I have been only a small cog in the giant wheels of progress.' In speaking of a difficult period at his college, he wrote, 'I would characterize the two-year period in the language of the Negro maid who quit her job: "There's too much shiftin' uv the dishes fuh de fewness uv de vittles!" '

At one point in his short memoir my grandfather wrote: 'Since I was reared in the West where there were comparatively few members of the colored race, I am often asked how I became interested in Negro stories. In the first place, I had a Southern background. My father used to tell amusing incidents about colored folks in Louisiana. Then about 1890, my father used to read to us the Uncle Remus stories by Joel Chandler Harris, which were first published serially in the *Atlanta Constitution*, a paper that we read with great zeal. I was well prepared for the fun I was to have later.'

Dean White's laws for a good Negro story included observing the 'truths' of Negro psychology and recounting them in Negro dialect, as outlined in his memoir. His collections, such as *Senegambian Sizzles* and *Chocolate Drops from the South*, were his homage to this 'lovable and amusing race' and their 'antics.' As a child I learned that my grandfather was a member of the Ku Klux Klan only because on one occasion I had mispronounced the 'Ku' as 'Cue' instead of 'Coo' and Dean White corrected me with a big laugh. My father told me with a wink that Granddaddy should know.

Granddaddy loved to hold forth for hours. I can remember sitting with him and my father on the veranda of the big hotel in Mineral Wells, Texas, where he'd gone to take a cure. For squirming, sweating, panicky hours he'd tell us his cursed nigger jokes, spitting tobacco into a cuspidor beside his rocking chair and drawing everything out at a snail's pace: 'Now, Eddie, did you ever hear the one about Old Sambo who wanted to go coon hunting?' I'd frown and squint into the sunlight and shake my head no and he'd get lost in a brown study as he tried to resurrect in advance every twist and turn in his tale. Suddenly his eyes would light up, he'd lift his straw hat, then resettle it farther back on his hair, which was slick and pressed down from the sweatband. He'd stagily slap his knee with his gnarled, liver-spotted hand – or maybe those spots were just the ghosts of freckles, for he'd told us he'd been a redhead as a lad and covered with big, overlapping freckles, his hair so bright that the boy behind him in school pretended to warm his hands above the fiery locks. The story ended with the first Edmund turning on the boy and knocking him flat. In all his stories there was violence. When he was still a teenager he began teaching in a one-room schoolhouse where there were three boys bigger and older than he. His superior worried about hiring so young a teacher because he wasn't certain my grandfather could discipline the three boys, but he ended up birching them all, though first he had to box one into submission. He was a lifelong advocate of corporal punishment.

My grandfather, my father and my Uncle Bill all had a cold self-sufficiency, something approaching smugness except there was no real joy in any form, no eagerness to communicate one's own importance to anyone else. They were self-contained, distant men, though my father was given to towering, furniture-breaking rages and Uncle Bill was too crazily angry for his wife and two daughters to live with him. My father supported them all, none too grandly, Bill in a trailer where he menaced his neighbors by waving a loaded pistol at them. Twice he had to be hospitalized for getting out of control. Late in life he had brain surgery – was it a lobotomy? All three of them – Bill and the first two Edmunds – picked their teeth and told long, unfunny stories that gloried in other people's ignorance or naïveté, often tales of happy but dim Negroes trying out big words or learned theories and getting them all mixed up. My grandfather told the one about the black recruit who nodded enthusiastically rather than looking to one side when his commanding officer called out, 'Eyes right.' When the officer said, 'Solomon, I said eyes right,' Solomon replied, 'Yassuh, boss, you's always right.'

When he wasn't telling me funny stories my grandfather was asking me to solve mental arithmetic riddles or poking fun at me while digging an elbow into my father's side. I'd been assured by my mother that I was a genius, but I couldn't do the sums in my head. Nor could I laugh at his jokes, or respond to his taunts except by squirming in my seat and blushing with confusion and the desire to disappear. I was supposed to defend myself politely, standing up straight, throwing in lots of 'sirs,' but I was too much of a neurotic sissy and too much of a Yankee to know how to behave in the right way, like a manly cadet. My father, I could see, was ashamed of me – of my lack of feistiness, of my slovenly rudeness, of my babyish pouting.

Sometimes I've feared that I was dying inside and becoming as gloomily self-regarding as my predecessors – those Roman numerals after our names seeming to denote doom. Once, in my thirties, I dreamed that I was buried alive inside a mummiform coffin that resembled me exactly. The dream occurred during a period when my work was being rejected and I was living with a young man who didn't love me – though I was besotted by him, both as a writer and as a human being. I feared the slow extinction of my feelings. I kept picturing my father asleep by day in his shuttered, air-conditioned room, as motionless as Dracula in his diurnal casket.

Living up North, even in such a conservative, racist city as Cincinnati, my father had learned to keep his condescension toward blacks to himself. He was a misanthrope who slept all day and stayed up all night, working at his blond mahogany desk under a big, tacky painting of ocean waves in the moonlight. The whole time he listened to 78s and later LPs of classical music, everything from Bach to early Stravinsky (he often played a suite from *The Nightingale*). He disliked the human voice and avoided the opera, though he permitted me to attend the summer opera in the zoo and even volunteer there as a supernumerary.

The janitor in his office (and in his warehouse) was an ageless black man named Charles, whom he enjoyed lightly chiding to his face and ridiculing behind his back. Charles was a deacon in his Baptist church who'd memorized much of the Bible, his only book but one he knew thoroughly. Whenever Charles quoted long passages from it to me my father would stand behind him winking at me, as if we were watching a performing monkey. Yankee intellectuals, spoon-fed on Freud, often asserted that Southern whites were afraid of black male sexuality and that this fear was the source of their racism. This supposition has been widely accepted, perhaps because it can't be verified or disproved, since an entirely unconscious motive eludes study or introspection. Ascribing racism to sexual fear is both demeaning to the resentful whites and flattering to the erotically superior blacks; the matter is complicated by an ambiguity about whether such superiority is real or assigned. I suppose a cynic might say that whites are willing to concede excessive virility to black men as long as they can retain wealth and power; it's an easy trade-off.

But I who've lived among real racists believe that their condescension is far more withering than sexual envy. For them a black is shiftless and stupid, smells bad and is easily confused, childishly frightened by ghosts, boasting about chimerical victories, clever only in avoiding work or punishment, naturally musical and athletic, quickly deflated, and finally all too happy to obey a firm and fatherly white master. My nephew, who married a Japanese woman and lived with her in Tokyo, told me that his Japanese friends speak of American whites in the same terms – lazy workers, great dancers, undependable friends, good in bed, reeking of foul odors; his wife said it was torture to ride in a closed subway with whites smelling of fermented dairy products.

Charles, standing in his old work clothes and smelling of sweat and labor, would cite biblical passages, demonstrating how the Old Testament prefigured the New, and my father would always be there behind him, smiling faintly through a cloud of cigar smoke and winking conspiratorially at me. After all, Dad was the boss man who paid Charles thirty dollars a week, with a twenty-dollar bonus at Christmas.

Whereas Charles might lecture me vehemently when we were alone (one of my summer jobs was whitewashing Dad's warehouse with him), the minute my father showed up, Charles would shift into a grinning, soft-shoe parody of his own erudition. My father, in his stained tailor-made trousers, his cast-off work clothes, would join in and whitewash with us, but despite his democratic ways Dad's simple presence always reduced Charles to Steppin Fetchit. In the waning years of the twentieth century, fifty years later, I once happened to take a long taxi ride in St. Louis, and there, suddenly, I had Charles vividly re-created. If I'd say, 'It sure is hot,' the white-haired black driver would chuckle and repeat, 'Hot, yassuh, boss, it be real hot, thas right, it hot, it *real* hot,' and no matter what inanity I'd utter he'd do his affirmative riff on it. That style had nearly disappeared from the world except in remote places or in expensive Southern private clubs where the Amos and Andy servants are paid dearly to flatter the illusions of old white men. 'Yassuh,' the taxi driver said, 'you's one hunnerd percent right!'

If a black succeeded in school or the army or business, my father would say, 'He must have a lot of white blood.' It was as impregnable a position as those Freudian theories that ascribed all behavior to the unconscious.

After my parents divorced, my mother, my sister and I moved to Chicago, but the divorce agreement stipulated that my sister and I were to spend one weekend out of every month with our father, as well as every summer. My father and his second wife (Kay Beard, the woman who'd been his secretary for the past seven years) at first lived in a two-bedroom apartment in the Cincinnati suburb of Kenwood; the apartment occupied half a floor in a big brick and white-plaster house. Whereas our small family house, at the end of a lane in Hyde Park, had been filled with leather armchairs, dark tables and cream-colored flowered upholstery, our father's new apartment was resolutely up-to-date. It had blond Swedish modern furniture, slender brass floor lamps with cherry-red shades, wall-to-wall carpet. In the terrible, humid, stifling summers the shades were lowered and the windows outfitted with powerful exhaust fans. My father also had floor fans housed in round, squat units slatted with protective louvers; each fan looked like a stylized mushroom breathing heavily through its gills. Everything was modern, the massive furniture with the inset retractable brass drawer pulls, the plain aluminum tableware, the dimpled hand-blown water glasses – church blue, police-siren red, emerald green. On the walls were two semiabstract sub-Douanier Rousseau paintings of close-up jungle growth and passionately red flowers, which Dad and Kay bought for a song at the Court of Two Sisters in New Orleans during their honeymoon. In this apartment I'd spend hours alone, tiptoeing up to my stepmother's vanity table and trying on her perfumes, just one drop at a time as if any more would summon the genie out of the bottle: my father, angry at his sissy son and fuming through his hot cigar smoke.

I once asked Louis Stettner, when he showed me his photos from the 1940s, taken in the New York subway, why faces back then were so different from those one sees now. He said, 'That was before the era of self-improvement. People just looked the way they looked. They had little idea about how to change.' That was the era of baked potatoes, of vegetables boiled so long they'd go from green to tan, of Wonder Bread stacked on a plate and, for dessert, a dish of canned Queen Anne cherries. Certainly no one we knew had plastic surgery back then – or if, like my father, they had their noses straightened they claimed it was for medical, not cosmetic, reasons. No one jogged or went to the gym and young couples became middle-aged adults soon after marriage. Women might fuss a bit over slimming but men were proud of their 'bay windows.' Men donned their brown or gray hats, cocked ever so slightly to the right or left, the sides artfully dimpled, the brim lowered just above the face, the crown reblocked every few months to maintain its stiffness. They wore their plain lace-up shoes and double-breasted suits and heavy overcoats and these uniforms elevated and concealed them in ageless anonymity – from twenty to fifty they were men, nothing more nor less. The women wore cheap housedresses at home to perform their chores of cleaning and cooking but emerged to do the shopping or to walk the dog in trim suits decorated with a gold brooch or silk dresses, their heads covered with hats, their bodies heavily perfumed with Shalimar or Chanel: mature women's scents. If their ankles thickened or their hips ballooned out under their skirts, no one found such amplitude regrettable. Just a bit funny, that was all.

Cincinnati was, perhaps, unusually dowdy with its German stylelessness, its heavy schnitzels and wursts, its beer, its sweaty, shouting baseball fans, its fake Tudor houses and century-old trees, its brick warehouses in the blocks leading down to the Ohio River, its 1880 Symphony Hall with the modest and yellowing allegorical paintings on the ceiling, its department stores (Pogue's, Shillitoe's) with their system of payment and change-making flying overhead in pneumatic tubes. I can remember going to town with my mother in her old Ford, parking and wandering through the perfumed, muted clamor and dazzle of Shillitoe's, becoming groggy with overstimulation and passivity, watching the pneumatic tubes snap into place with their sudden whooshing arrival, hearing the bells softly chiming in secret codes to summon one saleslady or another, the voice of the uniformed elevator operator sliding his control lever to two o'clock to go up or ten o'clock to go down or high noon to stop as he called out, 'Third floor, home furnishings, fourth floor, lingerie!' After a drugged morning of stumbling around in my mother's wake I'd head over with her to the Netherland Plaza Hotel, all Art Deco engraved silver panels of long-limbed nymphs in profile walking among hieratic stags, where we'd eat chicken pot pie and chocolate sundaes and watch the skaters with their frozen grins brake in a spray of ice under pink and amber gels.

Cincinnati dowdiness, I guess, was best symbolized by Mrs. Taft sitting in her box sipping a Coke right out of the bottle at the Friday afternoon rehearsals of the Symphony. My father never read a book, fantasy irritated him. He never had time for a movie and painting left him annoyed. But serious music consumed him and once LPs had resolved the problems of sustained hours of listening he'd stack the spindle high. It was rare for him to interrupt his night of work by going out socially in the evening, so soon after arising and eating breakfast, but he would accompany his wife on Saturday evenings to the Symphony, dressed in one of his dark suits, with a stiffly peaked white handkerchief, Countess Mara silk tie and mirror-polished black shoes. He didn't fidget or lean his chin on his fist or close his eyes. He sat there regally neutral, though if the work was modern and 'a bit hard on the ears' he'd read through the scholarly program notes about Frank Martin or Carl Orff.

He was a terribly lonely man, gliding home from the Symphony through the night in his Cadillac, drawing on his cigar that pulsed red like the belly of a poisonous fly, obeying the traffic signals even in the empty downtown streets. It would probably never have occurred to him to say he was lonely since he had Kay and his pets and his work and had so strenuously sought out solitude. In some ways he had an old Texas subsistence view of life and he would say proudly, 'I've got a roof over my head and a steak on the table. I don't owe a thing to any man, and I've never spent a night in jail.'

In another way he had shared his thoughts so little that they had scarcely developed; loneliness was not a sentiment he was capable of isolating or registering. Rolling home in the backseat I couldn't have felt more a prisoner if I'd been in a paddy wagon. Though I knew no one at the Symphony, nevertheless there I was surrounded by all those furred and cravatted presences, their eyes raking the crowds like a bodyguard's looking for trouble. The chaotic clamor of the orchestra tuning up – the tuba chuckling down and down through a difficult passage, a trumpet tut-tutting the staccato passage, the timpanist leaning down to press his ear virtually to the drumhead to verify its pitch – brought a note of methodical disorder to this hall of burghers, as stoically resigned to the concert as churchgoers to the sermon. And then, to a patter of applause, the conductor makes his entrance and rushes to the podium, flicks his hair, and launches into the Leonora Overture.

Spending the long, hot, humid summers with my father and Kay, I was bored not to death but into nervous, frantic life so acute I wanted to jump out of my skin. On some days I'd stay home with Kay. On others her slow, slovenly maid, Naomi, who took snuff while she ironed, would look after me though I could scarcely understand her drawl. (My sister was often away at camp.) If Naomi wasn't free to babysit me, Dad would take me to the office with him. I'd sit there and read Kay's racy novels (*Forever Amber* or the latest Taylor Caldwell) or *War and Peace*, though Tolstoy's untranslated conversations in French frustrated me. I'd make mobiles out of paper clips and the almost amber scotch tape of the period. I'd walk back to the water cooler a hundred times.

At home, my father and stepmother left cigarettes out in silver cups for guests, but since no guests ever came the cigarettes turned dry and brittle. I'd sneak out to the backyard and smoke them, even when I was only eight or nine. When there was no one to look after me my father would park me in day care with other kids in a grim section of Cincinnati. None of the kids seemed to know each other and they disliked one another as if we were each a reminder of our collective abandonment. I would sneak down to the toilet in the basement to smoke a cigarette stolen from home. That felt like a way of evening the score – an invisible, pointless, furious way. I didn't know how to inhale or even how to hold a cigarette – I held it rakishly between my ring and little fingers, as if it were a fan, say, used to jab emphasis into a conversation.

After my father and Kay moved out of Kenwood they bought a three-bedroom Spanish house back in Hyde Park, a stucco house built around a courtyard into which Kay had installed a plaster fountain of a boy holding a dolphin dripping from the mouth. My father appalled the neighbors by painting the house a light, sunny pink, but he relished that sort of scandal, which would make sure there'd be no welcome wagons, no smiling couples trying to get up a bridge game. Anyway, he insisted that Spanish-style houses in Mexico or Texas were often painted pink. His Texas past emerged in only a few stories about shooting rattlesnakes from a horse; my father had worked as a cowboy during several summers when he was still a student. He also spoke of looking out for copperheads when he went swimming.

In seventh grade I lived the whole year in that pink house with my father and stepmother and attended Walnut Hills, a public school for gifted students. My sister stayed with my mother in Evanston but I had my own room in Cincinnati, one that Dad had had built in the attic above the garage. My twin beds were covered with mustard and brown twill spreads. Kay had bought a Danish modern dark-wood armchair with a black leather seat and a wire back, and a small study lamp. I had to walk through the guestroom to get to the bathroom, but we never had guests and the bathroom was outfitted both with a tub and a shower stall that had side sprays. And there were thick pale-blue bath towels of several sizes, coordinated with the bath mat and the toilet seat cozy. I reveled in all this luxury and the solid bank account on which it floated like a yacht on a calm inland sea. Whereas our mother often ran out of money toward the end of the month and fed us canned peas and canned potatoes and a pork tenderloin that she fried in careless despair until the smoke filled the apartment, Kay and my father had expensive matching furniture in every room and stacks of gold-rimmed dishes in the cabinets, each insulated in its own purple velvet bag, and velvet-wrapped gold knives and forks, which even I thought seemed a bit showy. All of that was for the guests who never came; our everyday dishes were bright Fiestaware. We ate steak and corn and iceberg lettuce. Toward dawn Dad drank a glass of milk and ate a box of chocolate grahams, each freighted with a pat of cold butter.

After our mother's moodiness, her childishly excited moments of wild enthusiasm and her bleak hours of depression as she listened to the same record over and over ('Now is the hour when we must say good-bye' was a ten-inch 78 favorite she'd played so often it had an enlarged hole in its heart that made the English soprano's voice slow down into a Boris Karloff baritone), after her long evenings of downing one highball after another and her endless speculation as to whether E.V. would come back to her or not, and if so when, after her suffocating, tentacular closeness and weepy neediness, her fruitless hours of waiting for her latest boyfriend to phone her – after all that, my father's remoteness seemed restorative.

That isn't to say it was particularly stable or sane, since he too was highly volatile and appeared to be constantly medicating himself with cigars or, shortly before dawn, a pipe. He didn't mind it if I sat on the silk green-and-white loveseat in his study while he worked at his desk. He had astonishing powers of sustained concentration and could hover for hours adding up columns of figures, checking them on his calculating machine and printing out specifications by hand in neat block letters which he would drive into town and put on a secretary's desk at five in the morning, for her to find and type up when she arrived at eight-thirty. Sometimes he'd dictate business letters into a Dictaphone and leave the wire spools on the 'girl's' desk.

He owned his own business, White Industrial Sales and Equipment Co. His two Cadillacs were company cars, traded in every two years, and most of his travels counted as business trips. He was a broker of chemical equipment. If someone wanted to open a new factory making soap or brewing beer, my father and the twenty-five engineers who worked for him set up the entire process and assembly line, ordered the equipment and installed it for a commission as high as twenty-five percent of the total price. He represented manufacturers who made chemical mixers, porcelain fittings, copper tubes and vats, and rubber V-belts. Because he started his business in 1940, just before America entered the war, he was perfectly placed to ride on the immense industrial surge of World War II, when the country was required almost overnight to supply and arm its soldiers and those of England. Within a decade he had offices in five Midwestern cities. He told me proudly that he was the most successful broker of chemical equipment in the States.

It didn't last.

His achievement is probably impossible to ascertain now. The historian is only interested in spectacular wealth and innovation in business. On the thirtieth anniversary of Truman Capote's famous Black-and-White Ball, once considered the world's most sought-after invitation, *Vanity Fair* sent me a photo of all the guests and asked me to help identify the third of them whom no one could name. They were just rich people, couples who owned something big in Akron, and the world forgets these people as soon as the coffin lid closes over them.

A year or two after my father died in the late 1970s I was riding in a New York taxi and the driver was smoking a cigar. Tears sprang to my eyes as I realized that my father – who'd bullied us, terrorized his employees and impressed hatcheck girls with big tips and his jaundiced smile – was now even less substantial than this smoke. In another generation he would be erased from all existing memory banks, no more identifiable than Capote's white-tie-and-tiara-wearing nobody millionaires.

In my father's pink villa I seduced the neighbor boy, reluctantly practiced the piano and sat on the carpeted steps outside my father's closed door, behind which he slept his deep Transylvanian daytime sleep. I was thirteen, hairless, not yet full grown, big-eared, erect, and I longed to slip into bed beside my father. His wife left the house early every morning – well, by eleven. She had her piano lessons, her work as a volunteer museum docent, she had to stop by White Industrial to make sure everyone was hard at work. She attended luncheons at the Queen City Club and teas at the Keyboard Club – a full program that kept her busy and idle. My father was alone in his bed. The heavy pleated silk curtains were drawn shut under their boxy cornices covered with the same fabric – a dull sea green that slithered into a chartreuse sheen if held in a particular way to the light. In his bedroom there was no light of any kind and only the distant hum of traffic on Madison Avenue could be heard.

My mind raced with the scenario: I'd shed my clothes at the door and press my slender smoothness against his body, for I knew he slept in the nude. He'd awaken to discover himself covering me with kisses and already penetrating me – at last Daddy would have come back to 'us,' if not exactly to mother at least to her emissary.

My father did try to seduce my sister, who many years later remembered that Daddy had come on to her when she was thirteen or fourteen. He'd tried to kiss her and fondle her. She'd said, 'No, Daddy, that's not right.' She'd been a bit proud that she appealed to him – after all, our mother had often spoken of the elaborate ruses she'd imagined to reawaken his sexual attachment to her. Once I walked in on them as he stood behind my seated sister. He was brushing her long blonde hair; he had tears in his eyes.

We'd grown up in harem conditions, our ears filled nightly with the counsels and complaints of the Sultan's former favorite. There were few people in our lives. Like my father, my mother had few friends. She seldom called anyone, never had a long chat, a casual exchange of gossip and intimacies. Everyone she knew was a family member or connected to her work or was an ex sexual partner. Dad lived in total isolation and seldom encountered anyone who wasn't a relative or employee. His wife Kay knew other club ladies but even with them she was (by today's standards) extremely reserved. My sister and I were both weird and had few friends, though we were always desperately in love. My sister would wait by a silent phone for some tall, pimply boy at school to call. Perhaps this absence of intimacy (and of simple observation by other people) meant that all possible feelings – love, hate, anger, merriment, lust, frustration – were played out in the family circle alone. Only decades later, when I'd become worldlier and better-liked, did it occur to me that both my parents were in truth unfit for society. Just before she retired, one of my mother's colleagues said to me with disgust, 'You mother is really crazy, you know.' I realized belatedly that my father had been one of the most boring men ever to draw breath and that people had fled him. His idea of good conversation was discussing the various advantages of stocks versus bonds or explaining exactly what convection was. He also knew baseball scores, even *historic* scores and averages.

Through friends my age I have noticed that as teenage boys and girls become more and more beautiful their parents are reduced to continual spluttering rages against them. It's enough for a slim-waisted, broad-shouldered lad to come skateboarding up to the curb with a flick of his full black hair and two dark red roses surfacing in his white cheeks to make his balding, stooped father yelp with hate-heavy vituperation. I suppose hate is the only way to divert criminal desire – or an equally disagreeable acknowledgment of envy and spite.

My father never envied me. I was flighty and effeminate, I was already in the grip of a deviant sexuality, I got good grades but my academic seriousness fell far short of his own in his day – I studied only what appealed to me and flunked science and math, his best subjects. I couldn't hit a tennis ball or baseball. I wasn't as tall as my father, who stood squarely, massively, on thin legs (his 'race-horse legs,' as he called them) – whereas I dawdled self-consciously behind him, hand on hip, hip cocked out, my heavy head wilting to one side. I looked like an overcooked asparagus.

I wanted to sleep with him not because I found him handsome or seductive. He was considered 'distinguished,' just as in France a woman is said to have 'charm' when she's not beautiful. I never envied my father's sunken chest, swollen belly or skinny legs, but I longed for him anyway – he was the pasha, and more importantly he was the only man living under the same roof.

Once when I was living with my father that one school year, Kay left Cincinnati for a few days. This absence was highly unusual – perhaps her parents were ill. My father invited me out to dinner, not just to any restaurant but to the Gourmet Room – an expensive place atop the Terrace Hilton with a mural by Miró and a mobile by Calder, fine wines and French food. We sat there in our coats and ties and I 'drew him out,' as I'd learned women and children and inferiors should do with important men. Dad almost never drank and kept the bottles locked up in his bar in the basement; his usual drink was spring water, delivered in ten-gallon jugs and inverted over an office-style cooler. Now he was downing a whole bottle of Bordeaux and slowly melting in the high-backed chair opposite me.

We were looking out at the illuminated city below. He said, 'You look like your mother – you have her eyes – but then again boys

48

your age aren't so different from girls. At your age boys and girls look alike.'

Maybe he meant nothing by it, but attuned as I was to every nuance in his mood I thought he'd never been this ambiguous, this personal with me before. He spoke in a low voice and didn't lecture me. I felt pure and appealing in the candlelight, as appealing as a girl. A great formality came over me.

My father's amorousness was a thing of just one night. His angry outbursts were almost daily. He and his wife could fight over the most trivial details – the opening date of the new turnpike ('No, goddam it, Kay, it's on the seventh!'), an exorbitant bill for the summer slipcovers ('Goddam it, Kay, I said no more than three hundred dollars and I meant three hundred dollars'), or even the slightest delay ('Goddam it, woman, get your goddam shoes on and get into the goddam car') – though sometimes he was just clowning and might wink at me as he bellowed up the staircase after her. But usually he was serious, his veins bursting on his forehead and his neck, and he'd pound the table with his fist and Kay would wail, 'E.V., don't yell at me,' and break into tears then sob until Daddy finally simmered down and said, 'Oh come on, Kay, let's go.'

'E.V.' – she'd stress each letter equally, the 'E' on a higher pitch, the 'V' much lower, as one might say, 'Bad boy' – 'I can't get my feet in my shoes, they're so badly swollen up.'

'I don't see how that's my fault,' he grumbled.

'But, E.V., you know I have high blood pressure, and now I've sweated through my dress, sweated clear through – you've upset me, look!'

Once my father, who was reading his paper at the dinner table, was so irritated by my chatting with my stepmother he hurled a spoon at me and hit my forehead, where a lump quickly rose. 'Goddam it, can't I have some peace and quiet in my own house!' Maybe he thought Kay and I sounded like two women.

'E.V.,' my stepmother wailed in horror, 'look what you've done, and just when he's going home to Delilah' (my mother). 'Are you losing your mind? Are you? Only a madman acts like that, E.V.' She rushed off to the kitchen to put some ice cubes in a tea towel and pressed them to my forehead. 'You could have put out his eye, E.V. Can't you control yourself at all?'

My father gathered his paper and retreated up the staircase to his study, from whence a moment later a huge choral Mahler symphony thundered down. He never apologized though he did say, the next time I crossed his path, 'Here, young fella, let me look at that.' He tilted my head back and studied the wound and said, 'It's nothing. It didn't even break the skin,' as if I were a hypochondriac instead of the injured party.

A few years after my sister Margaret married, she visited Daddy at his northern Michigan summer house with her husband and first son. Daddy had never approved of Roy, Margie's husband – mainly, I think, because he snickered and gave Dad a limp handshake. 'He has no backbone, that guy, and he makes a bad impression,' Dad said. If the earth was to be inherited by strong-jawed, ambitious white men, Roy didn't fit the profile. As Daddy fulminated against the Democrats and Russians, Roy snickered.

Margie's son Keith was a sturdy, active three-year-old who raced about the Michigan living room – and finally overturned a coffee table and broke one of the four hand-painted tiles that formed the top surface. Dad went quickly from a cold smolder into a red-hot rage. 'That child is going to grow up to be a criminal,' my father shouted. 'I want you, Marg, and that sniveling husband of yours and that criminal psychopath of a child out of here. I'm giving you an hour to get out of here.'

'Daddy,' Margie sobbed, 'he's just a little boy, he didn't know what he was doing.'

'That's because he can't tell right from wrong since he's a criminal. Mark my words, he's got a screw loose and he's going to grow up to be an evil man. It's Roy's bad genes. I want all three of you out of here pronto.'

Margaret turned to Kay as one woman to another but Kay was brooding about the broken tile. And she'd never much liked Margaret, whom she knew had spent her adolescence helping plot Kay's downfall and our mother's restitution.

I kept thinking Dad would back down and perhaps he might have if Kay had intervened. Incredibly, Marg and Roy packed and fled the house having spent only a single night there, though the cottage was a full day's drive from their house in Chicago.

At every meal for the next few days Dad grumbled against Roy

50

and Keith, especially that sniggering Roy who'd polluted our bloodlines with his white trash genes.

Dad and Kay criticized everyone they came into contact with. Kay was a convinced if not very skillful mimic. All her impersonations of people sounded alike – a high, funny whine and a scrunched-up grimace. She'd seize on something someone had said – anything – and repeat it in her high-pitched mimicry voice, even if the person in question had an abnormally low voice.

She and Dad speculated about other people's motives, invariably attributing to them the crassest, most venal ambitions. 'Roy is just sticking around,' Kay said, 'because he thinks Margaret is a hairress' (she mispronounced 'heiress' as if that were an example of Roy's illiteracy, though in fact he did mumble an educated English). 'Well,' Dad said, 'you can't say I didn't warn her.' When she'd first announced she wanted to marry Roy, Dad had sent her on a month-long trip to Europe, hoping she'd meet someone more suitable. When she decided to go ahead with the marriage, Dad refused to give her away. Nor did he attend or pay for the wedding.

Dad and Kay saw nothing but greed, envy and spite on every side, and their only way to think of other people was to patronize or snub them. Dad could be a bit more egalitarian if he was dealing with another engineer on the job or even a garage mechanic. Incompatible myths about society shifted violently about in his head like tectonic plates: some people were better than others, which you could tell by their wealth. A 'good family' or a 'fine man' or 'lovely lady' were always rich, though some rich people were climbers and upstarts and crooks (Jews). On the other hand, one man was as good as another, so long as he was white and Christian and didn't wear brown shoes with blue suits or grow a mustache or affect a wristwatch or cigarettes or mumble or have a weak handshake. In fact the exact bandwidth of acceptability was extremely narrow. If a man strayed a fraction too far from the precise signal of masculine firmness and attractive modesty he'd reveal himself as a weakling or blowhard. My father was always judging people. Almost no one passed muster.

His business grew and my father moved into a ten-room house with a two-acre back lawn in Watch Hill. From the windows one could look down through a valley to the distant silver gleam of the Ohio River. It was the late 1950s and the house was entirely air-conditioned, unusual for those days. Now my father could seal us all in and circulate his cigar smoke and constant music into every room. At night as he worked the windows blazed with light; from the backyard it looked like an ocean liner. In the open-sided carport sat his and Kay's late-model Cadillacs, his the larger one and dark blue, hers powder blue and more compact. He told me in 1958 that he was earning about eighty thousand dollars a year, which in the terms of the early twenty-first century would have been the equivalent of half a million.

His father had had a dog called Ol' Boy. Now my father owned a faithful collie-like mutt with the same name – I wonder if I too should obey my destiny and acquire an Ol' Boy III. Dad's favorite cat, Baby, striped gray and white, would stretch then tiptoe discreetly across his desk through the piles of onionskin paper. Incredibly, he'd trained her to fetch the coiled pipe cleaners he tossed into the corner. Ol' Boy, gorged on hamburger ground from prime beef, would doze beside his desk and wait for his morning walk outside in the hot, humid neighborhood. As he waited he drowned in Dad's oceans of Mahler or Brahms, which never made him lift so much as the tip of an ear, though the slightest rustle from my father caused his eyes to fly open. He'd stand, excited, then seeing it was a false alarm and that Dad was still hard at work, Ol' Boy would cover his embarrassment by pretending to stretch and yawn, arching his back. Then he'd slump back to the floor into his light, vigilant sleep.

My father had voted for Roosevelt the first two times. Something drastic had to be done to save the country, he thought. When Roosevelt died Dad seemed stunned, certainly sobered and respectful, though he was appalled that his replacement would be the cornpone moron Harry Truman. Public welfare handed down by a patrician like Roosevelt was almost acceptable to Dad as a form of noblesse oblige, but it was repellant when proposed by a presumptuous little shop owner from Missouri.

Dad was a conservative Republican who worried about the growing national debt and was opposed to the racial integration of the armed forces and the graduated income tax, which only penalized the successful. But in his palmy days he wasn't rabidly fanatical. When a neighbor at the summer resort of Walloon Lake, Michigan, had us over for drinks in the mid-1950s and spent the whole time fulminating against Commies in our midst and praising Senator McCarthy, my father, once we were back home, made the classic he's-a-loony gesture of drawing circles in the air with a finger pointed at his ear. He thought every American should have a fair chance – good health care, free education, equal opportunity. If he wasn't in favor of opening the doors of opportunity to blacks it was because he believed they were like big retarded children incapable of bettering themselves. Nor did he think much of women, who were irrational, governed by their emotions, and swayed by mere appearances. It was no accident that when women had won the vote they'd elected a handsome Dodo and crook like Warren G. Harding. Homosexuals, of course, were beyond the pale, unmentionable perverts. He had once fired a thirty-year-old man who'd failed to find a wife and who wore 'unusual' clothes, cologne and a wristwatch – all causes for suspicion, since White Industrial must be above reproach.

Politically, Dad sympathized with hardworking and upstanding white men, young married men, and he was all for giving them every chance in the world. If an employee got married, Dad would automatically give him a raise. These admirable guys had defended the country in both wars and now were holding the line against Oriental Commies in Korea. If only that little bastard Truman would have let a real man like MacArthur go all the way in after them and wipe them out!

Dad always said that his business was worth little except as a name, a reputation for excellence, but as the years wore on his reputation became more and more irrelevant. Once the exultation and anxiety of the war years were passed, the manufacturers Dad represented no longer needed a middleman pulling in a twenty-five-percent commission for himself. They could put in the field an employee drawing a small salary who could deal directly with their by now long-established customers.

Dad's great scheme had been to reserve large sums in the profit-sharing accounts of each of his engineers and then, at a precise moment, turn these funds over to the men and let Hal, say, buy the

White Industrial name for Akron and Bill buy out the Charleston, West Virginia, office. Except that by the time Dad got around to it White Industrial had been dealt out and the individual offices were worthless except as real estate.

It was all the fault of those Jews who'd taken over Mixing Equipment, I recall, or was it Union Carbide? Here he, Edmund Valentine White II, had built up the business for them during the chaos of war, had created vast markets for them and patriotically helped arm the nation in the great transition, for instance, from real rubber (no longer available from Jap-controlled Malaysia) to synthetic. And now these Jewboy Johnny-come-latelies were squeezing him out, the very man who'd made them rich.

Dad bought a gun. He stopped shaving. He stopped playing classical music on the record player, as if he had undergone some metamorphosis and could no longer swim in those salty seas. He muttered to himself. He couldn't sleep any more and was visibly aging. He sold off the various buildings that had housed the five branch offices of his business. His top salesmen took their profit sharing, shrugged, and ran. He vowed vengeance against the Jewboys, whom he was going to stalk and gun down. They weren't gentlemen. They didn't play by the rules. The Germans had been right.

They sold their house and moved to Lake Forest, a wealthy suburb of Chicago. In his mid-sixties Dad entered a new field, janitorial supplies. He wore coveralls and a cap with a bill and delivered paper towels and toilet paper to offices throughout the Chicago area. He mopped toilet floors and installed the paper rolls himself. On his coveralls was sewn a badge that said 'White Janitorial Supplies.' No longer did he don his tailor-made suits, or order two new ones to add to his collection every season, year in and year out. Now they hung in the closet untouched. He took a sort of regular-guy humble pride in his knack for adapting to reduced circumstances. But if provoked he'd start waving his gun and shouting about the Jews – and all this dead sober. He'd become as mad as his brother. He invited Margaret, my sister, out from Evanston to Lake Forest many times, but she visited him only once. She sensed he was still in love with her and now his proximity disturbed her. Nor had she forgiven him for throwing her and her husband and son out of his summer house ten years earlier.

The janitorial business failed and Dad and Kay moved back to Cincinnati, to Indian Hill this time, their last house. When he was in his late sixties he had a serious heart attack. After that, Kay told me, he spent hours monitoring his heartbeat with a stopwatch. Day in and day out he kept track of his pulse. The doctor had told him he had no more than ten years to live – and Dad measured every second of that decade. One day he was watching TV in the evening and lit a cigar. Suddenly he stood up and said, alarmed, 'Kay, I can feel butterflies all over me. They're in my feet, my legs, they're rising—'

'Oh, for Pete's sake, E.V., sit down,' she said, and he did and he died.

I'd ignored him for years before his death. When I was a boy I'd forgiven him for his foul temper by saying to myself, Poor man, he works so hard, he has all of us to support. But later, in my thirties, I gave my sister money to go back to graduate school and then I took in my nephew. Dad refused to contribute a dime. I worked long hours ghostwriting textbooks as well as biographical sketches of composers for Time-Life Records and half of a book on *Homo erectus*, *The First Men*, and half of another one called *When Zeppelins Flew*. I even did publicity for Celanese, the chemical company. But during all these trials I never shouted at anyone or pounded the table or threw a spoon. As I lived into the age my father had been when I was a young teenager, I was less and less forgiving of him. I would spend sleepless nights worrying about where I'd find my nephew's tuition or how I'd pay the rent, but I never lost my temper. I decided my father simply had a bad character. He was a bore and a baby.

In his will he'd left my sister and me just fifteen thousand dollars each and the rest, whatever it was, went to my stepmother. He gave our mother, his first wife, who didn't have a retirement plan or pension, a minuscule sum. I suppose my sister and I had attributed a large fortune to him since how else could we justify all the temper tantrums he'd made? We had all participated in the agony. When Kay died a decade later she left Margaret and me five thousand dollars each but only on condition that we not challenge the will. If we sought to know who her other beneficiaries were or how much she'd left them we wouldn't receive anything at all. Margie and I just shrugged and took the money. We'd always daydreamed about how our inheritance would someday transform our lives, but in the end it was a pittance that went toward ordinary living expenses.

Not so long ago my nephew read through the letters my father had sent my mother after the divorce. She had kept everything in a manila folder. From those letters I realized how much he'd worried about my homosexuality. His theory, as expressed in his letters, was that I hadn't had enough 'yard life' – manual labor – to balance me out. My life with my mother, he thought, had been all cocktail parties with adults and creative dramatics at school, emotional, overly analytical huddles with my mother, no sports, no discipline, no schedule, nothing but overstimulation and moody self-indulgence. He had a point.

When I look back on how exasperated he was with me, how stern a taskmaster, always meting out onerous chores, how willfully dull he could be, I think perhaps he'd designed all these horrors to cure me, as if I'd at last turn toward women and a life of sitting before a calculating machine, night after night – if only I could be made to mow one more lawn, fill one more wheelbarrow with pine needles, whitewash one more damp warehouse wall.

Edmund's mother, Delilah, aged twenty

Edmund with Delilah at Mullet Lake, Michigan, 1940

My Mother

I suppose it's the nature of mothers to make their children wince. A friend of mine from Munich with Austrian roots groans because his mother is always trying to make him read Goethe and listen to Mozart. People complain because their mothers are too nosy – or conversely too cold and indifferent. Some people say their mothers cling too much and then are shocked when their mothers enter a church-run old age home and lose interest in them because they're so taken up with the intrigues and organized trips of their new community. Some children complain because their parents fight or are divorced, without realizing the most neglected people of all are the offspring of love marriages. A husband and wife besotted with each other look at their children as annoying interlopers.

My mother brought me up to be more cultured than anyone had ever been in her family – and when she succeeded I turned around and despised her for her 'crudeness.' Whereas I'd learned to think of conversation as an art, she blurted out anything that entered her head. Not only was she impulsive, she often sounded stupid to me: self-contradictory, imprecise, or just plain wrong. She stuck close to the nearest cliché and smiled triumphantly whenever she could locate it. Her egotism and incessant chatter could be truly punishing.

She'd been born in Texas at the beginning of the century. Her father, Jim Teddlie, was a railroad johnny, one of those men who repaired track or laid it. He died when my mother was seven or eight. She used to say he died of malaria while working in the swamps around Houston, but she still had a postcard he'd sent her from a hospital in Colorado, so perhaps he had tuberculosis. Was TB a more shameful disease than malaria? Was it the AIDS of its day?

Mother always spoke tenderly and admiringly of her father, though she seemed to know little about him. She thought of him as 'Irish' and indeed Teddlie, as I later discovered, is still a common name in County Antrim, on the Protestant side of the border. For Mother, being Irish meant being a 'dreamer,' 'poetic,' 'impractical.' I was supposed to have inherited these Irish traits, a mixed blessing since to the same degree that I was considered imaginative and artistic I was deemed incapable of earning a living or driving a car.

Mother thought the loss of her father when she was still a child had instilled in her a floating but permanent dread of being abandoned by a man, a crucial man, or just by men in general. She had a very posed photo (was it a tintype?) of her straight-nosed, square-jawed, wavy-haired father, looking no more than twenty-seven in a rocking chair, while her full-faced ageless mother hovered behind him in clean, copious laces, her glossy hair pulled back in a bun. She was standing and he was sitting – the reverse of the usual poses of men and women in photos from that day and age. My mother's brother stood off to one side in short pants with freckles and anger written all over his face. Beside him in a blur was my tiny five-year-old mother with a big, vague white bow in her hair. The blur seemed to have been generated by the intensity of her feelings – or by a sudden movement. I'm sure that even then she never stood still.

The only other tangible sign she had of her father's passage on earth was that postcard he'd sent her from the hospital, written in long, beautifully formed letters in purple ink. Perhaps the ink lost its original color with time; I imagine it was brown and metallic but I think this only by association, since that style of handwriting was known as 'copperplate.'

My mother's mother I knew well: Willie Lulu Oakes. She was one of the twelve Oakes children, from a family of homesteaders on a farm outside Stephenville, Texas. I suppose they'd started out in the 1880s, coming over from Louisiana in a covered wagon, built a sod house half underground, then a one-room log cabin, finally a proper house with several rooms added, with a barn and a smokehouse out behind. A stream ran through their property past fields of corn and cotton and a stand of pecan trees.

My first publication was a story I wrote about the Oakeses for the Stephenville newspaper when I was just nine. The article was published with a disturbing photo of me, looking like a timid sissy in short pants, white shoes and with huge eyes, seated with both knees to one side, my head resting against the tawny flanks of our collie, Timmy, like a starlet nestling into a great fur ruff. I looked small and expensive to maintain.

I remember I didn't much want to write the article since it entailed asking all our relatives for their recollections of Ma and Pa Oakes. I was too self-absorbed and neurotic to do the research, and I didn't want to dwell on our Texas past. I'd been born in Cincinnati and was attending grade school in Evanston, Illinois – a city I liked with its big Congregational and Episcopal churches no one seemed to take too seriously, since there religion was a pleasant social habit, not an occasion for red-faced fervor. In Evanston there were hundred-year-old elms shading wood houses behind their underclipped hedges. Plain girls straddled cellos at home and practiced for hours. Boys wrestled with one another after school in piles of autumn leaves. Everything smelled of quietly smoldering leaves. Fathers were professors of geography at Northwestern. Mothers got out the vote for liberal causes. But in Texas people were obese and talked with a country twang and laughed at Amos and Andy jokes. Their gardens turned to brown, burned-over patches by June. Those who weren't violent drunks were Church of Christ, Baptist or teetotaling fanatics.

My mother's brother, Uncle Jack, seemed an exception. He avoided church with a quip ('Hard to smoke in there'). A short little plump man, Uncle Jack was shaped like Tweedledum, with curly brown hair that grew low on his forehead and an unemphatic mutter people found killingly funny. He was the president of the Farmers' First National Bank, a position he'd reached, it seemed, merely by murmuring wisecracks, which he delivered with just a pained pass at a smile. He never looked at the person he was addressing. His eyes always rolled here and there like a dented metal ball ricocheting its lazy way down through a pinball machine – though every time it collided with something it lit the machine up

61

and drove the score higher. His talk and manner seemed just as random but racked up similarly spectacular results. People cackled and stepped in closer to hear the funny man and repeated his remarks to the eavesdroppers behind them. I suppose he had a dry wit like Will Rogers, although he indulged in none of that comedian's head-scratching Everyman wryness. Uncle Jack made no efforts, and his effects were so low-key they would have gone unnoticed in a big city. But in Stephenville with its courthouse, two dry-goods stores, four feed stores, its scattering of hat-doffing Negroes and overalled white farmers (thumbs hooked into their denim bibs, some of them driving tractors right into town) – in such a place even the smallest gesture and softest remark were sure to register. And Jack smelled of sweet bourbon at eleven in the morning, the liquor fumes seeping from his body. Sweat glowed on his crinkly hair with copper highlights as he stood in the sunlight, his heavily starched shirt blindingly white, his brown suit jacket neatly folded over one short arm – arms so short he could barely reach his belt buckle to fasten it. He had to have his lace-up brown-and-white spectator shoes tied by his kneeling wife. Aunt Margie was a pretty woman with light blue glasses and brownish-blonde straight hair carefully curled at the ends to frame her heart-shaped face. She was always wailing, 'Oh, Jack,' when she caught his joke, and turning to share her amused indignation with the other laughing listeners. I'm sure she really and truly disapproved of his quips but she'd learned to go along with the routine, for it was such a successful one.

Jack smoked Camels and drank all the time. I couldn't figure out his humor but then again I hadn't been exposed to many funny men nor did I understand why humor was prized at all. It seemed to me human communication was dangerously imperfect and intermittent at best and I thought that introducing crotchets and grace notes into it was perilously irresponsible. When I talked I couldn't get anyone to listen to me and if I ever won a moment of genuine attention I stammered with stage fright until the focus shifted away.

And yet Jack didn't torment me with questions about where I stood with Jesus or my progress at school or my (nonexistent) interest in sports. He'd stand outside his bank smoking, his pinball eyes ricocheting, the sweat pouring down his face and down under his starched white linen collar. 'Well, Eddie,' he'd say, 'are you for or against the communists?' 'Oh, *against* them, Uncle Jack.' 'Well now,' he'd mutter, 'so you're against them, are you? Don't like Joe Stalin? Can't tolerate Karl Marx?' I'd go silent, since now we were out of my depth. He'd sigh, grind out his cigarette, and say, 'Guess they ain't my kind of folks neither.' His bloodshot eyes would look around in a worried way that was somehow also detached and superior.

Later Jack would tell his wife he'd had an interesting discussion with me about communism and that he and I had both gotten to the bottom of it and decided it was a no-count system. 'Oh, *Jack*!' she'd moan, scandalized and even frightened that the merits of communism had been weighed at all with a strange Yankee nephew. Then it would dawn on her that it was all a big joke and she'd laugh silently, quaking, until she had to take off her pale blue glasses and dab at the tears in her eyes, whispering, 'No-*count*!' It had suddenly seemed to her so screwball for him to work up an opinion about a thing that was so obviously satanic.

Jack joined AA for a while every now and then, and despite the shame and secrecy attached to the organization his quips about his losing fight with 'Master Barleycorn' were soon repeated all over town, making defeat sound faintly glamorous. Anyone who succeeded in staying sober came off as . . . sort of . . . *unimaginative*. Because he was so entertaining he wasn't held to the same rules of conduct as other people. There was something so appealing about his quiet drolleries, his obvious vulnerability linked to a congenital detachment, and the falling cadence of his jokes, that no one wanted to cut off his fuel or quench his flame.

And then he was dead. His heart stopped and his eyes squirmed helplessly to the side one last time. He turned tomato red then potato pale. Half-empty pints of bourbon kept turning up months after his death – in the drawer of his rolltop desk at the bank behind the partitions of glass smoked only to shoulder height, in his tool chest in the garage at home, out in the gazebo erected in the back garden for his daughter's wedding, in the trunk of his Studebaker in a slot next to the spare tire. He'd always called his stomach his 'spare tire,' though it wasn't a defined cushion around his waist but rather a gradual slope.

When Jack died Willie Lulu, Jack's mother, transferred all her hopes to her daughter, my mother, whom she'd named Delilah (in Texas people called her Lila Mae). Jack and Lila Mae had had a difficult childhood. They'd always been poor and lived in a one-room house down next to the track, that was provided by the railroad company. But after Willie's husband Jim died, the mother and two children were turned out. Willie took refuge with her parents on the Oakes farm, where she worked dawn to dusk virtually as a servant and seldom met a man who wasn't a relative. Sometimes she cleaned for people in town. My mother could remember Grandpa Oakes's first Model T. She could also remember the first plane she ever saw, a frail single-motor glinting against the depthless, cloudless Texas skies. She could remember her grandfather giving her driving lessons when she was barely a teenager. All her life she looked young for her age since she never grew more than five feet tall, and back then she'd had to sit on cushions to see over the wheel. At the end of World War I an unknown young man had come running over the hills waving his arms and shouting the good news.

She had a naïve, cheerful delight in being up-to-date. She exulted in new inventions. When Americans walked on the moon she shook her fists in the air and yelled her funny croak and smiled a giant smile – while I stifled a yawn and wondered why billions of dollars should be spent to let these crew-cut bores trudge around on a pockmarked sphere. 'Space kitsch' was an almost instant category in my dismissively campy vocabulary, a sneering negativity my mother said was pointless: 'You can't turn back the hands of progress,' she said. Like me she was prone to malapropisms.

When my mother was still a child on the Oakes farm her family was nearly self-sufficient. They bought salt and pepper and sugar and needles and thread and matches from a traveling peddler and bolts of cloth from the dry-goods store in town but otherwise they produced all the pork and greens and nuts and fruit they ate and all the firewood they burned. Grandpa Oakes was quiet and hard-working. His wife was the matriarch in her rocker and black dress sniffing her snuff and holding her Bible. She could read it and was convinced she could resolve any dispute that arose by consulting it.

The most exciting time of year came in the fall when all the neighboring men, moving from farm to farm, took in the harvest. The workers would be seated at long tables for two big meals a day while the women dashed about serving fried chicken, okra and tomatoes, biscuits, ears of corn, iced tea and pecan pie. Only after the farmers hurried back to the fields would the women and children pick over their leavings. The one great exquisite rarity was citrus fruit. Even as an old lady my mother could remember finding an orange from Florida in her Christmas stocking and inhaling the royal, sinus-tingling smell of condensed sunlight and detecting it days afterward on her hands and eventually in the potpourri her mother made of the peel.

When my mother was ten or eleven one of her young uncles, a twenty-year-old guy with a slow smile and outgrown trousers, discovered her climbing a fence in a distant field all by herself. He sweet-talked her and rubbed his big brown farmer's hand against the crotch of her panties. 'I liked it,' my mother would say half a century later, which made her niece, Jack's daughter, widen her eyes, plant a big cold smile on her lips and say in her most metallic greeting-to-a-stranger voice, 'Is that right, Aunt Lila Mae? You liked it, did you?' The deliberateness of my cousin's question conveyed that she was humoring a mad or senile relative, but as a child psychologist my mother liked saying uncomfortable, even daring and original, things about children.

When I was seven and my sister Margaret ten, Mother asked Daddy to choose between her and Kay. As I recall he was mostly silent, but my sister and I were crouching on the stairs out of sight of the living room, where the fatal meeting was taking place, and we couldn't hear every word. The women were audible (our mother noble, Kay strident), but Daddy was mumbling miserably. I suppose Mother was asking him to choose between an ongoing sex life (Kay) and the long-standing sterility of the marriage bed. More important, Kay had devoted herself to the business night and day during its first years, whereas Mother was ignoring her husband and studying child psychology in order to earn a master's degree.

She wrote her thesis on the religious experiences of children.

Margaret and I must have provided her with disappointingly little spiritual behavior to observe beyond tearful burials for our rabbit and bizarre pantheistic rituals among the beech trees down in the hollow behind our house. Later, when I was ten or eleven, I decided I was Zeus and could make the traffic lights change by shaking my right hand in a particular way, but I didn't tell my mother about this form of religion (if that's what it was). On stormy days – by then we were living back in Texas – I could make the lightning flash.

As so many people do, as I do, our mother lived by the contradictory 'wisdom' offered by popular sayings. In this case I think it was 'returning to my roots.' For her, Texas and her parents were her roots, and we even drove slowly by the old Oakes farm, though it belonged to another family now.

Her hometown of Ranger, Texas, was a ghost town. Over the main street of boarded-up stores floated a ragged banner: 'Oil Capital of the World.' Their house was on the edge of town, on a slight rise – which afforded our grandmother, in spite of her thick cataracts that turned her brown eyes opal blue, a partial view of the comings and goings of her neighbors. She'd say, 'There's that new football coach going to visit Mrs. Cort. Yes, I think that must be him. He sees her three days a week in the early afternoon before football practice. Her husband's down at the bottling plant all day . . .' She would shake with contained amusement like a closed saucepan in which corn kernels are just beginning to pop.

The other scandal involved the rich rancher man a hundred miles south of Ranger who was having a drawn-out affair with a rancher woman a hundred miles north. They'd each drive into town in their big new Cadillacs, his red and hers pink, and park on opposite sides of the road before the small flyblown hotel. They'd take their regular room for several hours once a week then drive back home to their spouses.

These stories made her laugh but not slap her knee or howl. She had a detached though friendly relationship with humanity. Maybe because she was a working woman, who could read and write but who'd been forced to stop her studies at age ten or eleven, she'd not been inducted into the squeamish respectability of middle-class Texas ladies. Disabused about but not disappointed by the behavior of her neighbors, she had the gentle satirical humor of the old rural Texas.

Many of the stores and some of the houses near her stood empty. Their owners, ruined when the oil wells had run dry, moved away without being able to sell their property. Next door lived a family of millionaires whose wells were still pumping, but they lived just as they had before they'd struck it rich – in a narrow house with the curtains drawn against the glare of the sun, the living room kept as a sort of empty museum in anticipation of a day when they'd be visited by notables from out of town (a pledge of a distinguished future that never came).

Grandma's house was like a miniature reconstruction of the farm she'd grown up on. In the backyard there were four or five hens that laid eggs for our breakfast, and our favorite was named Biddy Hen. A vegetable garden was protected from the marauding fowl as was an arbor that in the fall produced plump, cloudy Concord grapes, the skins bitter, the pulp sweet. Inside, behind the screen door and up a step, the house smelled of biscuits and old age. There was an out-of-tune upright piano on which our grandmother banged her way through 'The Little Brown Church in the Dell,' and sang along in her choked, broken voice. Her big arthritic hands, shaking with a faint tremor, struck clumps of notes very approximately. She was roughly in favor of religion but she was not a churchgoer. She never spoke of God or Jesus. When my mother was a child she'd run off with a young aunt to a tent meeting staged by revivalists. At midnight little Lila Mae rushed home, red in the face, eyes glittering, and she shouted, 'I have been saved! I have been saved!' Willie Lulu told her calmly, 'You have been no such thing. Now go to bed.'

When we moved back to Texas after the divorce, I announced to everyone I was a Buddhist. The relatives were horrified, my mother embarrassed, but my grandmother said, 'Why, if that poor little thing wants to be a Buddha, let him.' I was surprised and gratified by her unconventionality. I even liked being called a 'poor little thing,' which seemed to address my inward condition.

After Jim Teddlie, the railroad worker, had died, Willie Lulu and her small children Jack and Lila Mae had been moving back and forth between the Oakes farm to town, where Willie earned bits and scraps cleaning house for folks and helping out. My mother remembered being the poorest child in town and seldom having a pair of shoes that matched. In the summer she wore no shoes at all.

One of the people Willie looked after was Mr. Snyder. He was a good fifteen years younger than she. When he was a boy in a rural one-room schoolhouse he'd snitched on some older boys to the teacher. Those boys had grabbed him after class, held him down and beaten his leg with a board until it had come off above the knee. Somehow he'd been saved, the blood stanched, the bone neatly amputated and the wound cleaned. After that he'd been babied night and day by his three older sisters for years and he'd grown fat and spoiled, the palace eunuch. Like a eunuch he had a sexuality that consisted of squeezing little girls and boys against himself for suffocatingly long minutes.

Mr. Snyder's older sisters realized they wouldn't be around forever to look after their invalid baby brother. He should be married off to the capable, walleyed cleaning lady, Willie Lulu. It was done. It was a good deal for her to have a father for her children and a good deal for him to have a full-time live-in care-taker.

Mr. Snyder taught math and English in a junior college. He was still going to college himself every summer in order to build his accreditation and rise in the system. On both sides, maternal and paternal, my grandfathers took years and years of summer classes to earn a BA and eventually a master's. Grandpa Snyder invited Lila Mae to study with him every summer – which transformed her life.

At the Texas State College for Women she met my father, whose father was dean of students there. They married secretly (she was two years older than he and he was just nineteen – his parents would never have approved of such an early marriage nor a union with such a poor girl). They went off to live in Colorado, where my father studied engineering in Boulder and my mother taught school in a cabin higher up in the mountains. He did not acknowledge her to his fraternity brothers but continued living in the house with them. The young couple met on a Sunday or stole an occasional evening together. By all accounts they were both virgins when they first married and had not consummated their matrimony till months later. Their inexperience, my mother always said, explained the low quality of their lovemaking. In her usual way of holding conflicting opinions about most subjects, she respected premarital male virginity as 'idealistic,' but she also had a 'Continental' notion that men should sow their wild oats first with older, more worldly women, then share the sensual dividends with their chaste young brides.

Lila Mae was tiny and slender with bobbed hair and a flapper's short skirt. E.V. was a tall skinny young man in a suit with a straw hat, a big nose and Adam's apple and a squint meant to be friendly and quizzical but which was invariably serious and disapproving.

Grandpa Snyder was a 'horny old bastard' – which is how I would describe myself now, half a century later. He slept in the same big bed with Willie, she wore a long flannel nightgown and he baggy white underpants and a sleeveless yoke-necked undershirt. They looked like dolls propped up on their many down pillows (Willie called them 'pillars'); I doubt if they ever touched. I can imagine Willie addressing him as she always did and saying, 'Why Mr. Snyder, I don't think that's called for, not one bit,' and laughing quietly at the very idea of sex. He was always teasing her for our benefit, as one might pretend to throw a stick to a beloved, but easily fooled, old dog in front of visitors. By the time I knew him he was retired. He'd sit in the same upholstered chair in the living room most of the day, next to the door leading down to the garden and arbor. The chair slid backwards and forwards on oiled grooves. In the summertime a revolving electric fan was trained on him. He'd peruse the newspaper or doze and let the fan riffle the pages. He shaved only every third day so he often had white stubble, making him look disreputable. His wooden leg, which didn't bend at the knee or anywhere else, was propped up beside the wooden post at the end of the bed. It had been painted a pale, shiny flesh color and when worn was strapped to Mr. Snyder's shoulders and waist by wide cloth bands and dressed with a black stocking and a lace-up shoe. The stocking, of course, Willie changed every morning to match the clean one on his real foot. He would show his stump with eyebrow-raising coquetry and a cruel, entranced smile, as if it might excite us. We were encouraged to feel for the bone inside the fat. It reminded me of one of those cheap cuts of beef that are nearly all fat and bone, that make delicious rump roasts.

My sister and mother complained to me, never to Willie, about his suffocating embraces, his denture breath, his powerful, irresistible arms built up from a lifetime on crutches. At the same time our mother insisted that we respect Mr. Snyder – who was a good man, a sweet person, devoted to Willie, the family's salvation. When Mr. Snyder started one of his anaconda squeezing sessions, Willie (with her slight palsy, her age-mottled hands, her flowered housedress, her walleye, her chopped-off gray hair) would chuckle away and keep busy, wandering into the kitchen to putter or stepping out into the backyard to scatter feed to Biddy Hen or to water the vegetable patch. Unlike Mr. Snyder she never touched us and when our mother told us to kiss her on her withered, crepey cheek, she never held us or stopped her modest, nervous little laugh. 'Well, I declare, Lila Mae,' she said in a soft shaky voice and with little emotion, 'these are the finest children I ever did see. My, my, this little Eddie is the sweetest boy and a fine upstanding boy he is, isn't he, Mr. Snyder? And Margaret Anne – why there's no finer little lady in all the world.'

'They sure are fine children, Willie,' Mr. Snyder added in a tone halfway between satire and sincerity. At that moment my sister, knowing what was in store, would skip out into the backyard to look at Biddy's troop of just-hatched, nearly bald chicks. 'Why don't you come over here, Eddie, and give your old grandpa a hug?' For if he reserved most of his hugs for girls, a boy would do just as well. He'd squeeze me between his thighs and wrap his fatty strong arms around my body, press his clean hands against my buttocks and rock me against his crotch and his heavily upholstered stomach and chest. 'Mm-*hmm*,' he'd exclaim, as if he'd just finished a tasty dish, 'this little boy is a fine little man, I'll tell you.' Unlike my sister, I didn't feel violated by the hug and no one seemed troubled when it went on for as long as ten minutes. 'I hope you love your old grandpa,' he'd say with his eyebrows wagging up and down and his grip getting tighter until I feared he'd break one of my ribs. The electric fan, shaking its head censoriously, laid down negations of cool air against my bare arms and legs. More often than not I was in a baggy blue wool swimsuit during the hundred-and-five-degree summer days, which as soon as I ran through the sprinkler in the backyard began to stink of lanolin. My button-up cotton shirt, which I'd nearly outgrown, would strangle me across the chest.

Not that I did anything to develop muscles. My body knew how to grow and that was all. I didn't compare myself to other boys or men. I didn't long for their round biceps or low voices or accurate overhand pitches, and in fact the minute I sensed the shadow of competition I gave up. Of course I admired other males and longed to have their arms around me or hear their low voices murmuring in my ear, wanting to be loved for the boy I was – an overly brainy, nervous kid with knobby elbows and knees, pale blue veins ticking beneath the pale white skin, a long, almost constricted torso (as if Mr. Snyder had squeezed too hard just there), and a small, rounded butt and big feet.

That closed world of Ranger, Texas, bored me; nevertheless I knew my endlessly puttering grandmother loved me, and that her understanding me was not a condition for giving me her affection. She patted me stiffly, sweating in the kitchen over her fried chicken and her biscuits and white gravy made from pan drippings and flour, and urged me to eat a tenth biscuit – an eleventh! – while she sang my praises in the most imprecise terms imaginable.

Maybe we've made a mistake in believing that love begins with understanding. Maybe a love that understands is the very one that can change most radically, can even come to an end. What if the lover finally understands just how worthless or offensive or irredeemable the beloved is? Maybe we should trust a warm, general love, the broadest loving gesture, a careless impulse of love.

Our mother had lost our father's love or interest, certainly his presence. She kept his last name but inserted her own first name. She went from being Mrs. E. V. White to Mrs. Delilah White. The loss this partial name change represented was a terrible blow she would only recover from forty years later, when she'd entered her eighties and our father had died. The first time she ever wrote a check she was in her mid-forties. Suddenly she'd found she liked working and making a career for herself, making her 'contribution to humanity,' as she put it. She'd lost prestige, was no longer the wife of a prominent businessman. But after the divorce she was able to work in her own name, cover herself with glory – though ultimately I knew that it was never enough.

She was someone with few insights into herself or others and at the same time she held comprehensive theories about how she and others behaved. She looked at her pitiful alimony of two hundred dollars a month (and one hundred fifty dollars for each of us) as poisoned money keeping her permanently attached to her ex-husband. She couldn't afford to refuse it, but she thought that symbolically it kept her married to him; he would stop the payments only when we came of age and if she remarried. Never mind that this was a standard legal provision.

I doubt if her theory of symbolic marriage through money was true. She would have been ready to marry virtually any man who asked her. Since no one did, she preferred to ascribe this failure to something darkly negative in her unconscious or fatally symbolic in the monthly check. At least such an explanation avoided the unflattering possibility that no one wanted her.

After the divorce she moved us first to Evanston, Illinois, then to Dallas. She wanted to be near her folks in Texas, and Ranger was just a half-day's drive away. I can still picture Lila Mae standing in front of her parents in Ranger with a scarily bright smile on her face as she explained how wonderfully everything was going to turn out. She worked first in Evanston, then in Dallas, and later Rockford, Illinois, earning a small salary driving long distances from one primary school to another, testing all the children, on the lookout for those who were 'exceptional' (very bright or very slow) or handicapped in some way and in need of special training, and carrying her testing materials in a brown leather attaché case. At night she perched her reading glasses on the tip of her nose and graded dozens and dozens of these IQ tests and personality tests.

When she explained herself to her parents, Mr. Snyder would sit in his big upholstered chair with the fan trained on his heavy body. Willie was constantly shaking, almost as if sitting were a penance and she needed to stay in some perpetual motion to remain in working order, and would sit on the edge of their double bed (which was in the living room of their small, three-room house). Every time she would start to get up to fetch more iced tea or bring out the peach ice cream she'd been churning all afternoon, Lila Mae would stop her. 'Mother,' she'd say, 'now you just sit still because I have something very, very important to tell you.' Then Lila Mae would stand in her absurdly fashionable and expensive clothes she'd bought at Neiman-Marcus, stiff and brocaded and sweat-stained under the arms, her short, squat body bedecked one season in the New Look with its ballooning, crinolined skirts, the next season in the Trapeze, cut on the bias – Paris couture styles that looked as unlikely as Kabuki costumes in the hot humble Ranger house beside Mr. Snyder with his collarless blue-and-white-striped shirt unbuttoned sufficiently to reveal his undershirt, his unbending wooden leg propped up on an ottoman, Willie in her loose housedress and carpet slippers, the baggy sleeves of her dress revealing her jiggly arms, fidgeting on the bed. Lila Mae was wearing her high heels and nylons, attached under her skirt to the garters that dangled from her fat-crushing girdle. She owned no casual clothes – no shorts or halter tops, no trousers or T-shirts, no denim. Nothing except these costumes as costly and constricting as ceremonial kimonos. Though she was just five feet tall she weighed one hundred sixty or even one hundred seventy pounds, which her dramatic dresses emphasized. She'd been given a quick makeup course by a salesgirl at Neiman's and now she wore her eyebrows plucked and penciled brown. Her cheeks were clown red, her eyelids smudged a faint blue. Above the right corner of her mouth was a large white mole she thought of as a beauty mark. In her twenties a doctor had burned the black mole, but instead of dropping off it had just turned white. 'Please, Mother, listen to my plan, because I'm going to go places in this world. I always try to present the best appearance possible, I never let myself just go, I've got my fine new Packard and, Brother,' (here she shook her fists and let her face go radiant) 'just watch me go!'

'That's right, Sister, I always did say you're going to go places,' Willie said, smiling to herself, almost embarrassed that she'd taken the floor, though she meant to be nothing more than the Greek chorus to Lila Mae's Protagonist. She called her own daughter 'Sister' and Jack 'Brother,' just as our mother called Margaret and me 'Sister' and 'Brother.' I guess it was a Southern custom but I imagined it derived from all those years Willie had lived alone with her children before her second marriage, just as my sister and I were our mother's only companions, siblings more than children.

People back then didn't have friends. They surrounded themselves with the families they'd been born into or had acquired through marriage. They knew many professional acquaintances, of course, and entertained them lavishly, but though they might become boozily chummy during an out-of-town convention, they never confided in one another and they did nothing to intensify these relationships. Mother would befriend people she met through her work but she always referred to them as 'the little people.' She'd say, 'I'm always very warm and open with the little people but I have to keep my distance or else they'd eat me alive.' She'd say with serene, unreflecting complacency, 'The little people just love me. No wonder. I'm so nice to them. It's not often they get to meet a fine lady like me.'

Like my father, she admired rich people. She didn't pursue them, however, and she would occasionally dismiss them as 'spoiled' and 'idle,' especially non-working wives. She admired scientists and doctors most of all, for contributing to the advancement of humanity. Research was the highest good and Mother would have ranked a poor medical researcher over a rich real estate agent. Yet she was not given to setting up such clarifying contrasts in her mind. She didn't torment herself over moral quandaries; for her everything coexisted in a general beige haze.

Not that she couldn't come down hard on cheating or stealing or cursing ('I don't like ugly talk,' she'd say). Nor did she approve of criticizing other people: 'When did you become so high and mighty?' she'd ask my sister, who had a nasty satirical streak. Mother was more likely to pity people than ridicule them. Although she believed in medicine and eventually worked in a free medical clinic for the retarded and brain-damaged at Cook County Hospital in Chicago, she continued all her life to read Mary Baker Eddy's texts as well as a magazine published by the Christian Scientists. The Scientists had 'uplift,' and a certitude that evil was only a form of ignorance that could be banished by wisdom. Mother described herself as 'bouncy.' The Ford she owned when I was an infant she named Bouncer. She longed to go on the Arthur Godfrey Show as a good-time gal who was also a mysterious femme fatale. She thought her name, Delilah, was so alluring that it made her a natural for a talk show.

She also read Emerson, not for his uncomfortable questions but for his reassuring answers. She liked his Yankee individuality, joined to German idealism and Hindu passivity, though she was not one to ferret out the contradictory sources of his thinking. She was a pantheist. She liked to believe we were all waves in a single big sea, that for a moment we rose as individuals before we crashed and were reabsorbed into the swelling mass. Sometimes we were all mirrors reflecting the sun, just slightly different glimpses of the same Oversoul. Even at an early age I found Mother's pantheism attractive but unconvincing. I never liked God in any form, even at his most universal. To me he was like Santa Claus – a grown-up conspiracy perpetrated on children to humiliate them. Too good to be true. Was I unconvinced by God because he was a man, an adult white authoritative male, and his son seemed an unfamiliar type to me back then in the 1940s and fifties: bearded, long-haired, liquid-eyed, compassionate to the point of morbidity? My mother loved the Christ of the Sermon on the Mount but her God she took in two incompatible forms – diffused through nature and concentrated at the same time in one kindly, attentive, all-forgiving grandfather, a Mr. Snyder with no unpleasant appetites. Christ himself she thought of as a wise man, nothing more, the Emerson of his day. Certainly not as God. She rejected Jesus the personal savior whom her niece (Jack's daughter) embraced so fervently. After Mother died I surmised that her niece believed she was writhing in hell and that all Mother's good works and her daily prayers to God counted for nothing since she'd not been born again, not been washed in the blood of the lamb.

As I was growing up Mother and I would go on long car trips. After we started living in Evanston we'd drive down to Texas in two or three long days. (My sister must have been in the backseat but I can't remember her.) Along the way Mother would like me to read aloud to her the hopeful, 'deep' books that caused her to look dreamy ('Read that again – we must remember that!'), or that would make her drum her hands with glee on the steering wheel and bounce up and down with the sheer excitement of absorbing beautiful words and inspiring ideas. Sometimes she'd forgo

Emerson and Eddy in favor of something meaty like Bruno Bettelheim's thoughts about death camp survivors or childhood schizophrenia.

For everything she did was oriented to her career. Her reading – or rather her listening, since she'd decided that audition was her natural 'modality' and that she was an aural rather than a visual learner – gave her ideas or strength for her work, and often I'd read her articles about retardation from a professional journal. Even her inspirational reading was destined to give her the fortitude and compassion necessary for the draining work of her profession.

She had no hobbies, though she could sew and cook. She never minded sewing a button back on or taking tiny neat stitches to repair a tear and I can still see her sitting on the couch, her short legs dangling, her reading glasses weirdly enlarging my view of her eyes, as she performed the humble task with admirable calm and efficiency, often still wearing her fancy work clothes. She'd stop anything, wherever she was, to do a bit of required sewing, and yet she would never have wasted her time gardening or playing the piano – much less playing cards or going for a walk. She collected nothing for herself though she bought me a music box for every birthday, each one 'improving' in that it played a Chopin waltz or a passage from Gounod's *Faust*. Everyone she spoke to during the day was a patient or parent, colleague or volunteer, a 'professional contact.' She worked a full day – at first in the schools, later in her Chicago clinic – and often filled her evenings performing private testing and consultations. She had no interest in therapy or purely psychological problems. For her all mental torment was ultimately due to chemical imbalance, genetic defects or brain traumas, usually sustained during birth. Her *own* suffering alone was due to genuine distress (caused, usually, by men's cruelty). As for the rest of us, she was convinced birth was so hard on an infant each invariably sustained some form of brain damage – a condition that was obvious if important functions had been disturbed such as speech or eye–hand coordination, less apparent if a subtler form of aphasia had been triggered (the interpretation of visual signals, for instance). When I had trouble learning to drive from a brusque, untalkative instructor who would demonstrate the right moves but never describe them, Mother assured me I'd make progress if I switched to a college student who'd talk me through everything and show me nothing. (She was right.) My birth, apparently, had been so long and difficult that her obstetrician had made her promise she would have no more babies. I had had several convulsions in my first few weeks. 'He told me to close the store,' she said, laughing one of her laughs, a low, humorless, even menacing chuckle. It strikes me only now that her decision to close the store was timed with (and may have caused) the beginning of Daddy's affair with Kay.

If my sister Margaret or I spoke of general apathy, a broken heart, listlessness, anxiety, Mother would nod and say, 'I think we should run an electroencephalogram on you,' or, 'Maybe what you need is a good neurological workup. After all, you did have those convulsions . . .' She saw deviance and neurosis as an unsoundable swamp, preferring a diagnosis of previously undetected petit mal seizures to philosophical despair or psychogenetic angst.

She was a hard worker, up at six, at the clinic by seven-thirty, not home till seven or eight, at which time she often saw private cases, as she also did on weekends. She loved the once-a-week open clinic every Wednesday morning at the hospital, when doctors of all different specialties would pool their expertise (she would take notes and write up the final report). She'd describe pitiful, grotesque children as 'a beautiful case of hydrocephalus' or 'a classic example of Down's syndrome.' She'd refer to sickle cell anemia or phenylketonuria. As a Southerner she was convinced she could communicate more effectively than a Yankee, Indian or Chinese doctor could with blacks. And if the doctor asked if a child drooled, Delilah was always on hand to translate: 'Mother, does your baby *pule?*'

She moved one twelve-year-old named Polly in with us. Polly was pretty and well-spoken, but she was alternately polite and violent, lewd and obscene or frightened and a bit vacant. I kept trying to remind myself, as Mother had reminded us, that we were 'privileged' to be able to 'observe' a patient with major cognitive and motor disorders, but I could never remain serenely scientific for long. I kept thinking that Polly was playacting or merely being a pest, and to my horror she'd suddenly be on the floor, writhing, flailing her limbs, her eyes turned back, her color green. I'd hop around on one foot and bite my fist, but Mother became icily calm.

She'd describe the unfolding stages to me in scientific jargon. She never called an ambulance but waited for the fit to exhaust itself. She comforted the 'awakening' Polly in a sweet, impersonal way. She murmured to me, as if we were doing rounds together, 'We must change her Dilantin level.' Poor Polly. She'd treat me with fawning affection the day after one of her attacks, as if she were afraid we'd send her away, which of course Mother did – a month later, when the period of observation was completed. Mother never identified with her patients. They needed her professional competence, not her tears, although once in a great while some little thing would trigger a good cry. 'I need to let go about once a month,' she'd say.

Like my father who bragged he'd never gone bankrupt or killed a man, my mother would also stress the basics. They were children of the frontier. She admired someone like her mother, who rose early, made her bed, cleaned her house and cooked at least one hot meal a day. 'When I'm alone in the house,' Mother would say, 'I set myself a place and even put a flower in a bud vase.'

She and her mother wrote each other one-page letters every day. Sometimes just two or three sentences scrawled in pencil: 'Hot here in the nineties. Need a good rain. Mr. Snyder still got his summer cold.' Sometimes Grandma added, ungrammatically, 'Tell Eddie never to smoke nor drank.' (I took up both vices quite brazenly as a teenager.) She'd seen Uncle Jack's health undermined by his smoking and his life ended early by drink. In the nineteenth century, when she'd been a girl, alcoholism had been such a general scourge that teetotaling had counted as the honorable exception, the mark of decency, just as chastity was the only way not to contract syphilis. I thought of myself in adolescence as an upstanding lad incapable of succumbing to bad habits and whose tragic flaw, homosexuality, was invisible to most people. I didn't like myself, I thought I was a total fake, but I was confident I fooled most grown-ups. I was often teacher's pet. And I was always on the honor roll for good grades. I was given a role in the eighth-grade Pageant, in which I represented Literature (I pronounced it in two syllables as 'Lit-chur' as I marched in solemnly, wearing a toga, to the slow music in Schubert's Unfinished). Grandma's injunctions seemed trivial; she'd forgotten the higher morality in order to focus on two minor addictions. Only in my early forties did I stop smoking and drinking with an enormous effort that consumed two years; only then did I appreciate Willie Lulu's homely advice.

My mother wanted to give me the blanket approval that Willie Lulu had bestowed on her. But Willie had led such a circumscribed life, seldom traveling out of Texas or even Ranger, that she never doubted for a moment what she thought about something. Either it was a part of her familiar, over-observed world, or it was utterly foreign and she said of it, 'Well I declare, will wonders never cease,' and conceded the matter was beyond her intellectual means.

Lila Mae had taken on whole new worlds for which she'd not been prepared. Not just the miracles of technology (men walking on the moon), for those innovations were precisely the ones she could take in her stride, since she had been programmed to believe in progress. No, what made her uncertain were the proper boundaries between children and adults, love and sex, work and play. And what bewildered her were her children – their strange, mocking sense of humor, their self-hatred, their duplicity or at least doubleness. Mother couldn't tolerate or even fathom our inexplicable suffering. 'I don't see what you're complaining about,' she'd say. 'You're not deformed, you're well housed and well fed, you attend good schools, your health is excellent, you're both intelligent, in the top percentile of the population, you're of normal height and average weight, you're good-looking kids, you weren't born in Armenia or Mongolia but in the greatest country on earth in a century of splendid medical care—'

She'd look offended and tired when Margaret and I laughed at her chirpiness. To my sister I was too obviously an egghead and nerd and pansy, but as teenagers she and I shared a bitter sense of humor. Our mother's brand of *statistical* reassurance struck us as grotesque since we didn't *want* to be of average weight or normal height but exceptionally beautiful and lovable. In fact we were obsessed by our flaws. I knew that I had a huge black mole growing between my shoulder blades, that I threw a ball like a faggot, that my big black glasses made me look like a creep. Margaret hated her teeth, which had gaps between them because our mother had been too cheap to pay for braces. She'd rather buy herself a mink coat and a matching mink hat – 'I *need* it,' she'd wail. 'A good

79

appearance is half of professional success. And I get cold in the winter going down to that ugly old Cook County Hospital when it's still dark outside in sub-zero weather. I'm with welfare mothers all day long and babies who are no more than monsters and I need a bit of luxury in my life. Your teeth look fine, Margaret Anne. It's all just your imagination. Why can't you accentuate the positive the way I do?'

But she, too, had something she was ashamed of: fat. The ninety pounds she'd once weighed still seemed to her her rightful, God-given size. That she now weighed seventy pounds more struck her as a horrible but temporary aberration. (I had no sympathy for her; being overweight seemed to me to be a form of adult carelessness, even moral failure.)

Her girdle was a medieval device called the Merry Widow that simultaneously cinched in her waist (making it hard for her to breathe) and pushed up her breasts with half-cups that barely came up to the nipples. The Widow molded her ass into one seamless, rounded sphere upon which no crack was detectable under her skirt. The girdle, which was French, was laced up the back. That was my job. First I'd thread the laces around the outer, easier vertical line of grommets. Once they were in place Mother inhaled deeply and sucked in her stomach, and like a professional torturer I'd shift the laces to the inner line of grommets, one by one. She would groan from the pain but stoically order me to go on pulling them as tight as I could. Her hair was wild, as brittle and blown-up as a tumbleweed from years and years of sitting under the dryer, her pale face not yet made up, featureless and shiny, her height minuscule since she wasn't wearing her high heels, to which she'd become so habituated that her back calf muscles had shrunk so that now she could walk no more than a few paces before stretching them painfully. Once she was strapped into the Merry Widow she could clip her nylons in place, apply her makeup, brush and spray her hair into shape, slip on her dress (my job to zip up, too), put on her woven white and yellow gold bracelet and matching brooch, her black oval ring with the carved intaglio of Athena's head in profile, and finally step into her immaculately polished high heels, douse herself with perfume, grab a purse that matched her shoes, then shrug into a three-quarter-length mink cape she'd had cut from her full-length coat, on the theory that people would think she'd been able to afford a new fur at the newly fashionable length.

There was no provision for wearing panties under the girdle. Maybe some women did but Mother would have been too obese to bend over and pull them down to urinate, which she had to do frequently during the day. Because she was pantyless her black bush was visible just below the bottom of her girdle when she was not wearing a dress. Margaret thought this situation repulsive and unhygienic and wouldn't help Mother into her foundation garment. 'Oh, God,' she'd moan to me, 'it's *so* yucky. Somebody could look up her skirt and see *everything*, and she wears that damn thing every day – it's not even clean! Most women wear big baggy panties over the girdle – why can't she? Is she a pervert?' Although even young slender women were expected to wear girdles under fitted suits and evening dresses, Margaret categorically refused. She herself had been plump as a ten- and eleven-year-old, but as a teen she'd become lean and athletic and she knew she didn't have to compress her hips and stomach into a rubberized tube. When I was a high school freshman I slow-danced at a school party with a famous local beauty. Under the chiffon I could feel the unyielding bones and webbing of the girdle. Girls were revealing their bare shoulders and arms to admiring men, but mothers made sure their daughters' bodies, the important parts at least, were armored inside strong, protective foundations.

The minute our mother would come home she'd say, 'Get me out of this girdle!' She'd throw off her dress and I had to unlace her as quickly as possible, keeping my eyes off the glossy bush below. Her extremely white skin was inflamed and waffled as it emerged out of the Widow. Mother visibly sagged into a bigger, rounder, shorter shape. She began to throw on her nightgown in the evening. She'd use cold cream to remove her elaborate makeup, believing a woman should never wash her face (in fact, water must never touch the skin), but must thoroughly slather it in cold cream then wipe it off with cotton balls. To this daily ritual she attributed her glowing, unwrinkled complexion – a claim she'd make loudly and clearly to anyone present despite the incontrovertible evidence that her face was covered with a mass of tiny wrinkles around her mouth and eyes and two deep creases across her forehead.

Once her face was stripped of paint she made her first highball of the evening. 'Ooh-eeh, I need a drink, Brother!' Mother diluted her inch of scotch with a tall glassful of water and ice, and kept a highball going throughout the evening. She'd write up reports in her neat, round hand, which her secretary at the clinic typed the next day. She didn't approve of television, though she liked it – 'I don't see how you can watch that dumb stuff' – just as she enjoyed popular music but usually only let herself listen to Mozart's Jupiter Symphony or Beethoven's Moonlight Sonata. 'I like fine music,' she'd remind us, 'beautiful deep music meant for the ages.' And though we laughed at her cruelly, I agreed with her completely.

Somewhere along the line my sister and I had decided our mother was a character, a caricature like Tennessee Williams's Blanche DuBois or Amanda Wingfield. Lila Mae's baseless optimism, her coquetry, her insistence that she was an old-fashioned gal and 'one hundred percent feminine' made us cackle like gargoyles. Adolescents are wretchedly conventional as they tiptoe nervously into the great crowded ballroom of adulthood. Margaret and I were ashamed that our mother was a divorcee – a 'gay divorcee' as she put it, to our minds as dubious a dubbing as a Merry Widow. In Evanston in the 1950s during the Eisenhower years a divorcee was just a step away from a prostitute. Our mother said she left Cincinnati because she needed a 'big stage, a big world – I need to think big and be with big people who have big ideas.' But if she'd stayed put she would have been humiliated every day, since there were no single men or women in their world back in Cincinnati, and all the couples they'd known would have sided – and did – with Daddy and Kay. A divorcee was seen as a potential husband stealer and home wrecker. When we'd lived in Dallas Mother was not allowed to sit at the bar or dine alone in the restaurant at the Baker: No Unaccompanied Women was their policy.

Moving back to Illinois, Mother had made up for lost time, becoming a habitué of supper clubs and piano bars. Her favorite place was Ricardo's, an Italian restaurant and bar in the Rush Street area of nightclubs near the Chicago River, down behind the Wrigley Building. The lighting was low, the creamy pasta dishes comforting, the waiters friendly, and Mrs. White was a good tipper and a real lady. Short and fat and girdled, smiling and drunk and fearless, Delilah would clamber with some difficulty up on a stool and eat her noodles alfredo at the demi-lune bar, behind which were illuminated full-length paintings of the vices or virtues, abstractions that struck a Christian Scientist as theatrical and unreal. I can remember one naked male figure transfixed pitilessly in a shaft of light. Another canvas by Ivan Albright, Chicago's best-known artist, showed a hag covered in sores and cellulite, which, to Mother's incredulity, Albright had worked on for ten years. There was also a leprous door by Albright with a long portentous title, and it was no accident that he had painted the picture of Dorian Gray for the movie – both the bland Before and the oozing, scary After.

When I accompanied my mother to Ricardo's we'd be seated at a corner table within hailing distance of the bar. We'd never have enough money to order without thinking; Mother would split a green salad with me and then we'd split a pasta dish. She claimed she ate like a bird and indeed most of her calories came from whiskey. An accordionist, always the same little deferential man, would come to our table and serenade us, his mouth producing a sad smile and his head cocked to one side. The old Mr. Ricardo would sometimes come by, too: Mother whispered to me that he was dying of paresis, the final stage of syphilis that destroys the brain, though I wondered how she came by such information. She liked to make extravagant, always-tragic diagnoses of the minor characters flickering past us at Ricardo's. There was no one to contradict her and the medical authority she assumed made her sound credible. Her diagnosis of old Mr. Ricardo thrilled me ('Look how he stumbled – that's called *ataxis*!'). Here was a distinguished gentleman in dark suit and white shirt, with an interesting accent, extremely thick lenses in his glasses ('Yes, paresis attacks the optic nerve!') and reserved good manners – and there, stumbling behind him, was his lurid venereal disease, contracted decades ago in the Old Country during a youthful lapse.

Young Ricky Ricardo (not to be confused with the Cuban TV star and Lucille Ball's husband) with his blond brush cut and regular features and his skin pitted from a newly banished case of acne, with his loud tenor voice which he'd unleash when he'd serenade Mrs. White and son with 'O Sole Mio,' was a well-judged compromise between Midwestern neighborliness and Old World hand-kissing, which he'd perform with a grin and a smart operetta click of the heels. Mother suspected the restaurant business bored him and that he wished to be a singer – 'Too bad,' she said, 'because he doesn't sing on tune, poor guy.'

From our corner table, where Mother kept the highballs coming, she'd turned her unfocused smile on the extremely tall businessman at the bar who kept glancing over. 'Roberto,' she whispered to her favorite waiter, 'do you know anything about that very tall man – don't look now! – that tall man at the bar?'

'Oh, that's Abe, Mrs. White. I don't know his last name – big tipper, owns a yacht he keeps down on the marina here. Lives somewhere nearby on the Gold Coast, I think he said.'

'That's interesting,' Mother said with a smile. 'That's *very* interesting.'

Maybe Abe noticed them conferring about him, because Roberto came over a moment later with a new highball and a ginger ale for me. 'Compliments of Abe,' he whispered. Rather than exclaiming with excitement, as I would have predicted, Mother merely smiled with boozy serenity and raised her glass to toast Abe, her head tilted slightly to one side. Her smile was pursed as if to reproach him tenderly for such an extravagance. A minute later he was standing at our table.

'May I join you?' he asked.

Mother smiled enigmatically and nodded and he slipped into the booth beside her and reached over to shake my hand. 'Abe Silverstein,' he said. It all seemed so easy to me and I wondered if Mother was sober enough not to ruin this chance. For it did appear a remarkable opportunity. Mother sat beside the silent phone night after night, anxious and depressed, because none of the men she'd given her number to at Ricardo's or at the Miller Steak House ever called her. At age fourteen I had replicated within myself all of her self-doubt – was she too old, too fat, too short, too drunk to attract this tall slender man in his forties with the unseasonable tan and the shiny dome circled by a monk's tonsure of dark curls, with the well-tailored suit that gave him staggeringly wide shoulders and exposed an elegant quarter inch of white shirt cuff, this man with the bright smile and the one winningly chipped tooth, with the big warm dry hands? I imagined his hands trying to unlace the complicated double helix of the Merry Widow. I felt anxiety building up inside me. Should I say something remarkable to win Abe over to our side? To lure him into a relationship with Mother, with us?

Mother spoke too much about herself, about her work with the retarded, and I squirmed with irritation at her social ineptness. Didn't she know that men needed to be drawn out, made to feel important? 'I love my work,' she said, 'because I feel I'm making a real contribution to retardation.'

But Abe wasn't put off. 'That's just great, Delilah,' he said. 'I didn't think I'd be meeting someone classy like you in a place like this.'

'Like me?' Mother asked disingenuously. 'Whatever do you mean?'

She wanted him to elaborate on how unexpectedly important and admirable she was, but he didn't pick up on his cue and instead started rambling on about other interesting men and women he'd met at Ricardo's. Naturally Mother didn't want to hear about them. She didn't want to be placed in a context, no matter how flattering. She wanted, as always, to hear that she was unique. Her smile faded from the goodwill she'd radiated when she'd been talking about herself into a drunken fragment of resentment and impatience. If I'd been in her pumps I would have produced all the appropriate little nods and murmurs of assent, but she went inert and heavy with frustration. I'd learned to make myself extremely agreeable to the two or three handsome guys my age I knew at Evanston High (in a year I'd be sent off to prep school). I knew they'd never sleep with me, but I wanted them to enjoy themselves so much in my company that they'd gravitate to me almost unconsciously. Mother had perfected none of my dark arts.

On the plane she'd met a Santa Barbara businessman who'd invited her to his Spanish-style mansion for a weekend. He'd woken her with a frozen cocktail shaker full of brandy, milk and white crème de menthe – brandy Alexanders for breakfast. 'It's not very appropriate for a mother to say this to a son,' she'd whisper, smiling, 'but boy was he a good lover! I'm so glad I met him or else I wouldn't have known what . . . *love* is. I mean what

all the fuss is about. I certainly learned nothing from your father.'
She might stray for a second into the glare of sex talk but she felt
more at ease in the soft shadows of romance and its vague
vocabulary. 'Of course I don't mean to suggest it's just . . . *animal*
between us. No, he's a very fine man, a fine spiritual man with a
lovely daughter who is very alone in that big adobe mansion, a
poor little rich girl if ever I saw one, badly in need of a new mother.
Her own died of breast cancer two years ago and Bill is at loose
ends, too, you can see.'

Bill, as it turned out, was Catholic, but our family was equal to
that. Mother twitched a veil over her head in the mirror and smiled
a Mona Lisa smile and Margie eagerly anticipated catechism
classes. She daydreamed about her new sister, Bill's teenage
daughter – they'd attend Vespers together! They would be insepar-
able, sisters! I myself would duck into a Catholic chapel and with
blushing self-consciousness sketch in a half-curtsy genuflection and
a watery sign of the cross, an insubstantial plus sign.

Margie and Mother and I sat around for hours speculating about
what went wrong when Bill stopped calling.

'Maybe he lost your number,' I said.

'I'm listed.'

'Maybe he's not sure you like him.'

'He can have no doubts in that department.'

'Do you think,' Marg asked, 'you were too . . . easy?'

'I was *always* a lady,' Mother said primly.

'Maybe *that's* the problem,' Marg threw in cynically.

'Maybe some men chase after cheap women, Margaret Anne,
but they don't respect them in the long run.'

I glanced at Mother and was surprised by her ruffled look of
virtue offended since she and I both knew she had been easy – an
accessibility eased by all those wake-up brandy Alexanders.

She went through a day of anxiety, two of tears, a night of anger
followed by a weekend of sodden self-pity – and then she took on a
crisp air of contempt. 'I'm afraid I was fooled by Bill,' she said as I
was lacing her into the Widow. 'He's not the upstanding, trust-
worthy person I imagined. It's just as well he stopped phoning –
that saves me from telling him politely but firmly that he needn't
call again. I'm far too busy a professional woman for men who are

cheap. Willie Lulu always taught me that I'm a fine person and should hold out for the best. I was brought up that way. I have no tolerance for cheapness.'

She could always fall back on Mr. Hamilton, a newspaperman who liked nothing more than to have Mother prepare him a hot buttery meal. Then they'd watch a variety show on television. He was half-blind and couldn't drive, which removed any reason for his going easy on the bourbons and branch water. He had been in the newspaper business for nearly forty years but he exhibited no interest in current events or office gossip and relayed no anecdotes of interest. I think he made up the pages, chose which stories would run where and for how many inches. His conversation was all boilerplate, the odd bits of information used to fill up columns. In some ways he was Mother's version of Mr. Snyder – a big soft man who was companionable. Mother kept hoping for someone better and when she thought things were working out with Bill or Abe she'd dismiss the thought of Mr. Hamilton with scorn. 'I need a *real* man,' she'd say. 'Someone who's got some oomph.'

But whenever better prospects vanished she'd go back to preparing homey dinners for Mr. Hamilton or let him invite her out for a big, sizzling steak at Miller's and a baked potato engorged with sour cream and chives.

Mr. Hamilton had a son, Bob, who was twenty-three when I was fourteen. Bob was a medical student the summer I got to know him but to earn money he'd been working in construction. He was tall and slender and deeply tanned and his hands were calloused and clobbered, which didn't really go with his neat blond hair and long straight nose.

The four of us went to the Lyric Opera House on Wacker to see one of the first performances of the Kabuki in America, a selection of highlights from various plays. I'd read a book about the Kabuki by Faubian Bowers, just as I'd read about the Floating World in James Michener's study of Japanese prints. We had orchestra seats – first Mr. Hamilton, then Mother, then Bob, then me. While the performers wailed and hissed, froze in mid-stride and ogled one another haughtily, and men dressed as maidens simpered and prattled in high, whiny voices, or suddenly, to a great clatter of drums and shriek of fifes, metamorphosed into evil white foxes as cherry blossoms fell from the proscenium, or an old crone (another man) singsonged her way through an interminable monologue about dynastic history interrupted only by the entrance of a red-eyed warrior in a helmet sprouting horsehair – while all this activity was going on onstage I was pressing my calf against Bob's iron-hard, heavily muscled and no doubt deeply tanned leg. I would swivel my shoe slowly from side to side in order to 'travel' almost imperceptibly into a snugger fit against his leg. Of course I knew that in a second he'd move away – irritated, if he registered my invasion at all.

But he didn't move away. Instead he flexed his calf muscles against mine. Seconds would tick by and neither of us would move. We were petrified, while an *onnagata* onstage trailed her hand-engulfing sleeves from side to side and spoke at length in a tiresome drone. Risking all, I edged my shoe so close to Bob's that he would have to retreat – but he didn't. He held his own, bracing his leg sturdily against mine. Some of the paper cherry blossoms drifted out and clung lightly to my sleeve, his shoulder.

At the intermission our parents toddled forth to buy their whiskey drinks. Bob and I sat the intermission out, afraid to reveal our erections. When Delilah and 'Mr. Ham' were out of earshot Bob turned to me and said, 'What's our plan?'

'We could go to the men's room and lock ourselves in a stall,' I said.

'That would never work. Besides, I want it to be nice. I'll come over to your place next week to watch the Perry Como Show. Then I'll pretend to be too drunk to drive home and ask to stay over at your place.'

A week later all went according to plan, though I could tell my mother suspected something and was reluctant to let Bob sleep in my room. Years later when I was in my fifties and Bob in his sixties, he looked me up in Paris and almost instantly we went to bed together in his hotel room.

My mother and I had such an intense, intimate relationship; no wonder I seduced her lover's son. When she was considering divorcing my father, she'd hug me and weep and say, 'If only I could find a man like you.' I'd stroke her hair. 'It's hard to believe you're just a little boy. You're so wise and feeling and sensitive.'

She wanted me to be artistic and cultured. She encouraged me to improvise on the piano. My big number was 'The Brook,' in which I'd start off as a soft trickle and end up as a mighty flood, hammering out rushing octaves. Not for me, assiduous practice devoted to learning the '*Marche Slave*' or 'The Spinning Wheel,' which Margaret perfected and performed at recitals, wearing a pale blue ribbon in her white-blonde hair, her legs encased in high white kneesocks. I had no interest in the patient acquisition of proficiency. My mother had told me I was a 'genius' with an IQ in the genius range (over 160 on the Stanford-Benet, over 140 on the Wechsler). She'd declared I was a musical genius as well – in fact a genius at whatever I took up. A genius, of course, must never be seen struggling. His impressive accomplishments are all instantaneous.

When I banged out 'The Brook' at ages four and five, adult visitors nodded and grinned at the prodigy, but when I was striking wildly, cacophonously at the keyboard at seven I could see my father was embarrassed and the guests appalled. 'I think we've had enough of that, Eddie. Hal, what about another Manhattan? Helen? Another martini?'

I immediately lost interest in the piano and never enjoyed playing again, at least not in the bravura, improvisational way that had sounded so magnificent to my childish ears. The next time my mother asked me to play for guests I said sullenly, 'I don't know how.' Margaret moved in and did a rapid, note-perfect rendition of 'The Spinning Wheel' and curtsied like a total prat to the general applause.

After the divorce Mother, who after all had just received a master's degree in child psychology, would sometimes say I needed a father figure. 'You need a man to teach you baseball and to teach you – well, how to be a man. Your own father is hopeless. He never wants to play catch with you. He's too competitive – he wants to win.'

'He plays tennis with me,' Margaret piped up.

'He's going to have a heart attack with that big bay window of his,' Mother said, 'lunging around that court. I suppose he always wins.'

'So far,' Margaret said, 'but I'm giving him a run for his money.'

The truth was Marg was good at sports, everything from field hockey to tennis to canoeing, and she lived for her summers at an all-girl camp, Bryn Haven, where she eventually became the captain of the Blues, one of the two main teams. Camp was a competitive, emotion-drenched experience for her. All winter long she'd daydream about her camp friends, to whom she sent very thick letters every few days. At the end of the summer my mother and I would drive three hundred miles up to Wisconsin and attend the closing ceremonies at Bryn Haven. There were races in big war canoes and archery contests and swimming competitions in the deep lake circled by towering pines. As dusk settled in and the night turned cool more canoes glided past freighted with cardboard and cellophane displays of Monticello, Mt. Vernon and the White House, the windows ablaze with powerful flashlights held behind them by girls wading unseen in the shallow water and pushing the boats along, humming 'America the Beautiful' in four-part harmony. Margie's team was victorious just as Margie herself, with short blonde hair, tanned, muscled legs and bright blue eyes, won every individual award including those for leadership and general citizenship and spirituality. She seemed pleased to have us present as her audience, but she might have wanted Mother slimmer, married and a homemaker rather than a hefty, self-praising, hard-drinking working woman, and she definitely would have preferred me in a checked short-sleeved shirt with the sleeves rolled up an inch, blue jeans, thick white socks and penny loafers, a regular guy with biceps rather than a pale bespectacled oddball in the Oleg Cassini designer shirt I'd bought on sale at Marshall Field's – the one with the big, embroidered gold ears of half-shucked corn going down the front like a priest's figured chasuble. Margie was always rushing off to the Friendship Circle in the woods for the exchange of one last vow or ring with Jeananne.

I suppose every once in a while Mother would remember I should be a real boy – independent, athletic, curt – but she wouldn't have liked a son like that. She wanted me to be her soul mate, her confessor, her advisor, by turns a wise child and a comforting adult, sexless as an angel.

When in my thirties I began to be known as a writer, people would ask her what her child-rearing method had been for me.

'With a gifted child,' she would say, opening her hands, palms up as if to display self-evident principles, 'you must let him set the pace. You must follow his lead.' She certainly indulged my whims when I was a child to the degree she had the time or money to do so. I'd want to eat sukiyaki in the Wisteria Tea House on the Near North Side, in a house so old and rundown it had become virtually a slum. Although I didn't think about it then, the year was 1952, just seven years after the end of the war and the confinement of Japanese-Americans in prison camps. No wonder the restaurant looked shabby and the waitress was so thin her hipbones poked through her rayon kimono. Neither I nor anyone I knew at that point had ever eaten Japanese food. Certainly no Japanese restaurant would have dreamed of serving raw fish back then. My mother and I were left in stocking feet alone at a table in a high-ceilinged tatami room of our own with smudged scrolls on the walls and rice paper glued to the windowpanes, filtering the already shadowy Chicago winter light. Beside us the vegetables and beef strips were cooking down in a thick, sweet-smelling sauce.

Although we were alone my mother and I dared not speak to each other above a whisper. The waitress came back periodically to fool with the setting on the tabletop stove and to feed the iron skillet with more chopped cabbage. The bubbling, the filtered light, the rich smells, the sound of tires outside sluicing through the melting snow – all tranquilized us, though when we'd arrived we'd been nearly hysterical with United Nations pep.

That meal had followed a disappointing service at the Chicago Buddhist Church on the South Side. Mother had encouraged Margaret and me to have our own religion, whatever it might be (perhaps this ecumenical spirit she'd acquired while writing her thesis on children and religion). I'd gone every afternoon for weeks to the neo-Gothic library at Northwestern to read Max Müller's *Sacred Books of the East*. I'd dipped into the Torah, the Koran and the Upanishads. But I'd been gripped by the Buddhist sutras. No matter how pessimistic I might become, I could never begin to approach the extent of Gotama's nihilism. He saw the self as an illusion, desire as the root of all evil, rebirth as the worst of fates and extinction as the only goal. In this world the most and the least one could expect was sickness, old age and death. Whereas the

Hindus posited an irreducible soul, the *atman*, the Buddha preached the doctrine of 'no soul,' *anatta*. In an unpeopled universe full of nothing but illusion and suffering, not a single entity existed, certainly no deity.

This is realism, I thought with grim satisfaction. No interceding ranks of angels, no accountancy of sins and good deeds, no heaven nor hell, no nosy-parkering into other people's bedroom hijinks. The opposite of hateful, intolerant Christianity.

But when we arrived at the Chicago Buddhist Church in a rundown South Side neighborhood nearly thirty miles from where we lived we encountered a group of smiling, waving Japanese men, women and children worshiping Amida, the Lord of the Western Paradise, a personage very much like a Catholic saint. He was a bodhisattva in the (to my eyes at least) 'degraded' form of Mahayana Buddhism, someone pledged to stave off the horrors of rebirth and the bleak solitude of nirvana by spiriting his followers away to a paradise where they could struggle toward enlightenment in comfort and in the busy, bustling society of like-minded souls.

I was bitterly disappointed – by the organ and hymns that sounded suspiciously Methodist, by the flutter of arriving parishioners in big hats exchanging kisses, by the depressingly secular announcements of upcoming bingo games and covered-dish suppers. I fled. Where I'd expected a bald abbot stony with meditation, a trickle of sandalwood smoke and a superb indifference to all forms of striving, I'd found a congregation of ordinary folks besotted in the ordinary way with the little pains and little rewards of everyday life.

'I thought it was nice,' Mother said, puzzled by my contempt.

'You liked it because it was just like some dismal Christian service,' I said nastily.

'I don't see what makes you so high and mighty.'

As I grew older I became more and more difficult with my mother just as she was becoming sadder and lonelier. When I turned fifteen she was fifty-three; she was finding fewer and fewer men to ask her out, she was nearly as wide as she was tall and constantly out of breath. When I'd let myself in at midnight after a date she'd want to know every detail about my evening. She'd be lying awake in bed in her darkened room just beside the front hallway. I knew she couldn't sleep until I came home and I resented this form of emotional blackmail. Nor did she suffer in silence. 'Remember,' she'd say, 'I won't be able to sleep a wink until you're safely back here, and I've got a killing schedule at the clinic tomorrow. Please don't keep me up all night, honey.'

When I'd stand in her doorway at midnight she'd want me to sit on the edge of her bed and rub her back. Sometimes she'd turn on a light and ask me to press out the blackheads. Her skin felt clammy. I could smell the whiskey seeping from her pores – kittenishly, she called it 'wicky.'

'Was she cute, that Helen of yours?' she'd ask.

I felt trapped, compromised by her nosiness, revolted by the touch of her skin which, however, was terribly familiar. I didn't want to discuss girls with her. I had bought a latch for my bedroom door and installed it myself so I'd have a little privacy, but she was always tapping at the door. If I didn't respond she'd say, 'Now, Eddie, you either open this door for your mother or I'm going to break it down.' I knew she would and could. If I stayed in the bath too long she'd shout through the locked door, 'You've washed it long enough.'

As a little boy I'd lived for her. I'd suffered when she wept over the divorce. I would read to her the beautiful words of Emerson and feel the same glow of admiration as she did, for such depth, such wisdom. I would sometimes cry hysterically when I was unable to console her. In my fantasies (and in my responses to the inkblot test she was learning by administering to me) I saw empty royal palaces and objects – jewels and graveyards – just as when I built castles of sand in the summer or of snow in the winter I peopled them with lonely, tragic tsarinas floating through crumbling wings of the Old Palace long since abandoned.

But as I grew older I resented my mother's dependence.

When she'd say, 'You and I are exactly alike,' I'd reply, 'Oh no we're not. You like to lump everything together. You prefer resemblance to difference – that's why you like the Bahai Temple in Glencoe, because they claim all the nine great religions of the world are *really* the same. But they're not! You have to make distinctions and not lump things together. That's your biggest mistake.'

Her 'mistakes' were legion to me. She was unafraid of the obvious. I lorded over her my more extensive reading, my better memory, my more critical approach to life, forgetting that if I had respect for the mind it was due to her. I attacked her for not keeping her distance, for not respecting my autonomy; I could make her cry but if I was nice to her even for a moment she'd be all smiles and forgive my trespasses against her. I felt she loved me without understanding me, just as her mother loved us all but knew little about us. Mother saw me as a sort of philosopher king, something like her secular vision of Christ. In her view I was eager to make my 'contribution' in order to reduce the sum total of human suffering. When she finally accepted that I was a gay writer, she'd say, 'You've truly become a spokesman for your people.' Gays were my tribe and I was leading them into the Promised Land. Only I knew how selfish and egotistical and too afraid of failure, obscurity and poverty I was to be able to afford the luxury of 'helping my people.'

In the late 1970s, when I was approaching forty and she was in her late seventies, she was drinking so much that she could scarcely walk to the corner. Her belly was a swollen watermelon under her girdle, her face resembled that of a squalling infant – creased, nearly toothless, red. She'd been forced to retire when the clinic she headed at Cook County Hospital closed its doors. It had been a private clinic within a public hospital and it had been financed by rich benefactors, friends of Abraham Levinson, the doctor who'd established the foundation after his son's early death and named it in his honor. Now Dr. Levinson was dead, too, as were most of his friends. Whereas the clinic (and my mother) had been pioneers in the diagnosis and treatment of retarded and brain-damaged children, now, thirty years later, better care had become common and there was no need for the Julius D. Levinson Foundation. She was forced into retirement with no pension and no savings. She had nothing but the pitiful monthly sums she received from Social Security.

And the money I gave her. I sent her a check every month for the next twenty years; in that way I'd replaced my father, who was now dead, and his alimony, which had run out. I maintained my mother in her fancy Gold Coast apartment with its doorman and view of Lake Michigan. I paid her dress bills at Neiman's and Saks

Fifth Avenue. Actually, she'd begun to economize so skillfully – she who had always been recklessly extravagant – that she was able to afford little luxuries even on the small sums I was able to spare.

At the same time my mother lost her job she had a second mastectomy. Her much younger boyfriend found a job in California, took his leave and was never heard from again. He'd been a self-serving drip, but Mother had loved him and losing him was a terrible blow. She felt he couldn't endure the loss of her second breast (nor endure her colostomy; altogether she would suffer from three primary cancers). As if these trials had not been harsh enough, she couldn't keep up the payments on her modest summer house and had to sell it. Jobless, loveless, breastless and homeless, she began drinking so heavily that one night, driving home to the house she was about to vacate, she crashed into the garage door, then staggered inside and fell in the bathroom. She cracked a rib and was unable to get up. No one knew she was there and no one came looking for her. One day went by, then a second. By now thoroughly sober but in excruciating pain and still immobilized, she began to worry about a new complication. She was too weak to irrigate her colostomy and her peristalsis seemed to have shut down. She knew that soon she'd be poisoned by her backed-up feces.

It was then she made her strange bargain with God. She told him that if he'd unplug her colostomy she'd never touch another drink. No sooner had she made this deal with the deity than shit began to shoot out of her side. And she honored her promise of abstinence ever after.

Once she stopped drinking she succumbed to the most terrible delusions. My sister and I failed to see that she had the DTs, though her symptoms were classic. She boarded a plane for Amarillo where she descended on her brother Jack's daughter. Two days later my cousin was on the phone: 'Eddie, you've got to come down here and get Aunt Lila Mae. She's gone crazy. You know those little bugs we have down here we call millers? Well, there were just three or four millers flying around the ceiling light last night but your mother saw *thousands*, revolving like devils at the mouth of hell. Now you know, Eddie, I keep a nice clean house, a Christian house. Your poor mother is out of control. I don't know anything about her business, but I kind of suspect she's not a rich, rich woman . . . ?'

'Not at all,' I said.

'Well, she's offering money, even very large sums, to just about everyone she meets. She's not at all nasty. She's as sweet as sweet can be. But she never draws a breath; I hear her in her room talking to herself, very excited and bubbly, like a little girl. You know I've always thought Aunt Lila Mae is a very special person. I love her to bits. She's believed in me all my life when my own mother did nothing but criticize me and tear me down. I owe your mother so much but I just don't know what to do now.'

I flew down to Amarillo and met Mother at the airport in a funny little costume she'd cobbled together, with pompoms in her hands. She had decided she was a cheerleader. Her eyes wouldn't meet mine, her smile was a manic blur and she was singing a little pep song of her own devising: 'Go, Eddie, go, go, go.'

I convinced her to fly back to Chicago with me the next day. On the plane she decided that the 'poor old woman' in the seat across the aisle had never enjoyed life and could be made so much happier with a check for ten thousand dollars. I knew Mother had only thirty-five thousand dollars to her name. The woman, who was younger and more focused than my mother, seemed shocked by the bizarre proposal. Mother said, in a calm businesslike voice, as if giving a diagnosis and prognosis to the parents of an exceptional child, 'Now just give me your name, dear, and I'll fill out this check for you. It's no trouble at all for me and it might bring a little color and gaiety into your life. If I might make a suggestion, you should cut your hair, perk up your makeup and wear bright, startling colors. There's no reason to succumb to drabness. With my little gift you'll be able to pay for a complete makeover and some lovely outfits at Neiman-Marcus. Why, you're on your way to a whole new exciting life!' She smiled a dazzling grimace at the woman, who'd turned away. I was intensely embarrassed yet hated myself for my emotional disloyalty.

I'd been in touch with a Chicago doctor friend of my mother's, an old colleague of hers, and he suggested I bring her directly to the psychiatric floor. The fifth floor of Cook County Hospital. But when in the midst of her ceaseless, merry prattling she realized I was going to leave her there her gaiety evaporated, and she sank to her knees, let out a wail and crawled over to me. 'You can't do this to your mother,' she said. 'If you have any love for me, any respect for me at all, you won't leave me here.' She kissed my shoe and gripped my leg with her hands, which were surprisingly strong. 'I'm begging you! If you have even the tiniest grain of decency – just imagine the humiliation! This is where I worked for twenty years! Oh, no,' she groaned, still on her knees, doubled over with painful sobs. I tried to pull her up and seat her beside me but now she was pounding the floor with her tiny fists – I could see flashes of her bright scarlet nails.

I remembered how cool and professional she would be in emergencies with her patients – with Polly, the epileptic who'd lived with us. I thought that the respect and autonomy we grant someone we love, even a parent, is in the end conditional. Yes, even the love of a son for a mother. If she sinks too deeply into madness or alcoholism or depression, if she becomes dangerous to herself, then even the most deferential son must go against her will and act in her better interests.

I left her there, not knowing that unless there was a sanity hearing before a judge with expert witnesses testifying she couldn't be confined against her will for more than a night. When I came by the next morning she'd already checked herself out. No one knew where she'd gone. I was furious that they'd released a madwoman; I thought that soon I'd have to rescue her all over again. Nor did I have the money to stay in Chicago or pursue her across country. I was a poor freelance writer who lived in one dirty room in New York, who often had to borrow small sums from friends to see me through till the next check arrived. I'd charged the tickets to and from Texas to my credit card, but I had no idea how I was going to pay for them.

When Mother surfaced a week later, she wouldn't tell me where she was. 'I can't trust you, Son.' She assured me she was safe and sound somewhere in the North.

I suggested she work on her memoirs. She still sounded pretty batty to me and I thought that putting together a book about her life would help her to 'integrate,' or so I told my sister, without knowing exactly what 'integration' was.

At this time my sister and I grew closer as it dawned on us that we were no longer neglected children but newly needed, if not officially designated guardians, to our mother. She had been too unhappy, too obsessed with her work and men, too alcoholic to be the serene, all-giving, nothing-taking goddess for whom our society reserves the label 'Good Mother.' But she'd given herself to us entirely, and we were the brats who rattled behind her like cans tied to a cat's tail, the excess baggage who'd prevented any man from ever proposing to her, or so she firmly believed.

When we were little children she'd sung lullabies to us, just as when we were ill she'd make us orange pekoe tea and toast sprinkled with sugar and cinnamon – those magical days home from school when we were free to listen to radio plays, *Our Maw Perkins* and *The Shadow*. She'd never looked at our report cards unless she was forced to sign them. She just assumed we were receiving the highest grades since we were both geniuses.

Although she'd rocked us and hugged us and wept as she did so when we were small, later my sister and I wouldn't let her touch us. We were repelled by her body, so fat, so corseted. I'm certain this distaste was inspired by her own self-loathing and her drunken, coquettish demands for massages.

I have replicated too many of her traits to be entitled to judge her. I alternate thin decades with fat decades; the thin periods have always been hard-won through medically supervised dieting, month in and month out, avid exercise and even surgery. Like her I am always pursuing one man or another, though unlike her I've usually lived with a lover for an average of five years at a time. Like her I'm work-obsessed, but I've certainly never put in the long, hard days she relished and bemoaned. Like her I've had my problems with alcohol and had to stop drinking altogether. Like her I alternate between low self-esteem and a prickly sense of my own importance. Like her I'm more intent on impressing total strangers than pleasing old friends. When my mother would speak to me in a crowded elevator her remarks were well enunciated and finely calibrated, so as to produce a favorable impression on the neighbors we did not know while remaining within the limits of something a mother might plausibly say to her son. I recognized her game because to this day I will leave my friends standing on a corner in the rain so that I can rush off to help complete strangers puzzling over a map or I will lose track of what my lover is telling me over dinner since I'm too busy worrying about the waiter's mix-up at the next table. Or I'm simply eavesdropping on the breath-takingly banal conversation of the couple behind me. My mother and I were oriented toward people if 'people' meant strangers. In that respect alone we might have been suitable to run for public office.

Eventually my mother straightened herself out. She hid out in a Michigan hotel as her DTs subsided, scribbling away at her memoirs, just as I'm doing now. She'd discovered the only effective cure for mental illness: room service. She was able to summon another living human being – a handsome young waiter – when-ever she wanted him. And since she was in small-town mid-America she could engage him in conversation as long as she liked. Whenever she felt threatened by his presence she could dismiss him with a smile and a large tip. Whenever he appeared he brought her warm, nourishing food. No hospital or clinic or doctor can provide this precise, winning formula.

I published her memoirs as I had promised to do. Stan Redfern, my first lover, had gone into book production and he took Mother's manuscript (which I'd edited) and brought it out as a hardcover with a paper slipcover, a photo section, an ISBN number, a plot summary and all the apparatus of a real book (including a foreword by Dr. Johanna Tabin and an afterword by me in which I wrote, 'More and more older people are experiencing and exposing the hoax of old age, and Delilah's way of blowing the myth sky high is one of the chief glories of her memoirs').

She called it *Delilah: A Life in Progress*, a title of Texas-size optimism for a lady in her seventies. We printed four hundred copies of it – all this before the days of desktop or on-demand publishing. She kept several boxes of it and sold it to the women in her church. By the time it came out my father had died but my stepmother Kay got hold of a copy. Was I foolish enough to give her one? Perhaps in my thoughtless, overworked way I'd forgotten that in it my mother said she'd first become aware of my father's 'philandering' when he gave her the clap. Nor did Mother present him as anything but the coldhearted egotist he was, someone who alternated between brand-the-flesh anger and the sort of drugged placidity he had to administer himself every day as if it were a nasty but necessary shot. Like most people who live far from the literary world, Kay overestimated the power of the written word; she didn't realize that literature is as much a part of the faceless, universal cacophony as speech.

My father's death left my mother nonplused. In her own mind she'd been involved year after year in the most dramatic communication with him, a dialogue constructed out of silent replies, some silences short, others heavy with irony or protest, still others staccato and excited and overlapping. Now all that artful combative silence had ended, replaced by the senseless low telephone buzz of death. Or what she'd always believed in good faith was just a subtle but heavily meaningful rupture in communication she now understood had long since gone dead for him and perhaps had never been interesting enough for him to notice.

She was so incapable of grasping that her long years of work as a psychologist were over that she rented a one-room office at the top of her building – the 'crow's nest' as she called it – and filled it with metal filing cabinets containing hundreds and hundreds of case histories. These were documents. They were official. They must be preserved. She might be held accountable, possibly before the law. She might be called on as an expert witness.

So her mental health was still fragile. When she'd been forced to sell her summer house she'd gotten rid of half her things but the other half she put in storage. Finally she decided to bring it all to her apartment. As the moving men unloaded furniture, clothes, books and dishes, she stood on the street behind the truck and said, 'apartment' or 'crow's nest.' Her manner was mock authoritarian and she expected the movers to be as amused by the situation as she was. She had to make it into a game or fall apart. When she couldn't decide where something should go she'd say, 'Wait! Now just wait!' and start to cry. I, who was always concerned about appearances more than the long-term welfare of my family or friends, said, 'Mother, just let them put it in your apartment and we can sort it out later.' My treachery frustrated more than infuriated her.

She teamed up with her grandson Keith, Margie's son. He and his mother were on the outs for the moment so his grandmother moved him into the crow's nest – which gave her a graceful excuse for no longer going up to her desk and files and staring dumbly at the yellowing folders and the names of retarded children who, if they were still alive, were now forty or fifty years old. My nephew was her new project. Mother would make him supper and then he'd read to her out loud, no longer from Bruno Bettelheim's but from my books. Yes, I'd replaced Mary Baker Eddy and all those wise men; no matter that my pages were too ironic to read comfortably, too descriptive and dirty to be uplifting. In a different way my nephew had replaced me, the young male person who could stimulate Delilah's reveries, plunge her into a serene ecstasy, no matter that he wasn't a worshipful seven-year-old sissy but an unhappy young adult who was laughing half the time at his cracked granny. She could thicken her skin willfully to signs of mockery so long as she could obtain a rough simulacrum of her old familiar rituals.

She'd turn down the lights and listen to Pavarotti singing Puccini. My nephew liked Bach or Morrissey but sentimental Italian warbling wasn't his demitasse of espresso. Yet he was tolerant. And how hard was it, to listen to his old granny praising his 'genius' (as a writer, as a guitarist and songwriter, as a student of literature)? She was certain that he, too, would make an important contribution, as his grandmother had done working with the retarded, as his mother was doing as a social worker and therapist, as his Uncle Eddie was doing liberating his homosexual tribe. She beamed with joy at the swooning beauty of 'Nessun dorma' and drummed her tiny fists against the invisible gong suspended just before her in the air – gleaming, the metal mottled, the surface immense.

New York, aged thirty-two

My Hustlers

When I was seventeen I worked for my father in Cincinnati all one summer, manning an Addressograph machine. By today's standards it was a cumbersome, labor-intensive way of running off mass mailings. One device stamped out names and addresses on metal plates and these plates were then inserted in a carousel, I believe, which noisily stamped inked letters on envelopes. My father had thousands of clients' names on his list. The Addressograph clattered away to itself for hours on end.

His office was only a few blocks away from Fountain Square, which by day was the slightly seedy heart of the small city. But at night the Square (which was in reality a long oval) became still seedier and attracted a few hustlers and johns. Adolescents from across the river in Covington, Kentucky, or the outskirts of Cincinnati would perch on the metal guardrails around the central raised oval with its verdigrised fountain. The young men would spit and nurse a cigarette inside a cupped hand. They might have another cigarette tucked behind an ear, which looked like a white barrette pushed into their carded hair. Their hands were big, raw, rough-skinned working hands. They usually wore white T-shirts and beltless, low-riding jeans and ordinary lace-up shoes, scuffed and worn down at the heels. Sometimes they might have on fancier trousers of a sleazy fabric, pleated and baggy. Their spitting gave them the air and appearance of dogs marking their territory.

Cars would creep around the oval and the older male drivers would look up at the guys sitting on the rails. If the car paused, the youngster would grudgingly slip down from his perch, throw away his cigarette, spit and lean into the open car window, his bare arm resting on the car roof. He might flash a smile that would reveal missing or ill-sorted teeth. The smile was so out of character in these faces with their thin lips, gnarled Adam's apples and crafty, pale blue eyes that it came across as incongruous, like a curtsy from a prisoner.

I knew intuitively what everyone was up to. I earned a small salary from my father. I thought I could hire one of these guys and have sex with him. Although I was seeing a shrink during the school term in order to 'mature' and go straight, my treatment had no effect on my imperious sexual desires. I was in the grip of a compulsion that didn't have much to do with pleasure. I mean, I didn't imagine a man stroking my naked body idly or kissing me or letting me enter him. I could conjure up the idea of love – doomed, crepuscular love – but not of pleasure. I had no specific sex positions or acts in mind. My ambition was to hire a guy, to touch his erect penis, to make him come, to be able to tell myself I had been with another male and put my lips on his penis. Maybe he would love me and we'd run away.

I had expended an infinite amount of time and energy arranging to seduce the neighbour boy, then a guy at camp, later two guys at boarding school, and to jerk off a few married men in various public toilets in Chicago where my mother lived. It seemed that almost no boys my age wanted to have sex with another fellow, though I was always quick to spot the one in a thousand who was willing. If someone's eyes lingered even a fraction of a second on mine, I went into instant alert.

How convenient that these young Kentucky men, smelling of beer and Camels, their bodies so lean they had no hips, a T-shirt sleeve swollen because it was folded back over a cigarette pack above a tattoo – how convenient that they were for hire.

I wasn't yet part of the homosexual subculture of the 1950s. I didn't know yet that a big penis was considered more desirable than a small one, that 'we' had finicky preferences for or against circumcision, and that a straight man was viewed as the highest good and another queen as nothing but shoddy goods, a pathetic 'sister.' For me almost any man would do. Not long before I'd been thrilled to be felt up in a nearly deserted Cincinnati movie theater by a man who smelled of licorice while we watched Hitler's dull, perfectly innocent home movies of Eva Braun at Berchtesgaden – innocent though the posters outside promised an orgy in the Bavarian Alps. She jerked from parapet to bench, stagily exclaiming over a new puppy or twirling to show off her new skirt as the man next to me, consuming his long black threads of candy and never looking at me, let one pale hand travel blindly up my thigh.

I was in a fever of desire for these hillbilly boys perched on the Fountain Square railing. As the city baked and sweated and the cars pulsed light and crept around, the air refusing to stir, I looked and looked. Here was a big blond with strong arms and slicked-back hair and a square, dimpled jaw – he saw me across two lanes of cars and his eyes tightened with curiosity. When he was sure my glances were intentional he broke into a big smile and waved me over, his eyes suddenly catching the stinging smoke from his cigarette and watering.

Crossing the street and jogging up the two steps to the raised platform made me almost faint. But I wasn't timid, or rather my timidity in no way put a brake on my resolve. I knew that all I would have to do was pay this man in order to be held in his powerful arms. No amount of friendship had been able to maneuver anyone into my arms, and no amount of silent praying.

'Hey, lil fella, har yü?' His hillbilly accent was nearly incomprehensible. He motioned me closer with an insider's sideways jerk of the head. He stood. He was wearing jeans. I noticed how his legs were slightly bowed, which made me picture him mounted on a horse. The area around his crotch was carefully bleached. It seemed he wasn't wearing underpants.

After some discussion I agreed to give him twenty dollars and I laid out another five for a room in a fleabag hotel two blocks away. I had on a short-sleeved white shirt and a black knit tie; I wore nerdy Steve Allen black glasses and had a longish brush cut. I was skinny and given to tics – my neck was always stiff and bobbing and I nodded it in little spasms that were so noticeable that I hated to sit in front of anyone at the movies. Although there were few people on the street I feared running into someone I knew – me, a seventeen-year-old nerd with a prissy way of talking and a constant tic, and he, an older, drawling hillbilly with a prominent crotch and a white T-shirt sticking to his chest.

Up in the room Hank undressed slowly, chatting away. For him tonight was typical, not transcendent. Despite the heat I pushed the wooden shutters closed but through the slatted openings the neon sign outside kept blinking. At last Hank was naked except for his white underpants (he was wearing some after all). He lay down on the bed, smiled and opened his arms.

'Whatya wanna dü?' he asked.

As I stumbled out of my suit trousers and up-to-the-knee black stockings and undid my tie and shirt, I just smiled and said, 'Oh, I don't know.'

'Yü gotta have sumpin' yü wanna dü,' he said, smiling and stretching his tan forearms and pale biceps.

'I just—'

'What? I can't hear yü.'

'I just want to be—'

'Pardon?'

'Held.'

I turned off the light and hopped into bed beside him. He slipped off his underpants and so did I. A blue neon glow from below the shutters alternated with a pink light from above. He asked me if I liked his muscles. I said I did. He flexed. I manifested enthusiasm, though for me the scenario was suddenly all wrong. I wanted him to stare into my eyes and sip kisses from my lips and hold me tightly and tell me he loved me while down there our genitals would do something ecstatic and nonspecific. And I wanted him to admire me, admire my soul and my very existence, since even unattractive people (*especially* the unattractive) harbor dreams of finally being loved not for their attributes but for their essence. In love I was an essentialist.

'Want me to flex?' he asked.

I thought that if I just shrugged he'd be annoyed, so I said with extra enthusiasm, 'Oh, *please* do.'

He wanted to be admired and so did I, but even though I was paying I felt his need was greater than mine. Or rather my sense of self could survive rejection since it was built on it, whereas his self-esteem was at once more masculine and more fragile. My desire for love obviously had to pay an admission price – admiration for his muscles. As he flexed and I expressed my enthusiasm, a faint smile came to his lips: I was a pansy after all, panting over a real man's body, and that felt comfortably familiar to him.

And then it was over. He was dressing, still wearing his benign, contemptuous smile. I'm sure he thought I had nothing to complain of since we'd both come and his come had shot halfway up his chest. My youth, my innocence, my capacity for devotion meant nothing to him. I was surprised he didn't even remark on my age, for surely I was at least ten years younger than he. But maybe it didn't show.

He playfully mimed socking my jaw and said, 'See yü around, kid.'

Those Kentucky boys also hung out at the Greyhound bus station a block off Fountain Square or loitered around a dirty bookstore right on the Square, a shop that cultivated anonymity by keeping innocuous, sun-bleached book covers in the dusty window behind Mercurochrome-colored plastic shades, half-lowered. Inside, the owner would fish up books with lurid covers and browning paper from under the counter only when customers requested them – all these middle-aged customers with white socks, brown shoes, black trousers and wristwatches (my father's catalogue of bad taste).

Once every two weeks I could afford one of the boys. I knew which ones I preferred – the compact blond beauties with hairless forearms and a certain spark-striking way of walking heel first and a constant need to pull their jeans up with thumbs hooked in the two front loops. They seemed to be concentrating on their crotches. They had a habit of looking me right in the eye while spitting to one side through compressed lips, as if it were a form of muttering or curse. Usually I was so flustered that I'd go with the first man who spoke to me, no matter what he looked like. I'd panic, afraid an outsider would see what was going on. I'd lower my head in shyness or assent, do anything rather than draw any more attention to my vicious desire. 'Hey!' was all they'd have to say and I was helpless. Usually I got someone spotty and mocking.

One day in the park I met a tall, weedy gay man in his early twenties who had been studying me and was on to my game. 'Well, hello!' he drawled, the 'lo' on a rising then a falling note, as if to suggest the importance of this encounter. He sounded like Mae

West. His forehead was shiny, his nose infected near the nostril. He came up to me as I was smoking a cigarette I'd stolen from home. I was standing in the doorway next to the bookstore. In those days the city was black with soot and I was framed by big black blocks.

'A lot of beef on the hoof tonight, wouldn't you say?'

I wasn't quite sure what he meant.

'The trade,' he said.

'I'm sorry?' I said.

'Don't you even know what trade is?'

He explained to me that all these dumb hillbillies were 'trade' – men who could be 'serviced' though of course they'd never reciprocate since they were real men and 'not at all light in the loafers.' 'But of course they like to be serviced. When a guy is horny he doesn't stop to wonder whether the nearest warm hole is male or female.' I wondered if that could possibly be true. It sounded unlikely.

He asked me how much I was forking out.

'Twenty,' I said.

'Drive a harder bargain, hon. You're ruining it for the rest of us. You can get them down to ten.'

At that rate I could have one every week, though at the end of each of my previous encounters I had felt wretchedly guilty and I'd vowed never to sleep with another man. As it turned out my hustlers would form a long sequence that I wanted to end with each new addition.

'I've been watching you,' he said. 'You're so fearless.'

'Driven,' I said, smiling. It felt good to acknowledge my compulsion with stylish rue.

He laughed. 'Don't you have a car?'

'Next year, but I'm just seventeen now,' I said. 'I'll have a car next summer.'

'Gawd, real jailbait. You look – well, you don't *look* older but you're so sure of yourself, such a saucy wench.' He smiled in an entirely harmless way to show me he was just fooling. He didn't look at me directly, no more than would a character actor – all powdered wig, black lips and beauty patch – allow himself to establish eye contact on stage.

Another friend of his drifted up, a plump young man with dark blue patches under the arms of his pale blue shirt. 'Mary, the joint is hopping tonight!' he said in a bored drawl, offering me a feverish little hand when we were introduced, which he confided to me as if it were a sleeping dachshund. 'So, how many of these guys have you had, Miss Thing?'

'Four,' I said. 'That big blond with the pompadour—'

'Oh, *her*, if she's straight she could die with the secret. Only bulldaggers are *that* masculine.'

There was a bored, careless camaraderie among us as our eyes kept wandering over the beef that thrilled me, though I didn't let on. The year before in Chicago I had met a gay man in his thirties who owned a bookshop on Rush Street and he, too, had befriended me in this same offhand way. The understanding was that though I was just a kid I was in training and their job was to instruct me in the arcana of gay life, though unemphatically, certainly with no excess of sentiment. When we were alone among ourselves we formed a secret sorority of flamboyant maenads in hot pursuit of an Orpheus to devour. We wanted a real man, a heterosexual man, but if he ever reciprocated our blandishments then he'd lose his virility and become as compromised as we were. A real man had to be primitive, angry, not too intelligent and, in conversation, a bit ludicrous, whereas we queens were clever but as sterile as eunuchs.

I didn't believe all these things, not yet, maybe I never would, but I understood that such was their view of the world. We knew that these men, these hustlers, had no interest in us physically (in fact they must despise us as sick queens, as freakish fairies). They wanted nothing but our money. So be it! At least this motive was simple, honest, and acted as an acceptable alibi for their availability. And hustling gave a lot of out-of-work people something to do in the empty summer city.

These two Cincinnati queens worked in a nearby downtown church, one as the deacon and the other as the organist. They wanted me to take a hustler down to the men's room in the basement of their church and suck him off in front of an open window. They'd be squatting in a darkened room on the other side of the air shaft outside the window. The window of their room looked out on the air shaft and was lined up with the bathroom window. They wanted me to provide them with titillation. In those days there were no gay bars except in faraway Toledo, no gay YMCAs except a fabled orgy palace of a Y in Milwaukee, no gay pornographic films except the secret ones passed from one 'amateur' to another, no places for gays to cruise each other ('And do *what* together?' the organist screamed: 'Two big girls? Bump pussies?'). But here in Cincinnati there were only these skinny straight hillbillies with million-mile stares, boyish torsos, grease-heavy DAs and tumescent crotches that could be opened and revealed, as in certain holy statues of Our Lord tearing open his chest to reveal his Sacred Heart.

I was burning with the desire, night after night, to see what these penises looked like, to know the size and girth and smell and taste of each one. I was possessed by literalism (I would never have been content with the description of a penis I couldn't see or touch). It was compulsive curiosity, a hunger for human flesh, a thirst for sperm.

I was glad to have someplace to take my hustlers, the church basement rather than hotels where I had to pay five dollars for a room and register under the contemptuous eye of the night clerk.

Nor did I mind exhibiting my tricks and talents to my invisible but attentive sisters on the other side of the air shaft. Their presence worked to make me feel more normal, one of the sorority. They also made me feel marginally safer, though I knew that if a hustler got tough with me they'd take to their heels and certainly never call the cops and risk probable imprisonment and exposure. But the hustlers didn't know this place and the unfamiliarity made them uneasy, just enough (we hoped) for them to take no chances.

We were alone in the big blackened brick church with its permanent smell of coal smoke and disinfectant, with its linoleum-lined halls lit by red exit signs. This unexpected solitude might have spooked the boys. They might have thought I was working for the cops. Maybe this was entrapment.

The hustlers were used to playing with themselves at a urinal and giving a john a sneak preview of what he could buy. But when I asked them to back up two paces and stand in front of the window where I could drop to my knees, they were puzzled and became uneasy, even though we were presumably alone in a silent, empty building. They were so accustomed to stepping fractionally closer to the urinal and hiding their excitement if a stranger walked in that they were reluctant to give up this useful reflex.

'Oh, Gawd, he was gorgeous!' the organist exclaimed half an hour later when I came back to the scene of the crime.

'You're such a huzzy,' the deacon told me with a mild smile. 'Hoovering away like that on that nice country boy, young, dumb and I presume full of come. Where'd you learn to swallow it, girl? I usually spit it out.'

The next summer when my dad let me drive a company car I picked up a half-drunk kid with beefy, freckled arms, red fuzz, jeans that smelled of beer piss and a florid face with small, puffy eyes and lips so full they looked as if they might split open. There's no point in mentioning him – his is just a face and a body and a big dark penis. It lay there on his stomach like a blood sausage.

An older guy with mutton-chop sideburns and a worried look insisted I park in a dark alleyway just a block from the bus station. As I was going down on his soft penis the car door on my side flew open and there was another guy, ugly, angry, who was saying, 'Now you're in big trouble. You're breaking the law, you know.'

I sat up, rigid with fear. 'Oh?' I said in a high, airy voice I didn't recognize. My heart was pounding and I was wondering how I was going to get out of this.

My hustler had already zipped up. Now I understood why he'd been limp – he was in a state of high alarm. I'd learned a valuable lesson: A soft dick means the guy is about to rob you. The hustler was looking around and in some peripheral pocket of my mind I thought that they, too, must fear the cops, for even if I had no rights or recourse surely what they were doing was illegal too, if in some lesser way.

'Okay,' the partner said, sliding into the driver's seat and closing the door. I was wedged between them and for a moment I hoped that after I'd paid up they'd let me service both of them. 'Damn, you're in hot water, Mister. You better show me all the money you got on you and if you hold anything back you'll be in deep shit.'

I pulled out my wallet and emptied the cash flap of the forty-two dollars I had. I dug into my pants pocket and fished out a small handful of coins, mostly pennies. The guy knocked the money out of my hand and the coins splashed on the rubber floor mat.

'Shit, this all you got?' He counted the bills carelessly, as if such a small sum was beneath his notice. 'If your pa knew you were out suckin' peter you'd be up the crick, wouldn't you?' I lowered my eyes. His big hand, resting on the seat behind me, knocked me hard on the back of my head. 'Wouldn't you?' he asked in a loud voice that had suddenly gone redneck.

'Hey, Jumbo,' my hustler said in a low voice, clearly embarrassed and miserable. 'Jess lay off and let's get out of here . . .'

'Shit, man, that's bogue. Don' be usin' my name.' A cruel smile turned his mouth up on one side. 'What else you got for us, cocksucker?' He grabbed my hand and looked at my class ring. 'I'll take that.'

'Oh, please don't,' I said in an overbred, fluty voice, which revealed to me how much of a victim I'd become. 'My father will notice it's missing. I won't be able to explain—'

'Let the kid keep his ring, Jumbo,' my hustler muttered. I was so irrational that I found myself liking him. I was already half-fantasizing that we'd get together some other time.

'I told you—' Jumbo shouted. But he broke off when the hustler jumped out of the car. A second later Jumbo was gone, too, and there I was in a parked car in the middle of the front seat, an empty wallet on my lap. Both front doors were open and the overhead light was glowing feebly and the cooling motor was ticking to itself as it contracted.

I was always reading novels, and I knowingly chuckled when a character was described as 'foolish' or 'naïve' but here I was: I was naïve, I was foolish, which until this moment I'd never suspected. The reader considers himself to be all-knowing, superior, but now I had to push this conventional flattery aside and recognize that cleverness is not a question of perspective but of accumulated experience in the world. I was slowly putting together my own fund of lived worldliness, more modest but more real than the reader's omniscience.

I was duped again in Cincinnati that summer when I was eighteen. I gave a hustler forty dollars to buy us both one-way Greyhound bus tickets to New York. Our plan was to meet on the corner near my father's new house in Watch Hill, an area of big estates and no sidewalks where any pedestrian, especially a teenage boy with a suitcase, would have attracted attention if anyone had been awake and driving past. I spent a sleepless night imagining how I'd become a blond with the bottle of peroxide I'd put in my bag; I'd be so transformed that my father would never be able to find me, neither he nor his private detectives. Kay, my stepmother, would go to awaken me and find my room empty. No note. A missing suitcase. A drained tub and a wisp of winking foam from my dawn bubble bath.

The guy never came. The hot, steamy Cincinnati sun rose and became more intense, like an alcohol lab burner concentrating and flaming whiter and whiter. I felt so foolish. I was grateful I hadn't already dyed my hair. Then for a second I'd become hopeful again and imagine he'd been held up and would appear in another minute or two if I would just be patient. Then I would remember how uninterested he'd been in the directions to this exact corner – at the time I'd thought it was proof of his quickness that he'd been able to grasp the baffling directions so easily. At last it came to me with pitiless clarity that he was a con man. He'd conned me. He'd taken my money and run. How he must have laughed at my naïveté. When I saw him on the Square a few nights later, he waved merrily.

One could learn about life from literature – one could learn to spot a confidence man – but only if one woke up from the smug, dreamlike superiority of the reader, which blinded one to the actual slippery manifestations of vice and dishonesty in the shadowy world of reality. In the novel, at least the reassuring nineteenth-century novel, one was always privy to everyone's well-lit motives and alerted to even the first sign of corruption. But in life – how could one navigate in an unnarrated world? Of course I was always narrating my life to myself but unfortunately I had no access to the private thoughts of the other characters around me. Even my own mind was too prolific to be comprehensible. It was certainly true that I was fashioning the book of my life at all times, trying out sentences, sketching out plot lines, hoarding impressions, restaging the scenes I'd just lived through. I'd already written and typed two novels in boarding school, one about me and the other (my senior thesis) about my mother or some more driven version of my mother to whom I attributed my own sexual obsessions. At every moment I convinced myself that I was gathering material for the novel of my life – all experienced from the philosophical distance of the author. Even these humiliating occasions when I was robbed could be used as material. Life was a field trip. My writing would turn all this evil into flowers.

I mentioned just now my 'sexual obsessions,' but all these encounters with hustlers were as much an expression of fear as of desire, and above all they were animated by curiosity. I was swallowing the sperm of strangers and this feast convinced me I was *possessing* all these men. I was like one of those nearly insane saints who must take communion several times a day, who are driven by a desire to eat the body and drink the blood of a long-dead historical human being. That man may also have been a god, but the saint longs for the pulse and crunch of a thirty-three-year-old Jew nailed to crossed boards. In the same way I had this permanent, gnawing hunger for all these street-corner Hanks or Orvilles, for their penises fat or thin, crooked or straight, eager or reluctant.

Hustling in the gay world is quite different from female prostitution aimed at heterosexual males. A straight man can assume that almost every woman he meets is attracted to some man, if not to him in particular, whereas the total number of gay men is very small, never more than five percent, and prostitution is an obvious way of enlarging that proportion. In poorer populations or in those where women may not have sex before marriage even many heterosexual men are available to other men, if they're paid something. *They*, of course, don't consider themselves homosexual – only their partners are.

In the 1950s I could walk for hours down the beach on Lake Michigan past hundreds and hundreds of sunbathers of all ages and several races – and everywhere I saw nothing but straight couples and families. Never did faunlike eyes flicker toward me through bangs, never did a hairy brute adjust himself and look at a passing lad's butt with an open mouth. There were no gay men in the world, or just a few here and there, hissing, theatrical queens, alcoholic and suicidal. But in Cincinnati there were *hired* men and the idea that twenty – or even ten – dollars could open their flies and make them lie back with a sneer and flex their muscles excited me. They were like dolls in a toy store that I could play with promiscuously but whose mechanisms would permit them to perform only one action – turn their head or open their arms – and that would exhaust their entire repertory.

My father and stepmother wanted me to attend debutante parties. I'd put on my tux and black tie and squire Mitzi or Taffy about or stand in a ballroom at the Netherland Hilton, alone in a crowd of extra men, afraid to strike up a conversation, even more afraid to appear conspicuously alone. But after I'd driven home my buxom, freckled date to her dimly lit mansion and pecked her chastely at the huge oak door, I'd head right back downtown in the company car, still wearing all my finery and still feeling the slight buzz of the champagne punch. I'd cruise slowly around Fountain Square, the swerving car lights suddenly snapshotting a white T-shirt, tanned hand and a thin arm raised to brush back thick hair. If I idled for a moment a guy in tight jeans and with ribs that could be counted through a T-shirt and huge, knobby shoulders standing up like bookends would be leaning down to smile through my open window, his breath smelling of tobacco. He'd slip in on the passenger side and say, 'Just get off work?' and I'd realize he thought I was a waiter in a monkey suit and I'd say, 'Yeah. Where should we go?'

'What you got in mind?'

'Just a quiet place where we can relax.'

'How much is me relaxin' worth to you?'

'Ten bucks.'

'Twenty?'

'Fifteen.'

'Deal. I know a itty-bitty little lane up the hill in Hyde Park, you'll feel you're in the country.'

I reached over at the light and he spread his legs and pushed his pelvis forward. 'Hmm . . .' I purred.

'You like that?'

'Sure do.'

'You gonna take care of me real good?'

'Sure will.'

*　　*　　*

When I was in college I spent one summer in Chicago. My mother went off to work in a clinic in Munich. She let me stay alone in her apartment and even gave me four postdated checks of twenty-five dollars each to see me through the month – enough to make sure I didn't starve to death but so little that I'd be forced to get a job. I worked on the South Side loading trucks which, in that day before containerization, was all done by hand. In order to get the job I had to lie and promise I wouldn't abandon it at the end of the summer in order to go back to school. I told them I'd dropped out. But one by one the men I worked with came up to me and urged me to return to the university. 'If you don't, you'll be like us, doing a shit job the rest of your life.'

I have no idea how they survived that job year after year. I couldn't stand it even a week, working in the hundred-degree weather. I worked nights and got off at dawn. The loading docks weren't air-conditioned and in the Chicago heat and humidity my eyes were stung and blinded by sweat, every muscle in my body ached. Although I'd lived by the bell in boarding school, I'd always been interested in my studies and the long afternoons, from two to six, had been free. During my freshman year at college I'd studied hard but at least I'd been exhilarated by my exotic courses (Chinese social structure, beginning Chinese, the music of Bartok, Buddhist art) and in any event I still had vacant hours for bull sessions around the dorm.

Now I was alone in a big city full of laboring, sweating adults. In my dirty work clothes I'd return at dawn from the South Side trucking district to my mother's elegant Near North apartment on the thirty-second floor overlooking the Loop and a swipe of the Lake Michigan shore. Coming home I'd walk down Michigan Avenue in my jeans and T-shirt, breasting waves of executives in seersucker suits and nurses in static-clinging white uniforms and elevator men in pale brown short-sleeved shirts and secretaries in pastel dresses and matching high heels, this whole disorganized army of wage earners walking through the slanting early light projected past the office buildings, like aisles of light in a morning forest. I was exhausted, but it felt disconcerting to sleep by day on my mother's gold-thread upholstered couch. Nevertheless I curled up on the couch in the sun-bright living room, as if I were the fertilized speck inside a warm yellow yolk, anything rather than lie down on the bed in the darkened bedroom. A nap on the couch, no matter how long, felt less sodden, less resigned than a more methodical turning of day into night. Late in the afternoon I'd scramble some eggs and then go down to the Oak Street beach, a wide band of white sand glowing beside Michigan Avenue with its six lanes of traffic and high-rise apartment buildings. This was the first time in my life I'd ever lived alone, if only for four weeks. The sexy, unknown city was rustling all around me. I'd grab a sandwich and head back to my all-night job loading trucks.

I didn't work long but I did earn enough to treat myself to a hustler. I'd seen them off Rush Street at 'Bughouse' Square, an open park covered with old trees where stump speakers harangued small crowds about crank causes. Whereas nearby Rush Street was brightly lit and at night echoed with loud laughter, the sudden gust of jazz and slamming car doors, Bughouse Square was leafy, solemn, shabby. In the midst of the Trotskyites and vagrants, a few hustlers threaded their way past overflowing trash cans or leaned against a tree, deriving precious sustenance from a cigarette.

I saw a sixteen-year-old with black, wavy hair wearing a well-pressed white shirt, its dandified, foreign collar wide, long and pointed. He had full lips, soft dark eyes heavily lashed and a certain luxurious fleshiness of ass inside trousers that were loose in the legs but binding just to the right degree across the crotch and hips. He saw me looking at him. My eyes must have been shockingly hungry – the sort of eyes that have lost all self-awareness and glint with pure emptiness. If someone had whispered, 'Ed,' in my ear, I'd have had to dial my way painfully back from the boy's handsome face toward earth, toward *me*, like a diver rapturous with oxygen deprivation who is drawn against his will up out of a storm-dark sea.

'Hi, there,' he said, and even those two syllables revealed he had an accent of some sort, the perilous *th* slurring off into the more universal *z*, the final *r* too faint to be Midwestern. His smile was soft, a bit sad, as if it, too, were a translation filmed through gauze, as if his friendliness had been rebuffed once too often and now hesitated on his lips.

'Hot enough for you?' I asked in a parody of Illinois ordinariness.

He looked puzzled, smiled with his full lips and shrugged, again in a delightfully foreign way, for Midwestern men dared not risk a gesture that might invoke a sliding shoulder strap or an imaginary flash of pink silk.

'Ed,' I said, extending my hand, shaking his warm, yielding hand, which *his* father had not taught him to firm up into a pledge of friendship nuanced by an arm-wrestler's strength.

'Roberto,' he said, lowering his heavy lashes operatically and nodding slightly off to one side, as if in deference to an unfamiliar but harmless custom of exchanging names.

He wanted twenty dollars, which was what I'd earned crouching all night inside the stifling hold of a truck – the exchange seemed fair, for how else did I deserve to talk to this beauty with his small hands that relaxed naturally into a closing curve? His feet were encased in loafers the mellow color of a Stradivarius. When I touched his waist with my right hand as we hurried toward a little hotel he knew about he turned his head toward me, stared, then smiled with an intimate half-smile. I fell just one step behind so I could admire that abundant ass I longed to feel. He was shorter than I though he held his shoulders back with almost childlike bravado.

'Are you Italian?' I asked.

'Yes,' he said, clicking his tongue and jerking his head back to one side in a gesture I discovered only years later was the standard Greek way of indicating agreement.

The room was big and clean and the wide window looked out on the square below, and afforded enough illumination so that we didn't need to turn on the overhead light. In the half-darkness his white shirt glowed. He let me unbutton it as we kissed. As soon as we began to touch, Roberto had the sort of gleeful, complicitous smile that says, 'Look how wicked we're being.' Never before had I associated irony with sex between men. For a moment I even suspected that Roberto might be gay or bisexual and surprisingly I still found him attractive. He held my naked body against his and quaked with silent laughter, then moved without transition into long, languorous kisses, letting his eyes rise and wander along the line between the ceiling and the wall.

Roberto's white shirt and tanned skin, his compact body with the sensual ass, his sense of irony and romantic air – all these properties came together to inspire me. That fall I wrote a novel about him while I was in my junior year at the University of Michigan. Like many novels by young people it was derived more from my reading than from my experience, but the character of the younger brother 'Roberto' was based on my very own Lafcadio, my own Tancredi, my own Felix Krull, my own Fabrizio. I had in mind a synthesis of all these gallant young men from Continental literature, plucky characters who had as strong a sense of personal style as my hustler, who were as romantic and long-lashed as a silent movie star and as streetwise as a Neapolitan shoeshine boy. My Roberto (my hustler and my character) was quiveringly and richly fleshed, his smile soft and unfocused, his body instinct with laughter. I knew almost nothing about him but I could keep returning to my memory of having held him in my arms for a moment, and having rented an hour of his time and leased on short term the use of his torso and hips and lightly downed legs and tan arms flung back to reveal his soft, creased, axial paleness. I liked the notion behind the English term *rent boy* more than our *hustler*, since the American word suggested something dishonest and on the make.

Roberto was my first male muse, a mental snapshot I worked up into a full-dress portrait in oil. I wanted to recapture that moment I'd bought and present him with a portrait in words. I wanted to convey to the reader as well my fascination with the boy. I was like Caravaggio, who paints in a saint's halo behind the curly head of a street urchin with a farmer's tan and a cynical smile. In my novel an older, richer, blonder brother hires a darker, smaller kid – and discovers they are half-brothers, the offspring of the same father but of different mothers, one fair and legitimate, the other an Italian mistress.

I've never reread the manuscript but as a junior I entered it into a fiction contest at the University of Michigan, which I lost. The judge said she found it unbearably facetious. Of course I'm sure it was a grating book to read, partly because it was relentlessly frivolous and supercilious about a subject, homosexuality, that at that time was routinely labeled disquieting or tragic at best. I couldn't subscribe to this lugubriousness and wanted to laugh at everyone's solemnity. The imp of the perverse guided my pen, but I wasn't a mature and cultured European, like my idols, but a bumptious Midwestern teenager. In my failed fantasy the first contact with Roberto had been commercial but before long the rapport was elevated to brotherhood and, finally, impossibly, to an almost marital love. The title of the book was *The Amorous History of Our Youth*, a pedantic fusion of Lermontov's Byronic parody, *A Hero of Our Times*, and of *The Amorous History of the Gauls*, a seventeenth-century satire of the court by Roger de Rabutin, Count de Bussy, which caused this sharp-tongued cousin of Madame de Sévigné to be banished to his comely little château in Burgundy.

Pedantry, satire, literary ostentation, an irritating lack of sincerity – none of these faults could conceal from my eye, at least, that I was quite humbly and gratefully in love with an Italian boy I had met once who had a strangely low and almost strangled way of whispering his words into the big ear of a bespectacled American geek, his awestruck client. If in my novel inappropriate emotions kept firing off, all these missteps just revealed how inadequate I was to the occasion.

I looked for him the next summer and all the other times I was in Chicago, but I never found him again. Of course I was looking for an Italian named Roberto and he was probably a Greek named Constantine. And he'd probably vanished, as a million runaways disappeared every year in America. If that Cincinnati hustler had been on the corner with the bus tickets in hand as he promised, I might have ended up like Roberto, though I would have been a bleached-blond, well-spoken kid too sissy to get more than five bucks on the open market. Surely that was the source of my novel, the fantasy that I could save one of these boys as I myself so easily might have needed to be rescued.

After I was graduated from the University of Michigan I lived in Evanston half a summer with my best friend, Steve Turner, a handsome, intelligent straight guy. Neither of us knew what to do with our lives. He was driving a city bus and I was driving a panel truck delivering eggs and fruit juice in a suburb as desolate as its name, Des Plaines. We slept in Steve's basement bedroom, smoked cigarettes and joked our way through the depression and disorientation caused by graduation, change, lovelessness and our grueling, low-prestige jobs. I was intending to go to Harvard in the fall to get an advanced degree in Chinese, which had been my undergraduate major. But one night I went down to Clark and Diversey, a gay crossroads in those days. At a coffee shop I started talking to a hustler with streaked blond hair, a gold lavaliere and tight black trousers. He wanted me to pay him ten bucks to fuck him, which I did partly because I'd never been with an avowedly gay hustler before. But two days later my penis burned when I urinated and my balls ached. On the third morning my underpants were stiff with a gray creamy discharge. I was mortified and told my mother I had to see a doctor. When she asked me why I said I had a 'male problem,' my improvised version of the mysterious 'female trouble' that, once invoked, usually warded off all further questions. No such luck. My mother wanted to know everything in detail. I told her as little as possible. Her doctor assumed I'd been with a female prostitute and winked before shooting me full of penicillin and giving me a prescription for a lotion that would rid me of the crab lice I'd also picked up. The whole experience was so shaming that it made me question my life, my values, my future. This one experience with a hustler had major consequences. I decided to take the two hundred dollars I'd saved, fly to New York in pursuit of Stanley, another student I'd met in Ann Arbor and who was now in New York striving to become an actor. A sustained love with someone from my own world seemed far preferable to these fly-by-night encounters with prostitutes.

I stayed in New York, got a job working as a staff writer for Time-Life Books and eventually started living with Stanley. I skipped Harvard and a PhD in Chinese, and all because a hustler had given me the clap.

In my twenties I seldom hired a hustler, mainly because I didn't know where to find them. Early on I picked up an ugly kid on Times Square. He led me back to a nearby room and to a little alcove separated from the room by a curtain. He was very insistent that I pay him in advance and leave my clothes on the only chair in the main room. He then drew me into the alcove, closed the curtain and rushed me through sex. Then he dressed me as fast as possible, accompanied me down to the front door, pushed me out of it and rushed back upstairs. The door closed behind him with a click and the sliding of a bolt. Something made me pull out my wallet and inspect it. His invisible partner had emptied it while I was in the alcove sucking that telltale limp dick. Now I recalled I'd heard the floorboards creak. I didn't know which bell was theirs. Anyway, they were two against one and I had no legal recourse.

One night a friend of mine called me at my office in the Time-Life Building and asked if I'd like to join him on a 'double date' with two johns from out of town. My friend was a highly paid advertising copywriter but he liked to work occasionally as a hustler to prove to himself that at thirty he still looked twenty, that as a confident young executive he could still come off as an insecure, skinny little street kid. The thirty dollars he earned turning a trick was worth more to him than his three-hundred-dollar day rate selling vodka and toothpaste. I joined him and two drunk middle-aged businessmen in a hotel room. My hustling buddy had told me to be sure to play dumb: 'There's nothing that's more of a turnoff than intelligence.' Our customers, who in any event were more interested in mixing Manhattans than in bedding us, kept trying to explain to us who Beethoven was; they had a novelty tape on which someone had added a congo beat to the 'Ode to Joy.' For a moment I'd *almost* grasp what they were talking about but then I'd pretend to get confused and I'd mutter, 'Fuck it!' and the two johns would wink furiously at each other over our heads.

I could never have been a professional hustler for even though I had a beautiful body my penis was too small and I was more passive than active in sex. Bottoms were a dime a dozen; real money was spent only on tops. Occasionally now I'll see an ad for a bottom in listings for escorts, but the fee he's asking is always small – and he's always outnumbered ten to one by those who describe themselves as 'VGL XXX horny dominant top WS, FF, C&B torture, BB, verbal' – which for my few heterosexual readers I'll translate as 'very good-looking, very well-hung dominant man into water sports, fist-fucking, cock-and-ball torture, a bodybuilder capable of handing out verbal abuse.' Now there is a winning profile. God made many masochists and very few natural sadists – no wonder all those bottoms must pay for their tops. To be sure we read every day about violent men raping women, and that sort of 'domination' is neither rare nor sought-after. True, refined sadism is so focused on the victim that it could be said to be selfless; life turns up few disinterested saintly masters.

Although I only hustled once, that unique experience I'd regularly inflate later into a whole career when attempting to be fraternal with hustlers: 'Oh, I used to turn tricks myself,' I'd say modestly, 'when I was a kid. I know what it's like to be in the business.' My hustler of the moment would eye me suspiciously – had I ever been young? he'd wonder.

In the late 1960s alternative newspapers like the *Eye* and the *East Village Other* began to run ads for gay escorts. At that moment I entered into a new period of my life that has extended all the way to the present moment – the excitement of ordering up an unknown guy on the phone. In the early seventies I was earning a miserable living ghostwriting college textbooks (I did two psychology books and one US history). I would get three hundred fifty dollars for a chapter. I hated the work but I set myself a goal: I'd stay in, type my pages on perception or Bull Run and then at four in the morning my hustler, who I'd ordered up earlier in the evening, was scheduled to appear. He was my reward.

Half an hour before he was due to arrive I'd empty my over-flowing ashtray, make the bed, dim the lights, open a bottle of wine and spray the roaches into temporary submission.

For a while I had a (male) madam, one I never laid eyes on but who would call up boys in his stable while I hung on the other line. He'd describe the boys and talk to me in an old-fashioned, queeny way: 'Now, hon, would you be that rare gay man who just happens to like – not to put too fine a point on it – Big Dick?'

The idea that a twenty-eight-year-old blond, six-foot-two, with an eight-inch penis was headed my way would excite me to the point my hands would shake. I'd force myself to concentrate on my textbook, on the principle of primacy-recency in the chapter I was cobbling together, or on the implications of the Dred Scott Decision, but if for a moment I dropped the reins, my mind would plunge over the precipice of this secret, this thrill in store for me. As the hour approached I'd convince myself he'd probably fallen asleep or gone out carousing and hooked up with someone at the bar. I'd clattered away at my typewriter hour after hour in order to deserve (and afford) this man, who became taller, better hung, lower-voiced, more crudely passionate by the second.

At last, as I heard those feet pounding up the three flights of wooden stairs, I'd breathe faster, I could feel my nipples stiffening under the friction of my T-shirt and my ass filling out my jeans fractionally. My cock was swelling in the pouch of my jeans and a blush blossom was floating up my chest and neck and invading my face. I became lightheaded.

This was the high point, the instant before he came into sight on the landing below and trotted up to my door. Sometimes I was already stoned, for even if I risked mumbling and stumbling when high nonetheless that state of mind released my deepest passions; my mood was a bit impersonal but at least intense. If I started fantasizing about doing something with this guy, a second later I found myself actually doing it. There was no membrane between thought and act. Of course some hustlers were recovering addicts or drunks and my slurred speech and glazed eyes disgusted them – they were no doubt afraid I'd offer them a joint or quaalude or some PCP and they'd fall once again into the abyss. I can remember one short, muscular guy I'd ordered up. He turned out to be someone I knew from my gym and he was so turned off by the puddle I'd turned into on downs that he said, 'Yeah, you're way out there, aren't you?'

In those days there were suddenly very few taboos against hiring oneself out. Many young gay men in the 1970s, at least in New York, thought it was cool, a source of money and adventure and a way to enter other worlds. Grad students who had high tuitions to pay, long, irregular hours and no time to cruise their equals at bars, welcomed the constant possibilities for paid sex offered nearly round the clock. If a medical intern stumbled home at midnight, exhausted from an eighteen-hour stint, his muscles tense and his nerves sparking, he could always plug in his special red phone and answer it, play his friendly cowboy character Jarvis or Will rather than his real Philadelphia persona of Edwin, so intimidating to everyone and so unforthcoming: so unsexy.

I'd get these guys pounding up my steps wearing chaps and cowboy hat, as I'd instructed them, or policeman's uniforms, or work boots and hard hat, which I'd remove as gently as Amfortas assisting Parsifal when the knight returns with the holy spear and must be disarmed.

Too often the reality wasn't as hot as my fantasy. Not because I demanded perfection. On the contrary. Some of these boys were too perfect. I liked a flaw, a wound, which acted as an opening to the communion of shared humanity. For instance, a guy named Hal lived upstairs from me and sometimes he'd drop by for sex. He had a badly mended harelip which made his taut, muscled torso and hairy chest and pale, narrow loins seem vulnerable, touching. The most poignant moment in *Lady Chatterley's Lover* occurs when, unannounced, her ladyship visits the gamekeeper's cottage and sees him, all unawares, washing himself in an outdoor shower. She glances at his white, narrow hips and his thin back and he never realizes she is there. His back, so pale and thin, is wholly male and vulnerable. If, instead, a big blond showboat, perfect with a blinding smile, an ever-ready penis, came bounding up my steps, his very perfection made me feel somehow . . . orphaned.

Of course I was young and attractive, in my thirties. I went to the gym three times a week. I had a powerful chest and strong arms, and my peasant ancestors had bequeathed me their mighty legs. I kept waiting to see how these hired hands would respond to the way I looked with my soulful eyes, drooping mustache and shoulder-length hair.

Sometimes they scarcely seemed to register me or my age at all. Later I learned that some hustlers preferred their johns to be old and adulatory. Then the john's gratitude would allow the overhead spotlight to narrow and isolate the hustler in a pool of intense desire, transform him into a St. Michael stabbing a St. Theresa left suitably vague in a swirl of shadows, fold upon fold. The hustler generates the passion, he is the one who drips with sweat, his own penis is what he watches swell and stiffen in the mirror. The john merely officiates, like a priest fussing over the chalice. The priest shouldn't be handsome or distractingly young or even too definite an entity; he is just the penumbra around a radiance. The altar boy is the one who should be beautiful.

My favorite hustler was Charles, whom I knew in the late 1970s and early 1980s. I must have seen his ad in an alternative newspaper as a leather-wearing master. He was about thirty, shorter than me, and had an overbite and an emaciated body. His bony face was concealed in the shadow of his visor. His voice was nasal but low.

'Take off all your clothes,' he said when he arrived. I stripped and he remained fully dressed, cap, boots, leather jacket and all. It was an inspired move, since I was entirely exposed and he armored. He told me to kneel on the floor between his legs. He sat on the couch and lit a cigar, turning it carefully to make sure it would burn evenly. He didn't say anything nor was I invited to speak.

The smell of the cigar enraged me – my father! – this stupid hustler polluting my house, how dare he – and suddenly tears were splashing down my face. My father had died just two years earlier and here he was again in the guise of a small, bony sadist. This was the smell of my father's cigar, repulsive and endearing. As Charles inhaled, the tip glowed briefly and lit up his face.

He stood and went over to the hardwood floor and ordered me to crawl on my knees to him. He pulled out his penis, which was only half-hard. He said, 'Pay me.'

At first I didn't understand and then I did and I fetched the money I had already laid out on the table. I came back and knelt and handed the bills to him. As I did he became erect. It was a single moment: I handed him the money and he got hard.

I couldn't afford to see him more than once a week, but I had an appointment with him week after week, year after year. He never varied the winning routine. I stripped, he never did. In fact I never saw his body. He'd light his cigar and have me suck him while he smoked, seated. Then he'd stand and become violent, insulting me. He'd kick me with his boots, but he never left any bruises or even created any residual pain. He knew what he was doing. He was a professional. He'd order me to get on all fours and he'd put on tight black leather gloves and stick one finger in me and then make me smell it. Then he'd fuck me hard; he wore a condom, unusual back then, even degrading, as if he were too good to touch my flesh. He never kissed me, though sometimes he'd drool in my mouth from far above as I knelt below him. The long string of saliva slowly unspooled to my open lips. He never smiled, though I smiled at him. He seldom came. Like a Taoist, he preferred to conserve his *ch'i*.

I asked him once if our kind of sex turned him on.

'Obviously.'

'But do you think of me afterwards?'

'No.'

Once I ran into him and his lover outside a leather bar near the docks. His lover was no younger than I nor any better looking. He didn't seem submissive or meek in any way – he was just a big Irish balding blond with some meat on his bones, regular features and a friendly face quick with curiosity. He was wearing a faded denim jacket and jeans and had a wide but not fat ass. Charles introduced us and acted normally sociable. Though it was a late spring night a cold fog was pouring off the nearby Hudson and swirling dramatically below the sodium-vapor streetlights above us. Half the bar was on the street sipping beers and leaning against parked motorcycles. Charles drove his lover away on his Harley.

Soon after that the hot weather set in for the duration. I was working for the New York Institute for the Humanities, which was housed at New York University. I'd sit in one of the back cubicles attempting to write my novel, *A Boy's Own Story*, fighting the anxiety I usually felt when I wrote. The offices were nearly empty. My cubicle was windowless. The heat and my hangover tempted me to put my head down on my desk and fall asleep. I was so sleepy I would write portmanteau words, which collapsed the syllables of two or three words I'd already sounded in my head. I even started to spell phonetically.

My clothes would stick to me. I'd sigh and shift in my chair from one side to the other. One more trip to the water cooler. I'd come back and read through my latest pages and make microscopic changes. I'd sprawl on my desk. Then I'd get fed up with myself, sit up straight, as tall as possible in the chair, and I'd hold my pen as if it were a scalpel. Now, I'd say to myself, I'm going to write a *good* page. Usually my head was so fuzzy with the morning-after effects of wine and marijuana that I was pleased if I could form real sentences, nothing more. But one day I did make a conscious decision to write *well*, and with my scalpel-pen in hand and my perfect posture I felt I was about to *attack* the page, as a conductor might ask the strings to have a cleaner attack on the opening phrases. The stern commands that I issued to myself were the mental equivalent to stabbing my leg with a straight pin in order to stay awake.

I would be horny, if that meant lonely and anxious to such a degree that only sex could lift me out of this mire with enough immediacy and absoluteness. I didn't have the patience to cruise someone in a bar, chitchat through three drinks and ninety minutes on the off-chance he might ask me back. Anyway it was the middle of the day. I phoned Charles and asked him if I could come over to his house in Prospect Park in Brooklyn. He said yes and gave me careful instructions. In those days middle-class white people thought of themselves as pioneers if they lived in Prospect Park.

He opened the heavy oak door after I rang just once and he ushered me into a hallway and stairs gleaming with beeswax and lit by a stained-glass window on the landing above. A small silk carpet glowed under my feet as if it were the light cast by the stained glass above. Charles was dressed in a white T-shirt and sleeveless black leather vest, which exposed his blue skin and knobby elbows. In the daylight his overbite looked comic, his protruding bones tragic. He asked me if I wanted to see the house. It was all carved massive four-posters and chenille spreads, electrified gas lamps and old wood sewing tables balanced on scrolled, cast-iron legs.

He unbolted and opened one door and showed me a bare room with a mattress on the floor and one small window high up, close to the ceiling. 'This is where I'm going to keep you,' he said. I didn't know if he was joking, but when I smiled he said, 'This is where you'll live.'

His words gave me an instant erection – the bliss of total passivity edged with the fear of total passivity. What would it be like to live here, to watch the daylight come and go through the little window, to be led naked in chains to the toilet, to be wiped, to be spoon-fed, to be fucked and threatened with the working end of a cigar?

No more taxes to pay, I thought. No more chapters to write. Time a blur of longing, excitement, boredom and loneliness. Come to think of it, that sounded more or less like my life right now but formalized and condensed.

After the release of my novel I moved to Paris and lost touch with Charles. I remained in France for the next sixteen years.

One night early on in France I picked up two boys on the rue Sainte-Anne, between the Palais Royal and the Palais Garnier, the old opera house. Now it's a street of art galleries and Japanese restaurants, but then it was still gay, the scene of the last days of the Club Sept, which had been *the* center of gay life in the 1970s. Even when I arrived during the summer of 1983 it was still staggering along, with candlelit eleven-o'clock dinners upstairs for theater people and their publicists as well as for a sprinkling of minor celebrities known only to a thousand other Parisians – that is, they were 'topmodels' (one word in French), hairdressers, jewelers, shoe designers and *maquilleurs*. The men wore dark suits cinched in at the waist, blindingly white shirts and sumptuous silk ties. The women had short asymmetrical haircuts, almost a crew cut on one side and a long Veronica Lake swoop on the other, all of it carefully stapled in place with hairspray. The conversation seemed to be nothing but bored bouts of silence punctuated with murmured catty remarks about new arrivals and shrill denials ('Now you're going too far'). Downstairs at the bar beside the small disco floor, well-dressed Italian gigolos in suits with long fragrant black hair pushed back behind small ears, toyed with drinks ordered because they phosphoresced under the black lights and turned their hands into elegant dark silhouettes.

To me they looked like the sort of young men one would have to install in an apartment and supply with a sports car – in any event way beyond my means. I could picture one of these gigolos studying himself in the mirror before going out, reknotting his scarf and lightly recoiffing himself with fingers bright with brilliantine. A definite turnoff.

More my speed were the boys outside, the ones who (since it was Paris) wore a sports jacket (but two sizes too large) and a dress shirt (but no longer all that clean). I picked up a pair of them – a skinny con man with purple lips and lead-white skin who kept steering me along by the elbow as if I were a dowager in perilous heels. The other was a little blond with a macho swagger and the improbable name of 'Stam,' which he insisted was English. He had an English father, he said. In our cheap hotel room near the Gare du Nord I was unable to satisfy my impulses as a voyeur. The two boys were too embarrassed to touch each other. Suddenly I was back in

Cincinnati in the 1950s: they were straight and I was gay. But there was a nice comradely air in the room, three guys together, or rather two paid performers and their American john with his dollars and paunch and funny accent.

I asked the boys to embrace but they touched each other awkwardly while looking at me. Left to their own devices they were like strangers dancing together at the moment when the music is switched off. But the minute they had me to reckon with, they went into action. Never in a hundred years would they have *chosen* me, but the point was I'd chosen *them*. As one of my friends used to say about hustlers, 'These boys want the arms of the whole world around them.'

The tall, pale boy had a big dick but it never got hard. Soon he fell asleep, not from drugs, I'd wager, but from exhaustion. When he awakened twenty minutes later he took a long hot shower, pulled a used Bic razor out of his backpack and submitted himself to careful grooming. He even washed out a pair of dirty socks and maroon bikini underwear with the cheap tiny bar of soap in the bathroom and put them on the radiator to dry.

But while that guy dozed or did his toilette, Stam and I had a great time. Stam was just a kid, maybe seventeen, but tiny, no more than five feet tall, with small blue eyes, dark blond hair that shot straight up out of his head like grass sprouting from a Toby jar. His brow was low. His ears were as small and intricately furled as a plant just before it breaks through the soil. His skin was closely pored and smooth, like chamois, and his body temperature was one degree higher than mine. His body was smooth and compact and hairless, with the silky skin of a true blond. But he was by no means handsome. He was too squat, his eyes too small, his swagger absurd in someone so short and young. Once in a while his macho dignity would break down and he'd giggle like a little child. On that first night he made a muscle and laughed at how small his bicep was, then squinted and wept tears of mirth.

I came to think of him as a character out of Genet, whose biography I began to research in 1986. Stam would disappear for long stretches of time and then resurface with tales of his adventures. He was always helping older and bolder and brighter friends bring in a shipment of hash from Spain and getting almost nothing out of it except a pat on his small but strong shoulders. He would try out on me three or four words in English or German, which I could never understand; he'd collapse into a sharp, barking laugh at his own expense and dab tears from his small blue eyes.

He wore baggy shirts with dubious designs – pale green isosceles triangles on a sickly yellow background or big gold tigers on black velveteen. Sometimes he smoked cigarettes. He had an un-Gallic weakness for whiskey which grew more pronounced over the years. Every time I saw him he was a bit worse for wear. Mostly he was a street person. Sometimes he'd have a room somewhere, a maid's room tucked up under the eaves of an old slate roof slick with rain, looking out over unpeopled courtyards. The toilet would be halfway down the winding stairs behind a small door cunningly shaped to conform to the curving wall.

He liked to talk to me for hours though he mocked my accent and vocabulary and incomprehension. He spoke in nothing but argot (*bagnole* for car, *gueule* for face, *tifs* for hair, *pognon* for money) and verlan (a reverse language in which bizarre became *zarbi* and femme became *meuf*). 'Instead of reading all those books,' he'd say, indicating them with a dismissive gesture, 'you should get out and talk to real people. You should learn how real fellows talk' ('*comment les vrais mecs causent*').

For me his attractive flaw, his redeeming wound, was his pint-size bravado. Even in bed he liked to lie on top of me and when we were seated on the couch he'd hook a tiny hairless arm around my neck and draw me to his chest and affectionately rub the knuckles of his other hand against my scalp and grunt, 'What am I ever going to do with you?'

I was almost three times his age, twice his weight, someone with a reputation if very little money, but I was delighted to be treated as a little brother by this tiny tough guy.

My American boyfriend, John Purcell, the man with whom I'd moved to Paris, returned to New York in 1985, where he would die of AIDS ten years later. After he left Paris I missed him. I felt old and formal coming home alone from a dinner in my dress-up Parisian clothes, walking past all those illuminated monuments along the Seine, then crossing it to the necropolis of the Île Saint-Louis. No matter how much I'd joked and nodded and exclaimed with the other guests over the salmon, now I was alone, lying in bed and looking at still more French shrugging knowingness on my little black-and-white TV.

How I welcomed Stam's visits! He'd call me from the corner. I'd remind him of the code needed to gain entry downstairs. I'd hear him rapping out his distinctive series of three short and two measured knocks and there he'd be, marginally more derelict than the last time. His eyelids were puffy from drink and his eyes slowly disappearing, his brush cut too long and limp, his sneakers mud-spattered and, when he removed them, his feet grotty. He'd grab my head and pull it down to his chest, which didn't smell very good. He laughed the gigolo's mirthless laugh, designed to en-courage himself.

He'd tell me about his latest adventure. He'd fallen in love with a diminutive girl who tended one of the rides in an itinerant street fair that moved from the gravel square in front of the Arsenal Library to Pigalle and on to the Place des Fêtes. She had become a victim to a sadistic carny man and Stam asked (suddenly I became more alert), 'Do you know how I can get a gun? I need a gun so I can kill him.'

I talked him out of his passionate lunacy, but soon he was weeping on my shoulder and I was holding his small hot hand. He angrily knocked the tears out of his eyes with the back of his other hand. By this time it felt as if I were deep into my Genet research as I consoled the little loner, this toy bulldog. He talked till dawn about Lucette – who swore she loved him, too, only she was so terribly afraid of Jean-Marc, and if only he had a gun . . .

'But you'd go to prison,' I said.

'*Je m'en fous*,' he said. 'I don't give a damn.'

His single-minded devotion, which crowded out all thoughts of his future, beat like a tocsin inside his hard, doll-like chest. After he'd worn himself out talking about his girl he took me, his old man, to bed. He still sat on top of me and burned his smooth knees into my biceps, he still force-fed his penis into my willing mouth, my hands still roamed over his hairless body with the silky armpits as white as the filaments in a calyx that the sun never sees.

Stam always stayed too long and talked too much, both effects of the quantities of the off-brand scotch I offered him, the Famous

Quail or Tudor Tartan. There is in most cases a practical advantage to hiring a hustler when the customer is a busy man (or a writer who insists on long patches of idleness in case he might become busy with inspiration). A hustler arrives within a half-hour of the appointment he's been given and usually is eager to hurry away. In New York, hustlers charge by the hour and usually save their come for the next client. Should a hustler linger, the john can always glance at his watch or stand up and say, offering his hand, 'We must get together very soon.' Holding out the prospect of a second rendezvous next week is always a way to get better service now and head off a petty theft, since the hustler hopes the john will become a steady customer, a 'regular.' But Stam had passed over that line into friendship. He was a buddy, and anyway he was a better drinker than a shrewd gigolo. And if the night was cold I didn't want to push him out into it.

We knew no one in common except a darkly handsome college student from Pau whom Stam sent me. The student needed a place to crash in Paris whenever he made trips there to deliver a briefcase full of Moroccan hash. He was educated and reserved and carefully coiffed and dressed, a fellow with a future who was at least two social classes above Stam. He shared Stam's sweetness, guilelessness and easy physical camaraderie (he, too, spoke of a girlfriend while cradling my big head on his narrow chest). Both of these guys were at the moment in their lives when everything, and nothing, seemed possible – everything because they saw no limit to their time, nothing because they had so few immediate opportunities and possibilities. In this great indeterminacy they talked and talked without an eye to consequences or the hour. They didn't think they were choosing their future since so little of it seemed under their control. I suppose they would have turned to me for advice if I hadn't been a foreigner, but they understood that France is a world apart, functioning as an elaborate system of reciprocal favors in which no outsider can ever play a real part. For them I was a benign witness to their lives. For me they were young bodies and fresh souls – proof that I was still alive.

I moved back to the States for a year and a half and when I returned to Paris it was to a different apartment where the phone was listed only in the owner's name, not in mine. I never saw Stam again.

Now I live back in New York. When I first returned, after being away so long, I fell into a gloom since AIDS and a tough mayor had closed down all the old familiar sex places, the back rooms and most of the saunas as well as most of the hustler bars.

Freud hypothesized that many of civilization's greatest accomplishments, including acts of altruism, were powered by repressed homosexuality. I thought of that when I first resurfaced in Manhattan. Now that no one would dream of repressing anything, I said to myself, civilization is crumbling, kindness has vanished, and altruism has evaporated. Certainly greed had become more naked, hearts were harder and there was no repressed desire investing music, painting or the dance. To be sure my own interest in the arts struck me as evidence against the veracity of Freud's theory, for I had never failed to act on my erotic impulses. Repression had played no role in my acquisition of culture or my accomplishments. Maybe gay life had just been dumbed down like the rest of American society. A duller cultural edge and the new Puritanism didn't add up to an attractive combination for an aesthete and sex addict like me.

I started exploring the gay Internet. One night at four a.m. on a rainy Tuesday in February I was staring at a chat room screen when a new name popped up: 'Kevin 20.' Although this was not a hustlers' site, I typed in, 'I'll pay $150 if u let me suck ur dick.' Kevin replied, 'Nice man.' I didn't ask him for a physical description nor did he demand any details from me. He just wanted to know what I expected him to do. I told him I wouldn't even undress – I'd just suck him off. As soon as he gave me his address I went barreling up in a taxi through the deserted streets of the Upper West Side.

The young man who opened the door looked like Michelangelo's *David*. He had the same deep-set eyes, heavy-browed, square-jawed manly face as the *David* and a similarly youthful body, except for a chest that was hairy and more developed. And in his beautiful sea-green eyes there was something shifty as he'd steal worried glances at me, almost as if he'd grown up mocked by older male cousins and expected me to laugh at him. After our second session, this time down at my place, I wrote him a schoolgirlish e-mail saying I couldn't stop 'replaying my mental film of him.' He called in a panic: 'Dude, did you make a video of me? Was there a hidden camera I didn't notice?'

'Not at all! No, I meant I kept *thinking* about you.'

'So, there wasn't a video?'

'Of course not.'

'Cuz if there was . . . I mean, Dude, I might want to run for office some day or be a model.'

Soon I was such a weekly fixture in his life that his doorman announced me before I gave my name. I'd realized right away that this boy didn't need my money, that he was a student living in a two-thousand-dollar-a-month studio with an elaborate computer and a plasma-screen TV. Kevin had a private trainer every day at his gym where he went for two or three hours. He'd attended Groton but had not been athletic there. Now, I guess, he was an 'athlete' because he pushed heavy weights around.

One day, when I was in his neighborhood by chance, I decided to drop in on him. The woman behind the desk, wearing the livery of the posh building, wasn't content with just the apartment number. She wanted the tenant's name as well.

'It's Kevin something,' I said. 'His last name has slipped my mind.'

'No, sir, Three-C belongs to Paul Thomas.'

'Oh. He wants to be an actor – I was remembering his stage name,' I said. In any event, he wasn't at home.

I quickly discovered I could please him if I brought him a new porno video every week, which he'd fast-forward and freeze-frame at strategic places as I knelt on the floor between his legs. Once in an e-mail I complained that he never looked at me. He replied, a bit hurt, that he was just trying to be macho and cruel in the way he thought I liked. I quickly conceded he was right. I found his eagerness to please touching. That was the wound in this otherwise perfect man – his granite-hard erections proved that he found our scenario exciting, too.

And yet the slave hopes that in the end the master will be kind, that he'll lift the bruised and flayed slave in his arms and murmur paternal things in his ear, just as the john wants the hustler one day to say, 'I don't want your money. I love you.' Once I asked an articulate, literary hustler, 'Did you ever fall for a john?' And he wrinkled his nose and said, 'Are you kidding?' I had hired him and told him he didn't need to climax if he had a client later on. That line ended up in one of his books as an example of unparalleled politeness.

Kevin was never cruel but he could be demanding, with all the imperiousness of youth. Sometimes I felt I was a vampire battening off his vitality. I was more than sixty. He was turning twenty-one.

Sometimes he seemed lonely to me, going from school to gym and back again, his habits already old-maidish. He instructed me to remove my shoes at the door and when we had sex on his couch he covered it with an old sheet. If the sheet was pulled even an inch aside in one of our maneuvers, I could see he was worrying about it until the cloth was back in place.

As the months ticked by I learned that the only porno movies he liked were of violent, hairy men in their thirties who thwacked each other on the ass and shouted when they came. A friend of mine gave me a film of a skinny boy bound and gagged and kept in a cage with a red rubber ball strapped into his mouth and round rubber mittens on his hands so that he couldn't masturbate, but Kevin didn't like it. He fast-forwarded all the way through it and handed it back to me reproachfully on my way out.

I think at first he imagined I wanted him to be a tough guy, working-class and taciturn and forbidding, but once he got over that idea he opened up and after sex he'd chatter away about show business. I invited him to a musical; he was quietly dressed and solemnly well behaved. He could have been my grandson if my son had married a great beauty.

I suppose part of what appealed to me was that I was his sole client. I began to click on to other unsuspecting people online and offer them money too. It worked about one time out of thirty. Just yesterday I had a visit from a twenty-three-year-old Aeroflot steward from Moscow who shrugged with bored Slavic indifference when I suggested we move into the bedroom. Only on his way out an hour later did he freeze at the front door and say, 'What about our agreement?'

I slapped my forehead. I had forgotten he was one of the men to whom I'd offered money. Suddenly I regretted the extraordinary gratitude I'd felt toward him when I thought I was getting a freebie.

Through my doctor I met a gifted painter my age or nearly who, like Robert Mapplethorpe, devoted his work to society portraits, pictures of flowers and male nudes. He invited me to his studio. One by one he hauled out Old Master-sized canvases of young men sprawling naked in chairs or standing in full command of the wood-slatted floor. Their hands were curving in around invisible rods or scrolls like those held by a kouros or pharoah.

'You should meet this guy I know,' I said. 'Kevin. He has the sort of body you like.'

'Wait – Kevin? A student? Big guy with muscles and a beautiful face, beautiful butt?'

'Lives on the Upper West Side?'

The painter said, 'That's the one. He was here last night. You see, given my great height and big body and beard, I have to pay someone if I want to be topped, and I always want to be topped.'

'You paid Kevin?'

'Sure. He's got his own website. Here . . .' He tapped out the address on his computer. There on the screen was a decapitated photo of Kevin, seated naked on the toilet gripping a fist full of dick. I wondered if our chance encounter, his and mine, had pointed his way toward a career in prostitution or whether he'd accepted my offer that first February night at four a.m. because he was already walking on the wild side.

Edmund with his sister, Margaret

Gretchen Pifer

Marilyn Schaefer

My Women

If women are in love with me they make me feel guilty. I believe that I should reciprocate their passion and, if I don't, I keep worrying that it's just obstinacy on my part. Even telling them I'm gay sounds to me like a nasty excuse; I scarcely believe it myself.

In the past, when homosexuality was considered especially shameful, I was slow to confess my stigma to anyone, which made my reluctance to return women's love appear all the more ill-natured: who was I to reject an honest woman's affection? Was I holding out for someone so much better? Like who, precisely? Of course straight men rejected women all the time, too, or worse, didn't notice them, or still worse, dropped them after toying with them. But in my mind that didn't happen. For me straight men were universally gallant, just as women were always dependent and ladylike.

In the 1950s and sixties, if I avowed, usually tearfully, to a woman that I was homosexual, she would smile forgivingly, even benignly. My neurosis or 'ego disorder' was considered curable. It seemed to my women friends that I'd simply met the wrong members of their sex – intimidating or professionally virginal or even castrating bitches. All I needed to go straight (they said with a dawning smile) was the love of a good woman.

From my mother I had learned just how violent and unquenchable a woman's loneliness could be. She was making her way professionally, and she took pleasure in her success, though she worried constantly that her luck there too would come to an early end. She'd been sheltered excessively by her husband and then, midway through her life, cut loose and told to earn a living. It was as if after hobbling around with bound feet she were suddenly unbandaged and told to become a marathon runner.

Because my mother suffered so much beside the silent phone, drinking highballs and listening to the same sad record, I came to think of men as monsters with absolute powers and women as victims, of men as the darlings of the Western world and women as never good enough to hold their attention. Even today, if a woman friend of mine is considering leaving her husband, I always counsel her against it. All I can foresee is loss of status, loneliness, poverty, whereas a man, a straight man, no matter how boring and abusive and ugly he might be will always find another woman to humor him, forgive him, even support him.

Unhappy women! How many of them I've known. Sniffling and drinking or with eyes big and reproachful, silent or complaining women, violent or depressed – a whole tribe of unhappy women has always surrounded me. I can't take it any more. Now I've turned them into a semi-humorous category, I've made them into a caricature of themselves, a category that subsumes and obliterates all the suffering individuals, but labeling them is only a recent strategy for me, a way of not rushing to comfort them. For most of my life I've been a shoulder to cry on. And for most of my life I've felt guilty for not easing the pain of all these women, starting with my mother. If I were straight, if I'd marry one of them, I'd know how to comfort her. I wouldn't run off with another woman. I wouldn't spend all my money on drink. I wouldn't wound her by cheating on her. I'd work hard to provide her with the security, and even luxury, she required. I'd be as sensitive to her needs as a sister and as protective as a father. I'd never have a bad mood of my own and certainly never get angry. I'd always tell her where I was going and exactly when I'd be coming home.

No wonder heterosexuality frightened me. Marriage, it seemed, was designed to make at least one unhappy woman happy, though at what an awful cost to the man. To me. Maybe a straight man is first and foremost someone who can piss off a woman and laugh it off.

I can be made to feel guilty by almost anyone, but when I experience guilt I become angry with whoever is inducing it. I am a social sort who enjoys joking and having a good time. 'Lightness' is a virtue in my scheme of things, rare and highly desirable. So many people are truly sad or bitter or incontestably in physical pain or in actual want. Women lose their looks and men their jobs – to stay in a cheerful mood after all that is the ultimate act of courage, even a fairly artificial one, given that groaning is a more natural response. In my pursuit of lightness, I sometimes feel like a spider monkey swinging through the trees in a world that is more and more deforested. If I look hard I can still find moments of frivolity, of silvery silliness, of merry complicity, even of pure cross-eyed joy. Till now I usually can spot the next branch but sometimes it's quite a stretch.

Once I read a study from the 1970s that showed that even when little boys were given dolls and little girls toy trucks, they still clung to gender differences with a burning commitment. '*She* plays with trucks – she's just a girl,' a little boy would say, proudly displaying his Barbie. For children, for all of us, no matter how we're programmed, male and female differences remain the world's binary code.

Which leads me to wonder how I feel about Woman as opposed to particular women. Unlike many gay men I've never idolized Woman or wanted to be female. I have never belonged to that tribe of fussy, perfectionist gays who displace their own feminine ambitions onto the women they adore to chastise. All those gay men who brush out their girlfriends' hair or dye their mother's lashes, who coif their balding aunt with a jewelled turban. I never wanted to wear a frock and only three or four times in my life have I tried to excite myself by imagining what it would be like to *be* a woman in a man's arms, to feel his penis penetrating my vagina, to hope that his semen would make me pregnant with his child.

To be honest, when I was a teenager I secretly thought that I was delicate and pretty in some invisible, essential way that even I couldn't quite fathom, but that might magically appeal to some tough, unsmiling man. As it turns out there are almost no gay men looking for a delicate, pretty man. A boy, perhaps, but not a man, and even the prettiest nelly boys, it seems, attract mostly nutty straight men who for some perverse reason want a chick with a dick. Even the fragile part of me longing for male protection I've never thought of as exactly female. Infantile, rather.

In the 1970s I was going out with my doctor and once, a bit tipsy over dinner, I winked at him. He said, 'I'm sure glad I've never picked up any cutesy little mannerisms.' Just the other day I said to a handsome young German, who's smart but too straightforward to understand devious charm, 'You are so kind to come all the way down here to see me.' I cringed, hearing my mother's lilting Southern cadences. He looked at me unsmilingly, kissed me and said, 'I'm here only because I want to be. It's certainly not out of any sense of duty.' I remember once I had my students read Tennessee Williams's *A Streetcar Named Desire*. One of the blue-jeaned young women, hair cropped short, nails unpainted, voice unmodulated, asked, 'Why is that woman Blanche DuBois so weird and girly-girly? What a Loser!' she said, holding the letter L with her fingers up to her forehead.

I was educated by my mother far more than by my father. From her I learned to be self-sacrificing. My mother made big, self-advertising sacrifices and sighed theatrically during her frequent martyrdoms: 'You kids go on and have a wonderful New Year's without me. I'll just stay here by myself and clean up. Now go on, don't worry about me one second. Just be sure to call me at midnight.'

My style of self-immolation is so subtle that the people around me feel bad but they're not sure whether I want them to. I am full of cheerful smiles and reassuring nods when I am caught by my guests, punching the bread a second time at dawn. Steal my lover away? Oh, be my guest! I'm not jealous, for heaven's sake . . . 'You're too good, Ed,' they say. 'Almost like a saint.'

So I've incorporated a large dose of the female principle without being feminine; and yet if I am to speak of the women in my life I must start with myself. I used to be careful about my looks, but now I have to remind myself to have my hair cut monthly or my teeth cleaned every six months. I wear the same sturdy, waterproof shoes every day. I've chosen comfort over style. When I'm confronted with the question, 'What's really more important – being slim and attractive or that second piece of cake?' the answer for me isn't always the obvious one. I'll have a dermatologist burn off the liver spots from the back of my hands, but when new ones grow in I don't care. My mother became a mild sort of exhibitionist in her eighties after both breasts had been lopped off and she wore a colostomy bag – she'd always arrange for us to see her naked. Now that I'm in my sixties with sagging breasts and a huge stomach I privately admire my body and am wounded when others despise it.

My young lover tells me I have a dated admiration for women who are 'ladylike' and a corresponding aversion to aggressive women, whom I call 'vulgar.' It's true I have a hard time warming up to a woman who says 'shit' or talks loudly. It's not that I don't want women to be pugnacious or ambitious or sexual. On the contrary, I admire ardor above all else in women, but I want their voices to be modulated and their manners elegant.

Women who imagine that I'm not quickly seduced by feminine charm because I'm gay are mistaken. I love young and not so young women who flirt with me, let me order for them, permit me to open doors and pick up checks, hold their coats and walk on the street side to protect them from runaway horses. If a woman is also intelligent and tells me her secrets I am soon eating out of her hand. If she is brilliant and original and stylish and lightly scheming, I can even be bridled and saddled. But a loud, nasal voice, hysterical giggling or dirty fingernails can cause me to bolt and run. When Michael points out that, illogically, I'm attracted to loud, brash, bullying, dirty boys, I have to admit he's perfectly right. Boys should be bad, girls good.

In my grade school, when I was ten and eleven, I accompanied bland, well-brought-up girls to the movies on 'dates' on Saturday afternoon that were our parents' idea of a harmless preparation for later, more perilous romantic and sexual encounters. Although I'd been a sweet three- or four-year-old, by the time I was eight, nine and ten I'd forgotten the urge to charm. In that paradise before I bit into the apple of social awareness, I had no idea that one could be ingratiating, seductive or even more or less likable. I hadn't yet learned to ask flattering questions, to 'lead people out,' to express sympathy for their pain and encouragement for their pleasures, to exonerate their failings as 'normal' and declare their modest successes to be 'triumphs.' I am sure I was a nice enough guy and even projected a low-wattage charm, but whatever glow I gave off was just the crumbling half-life of my sluggish existence. In the same way that I had no idea what I looked like and managed to stumble around ill-shod, badly dressed, unkempt and often dirty, I had no notion that some people were more popular than others, much less that there were acquirable techniques to insure popularity. Boys and girls alike were for me something like human furniture filling up rooms and corridors, as featureless as the real furniture we lived among. Just as we didn't notice the faded flowered slipcovers on sagging couches or the armchairs on which the green plush was worn down in browning patches, so we didn't see this kid or that as magnetic or repulsive. To be sure, I did fall under the physical spell of a Buster or Howie or Cam, but it seemed like a miracle if one of them liked me back. It never occurred to me that friendship was biddable.

Although I loved wrestling with boys, I would never have tried to wrestle a girl into submission. Not that girls were frilly at our school, or beauty queens. They were tomboys or colorless wrens with knobby knees and imitation tortoiseshell barrettes holding back limp hanks of hair. Their skinny pale arms pressed their books to their chests as they scurried along in full skirts and white bobby socks. But even so they seemed a bit remote and mysterious, at least physically. They were segregated from us in gym class, and during our weekly ballroom dancing class they were transformed by stiff organdy dresses, white gloves, shiny Mary Janes and faint circles of pink lipstick smudged into and then nearly wiped clean from their cheeks. Girls were neater, their lockers cleaner, their writing rounder and smaller, their drawings and sums impeccable, their singing more in tune, their skipping more agile than our movements, their playing of jacks just an excuse to whisper secrets to each other. We boys didn't have secrets. At least the Secretive was not an official genre of our conversations. As I grew older the women I was drawn to weren't epic Midwestern sufferers like my mother. My women were foreigners or bohemians or artists – and even back then, in the fifties and sixties, they were strong and independent.

In eighth grade my attitude toward girls changed. A block away from where we were living I met an English girl who was going to Nichols, the rougher junior high in South Evanston, not to Haven in the richer part of town, which my mother somehow had arranged for me to attend.

I'd met only one Brit before, a soldier I'd exchanged two words with. I thought she must in some way be 'aristocratic,' imbued with Shakespeare, sensitive, refined, a tea drinker, mild-mannered, but Alice had a tough, nearly incomprehensible Liverpudlian accent, small, discolored teeth, a way of going from wheedling to sharp pokes in the side, a fund of dirty talk and startlingly precocious ways. Our Evanston girls, the daughters of local dentists or North-western professors, were dowdy and faintly withdrawn and almost bovine in their frankness, whereas Alice would lead me into the garage under her building, press her hard pelvis against me, touch my erection and giggle, thrust her tongue in my mouth then wriggle away and laugh her unpleasant shriek of a laugh. She was skittish, unfocused, possessed by a demonic energy that quickly ran out, hard and thrusting then listless and bold, looking for something else. I felt she'd been kissed by older men, high school boys, even by dropouts. She told me I was 'wicked.'

When I'd see her she'd scarcely acknowledge me, just smiling faintly as if she weren't sure she knew me. Then something would shift inside her and she'd run up to me, embrace me and push her crotch into mine as she tilted her torso back in order to get a better look at me. She'd ask a question or two, not listen to the answer, then shake all over with private laughter that struck me as unsavory. Her tongue was as muscular and slippery as a carp.

For the first time it dawned on me that girls could be enjoyed in the boys' games of wrestling and grabbing and rubbing up against one another, except Alice wanted to kiss, sometimes uncritically with closed eyes and fluttering tongue, long sighs and a slump into my arms (she was taller than I), sometimes with a rough, mocking aggressiveness. She would rub my hand against her mons veneris, but only if I stayed outside her slick panties, which were of an anemic, foreign yellow-pinkness. Just when we'd both become truly aroused, she'd remember to slither away, slap my hand and run off, laughing her shrill laugh.

I didn't completely approve of her. There was something coarse about her. I didn't want my girlfriends from Haven, wearing their expensive braces and dressed in their powder-blue cashmere sweaters, to see me with Alice, to hear her shriek of a laugh and notice her bad teeth, but she excited me. She made me hard. I can still feel her thin, eel-like body wriggling out of my grasp. She would wag her finger at me ('You're a fine one'), as if I'd knowingly gone too far.

I'd studied the roughshod, horny world of boys closely, to make sure I wasn't being too queer for them. They didn't worry about pressing their hard-ons into my stomach through a double layer of denim, but they didn't want to be called pansies. Alice, too, was concerned by what people were saying about her. Would she get a 'reputation' as a 'slut'? Boys couldn't be sluts though they could be perverts. For me, all this fussing over labels was an obstacle to my obsessive needs. I wanted to be considered fast with girls and not a queer. That I dreaded: queer. I longed for contact with other men exactly to the degree I feared the label.

Once, years later, my sister told me that she thought boys who were oversexed automatically became homosexual. Early on, she said, they felt the pressure of a sex drive so compelling that it was irresistible; other boys but not girls were willing partners in erotic wrestling and circle jerks. These first experiences imprinted them for life. A neat theory, but it has more holes in it than a colander. Most boys who grow up to be gay men are afraid to roughhouse as teenagers. Alice was nearly as exciting to me as a boy, but my experiences with her didn't keep me on the lookout for a girl who glanced back, for a girl whose lips might part when she forgot herself and stared at me. And if someone said, 'You know, that girl with the big tits,' I faked it, but frankly I hadn't usually noticed.

I dreamed of linking my name to that of a girl who was a famous beauty. As a freshman in high school I fell in love with Sally, one of the most popular and beautiful girls at Evanston High. I had only one date with her, and that was a double date with my best friend

Steve and his girl. The four of us went to the movies. Steve, so kind, was trying to fix me up with someone. I scarcely exchanged two words with Sally; I listened to her as she chatted with the other couple about their friends, people I'd only seen or heard of. Actually, Sally said little, just murmured a few words now and then in her deep, well-modulated voice.

Sally was celebrated for her big breasts (which even I noticed) and her face, which was that of the Apollo Belvedere – bow-shaped lips, a long, straight nose, a wide, domed brow, an ensemble that was classical and noble and oddly mature. She looked like a woman, a grown-up woman, not a raddled adolescent. She said very little but she smiled dreamily with veiled eyes. Her smile had a way of lingering two beats too long, after the amusing part of the conversation had moved on to a different mood. Was she lost in her own thoughts and not paying attention? Had someone told her she was at her best when she smiled? She never guffawed or squealed with laughter or made violent movements, though catty classmates told me that when boys weren't around she was a real sow, rolling on the floor, drunk on beer, giggling herself sick with other girls over obscene speculations about particular penises they had known or divined through Speedos. Such a contrast to her usual dreamy composure seemed a calumny, but I'd seen how my prim sister collapsed into a squalor of obscene laughter with Penny, her best friend, but became more and more demure and posed by the second as she waited for a boy to ring the doorbell (my sister's dates were as rare as my mother's and caused just as much anguish).

I had no idea how boys wooed girls. It was no doubt a matter of joshing and shared nothings and hours and hours of scuffing through autumn leaves and even more hours of clenches during the slow numbers at the sock hop. Popular girls, I knew, were won by boys who were brave on the playing fields. But I suppose what later turned me into a writer – the belief that a few words in a particular order could work a magic spell, make an obscure person famous, a poor one rich, a nerd lovable – now led me to send Sally a long letter, written on heavy yellowing paper meant to resemble parchment, penned in the italic lettering I'd been teaching myself.

Once this missive had been sent off, my days (there were five of them) were spent in suspense and anxiety. I couldn't imagine Sally saying yes to me – and if she did, what would I do then? What if she didn't write me at all? I was no better than my mother, sitting by the silent phone, or my sister, longing for a date and at the same time fearing it.

I prepared myself to become Sally's lover by writing her a lascivious sonnet – trying to imagine that smooth skin under mine, those pillowy breasts under my heavy head, her narrow hips twisting under mine. She always seemed so calm, I could scarcely picture her thrashing about in ecstasy. No one, straight or gay, had mentioned sexual technique to me yet. Just as well: one less worry. For me love – at least love on the sublime level where I encountered it – wasn't a matter of performance nor a convergence of personal charm and popularity. No, love was the essence of one person communicating with the essence of another. It was a conversation that never approximated real talk. That's why to be rejected in love was so cataclysmic – one had been judged and found fundamentally wanting.

Being lonely for someone is much richer, more eventful and far more solitary than just being alone. I had had so little experience imagining myself in love that now I locked my bedroom door and made love to my pillow for hours. I would doze and awaken half a dozen times during the night only to climax yet again (I was fourteen). I thought Sally's love could make me popular, a real man (hadn't she gone out with college boys?), and secure (for in none of my scenarios did she break up with me once she'd accepted me), in the same way my mother's boyfriends were supposed to confer distinction on her, make her enviable and wealthy and triumphant with one simple ring slipped on her finger. I was expecting rejection, but if by some miracle she said yes our union would last forever (miracles are never temporary).

Love of that sort – behind a locked door, in the dark, caressing a pillow and whispering vows to it – was the purest form of love. Unlike real love with another human being, there was no sinking of the spirits, no halitosis, no fear of impotence, no impatience with the other's opinions, nor a panicky feeling of having become overcommitted, or a brusque impatience to be alone.

When I came home from school on Friday afternoon, the

envelope was waiting for me. In some part of my mind I felt surprised that I'd been able to make someone so important respond to me at all. Sally's handwriting was all circles and loops that twined around a straight, invisible guiding line. She told me that, alas, she didn't think of me as a boyfriend but as a very dear friend – which at first struck me as more a promotion than a rejection.

At last something public and decisive was happening to me. People would talk about this. I wondered why such a signal event was occurring in such weak daylight with no soundtrack beyond the whoosh of traffic on the wet road outside and the twittering of rainy-day birds. Closer to hand there was the ticktock of my mother's bedside clock in the next room, a little white face picked out in silver numerals and girded by blue sapphires.

If that afternoon I was capable of reading about my fate with detachment, by that evening I had collapsed into heavy sobs that weighed down on me and got tangled around my legs like wet sheets. I rolled in a hot, dirty, humid mangle of humiliation. Yes, of course, I was ugly, skinny, unathletic, worthless, uninteresting, stupid and I smelled bad. Sally had made me so. My mother and sister were weird and I was worse: invisible. First love is so painful precisely because it has no precedents, no rules to break or confirm. One has not yet been inducted into a fraternity of shared sufferers, of seasoned and congenial losers. One must go it alone, one is the first person ever to experience this unnamed thing called rejection. One can't shrug and submit gracefully to bad luck; one is the first angel ever to be cast out of heaven. And the damnation is eternal.

You would think that now, after decades of psychotherapy, I would have noticed long ago that what I've always yearned for is lovers of obvious (one could say banal) prestige. The women I loved, at least early on, were status symbols, though putting it that way makes it sound as if I wanted to add them like charms to a bracelet, whereas my despair was not the sort that anyone feels over the loss of something merely decorative. I suppose I was my mother's true disciple. She'd taught me by example that a man, though elusive, could transform one's whole life. So many novels in English, notably *Jane Eyre*, taught us that men did not necessarily marry their peers but from time to time might raise someone humble up in recognition of – well, of her virtues, though my mother and I believed in essential, not virtual love. We would be loved not for anything we did or were worth but for what we were, though we were nothing special.

Later, when I wrote the life of Jean Genet, I recognized myself in his characters whose very nature is subject to transubstantiation – through First Communion, for instance, or marriage. The bride changes her name, thus her entire identity. It's as if her molecules were being replaced. In the same way in Genet a boy, holding on to a pole in the subway car, suddenly thinks of himself as Joan of Arc grasping a lance – and instantly *becomes* Saint Joan. The idea of magical transformation arising out of a careless gesture, of the miraculous invading the quotidian: these notions were not unfamiliar to me when I first read Genet.

My suffering, however, was not metaphysical. Like my mother, who entertained the burning hope that that nice man from Santa Barbara, the one who'd awakened her with a cocktail shaker full of brandy Alexanders, would marry her and make her the rich mistress of a hacienda dominating the coast – like Mom I'd expected Sally to make me handsome, popular, normal, better than normal.

I left high school and went off to boarding school, where I fell in love with Marilyn Monroe. I knew she was the most beautiful woman in the world and yet she was also in pain, in need. She was unhappy. I knew I could help her. Perhaps I was powerless to help myself, nonetheless, I never doubted that I could bring her happiness. My fantasies weren't too exact as to what I would actually say to her or do for her. No, I never got beyond our little smiles of love and recognition, which burned with a brighter and brighter glow.

My favorite daydream was that she'd come with me to my senior prom. All the other guys (I was attending Cranbrook Boys' School in Bloomfield Hills, outside Detroit, Michigan) would be astonished: the frog, Eddie White, was really a prince. I had no concrete plans for inviting her. I just kept picturing her on my arm, her sequined gown glittering, her voluptuous body undulating seductively as we entered the dining hall, now transformed by crepe paper into a ballroom. It was like a mermaid's visitation. The thin boys with their brush cuts and spotty faces, wearing their powder-blue dinner jackets and burgundy cummerbunds with matching bow ties, would gape at us. No way, man, the biggest dweeb of them all with . . . Marilyn!?! Sheesh . . .

In fact I took Gretchen Pifer to the dance, a beauty in her own right who had been voted the most photogenic woman in Toledo the year before.

Gretchen's father was Bill, our dentist, and an old friend of my stepmother. The Pifers lived in Toledo in a big house that looked down on the Maumee River. It was a modern house with floating levels, lots of glass and a central living area two stories high – dramatic like everyone in the house. I didn't visit them often but every second I passed with them germinated in my mind in the long arid months that followed.

Compared to the silences of my father's house, the Pifers end-lessly chirped with sunny exuberance. They were all constantly talking, either in the central sitting room or off in little rooms – usually a dressing room. Mrs. Pifer ('Cathy,' as I was urged to call her) had been a dancer in the *Ziegfeld Follies* and she still thought of descending the stairs to join her guests as 'making my entrance.' She had an eccentric idea of good manners; she once pretended to call a local theater director Mr. Shakespeare, as though her confusion indicated her enormous respect. She made the mistake on purpose. She wasn't at all a narcissist, if narcissism relies on taking *pleasure* in one's own beauty. No, she cast a cold eye on time's inroads – the sagging chin, the pouchy eyes, the deepening marionette lines bracketing the mouth, the coarsening skin texture – and with workmanlike realism she sanded and spackled and painted them into temporary invisibility. Though a vague sense of emergency hung in the air, as if Cathy might go mad tomorrow, or, more accurately, had gone mad yesterday, just before my arrival, I never felt menaced by this coming or passing loss of control. Cathy wasn't crazy in the usual repetitious, soul-contracting, humiliating way. No, she was always fun – inspired, a bit lunatic, playful.

Surprisingly, my father liked her and especially Gretchen and indulged their caprices. I barely recognized him in this genial role. My sister resented the way Dad obviously preferred Gretchen to her.

Cathy wasn't interested in expensive clothes, just her own wardrobe trunk and the fanciful costumes she could dig up out of its odds and ends. She wasn't too good for ordinary work (changing beds, peeling potatoes) as long as she could wear rubber gloves and everything could be done 'backstage', unseen by her audience. Nor did she complain about Toledo – in fact, no one in the house complained about anything. The show must go on, and it was ongoing here on the humid banks of the Maumee. Every second of the day was tinged with fantasy – breakfast required an old feather hat, dark glasses and a simple 'day face.' The food was chosen as if no one had ever broken a fast before. ('Shall we pour orange juice on the strawberries? Shall we whip some cream for the rolls – that way we can call them scones.') The white, blue-striped bowls and napkins were lifted out of a Matisse painting. Someone lit and sipped ineffectually at a Gauloise just for the blue smoke rising in the sunlight and the forbidden odor of adventure blending with the smell of coffee. Cathy teetered downstairs on very high heels, her hair swept up in a disintegrating 'brioche,' her eyes glistening with belladonna drops. She had an unfocused, inconsequential giggle, whereas Gretchen had a raucous laugh that was at odds with her extravagant, slim beauty and smoky croak of a voice. She and her mother did lots of imitations, notably of Baby Snooks's infantile piping in which 'little' became 'widdle.' Cathy had known Fanny Brice in the *Follies*.

If Cathy was prattling away in baby talk and Gretchen was slapping her knee and laughing her bewitching shred of a laugh, Gretchen's older sister Dee-Dee stayed aloof: cool, classy and intellectual. She was getting an advanced degree in Spanish and on the mantelpiece in her room was a sumptuously bound edition of Rubén Darío's *Obras Completas*, the works of the nineteenth-century Romantic poet from Central America she was studying. Whereas Gretchen wore layers of makeup and had long, complicated black hair filled in with additional switches and falls, Dee-Dee was freshfaced with short dark blonde hair that she pushed back behind her ears. She'd read the just-published *Bonjour Tristesse* in French and could have been its sophisticated young author tooling along the Grande Corniche in a sports car. She, too, was funny, but in a muttered, muted way, not with Gretchen and Cathy's eye-rolling, belted-out patter that was designed to project to the top balcony. Once I was standing next to Dee-Dee when a log in the fireplace suddenly popped; without a pause she drew out imaginary pistols, aimed at the fire and muttered, 'Dance, pardner.'

Compared to my unhappy mother or my angry father the Pifers were playful people, interested in everyone, even in kids and teens, always ready for new excitement. Their generosity was all the more striking when I came down to Toledo from my boarding school – from a tough, motherless, comfortless world of sports, snow and study hall, to this big sunny house where I could sleep in, eat something French in a cream sauce and listen to Gretchen rehearse her lines.

Bill Pifer lived in an all-female world as a quiet, self-effacing provider. He was the nerd who got the showgirl. Cathy called him 'Pooky,' just as he called her 'Pooky,' but she said it with her lips pursed, leaning down from her spike heels to kiss his bald spot. She would assign him a minor role in the nonstop theatricals, plop a sombrero on him or twist a pink boa around his neck and he'd suddenly appear, pushing the temporary stage curtain aside and grinning sheepishly. 'Oh, Pooky,' Cathy would moan, catching my eye and winking, 'I told you not to come out until Gretchen says, "All hail, the sun is rising!" Pooky, you're hopeless, but a giant sweetie anyway,' and she'd blow him a kiss and he'd look terribly ashamed and pleased all at once.

When I'd visit him at his office he was a different man, smocked in white, his breath thoughtfully sweetened as he stared into my mouth, his whispered commands silently obeyed by his sturdy assistant, his hands gentle and competent, his solicitude never to cause even the slightest pain so at odds with the sadism of most dentists. His offices had been strangely decorated by Cathy but even the Expressionist landscapes on the walls and blown-glass marlins plunging out of a crystal sea in the waiting room – not even these artistic touches could diminish the cool, expensive efficiency of Dr. Pifer's domain. Like a busy prostitute who has three clients in various stages of arousal or detumescence in adjoining rooms, the good doctor had one patient waiting for the novocaine to numb his mouth, while another was biting down into a horseshoe of peppermint-flavored plaster and a third was submitting to the cold spray of the new high-speed drill.

He would keep the others waiting and would dismiss the assistant so that he could speak more playfully to me with his blue eyes dancing, his tiny gray mustache twitching, his big soft hands squeezing my arm or stroking my fingers or thigh or even massaging my shoulders.

Was he attracted to me, to men? I dared not pose the question, since what I loved at the Pifers' was precisely the air of permissiveness, of fluidity, and a dull call for definition would have killed it. Gretchen and Cathy were strong and charming but hounded by mental problems they refused to discuss; they seemed more drawn to the makeup kit than to boys or men. Bill was a shyly grinning little guy who'd learned to put on a 'wicked' smile whenever he was baffled or abashed; he tiptoed around with the air of a child who hopes to please his mother this time, though he's had to endure a lot of teasing.

During my last year in boarding school I spent a long weekend in Toledo with the Pifers. There I met an unshaved young man, already a sophomore in college, who took me out for a ride. We parked along a country road, lit cigarettes, cracked the window open and watched the November night rush in like a flock of crows, each of us half-leaning against his door and sprawled out toward the other. We talked and talked. In those days men rarely spoke of their homosexuality and at considerable peril. Maybe he wasn't gay but he did have some sort of burden he was carrying. He sighed, started to say something, and examined the tip of his cigarette as if it were the point of curiosity.

I can still remember that smoky parked car, with the sharp slice of cold air behind my head and the feeling of stalled frustration between us. It was one of my first adult moments, and I attribute it to the Pifers and the sensitive, good-looking young man who moved slowly, bravely around them. Maybe I remember that moment because it held a dark, suffering promise of sex and love with him that was never fulfilled.

When I was still at Cranbrook I met Marilyn Schaefer, a painting student at the adjoining Cranbrook Academy of Art. We've stayed friends all our lives – soon we'll be celebrating half a century of friendship. At the boys' school everything was stolidly, unreflectingly Midwestern. Half the boys were day students, the sons of the local 'automobility,' and the other half were the neglected or problem children of rich families who lived farther away. The art academy students, who were usually graduate students, had beards and long hair or, if they were women, sandals and no makeup and unshaved legs glimpsed under peasant skirts. They all listened to records of Wanda Landowska playing Bach on the harpsichord (God's seamstress, as we called her) or to twanging Indian ragas sliding up and down through a melisma of uncomfortably close chromatics. Whereas the boys' school was the Finnish architect Elie Saarinen's daydream about a traditional English public school, complete with brick walkways and carved gargoyles, the art academy was his tribute to Modernism, gardens and low buildings oriented toward a high peristyle framing a fountain that represented the souls soothed by Orpheus in the Underworld.

Marilyn was twenty-two and I just fifteen and though now I recognize that part of my appeal to her must have been that I was precocious, at the time I didn't play up my surprising intellectuality. I longed to be an equal, yet if something I said made her smile because suddenly I sounded like an old man (or like a little kid), I was happy to have earned the extra affection. I would go to her studio and watch her paint. I'd drink the bitter espresso she brewed up on her hotplate and talk about her enthusiasms – Marx, de Kooning, the American philosopher John Dewey, Walt Whitman. In the 1950s most people sneered at Whitman as a bardic blowhard; we liked small, tightly controlled impersonal lyrics filled with echoes of world culture that could be submitted to close reading – T. S. Eliot, in other words. The opposite of Whitman. But Marilyn liked America and American geniuses, which seemed unusual back then when American artists and thinkers still suffered from a national inferiority complex and thought of their countrymen as philistines. When heavyset, styleless tourists out from Detroit grazed through the Cranbrook grounds the art students laughed at them. Marilyn wasn't like that. She liked elderly Midwesterners. One of her favorite words was 'cozy.' If she was reverting to

German, which her parents had spoken at home, she'd say '*gemütlich*.' She praised Whitman's democratic vistas, his sweeping inclusiveness, his rhetorical punch; she made the rest of us feel like small-minded pedants. She also liked Dewey's egalitarian principles, his bold educational reforms, his utilitarian views of art. In the same way, she embraced Theodore Dreiser and declared *Sister Carrie* a masterpiece, whereas for us his novels were baggy monsters, uninspired reworkings of Zola's naturalism *and* (worst of all) corny and clunky. We liked irony, indeterminacy, bleak concision, whereas she favored bluff directness, simplicity, health. It seemed strange to me that someone who painted big, scary abstractions, which in the 1950s struck most Americans as criminally unusual, should have been so commonsensical in her literary tastes, though later I would discover that twelve-tone composers read Keats just as experimental poets listened to Glenn Miller – few people were avant-garde outside their own domain.

Just last night Marilyn said she hadn't known much about painting back then, whereas I had had the same unquestioning faith in her powers then that my students have in mine now. I suppose as Midwesterners, and as the children of chemical engineers and homemakers or of real estate developers and practical nurses, we experienced the arts as so foreign, even so preposterously unreasonable, that once we'd decided to embrace them we did so with lots of conviction and little discrimination. Surely it was no accident that T. S. Eliot and Ezra Pound, the two great poetic synthesists of our day, the very men who had ransacked all of world culture and could refer in the same poem to the Buddha and Sophocles or to Confucius and Jefferson – surely it was no accident that Eliot and Pound were both from the heartland. Like them we were public-library intellectuals, magpies of all knowledge, but like most autodidacts we were incapable of evaluating our sources: we usually read the wrong book. We had no notion that most writers and painters emerged out of artistic families or at least conformed to the artistic tradition of their country, time and class. As a teenager I tried to write verse like Milton's; later I wanted to write novels like Nabokov's. In one of my college novels I imitated Evelyn Waugh. If someone had said to me, 'But do you, as the stolid, graceless son of a Cincinnati broker of chemical equipment, do you seriously imagine you can just write a Renaissance Christian epic or something in the style of a Cambridge-educated Russian aristocrat or like the spokesman of the Bright Young Things of London circa 1925?' – if someone had spoken like this to me I wouldn't even have understood his point. Years later, when I was thirty, I met Erich Heller, a German-American literary critic, the author of *The Poet's Self and the Poem*, and he made just such an objection to my Nabokovian ambitions, which infuriated me.

I didn't believe in the social history of art. For me (as for Marilyn) writing or painting was private to the point of solipsism; it was a romantic expression of stormy individualism, not a classical reflection of a serene social milieu. The suggestion that our goals were limited or even inflected by what our parents did for a living made us writhe with impatience. We looked toward Keats, a five-foot-tall Cockney, not to the great Lord Byron, just as we preferred our own homemade giants Melville and Ryder over all those European writers and painters. No matter that they were both crackpots, that Melville had gotten tangled up in endless descriptions of rigging and whaling or that Ryder's paint was so thick it was now flaking off. We didn't respect competent technicians but rather American men, those who were possessed of genius but no talent.

I was intoxicated by the personal style of the Cranbrook Academy of Art. Everyone was silent and seldom spoke above a whisper. When they looked at each other's sculptures or paintings they didn't feel compelled to produce automatic praise. Rather, they stared at the piece quizzically for a long time, as if feeling it all over through long, sensitive antennae. Judgment was held in abeyance. No one was gossipy since no one took notice of eccentricity or financial failure or adultery, the usual three subjects of gossip. The students assumed all artists were oddballs; bohemia was a refuge for the *refusés*. They subscribed to the code of honorable poverty for 'martyrs to art,' as they jokingly called themselves. And adultery – well, the very concept was too suburban even to mention, though like everyone else they were subject to jealous fits and (given how much they drank) fights. Some burly, bearded sculptor, bare-chested with an acetylene torch in hand, might slam into his bird-like rival, but no one would tut-

tut when his girlfriend, the big-hipped Israeli potter, moved into his rival's bedroom.

The artists didn't read much but they carried around talismanic books – Susanne K. Langer's *Philosophy in a New Key*, the *I Ching* in the fancy Bollingen edition with the introduction by Jung, *The Songs of Maldoror* by the self-named Comte de Lautréamont. There were very drunken parties held downtown in Detroit by the favorite black male model with the tweezed eyebrows, in his rabbit warren of an apartment. All the male painters and sculptors would chug wine and drink beer and declare their sodden love to the same Wisconsin farm girl, a lithographer, her reddish-blonde hair twisted in plaits over a face that was crying out for mascara since her eyebrows were blonde to the point of invisibility and her lips nearly bloodless, so pale they made her teeth look yellow.

Marilyn loved all this craziness but after her own cool fashion. She tied her white men's shirt in front to reveal a sliver of her pale midriff above her black jeans. She puffed on cigarettes amateurishly. All evening she nursed the same glass of bad wine. She danced a bit by herself in the corner to a wailing Brenda Lee record but it was obvious she couldn't dance – she had the white girl's embarrassing habit of brandishing an invisible tambourine. And she was the one who ended up necking with the coveted Wisconsin girl in the corner. I stole glances at them. One moment Marilyn seemed as suave as Robert Taylor swooping in for the clinch with the pale girl and the next she was as calm and kissable as a starlet.

I was confused because she was also going out with an easygoing artist named Jay, a tall, bearded man whose neck and forearms were so massive and hairy that he looked like a beast captured in a man's shirt. He played the violin with a heavy Romantic vibrato; Marilyn said he and his brothers and their immigrant Jewish father played Mozart and Beethoven in their little Lower East Side family kitchen. Jay seemed permanently amused by everyone's exaggerations and failings and an ironic smile never stopped dancing over the lips that would have been mocking us had he not been so distant, squinting dimly at all this foolishness through layers and layers of scrims. Marilyn and Jay were lovers but no one ever said so. They never touched each other in public. Explicitness about one's romantic arrangements had apparently been deemed gauche.

In my teenage, middle-class world the whole apparatus of going steady, exchanging ID bracelets, of smooching at dances, of fighting, breaking up, submitting to the arbitration of friends – *that* was the point, the public drama, whereas at the art academy the heterosexuals were as furtive as the homosexuals. And even that firm distinction would have seemed primitive to them since the unstated ideal appeared to be bisexuality or, as it was called in that Freudian time, 'polymorphous perversity.'

People who have never seen Cranbrook can't imagine its extensive gardens and pavilions, the rolling hills covered with daffodils in the spring, the Greek temple and amphitheater in the woods, the girls' school, Kingswood, floating above a reflecting lake like a low Japanese palace. Of the five schools at Cranbrook, perhaps the art academy is closest to the Finnish vernacular version of Modernism that Saarinen had invented with its snug brick buildings, small leaded panes, and its couches covered with handwoven carpets that could be pulled back over the seated person as lap rugs. In the winter so few people seemed to be about – it was such a perfectly maintained institution – that it was like an architect's presentation maquette, and as if someone had placed a few human figures here and there just to give the scale.

I went home to Cincinnati for the long, hot summer during which I worked as a clerk at the haberdashery where my father bought his clothes, stacking and restacking dress shirts, but at the beginning of August I got a letter from Marilyn. I savored it by rereading it many times. She was working for a union newspaper in Iowa and she discussed her investigation into the nature of the paper's readership. Laughingly she admitted that workers didn't like drawings in the paper but preferred sharp-focused photographs.

She started a new paragraph, 'To use Aristotle's categories, what are you doing, thinking and making?' I was doing nothing but pushing a broom and stacking shirts, my thoughts were all vague and tormented and I was 'making' little beyond writing a few pages of a novel about my mother's sex life for advanced English class. But I was thrilled to receive this casual reference to socialism in McCarthy's America and to Aristotle in the land of know-nothings – and to have this chatty letter from my sophisticated older friend.

The art academy was usually just a one-year program but Marilyn came back a second year while I was still there. Jay was gone. Though I was seven years younger than she, a hint of love and even sex made itself felt. We mainly loved talking – about whether art should be for art's sake or should advance the cause of the revolution.

I learned that Marilyn was brought up by parents raised at Amana, Iowa, the German pietist colony. Their childhood and youth had been passed in the greatest austerity, though they looked back on Amana with real fondness and regularly visited 'Oba' ('Gramps') and a few old aunts who still lived there. They spoke English with a heavy German accent though they had been born in the United States; indeed, the colony had been in America since the middle of the nineteenth century. Amana had believed in continual revelation and well into the twentieth century God had spoken directly to various old men and women, whose outpourings in German (usually about the details of everyday life or character flaws) had been written down by devoted scribes. The boys and girls were kept apart, even in church, and if a young couple announced they wished to marry it was a cause for sadness. They were sent to far-apart villages. At the end of a year if the two persisted in their folly they were allowed to marry in a melancholy ceremony. Modesty and self-effacement were regarded as the highest state and bringing children into the world as a tragic mistake.

Marilyn's father had worked at Amana as a carpenter. When he and his new wife left the colony and moved to Davenport he became a builder. They had five children and Mr. Schaefer prospered. He built many churches and new communities. He and his family became Lutherans. Although he thought one must adapt to the modern world and embrace progress, he remained faithful to Amana and its ideals, although he despised its monastic structure. He was a gentle man, his wife even gentler, and both of them had a gently satiric sense of humor. Mr. Schaefer, however, refused to believe anything bad about Germany.

Marilyn hated religion or any dogma. When friends and family members would bow their heads to pray at Thanksgiving, I could tell her blood pressure was rising. She was shocked when her sister and her older brother converted to Catholicism, especially since that brother had been a longshoreman on the West Coast. I embraced Freudianism and once while I was parroting its doctrines over dinner Marilyn exploded and angrily denounced me. She told me I was ruining my mind with such shallow, unscientific trash. I smiled condescendingly at her need to 'resist' until in a lightning-flash of enlightenment as sudden as Gotama's I saw through all the pretenses of psychoanalysis – its sterile reductiveness, its hostility to unscripted experience, its vulgar mechanistic recourse to so many ergs of energy stored in the anus or some such tomfoolery. The more preposterous a theory is the more likely it is to appeal to an intellectual, since only what defies common sense can be entertained for long by anyone but a thinker. To believe in the un-believable, I suppose, is proof of the power of the mind.

In college I fell in with a fat, beautiful student named Anne Hall. She liked me to call her by the full 'Anne Hall,' just as she always addressed me as 'Ed White.' She joked that our one-syllable first names were too short to go unaccompanied into the world.

Anne had rented an old, falling-down wooden house in Ann Arbor behind another house. She'd furnished it with broken-backed armchairs and spavined couches. She was a painter and had set up an easel in the front living room. The easel itself and the wood floor were spattered with oil paint of every color; the smell of paint and turpentine rhymed with the taste of retsina we drank at a party Anne gave for a Greek poet. She'd read somewhere that a Greek male is not a man until he's cooked his first lamb. Anne barreled into Detroit fifty miles away in her Volkswagen and came back with a headless, hoofless and skinless lamb. She improvised a spit in her backyard over a bed of bricks and coals. The poet had to turn the blasted thing for hours as we gulped down cases of retsina and danced sideways in long lines, our hands linked by white handkerchiefs.

Anne was from a rich family in Indiana but she didn't care about assuring her social position or acquiring material objects. I suppose she always thought she would soon go on a diet and, when she was thin, buy a new wardrobe. In the meanwhile she'd pull down an Indian print, which was tacked up as a curtain, and wrap it around herself and fix it in place with a battered police badge. She often wore a white painter's smock, the sleeves stiff with dripping colors, her pudgy, pretty hands cerulean blue or madder pink, a wild dash of cadmium yellow licking her forehead.

She was often lost in her own thoughts and not really paying attention to what I was saying. I'd be looping forwards and backwards in my indirect, parenthetical, self-commenting style, a way of talking I abandoned much later when I gained confidence and could risk simple assertions. But back then I got tangled up in chains of qualifiers and contradictions. Anne Hall would suddenly realize she had blanked out on the last reversal of all that had preceded and she'd bite her lip and unfocus her eyes and shake her head as if to free it from the cobwebs. Sometimes she would blow a strand of hair up out of her face.

She wasn't a thinker in any organized way, but as an artist she had the distinct conviction that she should not just laugh and clown all the time, which was her natural bent. Maybe because she was from a 'social' family with lovely manners she had to resist the automatic reflex of measuring out her life in agreeableness. She'd suddenly sober up, make big eyes and say in a deep voice, all trace of frivolity banished from her face, 'Ed White. Ed White. Wh-what do you really, rilly th-think? Sincerely? Honestly?' Seriousness made her stutter. She suspected me of double-talk, which was unwarranted paranoia on her part, and of unnecessary elaboration, which was true and which I eventually got rid of. I came to despise nonessential verbal ornaments, though the reader may decide I'm still guilty of inconsequence.

I can picture her face as she screwed it up into her mask of high seriousness. Sometimes she'd beat her arms against her sides as if she were chasing a flock of trespassing geese. She wanted to call us all to order.

There were often friends sitting around watching Anne paint. She thought of herself as a bold abstractionist and she slashed and dabbed at her canvas with a palette knife or big wide housepainting brushes. The worst thing in those days was to be 'weak' or 'delicate' or 'unresolved.' We all subscribed to the belief that only men, only heterosexual men, were cut out to be painters. Only they had the visionary violence, the power to translate directly feeling into gesture, the nerve necessary to stick by bold, split-second decisions.

I'm sure Anne's relatives would have been horrified by her girth, the stray flecks of paint shining in her hair, her bohemian dress sense, and by the layabouts haunting her house and smoking cigarettes at all hours of the late afternoon and night. They drank white wine out of paper cups. Her relatives wouldn't have understood that she needed to live in squalor and talk about art till dawn in order to overcome the strictures of her upbringing.

Sometimes she could be fearfully masculine, driving all the riffraff out of the house because her patience had suddenly come to an end. She would tear through her rooms upstairs and downstairs, organizing her mess with military decisiveness. But on other days she could clean up real good – shampoo her silky hair until it glowed, scrub her face clean, immerse her hands in turpentine till they turned pink – and put on eyeliner and lipstick and two dabs of Guerlain.

She doted on me, which made my bones feel as if they were liquefying. She'd prop up my ego, which was always sliding like a drunk down into a puddle of self-hatred. I'd read all my stories to her, word for word, and she'd wear a look of solemn concentration on her face, though she'd blink and paddle a fat little hand through my verbal gossamer. 'Ed White,' she'd say. 'Back up. Whoa! Back *way* up!'

She cooked spaghetti and chicken breasts for me and boiled broccoli limp, though usually we just ordered in pizza. I'd write and she'd paint in her house which sailed like a pleasure ship all lit up through the night. She'd keep my paper cup full of chilled wine. We'd listen to scratchy 78s of Caruso. Once a week she'd let me borrow her old Beetle to drive over to Detroit to see my shrink, Dr. Moloney.

He would ask me if I was dating a two-hundred-twenty-pound girl because I felt inadequate to more obviously desirable ones. When I slept with her I certainly felt that I was slim and handsome – a prince! My main erotic interest was in how I imagined she was perceiving me, and to this day I wonder if straight men, at least some of them, feel that way, at least sometimes. A straight friend of mine said, 'When they're very young they feel that way.'

I never much liked myself when I had sex with men. I could never work up a persona for myself, never figure out who I was – a pockmarked rapist? A plucked and creamed effeminate monster? My mother? A dirty old man squatting beside a glory hole and sticking my grubby fingers through it to beckon any hard cocks on the loose? None of these images was appealing.

With Anne I liked myself. I was suddenly purpose-built, resplendent. It sounds appallingly vain to say so, but I felt I was conferring a favor on her. With another man I sometimes believed I was good company, a loyal friend, a benign influence, but I never thought I was doing him any favors by sleeping with him, much less any good. After all these years of liberation and psychotherapy I shouldn't admit my unease, but the last three decades have done little to ameliorate the negative effect of the first three. Perhaps I hang on to my shame because I've fetishized it; it excites me.

This edgy distrust of my instincts, this eroticized abjection, vanished when I made love to Anne. Not that it happened often – I was afraid of so much softness making me lose my hardness. She approved of me and my writing so enthusiastically that I was afraid of blunting my critical abilities and ending up a fool. But I loved her soft lips, her full, fragrant breasts, her full but remarkably firm body. We worked and read and I wrote and she painted and she cooked and I ate and I read out loud and she listened – but once in a great while we made love. Baudelaire writes, 'I know the art of evoking happy moments' ('*Je sais l'art d'évoquer les minutes heureuses*'), and he goes on to say it's pointless to look for 'your languorous beauty elsewhere than in your dear body and in your sweet heart.' I could never have such faith in my own past or present happiness (and surely he too is being a bit ironic) but I know what he means.

Marilyn (she seems to have forgotten this) and I tried to be lovers because I thought we should be all things to each other and should eventually marry. I even wrote my first published short story about her, 'Goldfish and Olives,' which was accepted by an anthology called *New Campus Writing*. Later, I would write about her often, calling her 'Maria.'

One weekend when she came up to visit me in Ann Arbor we kissed passionately and undressed but I was impotent. Today there are pills for that and behavioristic exercises; I sometimes wonder if I'd be married today if I'd been able to perform then and with other women? And if so would I be happier than I am now?

It seems to me that two men can never achieve the degree of tongue-and-groove intimacy of a man and a woman. Two men can be best friends, but that's a comfortable arrangement compared to the biological fit – or is it just the reciprocal role-playing? – of a man and a woman.

Today I saw two men walking along Eighth Avenue in New York, holding hands absentmindedly. They were both in their forties, one badly scarred from an ancient case of acne, both a bit Neanderthalish from their hours at the gym. Their eyes scanned their path like minesweepers. The one on the right had the overly male, deeply unpopular look of a double-X chromosome – I'm sure he had anger management 'issues.' The other one seemed happy to have a lover-friend all in one person. He didn't seem proud or possessive but just relieved. He was no beauty. And yet I could never imagine them flirting with each other or the double-X chasing his laughing partner through the house at dawn. Maybe flirtation would have made them snicker with evil embarrassment like Beavis and Butt-head. Maybe they were too unevolved from their primitive masculinity to live with women.

The other day I asked my sophisticated and sensitive hetero-sexual male friend a few questions.

'Don't you straight guys ever worry about becoming feminized by so much contact with women? It's not like in the past, when men played cards or shot pool or rode the range all day with their buddies. You and your wife are always together. So many elderly married couples start getting the same haircut, and from behind they look alike with their well-padded bodies, stiff gait, matching shorts and sensible shoes. How do men, especially after retirement, keep themselves from taking up their wives' hobbies – canning or tatting, say?'

'Travel is the solution,' he said. 'Retired middle-class people are always touring Birmanie or someplace where they must fret over the food and the bus without air-conditioning and the moral question of luxury tourism in a third-world country run by a few generals. Oh, the anxiety of travel takes precedence over all mere gender friction.'

'And don't straight men after all those years get awfully tired of playing the top?'

'You bet. Men my age are all interested in their butts; that's something we got from you gays: anal sex.'

'Yes, you keep stealing our perks – what about some of the burdens such as eternal damnation? You should have to share that, too. But you mean your wives fuck you with strap-ons?'

'Let's picture a demure personal vibrator. But it's more a question of submission to a dominatrix wife, or of looking at porno about cocks. The cock becomes a major preoccupation.'

'You're not joining our side, I trust.'

'I know some gay guys shave their bodies; if one wanted to be my boyfriend he'd have to shave off every last hair.'

'And yet even shaved glabrous smooth he'd still be a pal,' I said, ruefully. 'Other men have the most disheartening way of ending up each other's pals. Gay couples try everything to shake off the cold hand of pal-hood. A white middle-aged man takes up with a Thai twelve-year-old or with a black trannie or with a minuscule Ivy League redhead with a cock as long as his leg. One straight Australian friend of mine wrote an amazing story about a boys' school in the future where half the students are trained to be dainty, never to touch the penis and always to poke Kotex up their bums. They are kept out of sports. The other half are trained to be violent rapists, fiercely competing over the most demure lads.

'But even with all this role-playing and the added benefits of discordance in age, race, wealth and HIV-status, two men are still unable to shake the same-sex doldrums. A dinner party of men without a woman lacks sparkle.'

'At least two male lovers don't end up hating each other,' my friend said, 'but my divorced friends can't even speak to each other civilly. Those bad heterosexual values, as you put it.'

'And yet,' I said, 'this all-or-nothing love is the result of real, shared, reciprocal passion, the feeling that these organs, male and female, were designed to fit together, that these individuals, the man and the woman, are merely pawns in a bigger survivalist game, that women have been trained to pique a man and withhold sex until he is thoroughly seduced, then surrender in a lavish gift of a female body that will always be exotic to men. Feminists imagine that when men grumble, "Women," they're creating a category to rail against, but in truth they're complaining about a mystery that confounds and delights them. Like the queen at the end of a comedy, a woman can resolve tensions and confer blessings. If gays without women shriek and dance, it's because they've so scrupulously eliminated women from their lives that the feminine in themselves emerges and takes its revenge. The return of the repressed.'

'Yes, but marriage gets pretty old, too,' my friend said. 'You gays never seem to be very jealous, whereas women become dangerously like Medea when they suspect a rival. They're capable of strapping a suicide bomb to their backs and blowing up everyone around them. Gay men can have a *ménage à trois* or *à quatre* and the fourth wheel can blow out and be replaced several times and no one seems the worse for wear. Straight men dream of such flexibility but can never achieve it. Of course I know there are all those wife swappers. But that seems to be for women who chew gum and wear ankle bracelets and for elderly men with dyed hair who ride Harleys.'

As I walked home I thought yes, we gays have our precious freedom, though often we're merely free to be alone. Sometimes I stare at a lover of mine and remark the calculating look in his eye, the first sign he's already beginning to decide what to do with me ultimately. When two men live together they cohabit with their two careers, and the career is the only thing each man thinks defines him. Today career envy can divide a marriage, too, but most wives, no matter how driven, respect a successful husband. He will provide for her and their children (the problem arises when the man is a failure). But for two gay men, no matter how much they follow butch and femme roles in bed, these roles are just sexual fantasies, and like all turn-ons they can be switched off the moment the little helpmate rises from the sperm-streaked sheets and hurries off to a meeting where the new marketing director will be announced. Not even women are very successful at playing old-fashioned backseat women now; men are complete failures at it.

Perhaps because I grew up around unhappy women, I've always feared most females as mantraps. The stability and intimacy that might be gained by acceding to their needs has always been outweighed by my fear of succumbing to their power.

Well up into my twenties and even thirties I was still getting mixed up with unhappy women. For them I represented the solution. They thought I would love them, listen to them, learn to fuck them and they in turn would plump the pillow, go to the movie I wanted to see, make the lemonade according to the long boiling recipe I preferred, peel the tomatoes as I insisted, and despite all this deference to me, I was the one being housebroken. Domesticity doesn't have much appeal to someone whose happiest moments were spent in boarding school far from home.

I made all those women cry. One of them threatened suicide. Another threatened to kill me. One howled outside my door – all because I wasn't man enough to say to them, 'Are you kidding, Babe? I'm queer as the May breeze. Get used to it!'

What I loved about Marilyn was that she wasn't unhappy. She wanted nothing from me but friendship. She dreaded marriage. She believed in love, but for her the proper form of love was a short, romantic affair, just as a sonnet is the best form for a love lyric. She wasn't afraid to be alone. She preferred it. She had her stack of library books, her favorite music all programmed, she had her cozy bed and delicious snacks all ready. Quilts and cushions were tossed everywhere and on the wall were pictures of ancient Amana relatives smiling humbly at the camera. Her keyhole desk had been made for her by her father. An aunt had given her the pot of African violets. In the bathroom were art postcards sent to her from all over the world – many by me. She had created domesticity all alone. In love she was a bit like the Marschallin with her young lover, male or female, whom she knows she can't keep for long. Of course Marilyn kept us all enthralled by encouraging us to leave her for someone more suitable. She reminded her Chinese lover to buy a birthday gift for his wife. Her young Indian lover she counseled through his difficult divorce from a born-again storefront preacher. She advised her soubrette girlfriend to choose the stage over love. She gathered her friends around her year after year, dashed off to Oxford for a summer course in English history, hurried back to Iowa to see her mother. But mostly she stayed home, looking after her garden and her cats. Maybe because she was the first woman I knew who wasn't unhappy, who never once made me feel guilty, she showed me the way to friendship with women – which is another subject altogether.

At home in Paris, 1988

My Europe

I belong to the last generation of Americans obsessed with Europe and intimidated by it. When I was a small boy in Ohio, America was simultaneously isolationist and truly isolated. There were no foreign films. There were almost no foreigners. No one drank wine or used garlic or even ate in courses. We were served just one heaping plate of overcooked meat and fried potatoes and boiled beans, then chocolate pudding. Those who drank stuck to whiskey and water.

Travel to Europe was expensive and few people could afford it. For us 'Europe' was the symphony (all our conductors were foreign-born) and opera. We listened to the Texaco radio broadcast of the Metropolitan Opera every Saturday afternoon. During the intermissions there would be a quiz. Europeans with heavy accents and Hungarian or Russian names were asked to list all the scenes in opera in which (a) the tenor falls in love with his aunt, (b) the heroine is buried alive and (c) a witch switches two babies at birth. The jokey knowingness of the foreign participants, the unusual deliberation and circumflexion and secret mirth in their voices, seemed to us exotic and superior.

We longed to visit Europe, even live abroad for a whole year. Europe was where we would raise our general level of culture. Europe was where we might at last have experiences, even sexual ones. We deplored but were privately intrigued by 'European snobbishness,' since in Texas and the Midwest where I'd grown up the word *class* was never mentioned and if pressed we'd all have declared ourselves middle-class. The idea that we might be excluded from a club or a party because of our low birth seemed maddening and exciting to us.

In the 1950s Americans took extraordinary pride in the Marshall Plan. We were convinced we'd not only saved England and France, we also believed we'd single-handledly rebuilt the entire continent. We expected Europeans to be grateful ever after. Nor did most Americans realize how quickly and triumphantly Europe had emerged out of the war. As late as the 1970s ignorant friends and relatives of mine would say, 'I feel sorry for those folks, still living in bombed-out ruins.' Like some ninety percent of Americans they didn't have passports.

My first trip to Europe, for some reason, was to the Costa Brava in the mid-1960s when I was in my twenties. I guess I thought that sounded affordable and not as scary as Paris or London. My first lover, Stanley Redfern, and I flew to Paris, where our luggage was lost, and then we sprinted onto a waiting plane for Malaga. We hadn't made hotel reservations and in January the town was packed. A nice man who worked behind the desk at one of the hotels that turned us away offered us his mother's guest room. It smelled of backed-up sewage and was next door to an outdoor movie theater where people sat on folding wooden chairs half the night and listened to booming voices; from our window we could look down on the entranced, upraised faces strafed and submerged by alternating lights and shadows. Our luggage took a week to arrive. I made Stanley go with me to a bullfight even though we had to sit in the sun wearing our wool winter suits. We were too poor to buy new clothes or to afford tickets in the shade.

We visited the Alhambra on a guided tour in English. Two young gay Swiss guys came up to us (they'd taken our tour to improve their English) and told us that they just wanted us to know that they *approved* of our war in Vietnam. We were appalled and realized for the first time that we were being taken as Americans, as representatives of our national policy, and not just as Stan and Ed.

The luggage arrived on Stan's next-to-last day. We celebrated by taking a bus over to Torremolinos and going to a gay bar full of effeminate Germans in bits of jewelry and finery they could remove and hide when they walked home through the dark streets. I stayed on another week with Brookie, a pretty girl from my office, who insisted on wearing miniskirts everywhere in Malaga in Franco's Spain. We had big wolf packs of young men howling behind us wherever we went.

At night the restaurants were thronged. Twenty-two members of the same family would sit around adjoining tables in a café and eat ice cream. 'Europe' (at least the bit of it we'd seen) appeared eternal, poor but well-dressed, fiercely macho, Catholic and so little subject to change that all four generations of a family could laugh heartily at the same jokes.

Even fairly sophisticated Americans back home repeated over and over again, year after year, the same few clichés about Europeans. The English were 'terribly British,' wore bowlers, hunted foxes and had stiff upper lips. The French were blasé about sex, didn't bathe, studied Existentialism and ate rotting cheese. They were all unpleasant. The Italians were merry souls who sped around on Vespas, picked up girls, read photo romances instead of proper books, had innate artistic taste and liked everyone. The Irish were dour, downtrodden Catholics and problem drinkers.

After I moved to Paris in 1983 and stayed on for the next fifteen years I came to resent these ill-informed, primitive views. I noticed that American friends, especially New Yorkers, were irritated that the quality of life was so high in Paris and owed almost nothing to America. Americans would point out a McDonald's in Paris with glee, but they couldn't be persuaded that American eating habits had made few inroads in France.

And my American friends were puzzled when they discovered what the French admire about America: everything to do with cowboys; the delicious vulgarity of Las Vegas; the novels of Paul Auster and John Fante and the poetry of Charles Bukowski; jazz; anything 'alternative' from the Lower East Side; anything Zuni. The French knew next to nothing about American composers, including those who'd lived and studied in France such as Aaron Copland, Ned Rorem and Virgil Thomson. They knew nothing of our minor writers who'd celebrated Paris such as Kay Boyle, Djuna Barnes and James Jones. In front of Jones's apartment on the Île Saint-Louis there was no historic plaque nor would there ever be, though in the 1970s Gertrude Stein's rue de Fleurus address was finally commemorated. The French knew much more about American B-movie directors than we did and lamented our lack of 'film culture.' We weren't sure we thought 'film' and 'culture' belonged in the same sentence.

So strong was the American urban myth about disagreeable Parisians that it could not be modified through experience. My American friends would spend ten days with me and go out every night to a companionable dinner with French friends, often at their homes, but I'd catch them telling someone back in the States that no one ever invites you to his or her house in Paris, that all Parisians are nasty whereas the people in the provinces are adorable. The opposite is the truth, since Parisians travel, like foreigners, speak languages, crave novelty and live by their wits, whereas no city could be more closed and self-sufficient than Lyon or Bordeaux, no bourgeoisie more smug than that of Lille.

Because I learned French after the age of forty I could never eliminate my accent, though eventually I became enough at ease in the language to be able to give five half-hour radio broadcasts in a row. Because of my accent, however, I've always elicited a smile; if we English-speakers find a French accent supercilious or sexy, the French think an American accent is either charmingly or irritatingly childish – *bon enfant*, as they say. As someone who stammered as a child, still gropes for words and has always been guilty of malapropisms in English, I welcomed a built-in excuse for similar flaws in speaking French. My accent always provided new acquaintances with a ready-made subject. ('I think I detect a little accent when you speak,' the super-polite French would say. They would then always add, 'If only I spoke English as well as you speak French.') This scrim of foreignness through which I lived during my years in France made me more interesting than I was and as vulnerable as I felt. I didn't mind being *bon enfant*, even if the expression is condescending.

As a homosexual growing up in Cincinnati and Chicago and Texas and Michigan in the 1950s, 'Europe' represented a benign and mysterious alternative to the beastly oppression we knew at home, a time in the States when we were persecuted by shrinks on one side and priests on the other and deliberately entrapped by the police, the three institutions that corresponded to the three prevailing interpretations of homosexuality: as mental illness, as sin and as crime.

Although we ourselves had no other available model, we still could dimly hold out for 'tolerance' or even 'decadence,' and these qualities, piquant and somehow aristocratic, we located in 'Europe.' I remember when I was fifteen discussing Julius Caesar with Fred Mitchell, an abstract expressionist painter who taught at the art academy next door to my boarding school. Mr. Mitchell, a Southerner in his thirties who thrived on ambiguity and the unspoken, told me with a little smile that Caesar had 'married' several of his soldiers and that 'people in Rome are still talking about it.' Imagine all that said in a nearly inaudible Tidewater drawl.

I found his comment electrifying because a respected artist and teacher was referring to my most shameful vice lightly, and as if it were the most recent gossip. Even more extraordinary, he was suggesting that Caesar (the boring author of *The Gallic Wars* which I'd had to translate in class) had an off-color reputation that was being kept alive by the Romans of today. Europe, it seemed, was a place where homosexuality was joked about and rumors were passed down from one millennium to the next.

When I was sixteen I met a New Yorker in his thirties who was visiting Chicago. I understood that the man was married and therefore wouldn't be attracted to me, but a local queen I knew said, 'My dear, in New York they're very European.'

'In what way?'

'They're more bisexual. He may prefer women, but on a cold night in a strange city he might bed a boy.'

I added bisexuality to my profile of 'the Europeans.' The same queen told me that Europeans insisted on anal intercourse. 'Oh yes, my pet, we're all suck queens but they don't think that's even real sex. They go all the way – they're *brownie* queens.' Of course I knew that American gays could be versatile sexually, but this information suggested that Europeans had hierarchized sex acts. They thought we were childish with our oral fixations, which my shrink had warned me about. Anal sex wasn't designed for five dirty minutes in the dark, which was usually all we had to work with; rather, it required a bed, careful positioning, hygienic foresight, a lubricant – above all it required privacy and time. It was more committed, more grown-up, and it represented a more total surrender for the passive partner.

The dream of Europe for an American gay in the fifties was not only about our Continental counterparts; it was also about the entire bric-a-brac of society. Most of us were Anglophiles, read everything about the Queen's coronation, admired Auden and Britten; one of my friends bought his hat at Lock's and had his initials stamped in gold on the sweatband. Cologne from Penhaligon's, tea from Fortnum & Mason, shirts from Turnbull & Asser . . .

In the 1960s, when I was in my twenties, I would stay in London with a friend of mine who was just a few years older than me and who came to represent gay London for me – and more profoundly the English middle class. John acted in musicals and plays but mostly earned his living by giving acting lessons. He was thoroughly imbued with the pantomime / music-hall tradition and took me to see two elderly drag artists who impersonated two elderly sharp-tongued Cockney women. John had known and revered Noël Coward with a deference unfamiliar to Americans of my generation.

He was a socialist and a republican; the depth of his hatred for the lazy, ugly, bloodsucking royals shocked me out of my Anglophile fantasies. The mere mention of the Queen or Princess Margaret would elicit from him an angry snarl and a murderous mutter. He longed for a redistribution of wealth and took pride in the National Health Service. Once, when we visited a friend of his who'd just inherited a fortune and bought a grand house in Mayfair, John said, as soon as we were back on the street, 'It's criminal for people to live like that.' He thoroughly approved of another friend who became a successful movie star but didn't change friends, pub or basement flat. Whereas we Americans admired success and smiled over a rags-to-riches story, John obviously had more nuanced reactions. He followed politics carefully and read several papers a day.

He lived in a spacious flat for which he paid a curiously low rent on Marylebone High Street (he had to teach me how to say it, 'Marl-bun,' with the correct accent). Like Nancy Mitford he insisted on 'curtains' not 'drapes,' 'rugs' not 'carpet,' 'writing paper' not 'stationery.' The flat was unheated. Astonishingly, he provided me with a hot-water bottle for my bed at night and we'd hurl ourselves into the kitchen as soon as we arose; it was the only warm room. At teatime he insisted we drink our tea before the ineffective fire in the vast, arctic sitting room. It was a necessary ritual. In America we had no such rituals.

He was resourceful in making his minuscule earnings go far and he had not an iota of ambition to earn more, if more work meant losing one hour of his precious free time. He introduced me to Bovril and Marmite. He'd prepare cauliflower cheese for lunch, bangers and beans for supper, though as often as not I'd invite him to a fancy new restaurant (I remember one run by a glamorous sex-change who'd married a lord, another owned by John Schlesinger). In an expensive Italian restaurant I became so drunk I got up and danced a Highland fling all alone and knocked over the dessert trolley. (I no longer drink.)

If John was expert at paring cheese, he spared himself no pleasure. He was always finding cheap flights to the Greek Islands or to New York, where he'd stay with me or a theatrical agent he knew. Sometimes the agent would ask all of John's New York friends to chip in to buy him an airplane ticket. In London he attended almost every play and musical, buying cheap balcony seats or getting complimentary tickets through his acting school or from friends in the production. He knew every bus and tube route and would never let me hail a taxi.

He had a mentality born of deprivation and rationing. If I'd buy him a tea or bring home groceries or just offer him a cigarette, he was punctilious about thanking me for the lovely treat. Whereas in America we thought nothing of raiding a friend's fridge, in England I quickly learned to respect John's calibrated meal planning. He made an orange drink from powder, he washed out tomato tins and used the tinted water for cooking something else. Even though I could vaguely remember wartime rationing in the States, for the first time I realized how wasteful we were back home, how thoughtless. We always left the light blazing and the central heat roaring when we went out in America; John would have resented even the extravagance of a pilot light if his Aga had had one. He was stoic about heat or cold, damp or discomfort, and never ever mentioned them.

In those years we saw Margaret Leighton in an ephemeral comedy about an English family who installed central heating, which caused their house plants to grow rampant with tropical exuberance and finally choke off every room. The only good moment came when the son's beloved, whose gender is indeterminate, asks Margaret Leighton if she has 'a little man' to make her lovely clothes. 'Yes, tiny . . .,' Leighton said with icy nastiness. I found the whole play bewildering.

Whereas New York in the sixties had almost no gay bars, since Mayor Wagner had closed them all in an effort to clean up the city for the World's Fair, London had dozens and dozens – everything from old-fashioned East End pubs full of working men and smoke to candlelit gay restaurants and bars on the King's Road, from leather bars (which seemed genuinely menacing back then) in Earls Court to a suit-and-tie after-work bar upstairs off Leicester Square. Everything in London – the licensing laws, the variable bus fares, the freeholds and the ninety-nine-year leases, the guineas and half-crowns and florins and shillings – seemed unnecessarily complicated, the silt of centuries, but with John at my side I could steer my way through these traps.

John didn't read much beyond newspapers and he didn't own a television. He lived for activities, a disposition that seemed unusual and exhilarating to me, sedentary and bookish as I was. He would make me tour Chiswick House and Hogarth's House, race through the National Portrait Gallery or the Tower of London, take tea on the roof of Biba's, complete with ponds and swans – and cruise Hampstead Heath at night. In warm weather we'd take the last tube out to Hampstead, walk up the long hill to the Heath and work our way down through forests and clearings, our prey on a cloudy night visible only by the pulsing of a cigarette or the glint off glasses or the shockingly near clearing of a throat. I remember picking up an Oxford boy and bringing him back to John's flat. We had to walk miles and miles to get home. In the morning when I asked him if he wanted a 'scohn' (to rhyme with 'own'), he said in a languid drawl, 'I can't bear the thought I might know someone who'd fail to say "scon."' When I told another English friend that my mother always stayed in New York at the 'War-wick' Hotel, he whispered, 'You say that? I feel we're living in different worlds.'

The English thought Americans were good in bed, good dancers, violent, lazy. We did seem to be less inhibited, to feel more at ease in our bodies. American gays, at least New Yorkers, were already beginning to work out. John, who was an adept of the Alexander Technique, thought that bodybuilding led to a grotesque distortion of the muscles, a way of creating top-heavy Michelin men. Each time he saw me I was a bit bigger and more muscled. 'All that's going to run to fat,' he'd hiss – correctly, as it turned out. The English had to hire Americans to do jazz dancing in imported musical comedies.

John had been in the air force and studied Russian in the service. He hadn't been to university but he'd studied every aspect of Russian language and culture to prepare him for a job in intelligence. I suspect he hadn't gone on because his officers had discovered he was 'queer' (he didn't like the word 'gay,' which for the English spoiled a perfectly good word, though Americans couldn't make a similar objection, since we never used 'gay' to mean 'merry').

He spoke a very posh English which as a socialist he refused to associate with the middle class. 'It's standard English, my dear,' he'd say, closing his eyes as if to indicate the discussion was over. 'I feel sorry for you people from the colonies with your bizarre mispronunciations – why, you pronounce *Mary*, *merry* and *marry* all the same way. No wonder you're so confused.'

He would fly into a rage at the very thought of American naturalistic acting of the Actors Studio variety and even wrote a book-length polemic against it, which he never published. 'Why, those slovenly fools can't walk or talk, they don't know how to fence or manage a train or even sit simply and gracefully. The Alexander Technique teaches us to say no to our bad habits – what you'd wrongly call *instincts* – and to rethink vocal production and the entire head-neck-spine relationship.'

He tried to 'sort out' my neck which over the years, as he predicted, has become arthritic and nearly paralyzed. But the Alexander Technique, which requires months and months of one-on-one sessions and works only through tiny gradations, seemed quite alien to American rhythms. We believe in sudden conversions, weekend marathons, instant enlightenment. The notion of a technique that is built on small negations rather than one great affirmation made no sense to me as an American.

From his military background John had retained a neat mustache, a dignified bearing, a lonely, slightly bleak independence. He was tidy, energetic, red-haired. If he was almost hyper-masculine in repose, he'd willfully added an overlay of high camp. He and I spoke of every man in the feminine – in fact we never used a male pronoun or possessive from one day to the next. Everyone was titled 'Miss' (as in 'Miss Thing' or 'Miss Postman') – at the seaside we even once referred to 'Miss Wave.' We systematically suspected every man, no matter how podgy or uxorious, of being a flaming homosexual. We invented a fantasy in which I was a wayward young American heiress who'd been sent to London for John's instructions in deportment and elocution. He was always promising to turn me into a real lady. We exchanged dozens of letters in which we encoded all of our real experiences into this extravagant and fairly tiresome form of camp. Since it required constant translation of one thing into another even such a mechanical exercise kept us permanently self-amused.

In the sixties gender substitution and archness were passé in gay America except in small towns and among older queens. I'd known a dim, provincial version of camp in Cincinnati in the 1950s. But for John, who had lived in a theater milieu for most of his life, it was a living tradition. I suppose his ultimate point of reference was Lady Bracknell. Like her he pronounced girls as 'gells'; I was one of his 'gells.'

With me he couldn't stop camping. It was sometimes a relief to run into one of his students or a literary friend of mine. Then he'd revert to his clipped military politeness, though when the others weren't looking he'd arch an eyebrow or purse his lips or bug his eyes for my benefit. I wasn't sure which tone was his real one and which the put-on.

American gays with their muscles, facial hair and lumberjack masculinity repelled and alienated John, who for me represented the last link to a gay past that always had one foot (a very light, well-turned foot) in fantasy, that remained closeted out of necessity but took its revenge on dull normals by transforming all the men into women and all the women into enemies. His disapproval of the

American butch style didn't keep him from being attracted to individual clones. But he was always quick to say, 'The minute I got that big man in bed he started whimpering like a little girl.'

He was also very romantic in a melodramatic way, which struck me as vaguely 'period.' He told me that in the early sixties he'd had a lover named Nigel for several years. They'd been on tour in Scotland in a big musical. On their day off John was driving them along the coast in a hired car. Nigel said, 'I'm leaving you, John. I've found someone else.'

John, in true staccato Coward fashion, said, 'Very well,' rolling the *r*, turned the wheel and drove them both over the cliff. They survived but were in hospital for months.

As John and I grew older I retired from the bar scene but John, still slim and handsome, went out cruising four nights a week, always looking for love. I imagine he was a very good lover – faithful, generous, devoted – if slightly disapproving and nannyish.

American gays came to self-acceptance later than the English, and when it arrived we were already committed to the butch clone style, which excluded any excess of affection. John, however, had grown up on sentimental English wartime movies, on Shakespearean heroics and blockbuster musicals – three totally disparate forms that nonetheless shared a belief in exalted passion.

In London, and especially in the theater world, gay couples had lived out their loves discreetly and romantically from World War I on. All the Bloomsbury biographies and memoirs, for instance, attest to how well integrated gay men were in straight literary circles: Forster, John Lehmann, Keynes, Isherwood, Auden, Strachey – the whole buggery crowd in Virginia Woolf's generation. There was nothing comparable in New York. That some English gays had a niche and a style made them less susceptible, at least at first, to American machismo. In the same way the skeptical, combative style of English intellectuals ('What utter rubbish!') and the enduring English fear of sounding pretentious made them suspicious of American and French academic fads – or of all but feminism.

In 1949, when I was nine, I accompanied my father to New York for the first time. He liked Asti's, a Greenwich Village restaurant where the waiters sang opera arias and where famous singers dined. I introduced myself to the bass Jerome Hines, and we ended up sitting in his box the next night to hear him sing the role of the High Priest in *The Magic Flute*. We also befriended an English soldier who was eating alone at the next table.

I'd read Oscar Wilde and I assumed that because the soldier was English (my first!) he too must speak in constant quips and deliver polished epigrams. With my dull father and stepmother he sounded as tepid as they, but I felt that if I could recall one of Wilde's remarks he'd light up with recognition and deliver his own cascade of witticisms.

At last I got up my courage, interrupted my father, and said to the soldier, 'I know a widow who just buried her husband and her hair has gone quite gold with grief.' My father looked embarrassed at his sissy son's outburst. My stepmother knew perfectly well I'd never met a widow in my life.

The soldier looked genuinely repulsed. He winced with disgust and turned his attention to his chop.

I blushed bright red. I'd made an effort to communicate with my first European in a language – sophisticated and paradoxical – that I felt sure he would understand and appreciate, but he didn't get it. He'd been sickened by my effeminacy and crazy interjection. Here was this other continent – wise and humane and devoted to virtuoso conversation – to which I was beaming a signal, but the message hadn't been picked up.

Now I realize that 'Europe' isn't a thing at all except in the eyes of Americans and certain Japanese, that it has no unified culture or shared interests except in the eyes of optimistic architects of the European Union, and that nothing at all will ever join Swedish technocrats to Muslim farmers in the former Yugoslavia. Now I know that there are as many racists and dunderheads and violent criminals in Hungary or Germany, in Spain or in Greece as there are in the United States. Now when I contemplate the boy I once was mouthing an Oscar Wilde phrase to a crop-haired English major from Liverpool and counting on a sympathetic vibration bouncing back my way, I can only cringe at my illusions. Perhaps Europe is nothing but an outdated American fantasy, a utopia that is tolerant but not placid, scintillating but never cruel.

* * *

For a Midwesterner like me, Paris was a Leslie Caron musical, a heavy, grown-up perfume, exaggerated hem lengths dictated by the top five couturiers: Woman. La Parisienne. I read English translations of Balzac's novels or Zola's in which a dozen millionaires contended for the affections of a single mistress. I couldn't quite grasp how one of these rich men might be willing to kill himself over such a woman but could never bring himself to dishonor his family by marrying her. Faced with the alternative – death or madness – surely dishonor was a small price to pay for peace of mind? Yet marriage to a loose woman was never presented as a possible solution.

Nor could I understand why only this one woman would do, how she alone had become the focus for so much male lust and longing. Surely there were other beautiful women in Paris. Even in Cincinnati every third woman struck me as attractive.

Could it be that a *grande cocotte* served as the arbitrary prize, the agreed-upon organizing principle, in the competition among so many rivals? Apparently they had to accept a limited number of objects or women deemed worth struggling over.

Yes, France was ruled by women and certainly in French history there were inscribed more women's names than in the recorded past of any other nation. But these women were idols, not normal participants. They held a salon but didn't speak. They were queens detested for their excesses but they made few pronouncements beyond a thoughtlessly cruel 'Let them eat brioche!' Jules and Jim fell in love with a woman because her face resembled that of a particularly mysterious archaic statue. Her whims governed them (even killed one of them) but her motives remained unfathomable. The monuments to La Justice and La Patrie were all of women, but no real woman was ever a judge or president of the republic. In the old novels I was reading there was this uncannily impersonal essence called 'Woman' that superceded individual members of the subset. 'Woman' was feline. She reclined in a bed of flowers, attended by a round-faced black maid. Woman stared out at us shamelessly, her look as unconscious and as crippling as the Medusa's. She communicated syphilis, she consumed champagne by the hogshead and diamonds by the tiara, her main function was to ruin men by undermining their health and prospects. She was an open maw. She could scarcely be blamed for her maddening laugh, her insatiable appetites, her underhandedness, for she, too, was a passive victim of this larger potent abstraction, the female principle that glowered from within, though she always radiated malice. Femme was always fatale. She had polish smeared around her eyes, messy locks and a smell compounded of suet and sweat, yeast and youth, Guerlain and glands.

Oddly enough, she didn't crave sex. No, she submitted to it, licking sticky date goo from her pale fingers while Monsieur was pounding away at her infuriating nether parts. Woman wavered all the way across the spectrum from the grande dame, walking in her riding costume by Worth down the gravel paths of the Bois de Boulogne in the shadow of her blue silk parasol, to the slut, wallowing on a tiger skin in a 'feelthy' postcard bought from a stall along the Seine.

Nor did the men in their lives have to be young or fit or sexy. I have a photo of Dumas the elder – immensely fat and as jovial as Kriss Kringle, his eyes mere buttonholes and his whiskers somehow animated, his clothes as rumpled as they always look in a nineteenth-century daguerreotype (didn't those people have dry cleaners?) – balancing on his knee a pretty, childlike woman with a sweet face and a charming figure in a candy-colored shirtwaist. Later, during the Belle Époque, in the caricatures drawn by Sem, the men are bald with a monocle screwed into one eye, their blazing white shirtfronts polar, their lapels heavy with medals, mouths small and black with vice. And the women are showgirls the age of the men's grandchildren, their legs as busy and accurate as knitting needles, their small breasts breaking forth from a surf of lace and gauze. The men's avid eyes behind glinting lenses stare up the plump legs of the cancan dancers into a pantyless patch of fur and paradise.

In America men and women were not so different from one another. In our big practical hardworking land the wife was as likely to mow the lawn as the husband and he could go shopping as readily as she. Isolated in their suburban houses and sedated by the television light flickering over their faces in strange code, Man and Woman sat half-reclined, silent, widening, their hands blindly seeking the popcorn. Decent people were faithful, monogamous – in short, sexless. Love was cozy, not passionate, and the couple went to bed in matching flannel nightshirts.

I'd never known any French people growing up, except a French-Jewish boy in Cincinnati with thick straight hair combed back from his pale and strangely adult face. Our parents knew each other and we crossed paths at debutante parties and concerts. Somehow he and his family had escaped the death camps.

French people didn't emigrate, it seemed, as if their culture were too refined and above all, too pleasurable to be translated into flat foreign terms. I studied French at prep school, with an American, Mr. Cohen, who'd fought side by side with the French. He'd received, for his pains, a sort of diploma marked '*Pour Le Droit*' and inscribed with his name. I assume he'd fought with De Gaulle's Free French, though why with them rather than with his fellow Americans I have no idea (maybe he'd entered the war when America was still neutral). He was always wringing his large hands and massaging or constructing them on top of his desk like an offering to a minor deity. He rode his bicycle everywhere, and upon arriving in class he removed the clips from his tweed trousers. He had deep-set, heavy-lidded eyes, and if he was irritated by an interruption, he would stare fixedly at a point in space, produce a pained smile and pile one vast hand on the other, waiting ominously for the disturbance to go away. It was hard to imagine that such a sensitive spirit could coexist with his immense white veined hands, balding head and big, exaggerated features.

He looked like a convict but had the manners of a seminarian. He was so precise, so solemn, even prissy, that I suspected him of being homosexual – but then again he had a much younger pale, pale English wife with a wen on her chin and a bird-like chirp. They had somehow produced an eccentric daughter whom I babysat, and who one could imagine dancing in a sunbeam like Hawthorne's little Pearl.

In Mr. Cohen's class we were drilled in vocabulary and grammar, though we never actually spoke French. Did he know how? I wonder, since years later I was to meet Americans in Paris who could scarcely pronounce a comprehensible sentence – and yet they identified themselves as French teachers back in Dubuque or Waco.

His was the France of *Aucassin and Nicolette*, of Tartarin de Tarascon, of Gide's *La Symphonie pastorale*, of Babar – hierarchical, Catholic, agricultural, colonial. Mr. Cohen (or Monsieur

Cohen, as we were encouraged to call him) declared things to be 'correct' or 'incorrect.' This assurance about the acceptability of certain things and not others, whether it was our fashion of sitting upright on hardwood chairs and not sprawling or of copying out our homework, of conjugating a verb or making an adjective agree in gender and number with its noun – this pedantry I found intoxicating. If most Americans were laissez-faire and laissez-aller, their laxness came from an indifference to the life of the mind, not from an innate generosity of spirit. Exactitude was what M. Cohen promoted and he refused to let his affection for a particular student soften his sense of what was correct. In fact he never became friendly with a student. That kind of chumminess wouldn't have been 'correct.'

Over the 'correct' books we read in class I preferred the forbidden poems of Rimbaud, Verlaine, Baudelaire and, later, when I was older, the novels of Sade and Genet and Gide's *Journals* and his coming-out book, *If It Die*. Everything about Rimbaud confounded me when I was in boarding school. He was the boy in the affair with the much older Verlaine – but also the aggressor. Rimbaud was the 'infernal bridegroom' whereas Verlaine (though married to his Mathilde, a father and breadwinner) was 'the foolish virgin.' Rimbaud was the mentor, the inventor of a new vision of poetry, the bully, and Verlaine followed him, suffering and sobbing in the great female tradition of French lady martyrs. Neither man seemed very wholehearted about being gay; after they came out they kept slipping back in. Verlaine drifted back to his wife and in old age took up with many mistresses, and even his erotic verses were mostly about 'cunt,' just as Rimbaud in Abyssinia kept, it seemed, both boys and girls but mostly girls.

In the American gay mythology as propounded by the few older queers I was meeting in the 1950s, coming out was a one-way path – inevitable, irreversible, tragic – whereas these French gays lacked all sense of the irrevocable. Their bisexuality made them appear to me even more frivolous.

What impressed me just as much was that the French, though Cartesian and Catholic, seemed to respect whatever was satanic and irrational. An older student I met at the art academy gave me his fetish book to read, *The Songs of Maldoror* by the Comte de

186

Lautréamont. Written by a proto-surrealist, Uruguayan-born Parisian in the late nineteenth century, a man who bestowed an aristocratic title on himself in an act of dandified insolence before abjectly committing suicide at age twenty-one, *Maldoror* contained an episode in which a parent put a blindfold on his sleeping baby and then tortured it. Next the parent tiptoed away only to return a moment later, pull off the blindfold, and kiss away the infant's tears. Just when the baby was completely reassured the parent began to torture him again in the exact same way. The horror in the baby's eyes as it dawned on him that his torturer was his beloved father was particularly gratifying to the parent.

The French unblinking admiration for transgression, at least in literature, puzzled me; in America our idea of evil was a few lines of raunchy dialogue in a paperback novel.

A highly unstable concept of sex that included at least some forms of homosexuality, a worship of Woman, a demonic love of cruelty enshrined in expensive leather-bound 'classics,' a serious unsmiling defense of the avant-garde and a greater fear of appearing philistine than foolish – these were just some of the notions of France I picked up at my Midwestern boarding school.

Like M. Cohen, I couldn't speak French or understand it. I would say, 'I can't speak French but I can read it,' a complete lie, since my vocabulary was too small to get through a magazine article much less a poem by Mallarmé, whose cryptic utterances I would scroll before my scanning eyes with no result, even after I had looked up every word. My failure even to identify the verb or its subject in a string of seven words (*'M'introduire en héros effarouché dans ton histoire'*) I could pass off as my forgivable confusion in the face of a famously hermetic style – but I would have been just as incapable of reading a headline about Princess Grace.

I bought a record of Juliette Gréco. Her low voice, a compromise between song and speech, convinced me she was being sophisticated and even bleak (for wasn't she the Existentialists' muse, hadn't Sartre himself written the lyrics to several of her songs?). On a cold winter afternoon, when the snow outside the window was so blue it seemed a foretaste of oblivion, I'd regale myself by cooking up a pot of espresso on the transgressive hotplate and listening to Gréco's words rising and falling in alternating currents of desire and despair. Though her intonations were as intimate as the sound through the wall of lovers after sex, I could never make out what she was saying.

In college I majored in Chinese and I was graduated with honors after hundreds of hours of conversational Mandarin and repetitive work in the language lab, but, even as I received the parchment and sweated under a mortarboard on the University of Michigan football field, I knew I was a complete fraud, that I couldn't read or write or speak or understand Chinese. I'd memorized a four-line, twenty-word Tang Dynasty poem that I could trot out, with tones intact and a weird buzzing *r* produced with the tongue rolled back and touching the roof of the mouth, but that was my only linguistic achievement. I was as much a fraud in Chinese as in French. Chinese and French were the cornerstones of my identity, and neither one of them existed.

I abandoned Chinese completely, but I kept pegging away at French long after college. I would buy a bilingual version of *The Stranger* and force my eyes to slide over the hard, impenetrable French before sinking gratefully back into the absorbent English.

In the 1960s I worked for Time-Life Books (I suggested to some people I worked for *Time* itself, a publication I was careful to deplore ritualistically for its reactionary politics, though I longed in vain to work there). After eight years I quit (I'd just turned thirty) and moved to Rome for half a year. I'd intended all along to settle in Paris but my two brief visits there had so thoroughly intimidated me that I veered off toward Italy, which I regarded, as all Americans do, with fond condescension – unjustified, as it turned out, since the Romans I met in 1970 were not the smiling grape-treaders I'd imagined but chain-smoking, neurotic Marxists who stayed up all night and hated Nixon, but loved their twenty cats.

I took Italian lessons three times a week and after six months I could hold simple conversations with strangers and long, drunken, passionate ones with Diana, a painter with whom I was half in love. In any foreign language the most difficult exchange is with a group of people who all know each other at a party – no, even worse is listening to dialogue in a feature film since *verismo* requires that actors mumble even worse than people do in real life. After movies and parties come television newscasts because of the highly specialized vocabulary of political reporting. The easiest communication is a one-on-one conversation with someone who's in love with you. She can see in your eyes when you've not understood something and, since what she's trying to get across is essential to her happiness, she'll start again and again or rephrase everything much more simply.

When I came back from Rome to New York I spoke to cab drivers and waiters with an Italian accent. Since they usually had an accent of their own they seldom mentioned or noticed mine. New York is a city of foreign accents in which no one ever asks someone where he is from except out of hostility or as a form of flirtation.

Though I spoke my rudimentary Italian, the only language I took seriously was French. I'd buy books with names like *French Made Easy* and pepper my conversation and writing with French expressions as if nothing in English came to mind or was quite as appropriate. If two people were speaking in French on the street or beside me in a restaurant (and they seldom were, since in the 1970s the French rarely came to New York) I'd eavesdrop – and suddenly I'd have to admit to myself I understood nothing. Chinese symbolized the way I was different from my fellow Occidentals just as French stood for the way I was more sophisticated than other Americans. I clung to these two languages as my passports to cultural superiority, but neither was valid.

I agreed to do freelance a Time-Life book on, of all things, *Homo erectus*, titled *The First Men*. The head of research on the project was a Frenchwoman, who arranged a working lunch for me with two French consultants who'd discovered erectile fragments in a cave somewhere in the Jura. They were flown in for this conference. The chief researcher agreed to translate but soon, fueled by several glasses of white wine, I found myself speaking French with dreamlike fluency – until suddenly my colleague frowned and said, 'You know, you're not making any sense at all.'

At about the same time, in the early 1970s, I was cruising by the docks and met a short sailor from Marseilles with a very large penis. He didn't know a word of English and had decided I understood his language perfectly because I could say '*Bonjour*' or '*Merci*.' He'd rattle on and laugh at his own jokes and play the mini-macho patting my butt as we walked down the street or, standing on tiptoe, hook a possessive arm around my neck. He insisted I go with him to see *Les valseuses*, an early Depardieu movie about French hoodlums, and in the dark theater he pulled out his penis for me to play with. It radiated as much heat as bread fresh from the oven. I never knew what he was saying and after a long night of tromping the streets with him and listening to his nonstop murmuring, I'd develop a migraine. But what I did like was the impression we gave to passersby that both of us were French and lost in the midst of a long, thoroughly idiomatic conversation.

Even though I was frightfully embarrassed by his possessive affection in the streets, and his genital exposure in the cinema, nevertheless I half believed he and I were inoculated against blame by being foreign. We were French. We smelled of garlic and enjoyed immunity against prudishness.

One day in New York I received a phone call from someone named Gilles Barbedette except he pronounced his name 'Giles.' Although he had a French accent (the aspirated, deep-throat *r*, the *u*'s threatening to acquire a fluty umlaut, the machine-gun monotone phrases rising at the end into what today would sound Valley Girl upspeak) his *a*'s were almost adenoidal with Americanness (my name, Ed, became 'Add'). He said he was a French writer in New York on vacation and he'd just read a chapter from my novel-in-progress, *A Boy's Own Story*. The chapter had been published in the gay literary magazine *Christopher Street*. On the strength of that chapter he'd bought a copy of my preceding novel, *Nocturnes for the King of Naples*, and he hoped to translate it into French and to find a publisher for it. 'I have many connections in the French cultural world,' he said.

Gilles did most of the talking on the phone and interrupted if I attempted to say anything. Since I was his 'discovery' I had assumed he'd be interested in my opinions, but he wasn't.

When he showed up at my studio apartment I was startled to see he was nothing but a skinny kid. I suppose he was twenty-five at the time, but he looked like an adolescent. The year was 1980, AIDS was still a year away, and I was a young-looking, chain-smoking, heavy-drinking New York sex addict of forty. As we talked about books I sat on the floor beside him and kept touching his leg. I was sure he was a natural, if untutored, sadist and soon I had him naked except for my black leather jacket. He was 'shocked,' he said – and continued to say so for years to come. He always loved to tell the story of how he, a very young man, had approached me on a serious artistic and professional mission and I was, within minutes, kneeling on the floor before him and unzipping his fly, calling him 'Master.'

I suppose that even at age forty I still looked young enough or sexy enough (in my black T-shirt and torn jeans and with my flowing dark mustache and slender muscular body) that I wasn't used to being turned down. Of course American gay men rejected me all the time, but gently, and none who'd gone so far as to brave his way into my apartment would have appeared outraged by my smiling but unstoppable advances. Gilles, however, really wasn't attracted to me, as proven by his half-hard penis, nor did my behavior conform to his idea of his own importance. I was somehow insulting him. He was a cultural emissary, about to launch my career in France, and here I was treating him as just another trick.

Maybe Gilles's jauntiness and his way of doubling up in laughter and his adenoidal way of calling me 'Add' made me forget he wasn't American. Gilles kept a book, which he showed me, in which he wrote down funny, idiomatic expressions in English. He said lots of things like 'Later, alligator' – not what one expected from a middle-class guy from Brittany. With Diana in Rome and the sailor from Marseilles the extreme difficulty of communication had kept their foreignness topmost in my mind. But Gilles was so funny – or rather so boyishly eager to be amused – and his English was so up-to-date that, once I realized he wasn't going to put out, I felt he was a 'sister.'

In those days gay guys divided other gay men into three categories: forget-it; hot numbers; and sisters. A sister was a pal in whom there could never be any further sexual interest, even if the initial meeting had occurred through cruising. With a sister one let down one's hair and relaxed. One no longer had to look good or appear desirable or (depending on the target audience) vaguely menacing. With a sister one could 'dish,' that is, talk about real interests like dick size, one's own humiliation in the bar last night, the fight to lose weight or the latest Streisand record. Presumably one was more honest with a 'sister' than with a 'husband,' though some gay men found campiness more a strain than dull normality. Sisterhood, after all, was a link to the queer past and required imagination and flair.

Gilles had met Michael Denneny, the gay editor who'd published *Nocturnes for the King of Naples*. They'd gone together with Mark Blasius, a young professor and friend of Foucault, to the Saint, which I'd dubbed 'the Hindenburg of discos,' and indeed it did eventually implode. But at that moment it was the epicenter of New York gay culture with its industrial metal ramps leading up and up to a round dance floor under twisting and traveling spotlights. The lights were suspended from a planetarium dome through which people above, seated in row after row of balcony chairs, could look down on the action like shadowy ranks of bored angels observing the brilliant human drama below – that is if they weren't groping (or doing) their neighbor. At the Saint, Gilles and Michael could no longer squabble. The music drowned them out, their drugs kicked in, their shirts came off – and at dawn Gilles was leading Michael back to my place, just four blocks away (I was out of town and had given my keys to Gilles). When Michael saw Gilles's huge penis, he said, 'Is this a joke? I thought you were supposed to be a French intellectual,' and laughed. Gilles took offense.

Michael invited Gilles out for a week to Fire Island but was vexed when Gilles pedantically denounced the Pines as a boring gay ghetto, linked to a misguided American tendency to seek the ultimate meaning of the self in sexual identity. Gilles was in a black mood the whole time, hugged his skinny ribs and blue skin and laughed at Michael's housemates with their perfect teeth, swollen muscles and tans as dark as Greek honey. They were just about willing to welcome such an unwholesome-looking nerd into their Olympian midst but Gilles rejected them. Worse, he wanted to invite a guest of his own, a blond from Minnesota named Keith, but Michael's housemates strenuously objected: guests don't have guests.

At that time, just before AIDS challenged all our convictions, the New York gay community was entering its triumphant apogee. American gays had recently faced down Anita Bryant, the born-again orange juice queen who'd fought to have gay teachers fired across the country. She'd argued, rather subtly, that openly gay teachers set a dangerous example to their students precisely because so many of the teachers were attractive and accomplished. We'd rebutted her by saying that sexual identity was set in stone, determined in early childhood (Freud) or at birth (genetics). If an alluring gay mentor could 'convert' a youngster, why had so many gays persisted in following their homosexual destinies as teenagers despite their dreadful first experiences (with violent priests, drooling town idiots, grabby grandpas)? Gays had boycotted Florida orange juice until the company had fired Ms. Bryant, who was their spokesperson. In any case she'd lost interest in her cause, Save Our Children, and drifted off. Soon she was even pro-gay. The whole thing blew over, but in fighting Bryant we'd convinced ourselves that, first, gay identity did exist and, second, choice played no role in forming it.

Trivial as the Bryant incident sounds now, at the time it had mobilized tens of thousands of gays, just a year or two before Gilles denounced us all. We weren't in a mood to be scolded by another gay person, certainly not by a Frenchman, since we liked to imagine the French were wide-eyed with admiration for us and were following our glorious example, not taking exception to it. Weren't there gay bars in Paris named Fire Island and Le Bronx? we asked with condescending pride. Michael Denneny, who'd been the first editor in a major publishing house to sign up gay authors and launch a whole line of gay books, certainly didn't need to take lessons from Gilles – especially since his own intellectual credentials were in order. At the University of Chicago Michael had been one of Hannah Arendt's favorite students and had become her friend.

As for the rest of us American gays, we were Marxists or Maoists or Freudians or adherents to theories of biological determinism and as such we were all tinged with authoritarianism. We'd never wielded political power and had no hope of doing so. Our utopianism remained obdurate and pessimistic: pure. Certainly we had no need to compromise or evolve and nothing to gain from it. Although we read and admired Nietzsche, we'd picked up few of his habits of thought. For us paradox was a parlor trick associated with Oscar Wilde, not a key to wisdom; in that way too we were different from the French.

In 1980 I met Michel Foucault, the master of paradox. At first I knew and liked the man more than I understood his philosophy. For an American of my generation Foucault was scarcely a philosopher at all; between the Logical Positivists and the Ordinary Language technicians of my youth we'd come to see the proper domain of philosophy as the job of dispersing metaphysical murk and redefining moral quandaries as semantic confusion. Foucault seemed to be less a philosopher and more an historian who delighted in reversing received ideas about the past. Perhaps he was a structuralist, we said complacently, which made him sound like some sort of anthropologist.

I met Foucault because my friend Richard Sennett, the sociologist who'd founded a think tank at New York University called the New York Institute for the Humanities, had given me a job as its 'executive director.' It was a grand title but only a part-time position for which I earned twenty-five thousand dollars a year – money I badly needed to supplement the miserable sums I was earning as an adjunct teacher of creative writing at Columbia. Foucault conducted a seminar under our aegis on the history of sexuality, and on another occasion spoke with Richard Sennett before a standing-room-only audience. They both discussed masturbation in the early nineteenth century though from utterly dissimilar points of view; at the time no one seemed to notice the discrepancy. Perhaps Foucault noticed, but with us he was gentle and polite in a way that astonished us.

I invited Foucault to dinner at the Grand Ticino, a Village Italian restaurant that no longer exists. He was thin, narrow-shouldered, eager, with a mouthful of teeth somehow outlined in metal, his head shaved and gleaming. When he knew me better he asked if I thought he looked German. I said no and he seemed disappointed. He wore a suit which he'd thoroughly buttoned up and no tie, the shirt collar closed. It was as if he were trying to housebreak a wild puppy of a body, energetic and distractible. Like many French people he chose to eat what he thought would be the 'lightest' thing on the menu. 'It's not too heavy?' he asked the waiter anxiously. Later I discovered he would reject dinner invitations if he thought the food would be too rich.

During the dinner I regretted that I couldn't discuss his theories with him. Only later did I learn that he disliked such discussions outside the classroom. I asked him how he came to be so intelligent. He smiled and said, 'But I wasn't always so intelligent. As a child I was hyperactive and a poor student. My father was in despair. He was a middle-class provincial doctor. He sent me to a boarding school where I fell in love with a boy who was even worse than I in his studies. I began to apply myself so that I'd be able to do his homework for him – and that was the beginning of my settling down. Years later – thirty years later – I was coming back to Paris after the summer holidays on a crowded train. I stood next to a man who'd been a classmate of mine and we talked for hours. I asked him about everyone in our class but I was afraid even to mention the name of the boy I had been in love with lest I blush. Finally I asked about him and the man said, "That dirty fag?" "Why do you call him that?" I asked. "Oh, we all had him – didn't you?" '

I thought I'd had a strange and revealing answer to my nearly idle question.

Later that night Foucault went with me to Julius's, the oldest gay bar in the Village. Most of the customers were elderly but one was a teenager, tall and gawky and very drunk; when we left, the boy staggered after us and called out, 'So long, Pops!' 'What does "Pops" mean?' Foucault asked. 'My *friend*,' I said, 'it means *my friend*.' He smiled, pleased.

He told me that what he liked about giving seminars at Berkeley and NYU was that there was no formality separating students from professors as there was in France. 'At Berkeley they call me Mike. Whereas at the Collège de France we have enormous lectures where the students just hold up tape recorders – it's very dispiriting. There's no dialogue.'

Foucault's English, especially in the classroom, struck me as a pure product of the will. He'd decided he could speak English and so he could – the words dosed out, the grammar precise but precarious, the ideas leaping ahead and demanding expression. Linguistic facility appeared to be the natural result of his intelligence – and his relentless will.

One night he came to the Three Lives bookshop, when it was still on the corner of Seventh Avenue and Tenth Street, and he sat contentedly on the floor with dozens of other people in the upstairs room while I read a new chapter from *A Boy's Own Story*. No one recognized him, or at least no one made a fuss over him. A few days later he said, 'Of course I write as best I can, Edmund, but I'm not a real writer like you.' On another occasion he said, 'Some people complain about the obscurity of my early books, but they forget that I'm just like everyone else and that I'm only now learning how to write. Now I'm much, much clearer, but in France there are even those who accuse me of excessive clarity.'

'No,' I protested.

'Yes,' he said. 'I assure you.'

He was polite and almost docile, but he was capable of towering rages fueled by paranoia. Once in a seminar at New York University on questions he meant to include in the last volume of *The History of Sexuality* (still unpublished) he spoke at length about the difference between late pagan and early Christian conceptions of sexual morality. The contrast was so sharp that to this day I remember every link in his argument. At the end of the session someone tried to get him to say how these reflections might apply to us today, and he stormed out of the room shaking with rage. He was angry because he'd been so careful to establish that what he was doing was tracing out nothing but small historical clusters of related phenomena that influenced each other through a 'capillary' effect. Broad generalizations – especially across epochs – were what he detested most.

It struck me there was ample room for confusion. His work contrasting the pagan *Interpretation of Dreams* by Artemidorus and the early Christian rules for monastic life claimed to be nothing more general than what it was, but if we were hanging on every word surely we did so because we wanted to know exactly where our culture had gone wrong. We wanted to return to the golden, nuanced liberality of paganism. Foucault knew this – privately, as it were – but for methodological reasons, if nothing else, he wanted to limit his claims to contemporary relevance. He became very angry when a professor emeritus asked a mocking, ironic question during a seminar; Foucault was certain that the professor was out to get him (perhaps he was right).

Foucault, upon joining the prestigious Collège de France, had chosen a title for himself: professor of the history of systems of thought. In that denomination he had placed all that was dynamic and individual in his work. He would become easily fussed if careless people grouped him with the structuralists; unlike Lévi-Strauss, Foucault believed in history and thought it was both determinant and unrepeatable.

But I'm making a fool of myself discussing Foucault's ideas. He and I were acquaintances, nothing more, and I saw him no more than thirty times altogether in my life. I considered myself to be his dumb friend – but I thought hey, we all need one. When I first met him I was at the end of my drinking days. I'd lie in bed, my head turning late at night, and hold one eye closed while I read *Madness and Civilization*, just as over the previous decade I'd 'read' Nietzsche, Gramsci, Adorno, Roland Barthes and Walter Benjamin. Pages by these difficult but engaging thinkers had passed before my eyes and I'd underlined phrases that in my stupor I'd found to be significant or useful, but when I thumb through these volumes today I recognize I retained nothing and I can see no system in my cryptic marks.

But just as upper-class people and aristocrats have always assumed I must be one of them, in the same way intellectuals have often imagined I must have a trained and well-stocked mind, whereas in fact all I have is an alert face, a quick tongue and a few journalistic tricks. I pick up information easily and make use of it and then forget it. Over the years I've written paragraphs on Japanese gardens and the giant molecule, on the semiology of architecture, on Mexican movie stars and the Swedish royal palace at Drottningholm, on the American fondness for Proust and the French dislike of identity politics. I've written on Jasper Johns, Cy Twombly and Chinese scholar paintings of the Yuan Dynasty. I've written about the art of giving a dinner party and tricks for receiving weekend guests and about the quirky prose of Djuna Barnes.

In November 1980 Ronald Reagan was elected, which sent Foucault into a panic. He interpreted Reagan's victory as a return to fascism. He had been experimenting with LSD, which perhaps wasn't prudent since he'd once suffered from bouts of madness. One night Michael Denneny got a call at four in the morning, awakening him. It was from Mark Blasius, who asked Michael if he still had some of those tranquilizers they had once used to come down from bad LSD trips. Michael went to his medicine cabinet and found them. 'Michel Foucault is on a bad trip at Man's Country baths,' Mark said, 'and we have to go down there to rescue him. He's forgotten all his English and the only thing he could remember was my phone number.'

Mark and Michael taxied down to the East Village, checked in to the bathhouse, and went from room to room until they found a ball of naked French philosopher, crazed and hissing, in the corner of a cubicle. They went back with him to his New York University faculty apartment, made him take the tranquilizers and stayed with him for the next fourteen hours. Foucault was frightened by the Reagan victory but Denneny said, 'It's not all that bad.'

The following spring I was in Paris for a ten-day vacation. It happened to be at the moment when Mitterrand was elected – a socialist victory that caused leftists to dance in the street, though French capitalists were fleeing the country. Guy de Rothschild and his wife Marie-Hélène, two of the social leaders of Paris, moved to New York. There was talk of the French government confiscating the great fortunes of the land. Two communist party members were made cabinet ministers. Widows feared their gold ingots would be seized and Gaullists pictured Russian tanks at the gates of Paris.

Gilles and his lover Jean had a big apartment on the rue de la Goutte d'Or in the Arab Quarter. I stayed with them and slept on the couch. At that time the street was choked with vendors selling jellabahs and I bought one; I'd recently stopped smoking and acquired a big stomach that I hoped to hide in the folds of my robe. But the robe, though marked XL, was as tight as a sausage skin on me, and it was of a sleazy synthetic fabric made in China. Gilles and Jean had a good laugh at my expense.

Jean Blancard was three or four years older than Gilles. They'd met in Brittany at the University of Rennes in the mid-1970s, where Jean had been a student radical and a gay leader. He and Gilles had been militants together but now, in 1981, all that was over with. They laughed at gays, just as feminists made them yawn. All that was 'so seventies.' In France every fad has its day, but only one.

Jean spoke no English and his French was all argot. His word for bed, I remember, was '*piau*,' which means a pole and which few foreigners would have understood, even those who spoke French fluently. He had no imagination about linguistic difficulties since he spoke no other language. He was short and thick and had straight, dirty hair and a full mustache. He always wore a quizzical smile when I was around – irreproachable but *almost* satirical. His near sneer struck me as weak and offensive; he faced all the problems of the old-fashioned macho who is losing power. When he walked he trudged. He was too masculine to turn his head – no, he turned his whole body.

He and Gilles led a comfortable provincial life in the heart of Paris. Their dining room table was near the thrown-open French doors through which one could see the rooftops and chimney pots leading all the way down to the opera house, the verdigrised dome of the Palais Garnier. They shopped every morning a block away at the open-air market under the tracks of Barbès-Rochechouart, where the metro rushed out above ground. They ate every meal at home with a first course, a main course and a dessert, and during the meal they squabbled in muted French like an old couple. I couldn't understand what they were saying but Gilles pouted and whined and Jean was satirical or gruff. Gilles always seemed put out and 'hurt.' Although Gilles assured me that Jean had been an intellectual leader – *his* leader – now he was beyond all that. He worked at a university, Paris III, buying food for the cafeteria. He was a purchasing agent. It was a routine job, not very challenging, and in the evenings after their supper at home – the celeriac in mustard sauce, the frozen broccoli and chicken breast nuked in the microwave, the two old, badly battered cheeses unwrapped like mummy parts and, at the end of the meal, rewrapped, the chocolate mousse eaten directly out of the cartons, the thimbleful of bitter coffee – Jean would go out to the local gay bar, Le Moustache, to play pool with the fellows.

Jean and Gilles were fiercely patriotic, as I quickly discovered. In America one could always assume American artists and academics were routinely critical of their own country, but Gilles and Jean bristled at the slightest reservation about French culture, French fashion, French cuisine, French politics. Praise for France delighted them, and soon I was dishing it out. When I said I was addicted to the taste of Badoit, Gilles broke into a big smile: 'Oh, do you like our French waters? We have almost a hundred different waters and they all serve different purposes – to fortify the body, for pregnancy, for slimming, for rehydration, for digestion and so on.' He looked so radiant with promotional zeal that at first I thought he must be pulling my leg. I learned to praise everything French around him, including all classic French authors (living ones could be dismissed out of hand).

The first night I stayed at the rue de la Goutte d'Or I heard the most terrible grunts and howls coming out of Jean's room. As I discovered the next morning over breakfast, with Gilles translating for me, Jean had picked up an elderly Arab in the public toilets under the metro tracks, brought him home and convinced him to fist him.

'What!' I exclaimed. 'Was he dirty?'

Jean laughed and said, 'More or less. I had to make him shower. He smelled like a camel after a week in the desert.' No odor came immediately to mind. I was shocked that Jean had been able to persuade an Arab from the neighborhood to do something so exotic – after all, hadn't Foucault himself said that fisting was the only thing that the twentieth century had added to the sexual repertoire? And why would one confide such a delicate obstetrical intervention to an amateur?

Even more shocking was how undiscriminating Jean was in his choice of an elderly Arab. Back in Greenwich Village we felt we were daring if we went out with another middle-class white man who was *five years older* or *not college-educated* or *devoid of a gym membership*. To choose a dirty man in a smelly jellabah and with flashing gold teeth and to teach him to fist – it was all unimaginable.

Some of my readers, French ones, will think I'm ridiculing Gilles and Jean by mentioning sexual details of this sort. They'll say that I'm discrediting them by bringing up their eccentric sexual habits, just as I'm tarnishing Foucault's reputation by mentioning his bad trip at the baths. On the contrary. I want to suggest how heroic they were. They were intellectuals, but not feeble ones who'd chosen the mind over the body. As the golden age of promiscuity was shutting down, they were leading daring sex lives in which they were collapsing age and class and racial barriers. The Mitterrand victory owed a debt to the gay vote and the new government was quick to remove from the books crimes involving homosexuality. The special police force aimed at rooting out open-air cruising and sex was abolished; now the Tuilleries Gardens were jumping at night and in the Bois de Boulogne the Brazilian drag-queen prostitutes were openly soliciting business before retreating with customers to tents suspended from overhead branches. One night I watched a seven-foot-tall, brown-skinned Brazilian with Asian eyes, standing in silver lamé panties and bra on stack heels and wielding her full-length silver fox as a sort of torero's cape. As the cars rushed past, she'd whisper, '*Olé!*' and make a full *valencia* pass with her coat. This was the new France – multicultural, lawless, orgiastic.

Foucault invited me to the opera to see the revival of a Baroque work by Rameau, updated and starring Frederica von Stade in a mile-long black rubber cape surrounded by revolving mirrored walls and clouds of dry-ice smoke – I felt I was back at the Saint. After the opera I pressured Foucault to accompany me to a gay bar, though he said he would be mobbed there. I smiled at his pretentiousness. But sure enough, he had to flee the Central and hop in a cab almost immediately.

I invited Foucault and his lover, Daniel Defert, and Susan Sontag, who happened to be in town, to dinner at Gilles's and Jean's apartment. Gilles was meeting Foucault for the first time. I had learned, quite indirectly, that Gilles wasn't at all the Paris editor and translator he'd told everyone in New York that he was. No, he taught English in a high school in a dangerous housing development to the north of the city, though he had already done some literary journalism. His will was so strong and his sense of being limited by his family background so beautifully underdeveloped that within a year or two he was on the way toward realizing his ambitions.

What he wanted to be most of all was a writer, *un écrivain*, that highest of all accolades in France. I quickly learned that it was not conferred on just anyone. People would say modestly, 'I've written twelve books but I'm not a writer,' or they spat out, 'He's a sort of journalist, not a real writer.' Both Barthes and Foucault had announced the death of the writer, but their very efforts to desacralize the office revealed just how sacred it was in France; in America no one would have bothered.

I remember, as I was shopping for the Foucault dinner, I complained that all the green beans were so small in France and it would take forever to stem enough to eat. Jean looked at me with his sly, satirical smile and said, 'But Edmund, don't you know the small ones are the good ones?' I thought of myself as sophisticated culturally and psychologically, but I was a primitive in the arts of living.

That night we sat by the open French doors and looked out at the rooftops and the distant dome of the opera house. I said that friends of mine had been shocked I would invite such important guests to the rue de la Goutte d'Or, but Foucault was quick to remind me that ten years earlier he and Sartre and Genet had come to this very street to demonstrate in favor of a young Arab who'd been framed for murder by an older white man. When Susan Sontag went to the bathroom Foucault asked me, 'Why did you invite *her*?' Eventually I realized he rarely socialized with women. He lived in an all-male world, though he was devoted to his female students.

At home he entertained nothing but attractive young men, artists and intellectuals – and all gay. Not the big, grizzled sadists he reputedly sought out at the sex clubs in San Francisco, but the comely ephebes who reminded me of the small-sexed students surrounding the philosopher in Chassériau's painting of Plato and his Academy. I remember attending one of those parties on a Sunday afternoon. There they all were: Hervé Guibert, ringleted and beautiful as an archangel but with a permanently hoarse voice; his pal, Mathieu Lindon, a novelist whose father had published Samuel Beckett; the sweet-natured Jacques Almira, whose first novel had been prefaced by Foucault. He was an ex-beauty running to flesh who'd moved to Montpellier to be near the nude beach. Gilles was quick to enter Foucault's circle. After all, Gilles was young, looked younger, and he was so intelligent he could master Foucault's ideas after just a few exposures to them. Not that Foucault liked intellectual conversation. No, it was something far more intimate that he craved. Hervé Guibert had become his best friend because they were always trading secrets about their love lives.

Foucault had invited Gilles and me to dinner at his apartment on a high floor of a new building on the rue de Vaugirard. The unimpeded view of the sky outside was reflected in the floor-to-ceiling mirrored doors that concealed bookshelves. The furniture was sleek and modern, perhaps an echo of Foucault's years in Sweden. I told them about the new life-threatening disease that had struck a few gay men in New York. It was called GRID (gay-related immune deficiency) and no one knew what caused it. Gay men, most of them under fifty, were contracting a rare form of pneumonia and a skin cancer called Kaposi's sarcoma that usually was seen only in very old Jewish and Italian men. With the writer Larry Kramer and four other gay men I'd just founded something we called the Gay Men's Health Crisis because we wanted to make clear the disease struck gay men, not lesbians, and that it was a crisis, not a permanent condition. I, who equated personal liberation with sexual freedom, certainly didn't want to cut back on the number of my encounters. When I heard responsible community leaders talk about closing the baths and backrooms I broke out into a rash.

Foucault laughed at me and Gilles quickly followed suit. 'Oh, no, Edmund,' Foucault said. 'Leave it to the puritanical Americans to invent a disease that affects – that kills! – only gay men. That's too perfect. Maybe it will get rid of your blacks too.'

'As a matter of fact—'

'No, no! It's too perfect. Gays *and* blacks!' He and Gilles continued to tease me the rest of the evening. Foucault served hardboiled eggs and *foie gras en gelée* and a *poulet basquais* and *crème brûlée* but no vegetables or fruit. Nothing fresh. He smiled and said, 'I can buy all this ready-made at the caterer downstairs but the greengrocer is blocks away and I never have time to go there.'

Two years later, during the summer of 1983, I moved to Paris with John Purcell, my lover at the time. I thought we'd stay just a year. I'd received a Guggenheim fellowship for seventeen thousand dollars, which provided almost enough for us to live there for twelve months, especially since the franc was still weak due to fears of the socialist government. A New York friend put us on to a two-room apartment on the Île Saint-Louis where he'd stayed for a summer or two. It was furnished with broken-down furniture and collages by the ancient landlady downstairs, Madame Pflaum, an Austrian artist who'd come to live in Paris in the 1920s. Her husband, now deceased, had been an epigraphist and some of the Latin stone inscriptions he'd studied were mounted on the wall. The three sets of French doors looked out on the imposing white stone volute and sloped black roof of the church across the street, which had been built under Louis XIV. Next to the church was another seventeenth-century building, a convent, that seemed abandoned, though once in a while a light would glimmer through a dirty window. In warm weather a boy who lived in the church opposite – in an apartment right up in the eaves – would sit on his windowsill and smoke a joint. He had green hair. Once he gave a weak little wave in my direction.

I suppose some of my New York friends – Richard Sennett, Susan Sontag, the poet and translator Richard Howard – might have thought I'd go right to the heart of Parisian intellectual life. That's what they'd done in earlier sojourns. But my French was still nonexistent, though I'd been taking lessons in New York. John Purcell disliked long intellectual evenings. He preferred drinking and partying with average guys, usually older. But mainly I was feeling vulnerable after two decades in New York and my sudden departure.

I'd been addicted to the city as to a hard drug that doesn't kill you if you can get enough of it and if you remember to eat and exercise. I'd been addicted to copious New York sex, to long wine-soaked evenings of talk and cigarette smoking and exaggeration, to New York name-accumulating and name-dropping, but in spite of all my bad habits I'd always managed to keep working, reading and writing, even if I had to hold one eye shut. I never did too much of any one thing except drink and smoke and have sex. I'd gone out to Fire Island for many summers but then I'd stopped. I'd dropped acid twenty times but I'd never bought any drugs; I'd always cadged my joints. Recently I'd stopped drinking and smoking, gained weight and moved to Paris. I felt sleepy and unsure of myself. I knew few people and my identity, always shadowy in my own eyes, now seemed to waver into invisibility.

I got a job writing occasional cultural columns for American *Vogue*, which suited me fine since no one I knew ever stayed long enough under the hairdryer to read it. I'd been hired because I'd assured my boss in New York I was fluent in French. One of my first assignments was to interview Eric Rohmer, the most cerebral of all French film directors. Rohmer, an old, monk-like man obsessed with silly girls, received us in his spacious office. Gilles went with me. I taped everything. Although I could pronounce my questions in French, I understood none of his answers and couldn't follow up. Gilles and I rushed home and he translated everything for my article.

In 1983, Gilles was already on his way professionally. He was building on his 1980 deathbed interview of Sartre. Now he interviewed Foucault for *Christopher Street* magazine in New York. He found a publisher for his translation of my novel *Nocturnes for the King of Naples*. He took an indefinite, paid medical leave from his teaching job after a Turkish student pulled a knife on an Arab classmate. 'That was enough for me,' Gilles said. He claimed he'd had a nervous breakdown.

He published, with a co-author, a book about Paris gay life of the 1920s, based on extensive interviews, but he soon disowned it. I was never sure why. I think he was shedding his past as a gay liberationist. Foucault, too, was rejecting the gay ghetto and the idea of gay culture. He said that 'gay philosophy' and 'gay painting' were meaningless notions, though he insisted in the interview with Gilles that writing gay fiction was legitimate since it enabled us to imagine how gay men should live together. He felt that relationships between gay men were tenuous, undefined, still to be invented, and that gay fiction was the place where a vision of association could be worked out in concrete detail.

He told me that after working so many years on the history of sexuality he felt that nothing was duller than sex – the *idea* of sex, the sexual discourse – but he remained excited by experiments in living. He wanted to 'desexualize' our society if that meant rejecting the doctrine that we each contain a defining secret, that that secret is the nature of our sexuality, and that we have an obligation to 'avow' it. Ours, he said critically, was a culture of avowal.

Gilles began to publish fiction of his own – long, pallid allegories that strenuously avoided any resemblance to his own life. He wrote a novel called *Le Métromane* about a subway that started in Paris and came up in Manhattan and the etiolated, generic man who rode this surrealist conveyance and reveled in his own psychological deterioration. Later Gilles wrote a novel about a scholar named Baltimore obsessed with books and America. Yet another novel, *Les Volumes éphémères*, was about a fat woman who tries to start a utopian colony and her very thin male admirer.

Dull, dull, and arbitrary, which was odd work by someone so smart and combative who had such exquisite taste. Perhaps because of Foucault he'd come to so despise the autobiographical impulse that he banned anything he'd ever lived through from his writing. Of course certain inescapable preoccupations – books, America, skinniness – emerged anyway, but in sterile prose. The failure of his novels to interest anyone wounded him – worse, infuriated him, since in his personal life he was used to having his way.

Soon he became an editor and launched a publishing house called Éditions Rivages, which was twinned with a trendy, large-format, black-and-white magazine named *City*. Despite its international orientation and beautiful photos, *City* disappeared after a few years but Rivages, under Gilles's direction, became extraordinarily successful. Gilles published no new French novels (thereby avoiding vexing his contemporaries), just translations from other European languages and Japanese. He was a quick study and could grasp almost instantaneously what was new and dynamic in another culture. He swooped down on Vera Nabokov and published the Master's first, rather tawdry draft of the sublime *Lolita*, a draft written before he emigrated to America.

Gilles knew what the French wanted to airlift out of a foreign literature. There was little humor in recent French novels, so Gilles imported it in the form of comic fiction by David Lodge and Alison Lurie. The French liked short *récits* with a philosophical cast to them and Gilles brought over from English Eva Figes's *Light*, which was about one day in the life of Monet, and from Italian Daniele Del Giudice's playful *Wimbledon Stadium*. Never anything too long or too demanding. Then Gilles would force his French journalist friends (usually other gay men) to write glowing articles about these translated novels in *Le Monde* or *Le Nouvel Observateur* – and they were happy to oblige since Gilles was handing them what they craved most: novelty.

He also discovered whatever was fine and unusual – slim books by Grace Paley, Lorrie Moore, Steven Millhauser. He and Jean had moved to a bigger apartment not far from the Gare de l'Est and there would have small dinner parties for his writers and critics. Through Gilles I met all the American and English writers he was publishing; I was the inevitable American oak leaf in his table when it was fully extended.

Gilles developed two personalities – a jovial, boyish, exuberant, sometimes silly, always affectionate personality when he spoke English, and a gloomy, irritable, sharp-tongued, unsmiling personality in French. The contrast was absolute. With me, of course, he spoke English almost all the time. He assumed that I was an inexhaustible source of wise-cracking humor and light social satire, and even the blandest, unironic thing I said would send him off into paroxysms of laughter, as if I'd been especially wicked this time. He adored me and loved being my friend. I no longer thought of him as a sexual being and the transition into sisterhood relaxed me. Visiting Americans and Brits who met him through me remembered his hilarity, his big welcome, his instant comprehension of our in jokes. The disdain expressed in the damning English word 'quite' amused Gilles endlessly, the way a single syllable ('She's *quite* talented') could destroy a reputation. He laughed so violently with his hard, mirthless cackle that his legs would turn to rubber. He'd cling to my arm whenever we walked down the street. I'd have to hold him upright. His laugh, I thought, was more a signifier than a spontaneous response, but other people, visiting English speakers, fell for it. When he spoke English he produced, like us Americans, a constant chorus of affirmation, comments such as 'Wonderful,' 'Great,' 'Fabulous.' He would nod constantly, but a bit ahead of the beat, and his eyes roamed restlessly. He had a tic of saying 'Unh-unh,' the second sound a bit higher on the scale and louder. I suppose he was imitating our way of saying yes, 'Unh-hunh,' but that aspirated *h* was always tricky for the French and he just dropped it. When he was in the next room I'd hear him saying 'Unh-unh' to himself, almost as a rider prompts a horse into a gallop. When he spoke English with me or the 'adorable' Grace Paley or the 'darling' Susan Minot he was effervescent and adolescent, whereas in French he was already middle-aged, grim, tough. He was fond of the most acerbic literary critic in France,

Angelo Rinaldi, and of Rinaldi's lover, the rather Jesuitical Argentine novelist Hector Bianciotti, but their three-way friendship was like a conspiracy, a coven, and they sealed it in wormwood and gall. They were so at home with each other that they would speak in bored shorthand that floated on a yellow stream of poisonous laughter. They knew everything bad about everyone.

My struggle with the French language made me impatient with all longwinded formulas and pointless qualifiers, with those words like *bref* ('in short'), which introduced another digression, or *en principe*, which meant nothing more than a clearing of the throat. Whereas conversation in English overheard in a Parisian restaurant immediately sank a hook into my brain and dragged me behind the racing outboard of words and more words, in French I quickly became irritated and often I discovered I was watching lips flutter and purse with real hatred in my heart. I felt like a mouse running a maze, heading for the cheese at the heart of the labyrinth; whenever I encountered a barrier in speaking (a word I couldn't find), I had to be ready to reverse direction and scamper down a new alleyway.

The French Gilles was sour, disappointed, blasé, but when I'd visit him at Éditions Rivages he'd seem proud of himself, of his authors, even of his new suit and shaggy haircut. He'd been a provincial militant, then an exhausted, frightened high school teacher, but now he was a fashionable man about town, years younger.

Most nights he dined alone with Jean. They'd bought good furniture, imitations of Thonet chairs from Vienna. The Viennese Secession and Heian Japan were the two new obsessions in Paris that year. Their couch had sloping wood arms and pearly gray upholstery stamped with darker geometrical shapes, just as their armchairs were covered in a soft taupe, a perfect nest for their long-haired fluffy cat. Deep carpets, a fireplace, soft lamps and low wood tables intensified the impression of expensive comfort. After dinner Gilles would write his dull fiction and read leather-bound editions of Montaigne and Kafka and Nietzsche and put ticks in blue ink beside memorable or provocative passages. He eventually published *L'Invitation au mensonge*, a book of essays about liberating lies and the usefulness of masks. He invited French novelists to give up realism and imitate the fantastic aspects of

Nabokov, Melville and Wilde. I hated all this praise of lying. Far from feeling that a devotion to realism was hackneyed and self-evident (or that truth was nonexistent), I strove to segregate the truth as if it were some radiant isotope.

To the degree Gilles was bloodless as a writer, he was vigorous as a publisher. Everything he did – every phone call, every drink, every dinner – was calculated to advance his authors, those shadowy, benign beings who dropped into Paris only once every three years. Recently Alison Lurie told me that years ago Gilles accompanied her and a gay friend of hers, an American anthropologist, to Belle Île, where he said his family had originated. He claimed he could feel the presence of Celtic spirits in the air – sheer malarkey, since Gilles was, like me (like Alison!), a Voltairian atheist. Perhaps he permitted himself these folkloric touches, this alternative life, around foreigners.

Jean became ill. At first it seemed he had just a bad cold, maybe the flu. Being a good New Yorker (and an honorary New York Jew) I made chicken soup and brought it over but Gilles shouted at me, 'Do you think we're so poor we can't afford our own soup? How dare you treat us to your insulting acts of charity!' I tried to explain the idea of 'Jewish penicillin,' but he wouldn't come out of his sulk.

I rented a floor of a Renaissance Venetian house in Crete and Gilles and Jean spent a week there with John Purcell and me. We all rode motor scooters up into the mountains but Jean's hands turned blue the next day, a dark, uniform blue, and that struck us as ominous. 'Maybe the vibrations of the scooter broke some capillaries,' I said, as if that happened often.

Gilles said, 'Add, you don't know what you're talking about.'

They turned in their scooters and took taxis everywhere. Gilles said, 'That's the best thing about Crete, the taxis. There are always dozens of them just waiting. In Paris you can never find a taxi.' They hated the food, all the feta cheese and bits of charred squid and puff pastry swimming in honey. I went to the market and bought them a live chicken, which cost the earth and seemed to be the old woman's best friend, but the butcher didn't know how to slaughter or prepare fowl. He just hacked at it and Gilles and Jean were shocked by how it looked on the plate.

Jean had a rare blood disease and no platelets to protect him from bruising. He was wracked by a constant cough. He seldom left his bed and when I dropped by in Paris he never came out of the bedroom. The apartment became dirty and shabby and the cat box smelled. I'd seen the panic and hysteria in the eyes of my American friends with AIDS, but Gilles sank into despair as if he'd been preparing for it all his life. Not for a moment did he appear surprised by his bad luck. He kept up his job with his accustomed brilliance and I'd hear his hard laugh ringing out as he gabbled in his adenoidal English with his authors, but in French he made no effort to be cheerful. He sighed and complained and sulked. Never was a lip less stiff. His idea of an interesting conversational gambit was to puff his cheeks out and say, 'Oof! It's hot!'

Jean died in 1986. The cremation at Père Lachaise was appalling (it prefigured the cremation of my lover, Hubert Sorin, a decade later in the same place). Because Jean was a leftist and an atheist, there was no ceremony. We all stood around in the cold outside while the simple wood coffin was fed into the furnace – and I couldn't help looking up the length of the chimney towering above us to see if any black smoke was coming out. Then we gathered inside, row after row of us, in the properly neutral nondenominational chapel. Jean's mother was in the front row. Since Gilles, loyal to Jean's wishes, had ruled out all music and all eulogies, there was nothing to distract us or to commemorate Jean. We waited. And waited. I kept imagining that in a few minutes the guard would bring out a baguette, hot from the oven, and present it to Jean's mother, saying, 'Madame: your son.'

Gilles seemed so alone. He lived just a few blocks off the Canal Saint Martin where he'd halfheartedly cruise. I suppose his enormous penis got him dates, though he was becoming thinner and thinner and he walked with one shoulder pitched high and his head cast forward. His face was engraved with lines and his big nose and high cheekbones looked as if they'd break through the thinning parchment of his skin. I would have given him my time and sympathy if he'd ever opened his heart to me, but he was too proud and wounded.

He became impossible. One night we got into a taxi and Gilles barked out the name of his street, 'Rue des Vinaigriers,' which was only two blocks long and in a poor neighborhood where few people took taxis. The Vietnamese driver said he was newly arrived in Paris and didn't know the street. Gilles asked, 'You don't know how to do your job?' and refused to help. The poor driver had to look up the street on a huge map he could scarcely see in the dim car light. (I didn't dare offer assistance.) Gilles crossed his arms and slumped into his seat. He'd become a classic pain in the ass.

John Purcell got tired of Paris. He'd finished his studies in interior design at the Paris branch of Parsons and now he moved back to New York. He wanted to speak English, get a job, stay out late in the Village bars and flirt with the older men who doted on his Yankee good looks.

Finally I began to lead an entirely French life. Most of my friends were French and considerably younger than me. One night I invited one of the best novelists, Emmanuel Carrère, hailed by Updike as the greatest French writer since Camus, to dinner with my young, beautiful friends. Emmanuel and his wife made astonished fun at the '*ado*' (adolescent) paradise I'd constructed for myself.

During the solitary days I would lie on the couch and read new French novels and look up every word. I was so heavy-headed and ungifted for acquiring languages that I had to look up a word on the average of five times before I finally learned it. But I was acquiring a large and strange vocabulary. One day I picked up a poem by Baudelaire and I was astonished – I could read it right off! Not long after that I heard a recording of Juliette Gréco and she, too, I could understand.

And yet, when I traveled back to America for a week or two I was always afraid on the return flight to Paris that maybe I would have forgotten my French. It was not a passing anxiety, and I would hold imaginary conversations in my head to rehearse the next real one. I appeared on a book-chat show on French television and took a dozen French classes beforehand to prepare. The teacher would play me a videotape of a segment of the same show, then stop it and ask me what had just been said. Rarely had I understood the full import.

When I actually appeared on the show my French was adequate but I irritated the host by mentioning my homosexuality. I'd written a difficult novel, *Caracole*, in which none of the characters happened to be gay. There was lots of straight sex in it, but I didn't want to pass for straight myself on TV.

The book had been inspired by my reading of eighteenth-century French novels of gallantry such as *Les Liaisons dangereuses*. I thought it would be amusing to show a race of vain heterosexuals on the permanent make and to set the action in a place that blended eighteenth-century Venice, occupied Paris and contemporary New York. The novel was a result of all my hours of reading French during my marinades on the couch and of my years of living cross-culturally.

I told someone the book was as if a student was studying world literature and modern European history and fell asleep on the night before the final and dreamed a long, nasty dream. In it I settled scores with all the people who'd helped me and befriended me back in New York. The New York Institute for the Humanities became the Chat Box and starring appearances were made by characters based on my nephew and Richard Howard, Susan Sontag, her son and Richard Sennett. Sontag dropped me and asked for her blurb on the back of *A Boy's Own Story* to be withdrawn from future editions in English or any other language.

Now I felt all the more isolated, as if I could never go back to New York after I'd alienated so many people. Oddly enough, while writing *Caracole* I'd never thought my words would wound any-one. I'd imagined my friends would somehow be enlightened by my vision, which metamorphosed our wren-like New York lives into the parrot plumage of an extended carnival.

No one liked the book. Sontag's son, David Rieff, reportedly said, 'Pity we were attacked in such a mediocre effort.' Few American newspapers reviewed it and those that did were hostile or baffled. When the *Wall Street Journal* attacked Susan Sontag's *The Volcano Lover* it said that her novel was bad, weirdly enough, in the same way that *Caracole* was bad, a novel that had savaged her.

My editor, Bill Whitehead, hosted a masked ball in New York to celebrate the publication and to mirror the closing scene in *Caracole*. Now I realize that he knew he was ill with AIDS and would soon be dead; the party was his own farewell. Everyone was costumed and masked, but Bill's headdress was terrifying. He wore a black leather masochist's hood with zippers over his eyes and mouth. All the zippers were open. His liquid eyes blinked and shifted inside the narrow slits and his protruding lips were painted a glossy red. David Rieff, I heard, had come to the party with a bullwhip to thrash me but was turned away by the bouncers Bill had hired. A Tijuana brass band played deafeningly at one end of the rather small hired hall. It was a dismal occasion.

I hurried back to my muted eiderdown existence on the Île Saint-Louis with its hot-water heating that fizzed and knocked comfortingly through old pipes, its stone inscriptions from Roman graves unearthed in Algeria, its peeling wall hangings devised by Madame Pflaum in Montmartre fifty years earlier, its French doors framing the huge stone volute of the church roof across the street: a snail stopped in its track, defensive, but about to extrude an immense sticky foot and to slide fractionally forward.

In the winter, in the rain, the Île Saint-Louis at night looked abandoned or draped with blackout curtains, only a sliver of light escaping here or there from a hypothetical interior. The island rose up out of the water like a diving bell unexpectedly surfacing – or rather, since it was all balconies and spires and chimney pots soaring above massed façades, it resembled a drowned city splashing and dripping free of a suddenly drained sea. Some nights I half expected to see fish flopping on the pavement or algae trailing down from an overhanging arch. By day in February the island was quite visibly depopulated. Only a few tourists who'd strayed in from Notre Dame on the next island over peopled the streets, their voices muffled by the fog, the uniform smell of damp relieved only once in a great while when a shop door flew open and the intoxicating sweet odor of *pain aux raisins* drifted out or when one was assaulted by the fermenting, sickening stink of two hundred cheeses moldering in their straw beds. But usually there were just a few footsteps ringing off the walls, and, way down the long, straight rue Saint-Louis-en-l'Île, the flicker and glow of a red coat or a yellow slicker, as if only a handful of brave explorers were picking their way through the abandoned temples of a cold, northern Angkor Wat threatened not by the jungle but by the lights and loudspeakers of circling *bateaux mouches*.

Gilles became ill. I invited him to lunch and he cried when I made him walk two blocks to one of the big brasseries looking out on the Gare de l'Est. I said, 'Take my arm,' and he did with his little bird claw. He whined, 'I have neuropathy in my feet and they hurt and I can't walk on them. Why didn't you arrange for a taxi? Why aren't we back in Crete where there are all those lovely taxis just waiting?'

When we finally arrived the restaurant was empty. Gilles fully subscribed to the medieval French fear of drafts, now more than ever, and made us change our table three times. When the food arrived he picked at it and ate almost nothing, though he pronounced it 'correct.' He did some justice to his dessert. In the past he'd always had the appalling manners of a man whose mother died when he was still a child; Gilles tore at his food and ate with his mouth open. But now the look and taste of everything repelled him. He crossed his arms and defied me to find a topic. Finally he lay his head down on the table.

We went back to his apartment in a taxi that the restaurant had called for us and he stumbled out of his clothes, shivering, and fell into bed. I knew that he had his cadre of soft-spoken gay French friends to look after him, those cultured, murmuring civil servants, teachers and journalists with their whispering partners and comfortable apartments in the inexpensive twentieth arrondisement.

In the past Gilles may have dallied with me and laughed so hard at what he imagined were my jokes that he'd hold his stomach and twist out of his café chair until he was kneeling on the pavement on one knee and sobbing with hilarity, but now he didn't much enjoy my company. It tired him to speak English. He'd taken indefinite leave from his office. Edouard de Andréis, the handsome young straight aristocrat from Marseilles who owned Rivages, was also dying at an early age – in his case from a disfiguring cancer of the jaw. (Edouard died a few hours after Gilles; he lived long enough to learn of Gilles's death.) The good times were over. I knew that Gilles, ever ambitious, wanted to finish his best book, *Une saison en enfance*, about his mother's early death and his own painful childhood. He was also busy arranging his own memorial ceremony at the church just beside the Gallimard publishing house where all the chic literary funerals were celebrated.

I returned to America to teach for two years, traveling with my young French lover, Hubert Sorin, who himself was ill with AIDS. While I was away Gilles died. Marie-Claude de Brunhoff, who had become my closest friend, visited Gilles often and when he became too tired to talk but still craved company she would read to him from Dr. Johnson's *Dictionary*. Gilles loved old words and the capricious but imperious pronouncements of eighteenth-century savants. Gilles was still impressed by doctors who were famous professors and when I phoned him long distance he bragged about their frequent visits. Diane Johnson, the American novelist who lived in Paris, visited him often with her husband, John Murray, a well-known lung specialist, much honored by the French government for his work with AIDS patients in French Africa. But to the degree Gilles was touched or impressed by the visits of distinguished friends and doctors he was disdainful of the nurses. He was convinced they were ignoring him and had already written him off as a dead man. He complained loudly that when they drew blood they were hurting him with deliberate sadism. He reminded one nurse that when he died *Le Monde* would print several columns as his obituary, whereas she was a nobody whose death would pass unnoticed. Maddening and arrogant as he was, he was still so perceptive, so frustrated, that one could only respect his nastiness.

From among all his friends Gilles elected one, René de Ceccaty, to accompany him into death. René – an editor, translator from Italian and Japanese, cultural journalist and extraordinarily gifted novelist – was just four years older than Gilles and in many ways his counterpart, except René's novels were compulsively readable. After Gilles's death, René would fall in love with a young heterosexual doctor in the provinces who at first had been flattered by the attention of a real writer but later became troubled by what the neighbors might say. Nor was René's love a cool, discreet affection; no, it was the sort of violent passion his idol, Violette Leduc, had directed at the men and women she'd worshiped in vain, everyone from Genet to Beauvoir.

Gilles bullied René day and night, upbraided him when he was five minutes late and railed at him when some dreaded new symptom clicked in. Gilles had seen Jean through to the end with all the querulous homey love that had characterized their relationship. But Gilles had no one. Most of his friends, as writers/editors/journalists, had their own exhausting underpaid lives to attend to.

The famous foreign writers and French aristocrats and celebrated doctor-professors were good for the occasional visit but not for the panicked three a.m. telephone call. Nor would Gilles's duchesses push his wheelchair up the hospital ramp or run out in the rain to locate off-season raspberries in the hope they might tempt him to eat. Nor would they put up with his foul mouth and bad temper, his offhand insults and shouted denunciations. René hadn't even been a specially good friend before, but Gilles had obviously judged him well. He knew that René, despite his self-destructive passion in love and his cool courtliness in friendship, would serve Gilles faithfully. Perhaps René wouldn't hold him and kiss him but Gilles was too outraged, too bitter, to want that. Gilles wanted faithfulness, a commitment to accompany him to the grave that wouldn't waver in any way, that would depend on a single moral decision, objectively taken, and not on the vagaries of sentiment. Perhaps he even knew that René, the consummate writer, would write *L'Accompagnement*, an account of Gilles's last days but a discreet French book in which Gilles would never be named.

Gilles was lucky he was French and lived in France, where people could even be *admired* for being difficult and occasionally impossible. In America we must win every basic service with smiles and gratitude, since charity is part of our ever-vigorous Christian heritage, whereas in France the secular state has replaced charity with social services that are the same for everyone, nasty or nice. In addition, France is a country where people respect sincerity and interpret disagreeableness as proof of it. The worst thing is to be a hypocrite, *faux cul*, which means 'false ass,' for some reason (is it a reference to an actor's padding?).

But generalizing about 'the French' makes me uncomfortable, even if like all foreigners I do it constantly. The drift of this chapter from fantasies I had about France when I lived in Michigan to my first disconcerting glimpses of real French people, like the voluble little sailor with the big penis from Marseilles, and finally on to my living in Paris and my slow and painful mastery of the language, which put me in touch with all the nuance and staggering complexity of the most civilized people on earth – this progression has been mirrored in my pages by a movement away from broad and inaccurate ideas to portraits of specific people who like all actual individuals are never representative of anything. No man or woman can be a symbol.

One of the last times I saw Gilles he told me that he had found encouragement in something about me he'd picked up from translating *Nocturnes for the King of Naples*. He'd learned that I'd once been so dangerously skinny I'd had to gorge myself on bread and honey every day to fatten up. 'And look at you now,' he said, poking me in my well-padded side. 'Now you're a big guy. Plump as a . . . *perdrix?*'

'Partridge.' I didn't have the heart to tell him I'd borrowed the forced-honey diet from the life of Keith McDermott, whom I'd lived with in the 1970s.

Gilles died in 1992, six years after his lover Jean. I was in America. Mass was said for him in the literary church, which was packed with aristocratic women in publishing and all those solemn, soft-spoken young writers/editors/journalists who'd remained loyal to him despite his childish provocations. Everyone recognized he was an *emmerdeur* ('a pain in the ass' or, in the more colorful French, someone who daubs everything with shit) but his very violence had endeared him to his friends and colleagues. His father and stepmother were there as well as his stolid brother the engineer and his family. The priest, Benoît Lobet, gave a sermon that René de Ceccaty described as 'beautiful, intelligent, cultivated and humane.'

After I moved back to France in 1992 I spent an afternoon with Foucault's lover, Daniel Defert. Although Foucault had died of AIDS in 1984, he was still the most stimulating conversationalist I had known. Some gossips were trying to dishonor him by suggesting he'd concealed from everyone that he had AIDS and that he'd irresponsibly infected his numerous partners. To me the whole scandal was the height of absurdity. No one knew his own HIV status until 1984, when the viral nature of the disease was finally determined and a test for detecting it devised. Anyway, we all knew that Foucault was a total bottom and that bottoms didn't pass it on unless they suddenly became versatile, which Foucault hadn't.

By the beginning of January 1984 his doctors had surmised what was wrong but couldn't bring themselves to hand down such a diagnosis to a man who'd called into question all medical authority. Foucault didn't know he had AIDS because no one dared to tell him. To the degree he suspected something his suspicion was located in his fears that he had toxoplasmosis, a parasite that invades the brain. He didn't want his enemies to be able to dismiss his two new volumes of *The History of Sexuality* by claiming the author's brain was diseased. He feared that the instant this brain abnormality became known everyone would stop taking him seriously. It was only late in the spring that it suddenly dawned on him that he had AIDS, and that he might somehow, improbably, have transmitted the disease to his lover. In fact, Defert remained negative.

We knew nothing and said nothing. The don't ask-don't tell ethos of French society prevailed. In 1984 AIDS was still mysterious and shameful; it sent mature, beloved, self-accepting gay men scrambling backwards in time to their miserable adolescence with its isolation and self-hatred. Shame accompanied AIDS as if the 'victim' had contracted it deliberately, foolishly.

I can remember the last time I saw Foucault. A New York friend of mine, Howard Brookner, himself ill with AIDS, had made a documentary about William Burroughs. I'd pulled strings with Howard in order to land Gilles the job as the translator who provided the subtitles. I offered to help Gilles, but he assured me he wasn't working directly from the mumbled, on-screen speech but from a written transcript. I still worried that some of the slang might be beyond Gilles, but he peevishly waved me aside.

The Paris screening was a disaster, since Gilles had thought the constant use of 'fuckin'' this and 'fuckin'' that referred to actual copulation; he made many other mistakes and the official French translator of Burroughs denounced Gilles as soon as the lights came up – loudly and publicly. Gilles laughed at him and said he was just a jealous old incompetent, washed-up and envious. That was the same face-saving excuse Nureyev – ill with AIDS, weak and earthbound – was using when audiences hissed him offstage at the Paris Opera after he'd dared to dance in his own version of *Le Corsaire*.

Foucault gave a dinner for Burroughs and twenty of his own young men, ringletted and whispering. The bodily transformation in Foucault was dramatic. He was nearly skeletal, and with his shaved head, glinting metallic teeth and lightweight glasses, he finally did look German, his fondest ambition. He served everyone himself, carrying individually each plateful of catered food from the kitchen. Given how frail he was, his tottering about struck me as a Christian penance; he was like Elizabeth of Hungary, who wore a hair shirt under her robes of state since her husband forbade her to give up the throne for the convent.

Toward the end of his life Foucault spoke more and more of the value of friendship. If there was no God to whom we were accountable, then if we behaved morally we did so in order to turn our lives into beautiful, admirable examples. And of all the jewels in our diadem none glowed more brightly than friendship.

Burroughs and his assistant, James Grauerholz, and the dashing young director, Howard Brookner, surely had no idea of the honor that Foucault was paying them with this expenditure of energy. Burroughs, who resembled a Kansas undertaker, was wearing his old small-town and colorless tie. Although he spoke clearly enough at the beginning of the evening, soon he'd smoked a few joints and was mumbling. I had to translate for Foucault from Burroughs's English into normal English.

At one end of the room was Burroughs sucking on his joint. At the other was the full Platonic Academy, all those willowy anorexics, Gilles brooding in their midst. And Foucault, ill and smilingly patient, was staggering back and forth with plates of expensive and inedible food.

Three months later, on June 25, 1984, Foucault was dead at age fifty-seven, which surprised everyone, even him, since he'd just planned a trip to Elba with Hervé Guibert. Gilles, who'd conducted the last interview of Sartre four years earlier, now rushed in to get the 'deathbed' interview of Foucault on May 29, 1984. But when it was published after Foucault's death as 'The Return to Morality,' Daniel Defert realized it didn't read right. There was something thin about it, not really representative. Daniel insisted that Gilles hand over the tapes so that he could listen to them. Once he played them through he was appalled; Gilles had done all the talking and not let the feeble philosopher get a word in edgewise. Daniel denounced Gilles, who wept tears of rage at the ingratitude.

In Paris, aged forty-six

My Master

Here I am, way up in my mid-sixties, still suffering over young men just as I did in my teens and twenties. The spasms come less often and don't last as long (knock on wood) but they still drive every other thought out of my mind. I go to sleep grateful that I might find a few hours of peace, and yet I wake up before dawn to rush to the computer hoping that I'll find an e-mail from him: 'I made a terrible mistake. I want you back in my life.'

Not long ago I was interviewed by a gay magazine in Boston about the allure of physical beauty. In the next issue a disgusted reader wrote in to deplore that I, a sort of gay 'leader,' had lived so long and learned so little. Was I still mooning over mere physical beauty and scheming to get laid with cute boys? Had I obtained no inner serenity? Had I acquired no elder-statesmanlike dignity? Wasn't it just a bit repellant that I took no pride in my accomplishments and could find no solace in my wisdom? Was I, in fact, wise? Or was I only one more shallow hedonist, one more unhappy old queen?

I was obsessed by sex in my twenties, but it was invariably mixed up with love. I'd sit on the bus and look at the man across the aisle from me and wonder if I could be happy for the rest of my life with him. I'd imagine exchanging vows with him – the idea of true love excited me. Marriage got me hard. As I grew older (twenty-five, thirty) I feared that I'd never find a mate with whom to spend the rest of my life. Soon I'd be too old to attract anyone. Even though my own parents were divorced, as were half the couples I knew, nevertheless I believed in the sanctity of the marriage bond.

For me it was like being sealed together in a space capsule and launched into eternity. This prospect thrilled and frightened me. At last a partner and an end to loneliness. But what if he was the wrong choice? And could one bear to be looked at from such close quarters? Yet the idea so excited me that I was a menace to the boys I would court – convincing them to say yes to my proposals would become an obsession and I would be prepared to go down on one knee in public, hire a gondola, pledge undying devotion just to win their hand.

Invariably, I'd fall in love with a pretty boy, a boy younger and more delicate than I. If I should succeed in seducing such a boy, I scarcely knew what to do with him. By nature I was as passive as these boys were supposed to be; if I was lucky the pink-cheeked, full-lipped, flaxen-haired boy would have a sadistic streak; the foolish bride would become the infernal bridegroom. I fell in love with pretty boys, but I was aroused by masculine, demanding men.

I might as well begin at the beginning, which is the present. I'm writing this chapter now because my heart has just been broken by a thirty-three-year-old actor-writer-director named T. I met him two years and two months ago. He'd sent me a fan letter in which he'd added a note, 'You should meet me, I'm cute.' I was slow to respond since I was out of the country for four months; by the time I read his letter it was already several weeks old and he'd given up on me.

He came over one January afternoon and seemed boisterous, very much the young male. He had deep-set, steel-blue eyes, a big, thin-lipped mouth, and a long neck with an Adam's apple that wobbled like a cellist's bunched fingers playing a vibrato. His broad shoulders made him come off as a big man, though when he turned sideways his waist was breathtakingly slender. His eyes were just two gunshots in the snow, his huge nose like a keel lowered into the water, and his mouth was downturned like a shark's. There was something unreadable and tragic in his face, it gave the impression of having been constructed to serve as a disguise. Perhaps he laughed and leapt about and sprawled to inject animation into what was essentially a static mask. He often looked angry. If his thoughts were ever to wander away from the topic at hand, no one could tell since his face in repose emitted few signals.

222

At the same time, through all his words and smiles he was consummately charming. He was a Southerner, from Atlanta, and he'd attended Washington and Lee in Virginia. His city and his university translated, in my mind at least, as masculine and upper-middle-class in a heavy-drinking, sports-loving way. Since my parents were Texans I had a vague respect and sympathy for something I called the South, though Texas, so raw and extravagant, was a long way from patrician Virginia. T was the real thing – a good ole boy with Tidewater manners.

Meeting someone new, especially in the heavily interrogative American fashion, is a bit like fashioning and refashioning a clay figure – thickening something here, lengthening something there, smashing the whole thing flat and starting over again. Soon I'd seen that the patrician element was my addition; his father, I learned, was new rich and anyway not rich-rich but 'comfortable.' I pictured them in a McMansion on an acre and a half, the lawn freshly unrolled like wall-to-wall carpet. He'd grown up in the Pentecostal faith and had been frightened by the old people speaking in tongues every Sunday. American suburban life is perhaps, after all, nothing but a way of passing off its freaky religions as normal – its charismatic Catholics, polygamous Mormons, doctor-phobic Christian Scientists, total-immersion Baptists. These hard-shelled sects soften up in the land-scaped vistas of new, planned communities, or at least there they come across as nothing out of the ordinary.

I wondered if he'd mentioned how cute he was just to get a foot in the door, so he could tell other people he'd met me once, just as one might want to visit Ellis Island once, though it's not of particular interest. But no, I could tell from his conversation that he'd read most of my books, and in the next two years I discovered he was a real reader, always carrying around some new enthu-siasm, the latest fashionable fiction by Chuck Palahniuk or George Saunders. T really liked my work and soon was indignant that reviewers attacked it and that the gym bunnies living around us in Chelsea weren't aware of my existence and read nothing but beach books about dating teenage boys. He was careful to let me know he'd had a lover in his fifties when he was still an undergraduate.

From the very beginning I responded to something aggressive in him. He was trying to impress me, but that was just an oil slick floating over a deep undertow of confidence. I knew that even very masculine men have their doubts and worries, their weak points and shaky enthusiasms, that they think their nose should be straightened and their voices lowered, but T was courting me and he knew it was working. I was wary of filial respect; I didn't want to be respected. If a student said he thought of me as a father, I'd snap back, 'That's funny, I think of you as a father.' What I wanted was what this guy was offering me – eyes sizing me up, greedy, restless eyes, a lean face in need.

He was an out-of-work actor, one of the thousands in New York, maybe a hundred thousand. Most of them, like him, don't belong to the union, Actors' Equity, and like him they do office jobs and take classes from older, non-working actors who've developed almost a psychotherapeutic relationship with their tormented, self-conscious students. All those Indiana boys who sang Curly in *Oklahoma* back in high school were now studying to play blind, hapless Lucky in *Waiting for Godot*. T said he wasn't hungry enough as an actor, by which he meant he couldn't quite push himself into daredevil stunts of unspeakable effrontery while tackling someone who might help him. And yet here he was. He'd read my books and knew I was promiscuous, HIV-positive, passive – 'a whole program,' as the French would say, *tout un programme*. I'd also written a few plays.

Physically I had nothing to offer – I was old, fat, winded, impotent most of the time, hairy and with big breasts and a small dick. I was huge – only five-foot-nine inches but 260 pounds. Jean Genet once looked at Rembrandt's painting of the nude, sagging Jewish wife and said, 'That's me. That's the way I look.' In a suit with combed hair I was sometimes thrown the sop word 'distin-guished,' though I'd had to look at too many movies and taped TV shows of myself to lend much credence to that description, chari-table as it might be. I found my crooked smile, fat cheeks, swooping intonations and roguish side-glances grotesque, though I made other people laugh. I couldn't help mugging. My high, surprisingly young voice dripped with sarcasm and automatically put every other word between inverted commas. Perhaps the sort of people who go to readings and lectures and book signings want to enter into a pact of jovial, cultured complicity with the established elderly man up there on the stage; they want to be the recipient of his winks and giggles.

But my years of living in France had turned me into a realist about myself (the French are very realistic). Fame might be the best aphrodisiac, but I wasn't famous enough to excite anyone except the rare individual. When I was younger and less celebrated I had had more success; youth boosts the appeal of even quite mediocre fame. In any event it's women who are more susceptible to the lure of power and money. Men like youth and beauty; straight men might envy or compete with male success, but gay men seek out trophy boys, not unattractive if well-known older men. Perhaps a young gay man might convince himself I was appealing if he knew he could end up as Mrs. Edmund White, but only one person can fill that post at a time and for the last decade I'd lived in marital harmony with Michael Carroll.

T told me that he had a possessive lover. They didn't have an open relationship. Jake was a sexy rock musician and a New York Jew – a heady combination for a Southern WASP brought up in Atlanta. He said that he was fascinated by Jake and his lesbian sister and her partner, a psychiatrist. He liked their savvy, their humor, their passionate shopping and ever-vigilant standards. He liked the way the two women had bought a country house and fixed it up. He admired their efficiency in locating a donor of sperm of the highest quality to instigate 'their' pregnancy (only one of the two women actually bore a child). T liked the way they'd once greeted a skimpy nouvelle cuisine dish in a three-star Paris restaurant with 'You've gotta be kidding!' He thought their chutzpah and his own embarrassment were exciting, piquant. I knew what he meant.

'Do you think,' I asked, then hesitated, suddenly confused – 'Do you think Jake will be jealous about your coming over here?'

'Oh, he is jealous,' T said, wiping away his smile and leaning back, spreading his legs. 'The minute I told him you'd *finally* answered my letter he said, "You're going to have sex with him, I know it, you're going to become lovers, I'm sure of it."'

I looked back at T as levelly as possible, editing out all my nervous smiles: 'Sounds good to me.'

'Are we alone?' T asked.

'Michael's out for the evening. Didn't you notice his heavy-handed way of saying he was going to the movies and dinner? He wanted to leave us some time alone.'

T stood and walked as slowly toward me as a gunman down the center of the road in a Western. He cocked his chin up toward the ceiling and let his eyes shut halfway in a squint. His gait was relaxed, almost shambling, as if he might suddenly draw in a shootout. His mouth was a compressed line curving downward. There was something crafty and loose-jointed and almost cruel in his whole manner, but it was also a serious cowboy parody. I was excited and pleased. He was an actor (for the occasion so was I), by which I mean we weren't like the usual foolish intellectuals who snicker and talk and talk and get drunk and finally out of sheer exhaustion wobble off to bed, apologizing all the way. No, we were willing to act, to stare at each other, to break down the nearly sacred barriers between young and old, handsome and ugly, a hot man and a quickly cooling much older man.

The club chair I was sitting in was from the 1930s, and it was so deep and dwarfing that I always felt trapped in it, like a child-king. It guarded me with its dowdy arms, and could have been a challenge for T, but he simply pulled me to my feet, then pushed me to my knees, my face going to his crotch like a bucket down a well.

When I was listing all my faults as a potential lover, I forgot to mention one virtue: I'm an experienced cocksucker.

I'd let myself go disgracefully. I was so fat that at the theater or in a coach class airplane section I preferred an aisle seat and if by mischance I was wedged between two people I had to cross my arms over my chest like a pharaoh. I sweated profusely and huffed my way up even a single flight of stairs. At the baths a trick would say to me, 'You're nice. I like a *big* man. Do you mind my saying that? All this is mine!'

I'd submitted to long and painful lyposuction on my torso after which I'd spent a month tightly laced in a black surgical corset that prevented the excess skin from floating free or sagging. I'd seen a nutritional counselor once a week for a year and lost twenty-five pounds (with another twenty to go) by nibbling on carrots I had to carry around in baggies, by eating a can of tuna for breakfast (at that hour it smelled like cat food), by avoiding all bread and desserts. I hadn't drunk alcohol for twenty years; now I gave up fruit and fruit juice as well. When I stopped seeing the counselor I gained back the twenty-five pounds within a month and in another I put on an additional ten. My general practitioner worried about my heart (both my parents had died of heart attacks) and put me on three pills.

I hated buying clothes since soon – in a month! – surely I'd be thin again. And yet I didn't want to appear shabby. For a while I'd let my hair go white but then I began to have the hairdresser color it. I lived in an indelicate balance between a desire to look 'natural' and 'masculine' and a fear of surrendering altogether to extreme old age, which in my mind was synonymous with invisibility. Would I resemble a painted old queen or dumpy old bag? That was my choice.

Not that I was vain. I wanted only to attract other men, not compete with them, and I would have put rings through my eyebrows if that would have done the trick. I'd never liked my looks and it had astonished me when my previous agent told me not long before that thirty years ago she and everyone she knew had lusted after me. I'd never had the slightest notion back then that anyone desired me. I'd seldom felt desirable. I would have had more luck with women, I thought, since they responded to gallantry, humor, devotion, charm, worldliness, success – all the superficial qualities that had been lavished on me. In gay life what went over was a low, reedy voice, a powerful chest, a stiff dick and big balls and a smooth butt – everything that T had, as I was now discovering.

He was exactly the man I'd always wanted to have in my arms, and my admiration for him was not eccentric. Once we had lunch in Chelsea with my ex-lover Keith McDermott; Keith was on the phone soon afterwards asking me, 'Who's that guy? What a find! Gosh, he's so sexy and smart and charming and he seems fascinated by you. How do you do it?'

'He's a fan,' I said coolly, as if such a label dismissed T's interest in me, whereas in truth I knew that his admiration of my work testified to his intelligence and constituted my good fortune.

We started to see each other all the time. He'd be out jogging in the spring rain and he'd ring my bell and come up and fling himself, drenched and mud-spattered, across my bed. I'd kneel on the floor between his legs, which were dangling over the edge of the mattress, and I'd pull his gym shorts down and inhale the smell of his jockstrap, which was visibly swelling. In an instant the head of his dick would be poking up stickily over the elastic waistband. When I'd peel down the jock and release it, it would be hard as wood and smell at once sweet like sperm and bitter like urine. My temptation was to forgo undressing myself altogether and not even to touch my own cock. I just wanted to serve his, which had become the center of my world for the instant, to work for his climax and to lick it down like a greedy cat. Sometimes I felt sex – our sex – had little to do with pleasure and was a merely symbolic transaction, another notch on my belt, another performance in the long run he was racking up. Later we relaxed more, took our time, beguiled the hour, but in the beginning perhaps we were too anxious. I wanted to make sure it happened. I was worried that this much younger man would become irritated by my prolonged milking and would push me aside as someone sleeping might wave off a mosquito. I suppose I want to say the simple fact of our being together felt like a miraculous act of generosity on T's part. I was always grateful. Gratitude is my main erotic emotion, one that goes well with abjection.

I can imagine some of my friends reading this and muttering, 'T M I – Too Much Information,' or 'Are we to be spared nothing? Must we have every detail about these tiresome senile shenanigans?' What I am trying to demonstrate is that I had gone beyond the limits imposed on any self-respecting person because, precisely, I did not respect myself. I was content to worship at this living shrine, to probe his tender, lordly balls with my tongue, to plunge the full length of his cock down the scabbard of my throat, to brush my fingers lightly through the blond crotch hair, which was nearly invisible in the afternoon light, or to dare to crawl up beside him and lick out the sour salt taste from under his powerful arms. Sometimes when he was lying flat on his back he would crook his neck up to see what was happening to him only as he approached his painful, wracking climax; at that moment his glans would become so sensitive that he pushed me aside and jerked himself off, though a second later he would feed me the spunk off the warm side of his forefinger. When I picked up a bit of confidence I would end up by lying below him on the carpet; he'd stand and I would look up the length of his body. I'd jerk off and he'd shake the last drops of his cum onto me. I knew that now that he'd come he was already bored by the whole thing, but he would generously frown in concentration as he looked down at me. I seldom forgot that he was looking at a fat elderly man, but in the glow of his athleticism I sometimes felt like his partner, not just his slave.

That first year he had the usual young gay man's gym-built body with big biceps and strong shoulders and swelling chest, though his body was also unusual in some ways. His torso was disproportionately long, his blond skin hairless except for the lightest down, his buttocks weren't tight and tiny and rock-hard like the usual gym rat's. No, they were modest and real and appealingly normal looking, even just a bit soft, ripe melons you might like to weigh in your hands.

I pushed him toward sadism. I doubt if he'd ever been violent with anyone before me, at least not while sober (as a college boy, he'd told me, he'd been drawn into drunken fist fights he could scarcely remember the next morning, but a fight is not a fuck to be sure). I told him I had a kilt fetish and one day when he came over at an appointed time I left Michael's kilt – which I'd bought him but which he'd put on only twice – draped over a dining room chair with a cat-o'-nine-tails beside it. I was in the bedroom, naked and kneeling behind a closed door, curious as to what he'd make of the situation. 'Curious' scarcely gives an idea of my hopes and fears. I could hear the front door, which I'd left ajar, slam shut. Now he was in the apartment and I was feeling a cornered animal's excitement. I could hear the muffled clank of the kilt's metal buckles tap the wood chair. At last he opened my door. He was bare-chested and barefoot, just the kilt around him, the front of it severely tented by his erection. He looked as triumphant as a warrior. His legs appeared hairier than usual and his feet strong and prehensile. He had the splayed whip in his hand. His face had been copied in white steel, all the mitigating laugh lines and world-weariness whited out in this new, simpler mask. Of course he'd known what to do! He was an artist, not some middle-class twerp who wanted to be normal, and as an actor he was slipping into this surprise role, as if the new and under-rehearsed understudy had suddenly been forced to go on in a starring role as the villain. He'd never whipped anyone, nor had I ever been beat; I worried vaguely that he'd draw blood or leave marks, but that apprehension relaxed and suddenly I longed to wear his marks. Later I'd say to him, 'I want to tattoo your name across my ass.' I should have done it.

Though T complained of Jake now, when they'd first met they had something that looked like a Sanskrit bar code tattooed just below the navel in dark blue signs. They had matching tattoos. When I sucked T I stared into this symbol of another love but it didn't make me feel jealous. I refused to be jealous. One day I noticed T's pubic hair had been trimmed short. 'Yeah, Jake likes to do that,' T said, with a fond smile. I knew that gay guys often cut back their bush in order to make their cocks look bigger. I didn't like the practice – it seemed whorey, like a heart-shaped pussy patch.

I oscillated rapidly between mentally rebelling against the surprisingly sharp pain and welcoming the domination. A lanyard suddenly shot up between my buttocks and struck my balls. I yelped and cupped myself in defense, but T didn't stop. As he was flogging me I looked up and his face was red with anger and his jaw protruding. My instinct was to whimper and accept whatever he dealt out, but I learned I could provoke him to new heights of fury if I pretended to resist. All the while I would plant new ideas in his head. 'Please, don't hurt me. Don't make me suck your dick. Please, please don't put those handcuffs on me.' Resisting wasn't something I fell into naturally; all my fantasies were of surrender. T was usually tight-lipped, though he was always game for any action. Perhaps the ludicrous aspect of S&M sex embarrassed him. Perhaps language made him feel uncomfortably accountable.

I was more aware than anyone how ridiculous sadomasochism was. I joked about it all the time – it was obviously a last effort of the old to look sexy. On my street I could see paunchy graybeards in leather creaking stiffly off to the S&M bars. I subscribed to a website called slaves4masters.com on which lonely pudgy middle-aged men in remote towns in Kansas advertised for slaves who were seeking pain and torture; the masters looked like Rotarians. For me, illogically, being suburban was a fatal flaw in a master. On my first day listed on the site a medical worker in Cleveland ordered me to relocate there and live in a cage the rest of my life. When I thought, 'But I must finish my semester at Princeton, then there's Rome in June and Provence in July,' I failed to reply, and he wrote, 'You should be grateful for my offer at your age. You're old and overweight – no other master would have you. You will obey me, boy. Now!' He was forty-one.

The same day a twenty-nine-year-old Latvian offered to relocate me to Amsterdam where he'd turn me into a dog. I'd eat biscuits from a bowl at his feet and have a dog tail permanently attached some five inches into my asshole. That sounded tempting but I thought, 'What if I no longer want to wake up one morning and find myself sleeping on the floor at the foot of his bed? Eat canned dog meat? If I no longer want to be trained?' And then I thought, 'These men are serious. They'd flog someone into unconsciousness or break bones. T and I are just amateurs, thank God.'

My best friend, Marie-Claude, sent me the hit book of the French season, *The Notebooks of a Submissive Woman in the Provinces* (*Carnets d'une Soumise de Province*), which I described to another friend as 'the sort of book in which a bored housewife in a restaurant over Sunday dinner whispers, "Master, may I go pee?" and her husband roars, "No!"' Ridiculous. Old-fashioned. Born out of the tedium of malls and developments.

One day T and I were having lunch at the diner around the corner and I kept giving him my glass of water to drink after he'd emptied his. 'Did you ever think of pissing on someone?' I asked.

He smiled as an actor might if asked whether he knows how to fence. 'I've never done it. I might be piss-shy.' But when we got back to my place he said, 'Get into the tub' and I undressed and headed into the bathroom as he slapped my ass with teammate impatience. I knelt under a single ceiling spot as he stood beside the tub, still dressed but his cock out, swelling but not too stiff to keep him from urinating, and, though I wanted to beg for it, I kept quiet so as not to break his concentration. When he hesitated I turned on the water thinking the sound might help, but in fact it was probably just my looking away that released the hot, clear stream. He pissed all over me, and when I turned my face to feel it on my cheek he said, 'In your mouth. Take it all in your mouth. Swallow it.' He said it in a confidential tone, like a father saying, 'This is for your own good.'

Once he came over with a full bladder but both bathrooms were occupied so I led him into the little study and drank every drop with his penis in my mouth. He said he couldn't feel anything, which he regretted, though he admired my competence. As I swallowed and swallowed I kept my eyes trained on his, as though I were drinking directly from his soul.

I loved the look of his penis, heavy, drooping. I never wanted to anthropomorphize it or turn it into a one-eyed puppet or little fellow or fondle it idly. In this regard I truly was an idolater who looked with respect at its ancient repose on its sac like a water god splayed on a shaded rock. Or I bowed before its erectness, as if it were a numinous presence separate from me and from T.

We often had lunch at that neighborhood diner, sometimes before sex and sometimes afterwards. The diner was managed by a short, dark Mexican poet with bad skin and big, searching eyes. He always wore impeccably white dress shirts and he was powerfully drawn to T. One Sunday afternoon T went for a long walk with him beside the Hudson and Miguel said to him with sudden conviction, 'I hope to have T in my life for a long time.' T was struck by the ardor and intrigued: 'He's kinda hot, right?' he asked me, frowning and smiling at the same time, as if about to taste a new flavor of ice cream that sounds bad ('*fleur de tabac*') but everyone says is good.

I took a complicated pleasure in the way he could find something sexy in even the most unlikely men. I introduced him to someone close to seventy, portly and flush-faced; T said, 'I could fuck his butt. He's got a nice butt, doesn't he?'

T asked me not to send him dirty e-mails because he was afraid Jake would open his computer under the guise of having left his own behind at the office. Now I wonder if my obsessiveness was already wearing him out. Did he really want to waste time responding to my long-winded toilet fantasies? Once I was itching myself raw with horniness in London and I e-mailed him a long fantasy. I didn't notice that I'd pushed 'reply' and sent it to the law firm where he was proofreading at night. 'Not for the faint-hearted,' he wrote back sourly. Three times I got him to shit while I knelt beside him. He'd use the slave collar I'd just bought at the corner leather store to pull my mouth down onto his rock-hard dick while a rich, barnyard stink rose up around us. The first time he said, 'That was strangely intimate,' and I knew he was glad I'd pushed him that far (but no farther). That first time his climax had been especially powerful. I was always edging us toward the repulsive, where he met me halfway, but he didn't want to linger in those disturbing precincts and he started to steer me away from my excesses. Not that I had masturbated thinking about such things; it just marked another extreme I wanted to reach with him. I could imagine the captain of the baseball team seriously daring his best buddy to break another taboo ('Dude, I'm not pulling your chain. You'll see. It will be sweet').

One time I pretended that my newest mania was that I wanted to see him getting fucked by a piggy, balding, big-dicked hustler I'd hired once before. T said yes but a bit dubiously, almost as if he feared I'd lose respect for him if I witnessed him bottoming for another man. I didn't think it out, or not too clearly. Even when left vague, however, S&M is highly cerebral. Sometimes when I was kneeling before T he'd twist my head about and fuck my ears or nostrils or closed eyes before finding his way back into my mouth, as if he were looking for as many ways as possible into my head. We didn't discuss it; sex, like music, is its own language and parallels ordinary words but doesn't replicate them.

I'd invented the incident with the hustler because I was afraid of boring T, this nervous young man of mine. But once the hustler was fucking T, I nearly swooned from the beauty of T's blond, powerful but boyish legs being levered open by the hustler's hands and pushed back and down by the hustler's thick chest, weighting him.

What I hadn't anticipated was a varsity team nod from T to the hustler, almost as if they were the fairly normal, slightly inexperienced paid performers in a scenario dreamed up by the tubby sicko over there. Not that there was any hostility toward me. No, just a straight-arrow glance of friendly recognition offered by one of them to the other, captains of rival teams who at half-time nod to each other. T couldn't keep an erection and the guy was hurting him; we all called it a day and smiled and got dressed. No one had come. T looked at me and shook his head and said, 'You're amazing.'

If I was able to dramatize my abjection during sex, afterwards T and I were just buddies. I was always quick to laugh at his jokes and praise his ideas and T, who knew my books, said I was a bit like the narrator in *A Boy's Own Story* endlessly humoring Tommy. Bingo, I said. Of course in real life as an adolescent I'd been in love with Steve Turner, the model for Tommy, and I had indeed worked to be the best friend in the world to him, so T's comparison took my breath away. Later, T wrote a play and I thought I saw bits of myself in the hero's artistic woman friend who disguises her lust for him as a creative partnership in art.

As T wrote his play I urged him on. He'd always written back in college, stories and essays, and now I told him he shouldn't be like every other actor, passively waiting for a director to choose him for a voiceover. The word 'passive' irritated him. Soon he was reading his play to me in bits and pieces. I would fiddle with a word here or there.

His play was about a young man from the provinces who comes to New York in search of success as an actor. He lives with a young male shrink who wants to marry him and adopt a child. But the actor pushes him away. When the actor leaves him the shrink asks, 'Why were we ever together?' And the actor answers, 'I fucked you and you paid the rent.' Eventually the actor rejects everyone, family members and friends alike, and ends up alone and miserable.

Soon after we met I started to pay T a hundred fifty dollars every time we had sex. I said to him that I was used to hiring hustlers and he might as well be in on the game. Besides, you think it's fun to be paid for your body, right? Did you ever get paid before? No? Doesn't it make you feel sexy?

To take the hint of shame out of it I dramatized it. He'd lie on his back and I'd place the money on his hairless, smooth stomach while I knelt between his knees. He was good, very good – he counted the money, bill by bill, and muttered, 'Goddam faggot, you like paying for this hot jock dick.' We lived in this low-level world of industrialized porn dialogue, but we were always refining it. I was the bespectacled, nerdy high school math teacher; T was the greaser who kept flunking and Teach was always lurking around the station where T pumped gas. One day T burst into the filthy, shit-streaked, fly-buzzing toilet and started fucking Teach's face. Now he was getting A's and money.

I knew he needed the money. He worked one office temp job after another, but they paid poorly and Jake expected him to cover his expenses and pay almost his half of the rent. The one time T held down a salaried full-time job Jake was enthusiastic, but T hated the feeling he was being absorbed into the middle-class working world and quit after two months. Jake was furious, for hadn't he relegated his own 'art' to an occasional gig in an East Village venue, the seventh in a program of nine rock bands? 'Do you seriously think you're going to make money as an actor?' Jake asked.

For a while T considered entering law school. When he ran into a prosperous classmate and fraternity brother from Washington and Lee in a Burberry coat with his lovely wife in pearls and three children in little camel's hair coats, T felt shabby in his jeans and old flight jacket. 'I don't have to practice law,' T said to me. 'It's just a good fail-safe.' I didn't know what to say. If I endorsed the idea of law school I'd be casting doubts on his future as an artist and siding with his parents and Jake. But if I came out against law school I might be responsible for what he could become at forty or fifty – an eternal office temp. I said I didn't have an opinion. It did seem to me a shame for him to waste his best years in law school when he should be devoting them – to what? To letting the camera make love to his face, his big nose and throbbing Adam's apple.

Once T said, 'Of course I'd probably have sex with you even if you'd never started paying me.' I registered that *probably*. Once he said, 'I earned only twenty-four thousand dollars last year – I wonder how I get along.' I'd paid him twelve thousand dollars, I figured, over the previous year – the equivalent to another twenty thousand dollars before taxes. Of course he wasn't counting. He didn't give a fuck about money.

No one ever knew that I paid him, for though I loved to say shocking things, my usual desire to scandalize now was out-weighed by my pride in his apparent desire for me. Of course I knew people must be saying he was star fucking or exercising his power over a foolish old man. My only fear was that I wasn't a big enough star to hold his interest for long. As Michael, who was thirty-seven, said of T, who was thirty, 'Guys his age don't like to do the same thing for long. One day they wake up and change their minds for no good reason. Whereas a man your age wants some-thing good just to go on and on.'

One day that first spring Jake accused T of sleeping with me. T denied it – and then felt guilty about lying and did in fact stop. This hiatus made me panic, but I thought he'd drift back to me. Anyway I had other men I was having sex with.

T and I were (this sounds crazy but it's true) brothers, equals. He worked nights, so we were seldom free to go to the movies or the theater, which Jake would have opposed in any event. But after his gym class and on days when he didn't have an acting class we would linger over lunch in the corner diner, our laughter and talk jealously witnessed by the romantic Mexican poet. Michael went out of town to a wedding and I cooked a steak lunch for T – and before you knew it the no-sex resolve had melted away and he had me kneeling under the table sucking his dick, the full side panel of the tablecloth cutting off my view of his upper body. He was fully clothed and only his fly was open. For once T was into verbal games; he pretended he was talking to an imaginary business partner over lunch while I sucked him off, silently and secretly.

We never looked at porno films because we were the stars of our own fantasy. Once I switched on a DVD but it was a distraction and, for T, competition. The oiled bodies and huge organs, the wooden acting and unconvincing dialogue, the macho grunts and lisped lapses, the weird half-closed lids in feigned ecstasy, the dubbed groans that weren't quite synched with the lip motions, the glistening transparent condom that magically appeared in place between shots, the meth-driven passion that suddenly lent an unexpected wildness to a lackluster orgy – nothing in these films could compete with T's loping walk and subdued, elegant cockiness.

People sometimes stopped him on the street, insisting he was one movie star or another; when T would laugh and deny it, the skeptical fan would say, 'Come on, you're him, I know it.' The fan would end up saying a bit mockingly, 'Well, *sorry* to invade your *privacy*,' as if such an infringement were the only explanation of T's denial and a reprehensible lapse in the duties of a star to his fans.

That we had such an intense sex life was a tribute to T's ingenuity and energy – he was sexual enough for both of us. When people are asked on TV dating shows if they're good at sex they sometimes say, 'It all depends on my partner,' but I'm not sure that's a good sign. That probably means the partner carries the whole burden, provides all of the thrust, and the other person's participation amounts to little more than nerveless receptivity.

Because I am HIV-positive we were always safe – except no one seems sure what that means. No matter: If being penetrated anally without a condom was the most dangerous activity and being sucked the safest, then we were entirely safe. I never fucked him and most of the time I sucked him – and he never reciprocated. I think the only position T feared with me was being rimmed, though he never said so. Or maybe having his legs in the air didn't fit in with his image of himself.

If he ever called himself my master, he laughed or at least smiled and placed the word between quotation marks. We were friends who played at domination and submission. He respected me as a writer but not so much that it put any distance between us. Anyway, it was no big deal; most of the people he knew had never heard of me. His respect was balanced by his 'professional contempt' as a hired sadist. I was always trying to get him to mock me, but he never obliged. Once he did say, 'Did you come? Oh, whatever you're doing down there with that thing.'

Now that he's broken my heart the banal thing my friends, even those who are officially sympathetic, can't resist saying is: 'It's a little strange for a masochist to complain when a sadist hurts him.' But that shows a total misunderstanding; I agreed to be whipped but only as a boost to pleasure, just as I wanted to be humiliated if a sexy young man was making fun of what I most despised about myself – and was using his contempt to get a harder dick, a stronger climax.

And anyway, something else entirely was happening. We'd laid our bodies and souls bare to each other so many times, week after week, that each time the needle tracked the spinning groove it dug it deeper. Or maybe that was happening only to me, not to him. When I told him recently how unhappy he'd made me by breaking up with me he said, 'Breaking up? But that makes it sound like we were lovers. I'm confused. I thought we were friends who occasionally had sex, whereas you make it sound . . .' He didn't need to finish his cruel sentence.

Sometimes I wondered, even during the palmiest days, if I was making a mistake to have so much sex with him, so much violent sex, and accompany it with so little affection. Did the money I paid him and our unloving love fill him with real contempt for me? In my thirties I'd had a slave, and only during an acid trip in Key West did I recognize that I really did despise him – and I stopped seeing him.

Did T sometimes despise me?

Or did my mistake have nothing to do with S&M? Perhaps my real error was that I indulged in so much intense, sweaty sensuality without channeling it through any social forms, even the meager ones gay life provides. Our affair existed in no one else's eyes, we pledged no vows from a book, nor before our friends. I can just hear T exclaiming angrily, 'What is this bullshit! Affair! I never signed on for anything with this guy beyond a simple friendship which now is beginning to sound neither friendly nor simple.' T is someone who became gay because he hates female culture – all the tears and pledges, showers and candlelit dinners. In the past gay men were always hostile to marriage except the very few who wanted to be women; now they're all for it – except T.

And me? Yesterday I read about myself in a new book called *The Violet Hour* by David Bergman: 'White's way of avoiding the humiliation of falling prey to the domestic banality of marriage is to elevate love into some version of Courtly Love with its neoplatonic Christian metaphysics, a love that demands failure and pain as its keenest evidence of sincerity.' By that token my love for T must be the most sincere act of my life.

I was finally introduced to Jake who may have been a rock performer but who was very polite and affable, if in such constant motion he almost seemed to be an optical illusion, a blur where wings must have been beating impossibly fast. He cooked the first barbecue of the spring for T's thirty-first birthday and treated me with a certain deference and a lot of friendliness. He appeared to like cooking since it kept him in motion and in no need to converse for long. He could pop in with a wisecrack or an exclamation but he wasn't subjected to a sustained dialogue. When other people spoke he nodded his head cautiously and then only after a brief freeze frame. He was slight and wiry with a cleaned-up Brooklyn accent and something adenoidal reminiscent of Jerry Lewis – but muted, polite, played down. T complained he was too thin; what must he think of my imposing girth, I wondered.

I suppose I should have felt guilty in Jake's presence, but I didn't. I rationalized my indifference by saying I had known T long before I met Jake. I hadn't met them as a couple. I owed them nothing as a pair. But the truth was more elemental: T was such an event in my life, such a benediction, that I would have stolen him from my best friend. If the stakes are high enough any crime can be justified.

Jake remained jealous. He asked to read something I'd written and T gave him *A Boy's Own Story*. He read only the first chapter then tossed it aside, announcing, 'I'm sure you're sleeping with him!'

T said, 'Jake, that doesn't make sense. You just read a sex scene that happened when he was sixteen, he wrote it twenty years—'

'I don't care,' Jake shouted, more pleased with himself for his discovery than angered by my putative betrayal. 'I know I'm right. It doesn't make sense but I'm a hundred percent sure.'

Once when I spent some time with them T said to me in an aside, 'I build up the funny old professor side of you so he won't get jealous.' I smiled but until then I hadn't known I had a funny old professor side. I was terribly wounded.

In some Polynesian tribes young men will make love even to quite old women but they do so in a special position, both partners kneeling and joined at the crotch by their genitals but leaning radically away, their faces turned back to look up at the sky and their weight balanced on their hands, almost as if they were about to do backflips in opposite directions. I sometimes thought that our sex was like that: charitable and athletic and demanding only a minimum of contact. We seldom touched. I kissed him on both cheeks when he arrived or left but he must have excused that as some French affectation. Of course I touched his penis with my lips but we never held each other or caressed each other. Toward the end I gave him a few nude massages and I even said, 'This is great for me since the slave gets so few chances to touch his master.' He smiled sleepily. The best massage – and one of my happiest moments – occurred on a cold night when I built a fire and spread out a towel on the floor. I knelt between his legs as he lay naked on his stomach. I rubbed his shoulders and arms and back and buttocks and legs and feet and buttocks and shoulders and buttocks. The traveling orange and yellow firelight reflected off his oiled body, cleaned it with little sandy licks of warmth. I had total access to this superb animal, his high arched feet and uncalloused toes, his full, packed calves and long, cantilevered thighs, the mounded hips and narrow waist flaring up into the triangle of muscle suspended from the wide kite bar of his shoulders. There wasn't a single imperfection anywhere except a dark, yellow-black bruise on the inside of his forearm, a karate accident.

He'd given up the gym one year into my knowing him and started karate classes. Whereas the gym was by now a gay institution, almost all of the young men learning karate appeared to be straight, working-class guys from Brooklyn or Queens. T liked that world; it made him feel tough. Sometimes after a class he was unbearably aggressive. His voice, always loud, would clean out my sinuses, entering every last cranny of my head and resonating there. He had a teenage way of sprawling and going inert only to wake up a second later and spring into hectic action.

Karate gave him a new body. The smooth bubble biceps and shoulders and pecs earned through weightlifting thinned down and became striated with muscle. He no longer had a ridged, chocolate-bar stomach but rather long, lean muscles that ran up his stomach like thin barrel staves. His legs were now as supple as his arms and much stronger. He'd always had a bounce to his walk and a wary if reposeful way of scanning the horizon, his head turning and fixing, then re-achieving its balance at the end of his long neck. Now he'd added a fractional, panther-like crouch to his way of standing and walking. When I massaged him I felt like a child who wanders into the intricate works of the town hall clock – here something was whirring, though it would strike only in five more minutes. There a spring was released and another was coiling. The Princess was edging forward and the Moors had already raised their hammers to pound the gong.

One day after sex while we were both still naked and panting he told me to stand and he started showing me some karate moves he'd just learned. My body was big and unmanageable but I got the idea and our second of sparring was sexier than anything that had preceded it. I was the crazy professor reduced to crowing for my blue angel, but I was also a thick Roman boxer learning a move from a slender Greek youth.

He lived an indoor life, rushing from acting class to office job to karate to late-night drinking bouts with friends, and he had marble-white skin, long pale arms, a face carved out of ivory, only the top of his chest and his neck up to his Adam's apple glowing pink, like Galatea slowly turning human.

I incorporated T's loud voice into the character of Timothy McVeigh in the play I was writing for him. One day I'd said, 'Remember, you're my master and you can order me to do anything. You can tell me to write a play for you, for instance, but you must give me the theme.'

He smiled at this whimsical scepter I'd placed in his long, fine-boned hands. A few days later he said, 'Timothy McVeigh. I want you to write about Timothy McVeigh.'

I thought, McVeigh and Vidal! I could write my version of the elderly Europeanized man and the brainy, uneducated young killer. Wasn't their relationship a bit like T's and mine? The bored older man battening off the sap of this randy young guy? Of course there were differences. Vidal was rich and famous and McVeigh was a fanatic and probably a virgin. Vidal would never have mooned over anyone, especially a piece of skinny Upstate New York trade, as he eventually put it to me, objecting mildly to my portrayal; of course, what I'd ascribed to Vidal was my own lovesickness for T. But I could make other things in their relationship resemble the mechanism driving ours. The older man who doesn't appear abject only because he's so sophisticated and droll and cynical; the catlike young man who isn't frightening only because he defers to the man and courts him. The occasional acts of violence that are carefully limited and staged and almost assigned. The easygoing camaraderie when it's no longer a question of sex.

T and I were so easygoing that we often spoke of our other tricks. I had my regulars, as well as guys I met at the baths, and I'd excite T with my stories (though he was too cool to show it). He was turned on by a short, stocky bottom at his gym and was thrilled when he finally got him. He liked going to a leather bar, the Eagle's Nest, where he'd get drunk and have half-clothed sex in a dark corner; he was even proud when he was thrown out for testing the limits.

One night I went with him to the leather bar and when I came out of my building to join him he looked at me, all dressed in black, and he said, 'You look cute.' He said it almost in surprise and he made the *u* in *cute* somehow into a diphthong – an echo, as I heard it, of some high school, Atlanta pronunciation. It was the only time he ever said anything about my looks.

T was always talking about Tony, who was clearly the best sex he'd ever had and someone he had been drawn to from the very beginning. T spoke to me frankly about this love, since never for a second did he consider me to be anything other than a friend. In her novel *Foreign Affairs* Alison Lurie says that ugly women have a lot more sex than people imagine but they have to listen sympathetically to men's unhappy sagas about their love affairs with beautiful women. I was the ugly confidant. Not that I minded. I was happy with crumbs, golden crumbs that spilled off this full loaf.

I suppose I should also tell the reader that everything else in my life was going so well that I could afford a highly selective humility. I had begun to have a few new real friends in New York after returning to the States five years previously. I liked my job teaching at Princeton. I was in good health – I'd made several mournful television programs in the mid-1980s saying farewell to the world, but it turned out I was asymptomatic and not yet in need of medication.

I had a small but faithful readership, and I had always placed the overall longevity of my talent, such as it was, above the success of any one book. Perhaps I was the last writer to care about posterity; believing that there would be readers in the future had become an act of blind faith. Of course people would always read things (captions, e-mails), but would they want to read long imaginative or confessional works written by writers in the past, even the recent past? I'd been interviewed before an audience by a trendy English critic who was so scornful of Jean Genet's novels that I finally asked him, 'Let me get this straight. Do you think works of art wear out? That one generation can't read the books of an earlier one? That Shakespeare has nothing to tell us now?' 'Yes,' he said, 'that's what I believe.'

Suddenly all the pretensions of 'universal' and 'eternal' art were called into question. I, who'd long since doubted that a 'canon' of white European male books should be read and studied by everyone, was now being asked to frame a more radical question about the relevance of a work by one generation to the next. We still hailed writers for being as original and profound and lasting as Hemingway or Flaubert, but maybe it was an empty rhetorical gesture. Maybe even libraries had a short shelf life.

No matter. I thought you, the reader of the future, the solitary twenty-year-old in Kansas, might be able to hear my voice, scratchy and bleating as it may be, as we can still hear Caruso's. Like Walt Whitman I want to excite at least one young man not yet born; the kid in Singapore or Salt Lake City who gets an erection at the thought of humiliating his teacher.

Whereas I was almost always available in the afternoon or even the morning or very late at night and functioned as a sort of sexual pit stop for T, Tony was more complicated to line up. He had other men in his life, even many men; his shrink had wondered if Tony might not be a sex addict. T would get jealous thinking about those other men. Since T resented Jake's possessiveness I looked for a little smile, but T didn't recognize how inconsistent he was being; he was as childish and moody as a Homeric hero, and as irrational.

I loved cooking for T after sex; even though he was a sensitive, civilized man, there was something so alert about his body, as focused on my movements as a bird dog on a quail, that I enjoyed being the object of so much attention, though it made me clumsy and self-conscious. Was he the man and I the woman? He the son and I the mother? He the macho older brother and I the sissy kid brother, in love with (and afraid of disappointing) my idol, rushing about to bake him brownies? So many gay men want to *be* their lover, who is an idealized reflection, but I wanted to *have*, not to be.

Michael recalls that I said to him in a smug moment, 'If I play my cards right with T I may be able to spin this out to the end of my life.' And when would the end come? The actuarial charts said in ten years, which I knew would speed by given my sluggish metabolic clock (the contrary to how time creeps by for a flutter-hearted child). At this rate, how many more times could I suck T's cock? A thousand? And would he permit such greedy vampirism?

I made him promise he'd piss on my grave.

We went to the Noose, the leather shop around the corner. A stylish red neon noose hung in the window above a leather harness and *cache-sexe* kept closed by padlocks (on a website I'd read about 'enforced chastity'). Inside, everything smelled of leather, and black jackets and chaps and whips hung thickly from the ceiling like sleeping bats. The salesman, a thin, worked-out but worn man my age, said to T, as if it were information important to the fitting, 'Which one of you is the boss?' T said, 'I guess that would be me.' 'I figured,' he said without a smile. Very man-to-man.

T stripped off his T-shirt. We were standing in the back of the shop in an improvised fitting room before a three-way mirror. Just beyond was the workshop, with its leather-working tools and strips of black hide. The fitting room was open on both sides and two husky men, customers, stuck their heads in and gawked, as if T, too, were for sale. It felt like an episode in a dream, arbitrary and drenched with emotion.

T was fitted for a leather harness. The harness consisted of a big steel ring just below his chest and another one between his shoulder blades. Thick leather strips crossed each shoulder and came around to girdle the underside of his pecs; the strips snapped on to the rings fore and aft and held them in place. In front another piece of leather dangled straight down and attached to a steel cock ring – except T didn't let the man fit that one on him. Later he told me he'd had a hard-on the whole time. The salesman and I flanked him, our faces lost in shadow, while he stood directly under a powerful industrial light, as if under investigation, his ribs and his breathing stomach picked out by the overhead brightness. I was slow to pick up on T's excitement as an exhibitionist, but once I noticed the blush across his solar plexus I was delighted that I'd provoked this unforeseen pleasure. I knew that when we got home I'd benefit from it. As we were leaving I caught sight of a leather half-hood attached to a painful-looking bit and guided by reins and I wanted T in boots and spurs to ride me like a horse, urging me on with a crop striking my flanks, my mouth torn by the bit.

'Jesus,' he said once we were out on the street, the harness in an unmarked black bag. 'That was so hot having you guys looking at me like that.'

Would it have been just as hot no matter who was looking on? I decided anyone would have done, but that didn't matter since the observer had happened to be me. That must be the part of him that enjoys acting, I thought.

I bought him a German poster from 1900 of a champion boxer of the time. The boxer's nose had been smashed in but he had the stocky body and barrel chest T liked. It was so expensive I had to pay for it in installments. T told Jake that it was a cheap copy and I was giving it to them as a couple.

I went away for two months during the summer with Michael. Although T liked Michael I could see he envied him – after all, I supported Michael so that he'd be free to write and I dragged him along to Bavaria or Austria or Italy or Greece or Provence in the summers and to Key West in January. T never said so, but I felt I could have had him if I'd moved Michael out and T in, though the long standoff between T and Jake suggested how unsuccessful any attempt to possess T would be. After he'd contemplated Michael's situation he'd console himself by saying, 'I'm sure it's better for me to have to work for everything I get.'

He began to appear every weekend in a curious play, *Birdie's Bachelorette Party*. Troops of short dark-haired secretaries from New Jersey were bused in for a performance with lots of audience participation. I went one night. An actress greeted me on the stairway with studied calm, 'I'm so worried about Birdie, she doesn't know her fiancée is cheating on her.' Nothing makes me feel more awkward than let's pretend with a professional performer.

T was playing one of Birdie's gay friends, a big queen. He was bare-chested and dressed only in a white bikini covered with sequins. He wore pink boots and had sparkle on his eyelids and shoulders. That night he'd been eating garlic and his breath stank in a deliciously offensive way as he clung to me and told me in a high, whiny voice what a good husband he was sure I'd make. I did feel like a suburban retiree with a feather bolster for a stomach. He kept calling me 'doll' and leaning his hot bare body and bad breath in closer and closer before bounding away to greet a new party of giggling secretaries and confiding to them something inscrutable about Birdie and her make-believe dilemmas. He was such a good actor and so weirdly effeminate that his performance felt sacrilegious; how did the priest become the temple prostitute? When he was recast the next week as the macho master of ceremonies his fellow actors couldn't believe that he was the same person. I found this fraudulence exciting, like a child who realizes the veiled, bejeweled creature who comes to kiss him good night is his daytime, hausfrau mother in disguise. In T's case I wondered which role he preferred, or was the question itself naïve? Most of us are authentic through lack of choice; his roles he assumed and discarded like a woman feverishly trying on dresses. Each one he played so well that it seemed the real one. I saw him in one student film play a sort of holy idiot and in another a querulous, violent redneck.

Toward the end of July, after two months in Europe, I was frantic to see him. I called him from France and found out he'd be in Maine when we got back; he and Jake had rented a house near Blue Hill. I said that Michael and I were dying to spend that very week by the sea and we'd take two shares. Michael was so good-natured (he could see how frantic I was) that within twelve hours of flying into JFK from Nice we were airborne again, this time heading for Bangor.

We rented a car and followed the landlord's faxed directions ('Two miles from the second Dunkin' Donuts turn right on 4A'). The house had a pool in back and a vast meadow that curved down to an inlet. T showed me around. In the basement he pointed out a small wooden enclosure and whispered, 'This is where I'm going to tie you up and beat the shit out of you.' In the barn behind a door with peeling paint, he showed me a crude, smelly toilet: 'This is where I'm going to take a shit while you suck me off – you like that, don't you, Piggy?' He was whispering, jabbing me roughly in the ribs, and then he broke into a reckless smile that showed me how glad he was to see me.

One day Jake was going to drive his friends to a flea market since they couldn't manage his stick shift. But then he noticed we had an automatic and sent them off in our car while he prepared an elaborate meal for everyone and even found time to go for a romantic walk in the woods with T. At midnight I'd say I wasn't tired and was going to sit up reading, but T never crept down to join me. Jake was a light sleeper and the stairway and floors creaked. Everyone but Michael would sniff cocaine and talk and talk urgently about nothing, but T and I never had a moment alone. T decided we should all go to a contest of Maine lumberjacks and lumberjills. The line for the outdoor toilet was so long that T and I went into the woods to urinate. We stood beside each other. T whispered, 'I wish I was pissing this load on you,' and his cock grew in his hand. Jake was behind us, just out of earshot. Another night we went to the local fair and we all rode rides and ate cotton candy; when it began to drizzle we hurried home. I wondered if in New York T had ever noticed how inept I was physically and how easily frightened. Here even walking up the bleachers to watch the Jacks and Jills as they raced to saw their way through a tree trunk – even that slight rise, with a gap between levels through which I could see the ground fifteen feet below, panicked me. I crawled my way up, whereas even little children skipped nimbly past. Scrambling along the rocks above the beach and jumping down onto the sand was beyond me. Nor did I want to take T's hand for fear my weight would topple him. He was kind and made polite if untrue noises about how he, too, was subject to bouts of vertigo. He was treating me like a favorite uncle.

He drank too much and clowned around in the pool with an inflatable dinosaur and on land lived in his ugly lumberjack T-shirt and a reversed baseball cap for a local minor league team. He drank Coors and joked around and spoke with a redneck accent. No one could take his eyes off T. He wasn't dominating the conversation. He was just first among equals. And he exuded his panther-like sex appeal; we all wanted his babies. I don't think he worried about my being vexed at our abstinence because he'd warned me that Jake would be jealous and ubiquitous, but he escaped the tension by drinking and talking. Soft gray clouds drifted by, day after day. Pascal says we never live in the present, which is the only time we truly possess. No, we regret the past and long for the future. That week in Maine I was certainly longing to be back in New York. At Blue Hill the circus had only one ring and T was in the middle of it in top hat and with a whip.

That vision of the raw wood enclosure in the basement under metal bands holding up blocks of pink insulation – that cage burned a hole in my imagination. I daydreamed about renting this very house some other time and driving up with nothing but a car full of chains, a bullwhip and T's strong arm.

A few days after we returned to New York Jake left for Tokyo on business. T invited me over to his place the first evening he was alone. When he opened the door the lights were off but I could hear the cats thundering down the metal stairs to the basement. T was wearing nothing but his metal-cupped karate jockstrap and once he'd closed the door he instructed me to get on my knees and to lick around the edges. I'd brought over my slave collar in a paper bag, which he put on me with some difficulty since his hands were clumsy from drink. I found his drunkenness scary and appealing since he wasn't quite himself. He had me strip and then he pulled me down the metal stairs, which were painful on my bare feet. No sooner were we downstairs than he ordered me back up to fetch my own belt, which for a second I couldn't find. I felt stupid (slavery made me stupid); only later did I realize that that was the point. The slave was a fuckup so he could be punished. The boutique website on slaves4masters.com was called 'Stupidboy.com.' There the confused boy, whose judgment was undermined and self-esteem was eroded by servitude, could spend his last dollars on products (a genital cage, a locked-on butt plug, all the plastic wrap necessary for total mummification) which would render him all the more non-functioning in the real world, though more and more useful as a fool in constant need of correction. Because I took so long locating the belt I needed to be whipped with it right away.

The basement level (garden, bedroom, bathroom, TV room) was dank and narrow and smelled of cat piss. T ordered me to kneel on all fours facing the wall. When I heard him rooting around looking for a rubber and lubricant in the stash beside the marriage bed, I glanced back over my shoulder. Furious, he sprang forward and beat my ass with my belt: 'I told you to fuckin' stare at the wall, shithead!' A minute later he'd unrolled the rubber and was slamming his way inside me. He reached around to pinch my nipples. I felt so happy. After it was all over we sprawled naked together and watched a DVD of a beautiful first movie by a young American director. T and I didn't touch or kiss but his body, the body of Mercury the messenger, and my Jovian one sprawled side by side. One of the cats tiptoed into the room and sniffed the used condom, cast aside on the floor. T drank gin from the bottle. It was nearly dawn when I crept home, my skin stinging under my trousers. I've earned my stripes, I thought.

After Christmas T broke up with Jake and within two weeks he found a one-room fifth-floor walkup in Hell's Kitchen at the edge of the theater district. He rented a big Ryder truck, the same size as the one Timothy McVeigh had loaded with fertilizer and turned into a bomb. I helped him move but was alarmed to discover that because of my age or heart or size I was no good on the stairs carrying heavy things. Luckily he had a whole team of young friends including Jake's friends from the house in Maine. They seemed to be abashed, even mournful, over the break-up. The largest objects were a new double bed and the framed poster of the German boxer. I also gave him a lamp and a chair from the fifties. Michael was away in Florida in February and T and I had the apartment to ourselves but our sex wasn't free and dirty and inventive as in the past. It had become heartless and routine, and every other time he'd have trouble maintaining an erection. I blamed myself, but now I realize he had always been the source of all sexual energy and it was he who was losing interest. Although he had broken up with Jake so that he could finally live out his love for Tony, they kept sniffing around each other. On the phone I said to Michael, 'I'm a good enough novelist to know my days are numbered. I was a useful alternative to Jake, but now T is free of him. And when T was doing his dreary office jobs I reminded him he had a life in art, but now his play is going to be produced. No more need of Uncle Ed.' I said that but didn't even half believe it. Didn't he need my dribs and drabs of money now more than ever? And my own play, the one I had written for him, had found a producer who was about to option it; didn't T want to assure his role in it?

T would lie athwart the bed only half undressed and let me feast on him, but I was wary and confused.

Michael came back from Florida and I gave a large party for him. T attended and I introduced him to more than one person who said with a Marx Brothers waggle of the eyebrows and a puff on an imaginary cigar, 'I've heard a lot about *you.*' I could see T visibly darkening.

He and an actor he knew gave a backers' reading of my play for the interested producer. It went well but the next day the producer told me he didn't want T in it. 'Not that he was bad,' the producer said, 'it's just that we need a star. Two stars. It's hard enough to earn out even with stars.'

'I understand,' I said, 'but I wrote the play for T and I won't do it without him.'

A promising young director who'd had one long-running hit invited T and me to see something he was working on. We both liked the direction and discussed it with each other over dinner. This director had received an invitation to submit a project to a prestigious theater festival and he wanted to propose my play with T in it as virtually a co-author. T and I were both enthusiastic.

Over dinner T told me that at last he and Tony had spent the night together and had made love three times. As we stood on the curb after we left the restaurant, I said, 'You probably want to rest up . . .' But T insisted I accompany him back to his apartment. As I lumbered up the five flights I tried to make my step a bit lighter, my breathing less labored.

The apartment smelled of garbage, which I could see spilling out of a damp paper bag. A harsh ceiling light in the hall fell on me; I pictured myself as a jowly man, pale with exhaustion, sagging to his knees on the floor beside the bed. I could tell T's cock was too sensitive to touch after the exploits of the night before; I could still have saved the day by heaving myself up and leaving abruptly, but the inertia of politeness held me there on the floor though I myself felt not the slightest stirring of desire. To make it worse, when I was preparing to leave I fumbled with my wallet and said, 'I only have—'

'You don't have to *pay* me!' T said angrily.

The fatal words marched out of my lips like soldiers over a cliff: 'Maybe you don't want to have sex at all.'

'Yeah, I think we should give it a rest.'

I wasn't sure if stopping was something he'd been thinking about for a while and he'd seized on my words as the first occasion that had come along. Or was he irritated only this evening and I had done everything wrong? He must have seen how dismayed I looked. He said, 'I'm not saying we'll never have sex again.' He pulled me up to his side on the bed and we spooned for a moment. He was behind me and he draped an arm around my waist. It was the only time he ever held me. For the last few weeks we'd been talking about going somewhere – Boston? Washington? – for a weekend. Now he said, 'We should take a train up the Hudson and stay at this place near West Point for a night.'

'Sure,' I said.

Later I realized he had so little idea of suffering from love that he didn't mind provoking it, even in someone he said was his best friend.

As I headed out I said, 'That garbage really stinks. Do you want me to take it down?'

I left brusquely, the comical mess in my hands, but I could see from his lifted eyebrows and unsmiling mouth that my exit didn't register as something matter-of-fact for him but rather as 'sad.' He felt sorry for me.

I couldn't remember what T had just said. In fact for the next two months I cried every day over words I couldn't really remember. I started to write things down in a notebook. Even though all my observations about T were as sacred to me as the dream to Jung, I was never sure what they meant. Nothing really explained the panic and despair that took hold of me. My heart beat so hard and fast that I was afraid it would knock its way through the thoracic cage. I could think of nothing else and if for a moment I did, I'd feel my way back to my unhappiness just as a tongue keeps seeking out a cavity.

There was nothing melancholy or delicious about what I was feeling. As Madame de Staël wrote, 'Whoever can be melancholy, whoever can resign himself to pain, whoever can still take an interest in himself is not unhappy. You must be fed up with yourself and yet feel you're tied to your own being, as if you were two people worn out by each other; you must be incapable of any enjoyment, of any distraction, so that you'll feel just one thing: grief; finally there must be something somber, something that drains away all emotion and leaves behind in the soul a single impression, restless and burning. Suffering is at the heart of every thought, it becomes the sole principle of life and you recognize yourself only in your misery.'

Here are some of my notes and my comments now.

T says we might have sex again – but when? I don't want to have sex if it repulses him or wearies him. I certainly don't want to be in the position of having him politely but firmly tell me no.

Nor can I quite bear the heartless sex we've had in recent weeks.

A childish part of me could wish he'd fail with Tony – but that wouldn't bring him back to me.

Masochism gives the slave something sexy to do with his abjection, but rejection leaves him with nothing but self-hatred.

Here I was still plea bargaining with my suffering, stipulating what kind of sex I'd have and what kind I wouldn't. I thought I still had some cards to play. It hadn't yet sunk in I'd lost the game.

Proof: He came down on a Saturday already drunk on bourbon he'd been sipping all afternoon at home alone. When I went into the bedroom for a moment he came after me, eyes crossed, legs wobbly, spurs clinking. He pissed on me in the tub, then still half-dressed slumped to the floor and asked if I had any good porno. I turned on what was already in the VCR (a feeble film of flabby Swedish teens, its only virtue that there wasn't a condom in sight). T couldn't get it up again. We went off to a late dinner and a midnight play with a big, black-haired actress he used to sleep with and who was still in love with him, though the form her love took was silently watching him and taking note of everything, her huge eyes never blinking. I envied her her inscrutability.

I went to bed happy-bleak, thinking I don't have to go on seeing him forever. I can give it six months and then stop.

A day later:

This morning Michael said T had called twice last night, pleasantly drunk, flirty-weird and looking for me.

A twenty-two-year-old Norwegian snowboarder I'd met online came to stay with me for a week. T kept sniffing around. He asked Michael if I was sleeping with Pål. Michael said he didn't know. I let the cat out of the bag by saying no, I wasn't having sex with the Norwegian. I wasn't strong enough to keep any secrets from T, to play any games with him though I felt he wanted me to.

The next Thursday we had lunch under the gaze of the romantic Mexican. T said that he was sorry he'd confused things by having sex with me that last drunken time. Now I was alarmed – hadn't he'd said we'd hook up 'from time to time'?

T looks tired, third day of hangovers, his jawline sharp, almost dangerously sharp, from weight loss. Twice he tells me about a sexy writer friend of Tony's who admires my work – is this guy being pushed forward as a consolation prize? T tells me he's so happy, it only gets better. And I think, of course these two young but seasoned men, macho with hard hot dicks, of course they love each other and where am I in all this, a sixty-four-year-old man still in a rage for youth, sperm, love, for low, resonant voices?

T seemed to recognize that maybe the lunch hadn't gone well. At least when he sailed past on his bike, wearing his shiny yellow insect-head helmet, he waved and called out, 'Hey, Ed!'

I come home groaning every few steps, or am I mewing? Who wants a loser? Suddenly everything I do seems the wrong thing done in the wrong way. A break would end all this speculation.

I'm afraid of my suffering, afraid it will get worse, even become aggravated like an infection. I'm sort of afraid of going crazy.

In the house I broke down and cried and cried. All my life I'd only been able to cry by telling myself I was indulging in self-pity. That's what I was doing now, pitying myself.

It's this terrible feeling of living in a culture where everyone knows more than I do about love. I'm unrealistic, immature, unreasonable and my feelings (my terrible sadness) aren't even worthy of sympathy.

When I told T how much I was suffering he said, 'I'm rather flattered. I thought I was just one of twelve boys, I thought I was just another hot hard dick – not that there's anything wrong with that.'

'Oh, no,' I burbled, 'you were always much more than that. I love you!' He couldn't find anything to say, since my love was hardly news, and right now it made him feel guilty, though it was also a mild tribute of sorts, and all compliments are welcome to a hero of his own times.

Now I felt under a new constraint. Not to see him again would only confirm his theory that I considered him to be just a hot hard dick. And of course if I said I didn't want to see him again it would mean accepting that he would never love me again, the worst possibility of all.

T's phrase 'hot hard dick' keeps burning a brand into my mind.

There's something dishonest about denying that I liked him 'for sex only.' Of course I liked him for sex – but that word over-simplifies and betrays our thrice-weekly self-invention, the honor he conferred on me by admitting me to his band of young men. Sometimes I think that the whole notion of the wisdom of older men, their better judgment and longer perspective, is just an illusion invented by the old themselves to compensate for their loss of virility. Sex was the most splendid gift T could have given me. I wasn't even required to think every time how blessed I was. He let me take a frequent miracle for granted.

The terrible tiredness. Ten days in and I just want to sleep. I feel wobbly and my muscles ache. I wake up at six in the morning and in my e-mail I find a dirty message from a trick, Tom – which cheers me up.

T's own play had found a producer over Christmas. Now the plans for it were firming up. T was looking for a director, a theater and actors. He said to me, 'With the play and Tony I have a full plate.' Meaning he had no time for me.

Now, looking back on it, I suspect Tony was behind so much of T's cruelty. T was in love and wanted to please Tony; I was easy to sacrifice, especially since T seemed incapable of imagining my pain. 'You've always seemed so jolly and cynical about sex,' he said. Then, mitigating, 'I mean, we were both cynical, it was all a big joke, and why not?' I realized that my 'cynicism' was a cultivated indifference, since I had seen how poorly T responded to Jake's expectations.

At midnight the next day we spoke for a while on the phone about his play and mine. T was sipping bourbon but even so he was a bit guarded.

I realized that this grief over T resembled the mourning after my French lover, Hubert, had died – and then it dawned on me that this was exactly the tenth anniversary of Hubert's death. When he died I'd felt I was a balloon cut free of its moorings, sandbags thrown overboard, and that I was floating higher and higher into unbreathable oxygen, unfiltered sunlight. I felt so alone in Paris. Now my life was full, purposeful, directed: every waking moment was aimed at T. Cesare Pavese, the Italian novelist, said that when you're suffering over love at least you're not bored.

I sent him an e-mail: 'For a long time you and I made each other happy. Now I make you feel guilty and you make me miserable. I think we should stop seeing each other for a while.' He wrote back within the hour, 'I will miss you.' I'd hoped he'd argue with me or say something complex and considered, but he didn't.

Then I entered a terrible week. I woke up all through the night and rushed to the computer at four, at six, and looked for a message from him, but there was only silence.

I began a frantic period of cruising online. Suddenly I was drumming up relationships with an unknown eighteen-year-old soldier in Georgia, with a forty-five-year-old poet in Indianapolis, with a red-haired bear in Mobile whom I once met at a reading in Atlanta. I went back and forth from one site to another, sending hundreds of messages and occasionally receiving one ('Too old' or an automated brush-off: 'The person you contacted wishes you luck in your search but feels your profiles do not match.').

I was desperate to find a replacement for T. I thought of asking my literary friends if they might not have the spare acolyte. I considered going to the Town House, a coat-and-tie bar for old men and their young admirers (or well-dressed hookers), but any actual (as opposed to virtual) encounter required more self-confidence than I could muster. Nor did I want to hook up with a pale, pointy-featured intellectual who over-articulated. T was the only real athlete in our crowd, the only bad boy we knew, dunking our braids in the inkwell.

No, I preferred clicking on the computer and tapping out obscene messages, an old man with a belly hanging in the sling of his T-shirt, sitting for hours and hours in his underpants, bare feet getting cold from the air sluicing in through the badly insulated window. I would sit there until my left leg would fall asleep and I would have to hold it in my hands like a dead animal in order to walk it to the bathroom to pee. I left the light off so I wouldn't have to see myself in the mirror. And yet I went right back to judging the photos of young men on my screen. His legs are chicken thin. Is that a hint of blubber at the waist? Oh-oh, he's only five-foot-four: 'Dear Sir, I would like to be a slave to a young, small master.' I wrote, 'Have you ever been drawn to this role?'

Hours and hours would go by before the screen. When I was a teenager I kept imagining that in my fifties or sixties I'd be calm, my yearnings shed, my eyes trained on release from the pain of living. And yet here I was, sending messages in electronic bottles.

It did seem so unfair to me that we could have had sex a hundred eighty times together over twenty-six months and then one fine day he could decide unilaterally, almost as a whim, that it was all over. (Did I ever have so much sex with any one man before? Did he?) More than unfair, it seemed weird to me that society would say anyone anywhere was within his rights to pull out suddenly and definitively from a relationship. Of course divorce procedures slow things down a bit, but sometimes it seems everyone who can afford to get divorced does. When I think of all those wives who worked full days, attended soccer matches, took cooking classes, went jogging at dawn – and then got dropped at fifty for a thirty-year-old with less beauty and no accomplishments. The husband looks sheepish, but he's been coached by his new girlfriend and he knows he's doing the right thing: This way, toward youth, lies life.

Princeton became unbearable. On the Tuesday, my day for running the department, I barricaded myself in my office and drank quarts of San Pellegrino and wept (at least I wouldn't become dehydrated). I told everyone – my colleagues, the office staff, even my thesis students – about T. It felt as if I had some very important news to impart, but everyone looked embarrassed. I'd never mentioned T to them before. I had a partner, Michael, one partner, the way they had a husband or a wife, and they could hardly be expected to worry about some new person. To raise the ante I said, 'This is the worst thing I've ever been through,' and they said, 'It sounds banal, but time will heal everything, though of course that will mean it's really and truly over, which is not what you want to hear now.' A very womanly and sweet poet said, 'Oh, honey, I know what that's like,' and she touched my sleeve, hesitantly, as if a homosexual man might not appreciate being touched by a woman. My best friend at Princeton said, 'I wonder how many hearts you've broken over the years?' and I knew I'd broken many but I could barely remember the names of those men. Another time she said, 'It's as if T had a key and he opened a door and the whole building collapsed. You seem to be having a complete breakdown.' My friends in Paris were worried about me – it was going on too long. I was gratified that everyone was taking me seriously. And it was moving to hear other people say T's name.

Forty times a day I checked my e-mail, but never a word. On the train back from Princeton I wept openly, the tears flowing down my cheeks uncontrollably. I didn't have a tissue to blow my nose. No one noticed. If they would have they might have thought I was a grandfather mourning the death of his old wife, not an antique libertine bewailing the loss of a hot hard dick. Anyway, the heterosexual equivalent (bounder is dropped by showgirl) would have made everyone laugh, me included.

Exactly a week later I thought I couldn't go on. The week had been the moral equivalent of a year. My friends said, 'Don't call him. Just stick it out or you'll have to go through all this again. Surely you don't want him as a friend, do you? He's a nice enough guy, but seeing him arm in arm with Tony, that will be intolerable. Please, please stick to your guns. In another week you'll start to feel better.'

In another week, I thought, I'll be crazy. I sent him the e-mail I'd been expecting from him. Just one word: 'Hey!' Twenty-four hours later and he still hadn't written back. I called him and left a message. An hour later he called back and said wearily, 'Hey, Ed.'

'I missed you.'

'Oh yeah?' he asked with an edge, louder and nastier than he might have intended.

Great, I thought, now he's the injured party.

We had dinner at Joe Allen's, just two blocks from his new apartment. I think that made him nervous ('I could come down to your neighborhood just as easily,' he said) since he must have feared I'd finesse my way up to his room. It was April 12, 2004. He had on my favorite cerulean blue T-shirt. We sat knee to knee at a table beside the bar. The waiter was so solicitous, I could almost say tender, that I felt he knew this was a reconciliation. I told T I'd started seeing a middle-class shrink who was 'sure' T must have felt 'degraded and objectified' by being paid.

T: 'I didn't mind being paid for something I wanted to do, that was hot, earning money like a hustler, but then when I stopped wanting to do it I resented the money.'

T: 'I knew I wanted you to fall in love with me because I wanted to be part of your life. And, admit it, if I hadn't slept with you, you never would have thought about me twice.'

I said I was sorry I was being so neurotic, crying all the time and plaguing him with my neediness.

T: 'Yeah, it's been tough on me. But, yeah, I do have good stuff going for me, I have a new love affair, all that excitement, and my play, yeah – so yeah, it is harder on you, it seems funny that when I broke up with Jake, who was my lover for four and a half years, he barely blinked, whereas with you it's become such a pain in the ass.' I noticed that my love for him had gone from being 'flattering' to 'a pain in the ass.' I wondered if people still fell in love this way, my way. Was it a period piece, my love for T, something akin to Sarah Bernhardt's wooden leg? My students, it seemed, bumped shoulders, wore each other's clothes, slept in the same bed for weeks without having sex until one drunken night it half-happened, then the next morning it took place fully. Then they drifted away, cried a bit, hooked up one more time and it was over. So much better than this art nouveau passion of mine.

T said that he had made the right decision to stop sex between us forever. He said, 'Otherwise you'll go to Rome and think about me and not have a good time. And when we're together there'll be all this tension, will we or won't we, so it's best to say it's over!' He talked with a meat-cleaver assertiveness.

Suddenly I broke the rhythm and touched his hand and I said: 'I feel terrible.' He smiled in confusion, as if I was about to turn another compliment and he didn't quite get it.

Me: 'It's like you're so strong, such a bully, you can just say matter-of-factly, "No, we won't ever have sex again" – you can say that and I nod, then I go home and suffer and why should I suffer all alone? You should hold my hand and go through this with me.'

T said: 'I didn't want to feel I had to go to bed with you just to please you. That's too much like when I was a kid with my mother. I felt that if I didn't please her my whole life would fall apart and I'd lose everything. I don't want to have sex or do anything just to please someone else.'

Me: 'Well, the good thing is how we're talking. We never talked this honestly before, not when we were having sex.'

T: 'Most people your age have stopped feeling things but – this sounds fucked up – but you haven't,' as if he'd given me a gift by making me suffer.

He walked me to the corner but we stood under an awning for a moment out of the rain. He told me how he'd mentioned to Tony that here, on this very corner, a hot little Brazilian had stopped him two nights ago and asked him if he had a lover. I'm seeing someone, T had replied. Ten minutes later Tony had called back to say, 'You should have told him you have a lover. You do. You do have a lover.'

I asked T how that made him feel.

'Scared. Excited.'

In the taxi home I thought, People are scared not just of intimacy but also of being dropped, as well they might be. I woke up at four a.m. crying. There was a car alarm in the street below gabbling to itself, singing harsh scales. I wanted to e-mail him: 'No matter how you figure it I've been demoted from those days when you'd phone and tell me to get my faggot ass up there.'

I asked Michael if he'd realized in the past how much I was falling in love with T, because I hadn't. Michael said, 'Last night I thought it was exactly two years ago you stopped letting me hold you in bed. Maybe already back then you were in love with him.'

The shrink seemed shocked by everything I said. He was especially exercised over the money, though at the end of every session I fetched exactly the same amount out of my wallet and I didn't know if therapy had the same benefits.

The shrink approved when my doctor put me on Paxil. 'You've been so unhappy it's been hard to get much work done. You can't really . . . think.'

I saw him twice a week. One day I heard myself saying, 'It's as if T took me into the Fight Club with the other fellows and now he's pushing me out, toward women, toward the old. I've always had friends who were old but now when I see old people in the street they irritate me.'

One of my friends, who's eighty-seven, said to me: 'You're afraid of growing old.' When I talked about T, my friend said: 'Grow up!'

He was right, of course. There was a time when I would have thought sixty-four was old, but now, out at Princeton I was surrounded by senior faculty members in their seventies and eighties. One of them, a translator and novelist, said, 'If only I were in my sixties again. That was a good age. You'll see: In your seventies everything starts to fall apart.'

It was as if T had kept me suspended in a bubble, immune from the contagion of age, but now I'd been expelled and I was shrinking and withering visibly.

My two months of suffering over T were the most lacerating of my life. He made me feel I'd crossed that terrible line into old age and the feminization of the male body that old age brings. Over a lunch T said that yes, because he had a way of falling for strange and lonely and funny-looking girls, they were devastated by his attention. It sounded like the havoc the football captain might reek if he courted the bookworm, even on a dare, as a joke. He left the analogy hanging in the air, but I sent him an e-mail saying I hated the way he'd compared me to his guilt-inducing mother and to those strange girls, that I wanted back in with the boys. I said, 'You favored me by letting me be one of your boys. No one has ever disliked female culture more than you do. I'm sorry that my great unhappiness has weakened me in your eyes by making me cry and complain. But don't push me away.' He replied solemnly that he'd not intended to make any comparisons between me and those freaky girls, that it was well known all the world wanted to be my friend.

When I saw him after that long, long week of not speaking to him we sat on the couch holding hands and he drank and ate a huge platter of hors d'oeuvres. I was ravenous for his touch, for the sight of him, for his thrilling smile, for his maddeningly loud voice. As Roland Barthes writes: 'On one side, the soft, warm, downy, adorable body, and on the other, the ringing, well-formed, worldly voice – always the voice.'

Nothing gets resolved. Just before I left for Rome T came to dinner. We always referred to sex as 'steak' as in 'I fed him STEAK.' That's what I gave him that last night. He drank his two glasses of champagne and half a bottle of Bordeaux and when I went into the kitchen to fetch the dessert he came after me and held me and I was happy. My old dog T was nuzzling me with his cold nose and warm paws. I said, 'We should be good or else you'll end up telling Tony and he'll forbid you to see me—'

'Yes, we should be good. We don't want to go through all that again,' by which he probably meant my tears and e-mails and his firm delineations of his rights and my boundaries. So we just kissed and said good night at the door.

Stan Redfern

Keith McDermott

Jim Ruddy

My Blonds

As a teenager I was often in love – with my gym teacher, with a blond senior who shared the locker room at the same hour, with a painter at the art academy, with my best friend Steve, with a farmer I met on the train named Orville to whom I dedicated an opera I was composing (it was named *Orville*, too, and dealt with farming and incest and madness – my only Faulknerian work).

I imagined that ardor was enough, that if I felt strongly, then that intensity would inspire a reciprocal passion in anyone I fancied. Only later did I discover that people ranked one another, that what they wanted was not devotion but wealth or beauty or celebrity or social status and that if they themselves had very few of these attractions they would attempt to marry someone just a bit higher than they – and to trade up from there. In the gay world I can remember when I was fifteen I met someone in his thirties, a Texan who owned a bookstore on Rush Street in Chicago, and he asked me what I was looking for in a man.

'Someone rich who will take me away from my parents and support me.'

'But, Doll,' he drawled, 'the rich ones always end up with each other.'

I mentally protested. What about my youth, my pure, hairless body, my near-virginity, what about my love, the beauty and urgency of my feelings? I used to hear older teenage girls argue about who was sexier – Rock Hudson, Farley Granger or Tab Hunter – and these pimply, fat-ass girls with their braces and limp yellow hair would quibble with a sense of absolute privilege over the relative merits of these superb males (all gay, as it turned out). I was no different; since all my choices existed only in the realm of fantasy, I poured all my psychic energy into becoming a connoisseur of masculine desirability rather than doing anything to improve my viability on the open market.

If that was how I approached movie stars, of the real men I occasionally met I required only one thing – that they should want me. A rich man or a blond athlete might compete for me in my dreams but in my waking life anyone could have me if he showed the slightest interest. I slept with pockmarked, shiny-nosed heavy smokers with fetal bodies as pale and glabrous as plucked baby chickens. I slept with a big strapping redhead with an enormous uncircumcised bright red penis head smelling of Canöe, a sweet cinnamon-and-clove cologne popular in those days. I went with a fat black Chicago bus driver to the end of the line and to his apartment where he discarded his uniform and slid into fluffy angora slippers and a ruffled pink robe and put on scratchy records of what people called 'race music.' I slept with a handsome Mexican student from Northwestern whom I met in a lakeside park and within minutes I was in love with him and his penis, so much darker than the rest of his body. I brought him back to our apartment, assuring him that my mother was away until midnight, but as I was caressing his heavily oiled black hair I looked out the bay window and saw Mother, hood up, scuttling unexpectedly through the rain. I panicked and pushed him out the back door – and never saw him again. All that remained was his name, which I enshrined at the end of my first novel, *The Tower Window* (or, alternatively, *Dark Currents*), in which a teenage boy is torn between his love for a girl his age, based on Sally Gunn at high school, and the handsome Mexican. When Sally fails to return the love of 'Peter Cross' he ends up in the arms of Miguel.

After all these crushes, these flashes of sheet lightning crackling through the sky and sizzling down through this rod or that, everything condensed into one single bolt when I fell in love with Stanley Redfern. I was a senior at the University of Michigan. It was January 13, 1962, my twenty-second birthday. A grad student, Bart Wimble, had adapted Rilke's 'text,' *The Notebooks of Malte Laurids Brigge*, for the stage, and Stanley was playing Malte. I had never seen him around the campus. He looked three or four years younger than his twenty-one years. He was just five-foot-seven, solidly built, with a long, lean face of classical John Barrymore beauty. His nose descended in a straight line from his brow, without a bump to indicate the transition. Wasn't it Pascal who said, 'If Cleopatra's nose had been shorter, the whole face of the earth would have changed'?

Stanley was blond, very blond, and his skin glowed with a radiant health that contradicted his melancholy role. The play was static, post-Wagnerian in its preoccupation with death, solitude and love, but I welcomed its noble longueurs since I was so entranced by this blond god onstage with his slightly husky voice and extreme personal remoteness. He looked as if he had been hypnotized into believing he was moving slowly underwater, delighted by every hallucinated fish that brushed past him, leaving a streak of fluorescent glow on his skin that only he could see. He was dressed all in white.

I'd gone to the play with a wry, unhappy medical student from Scotland named Billy, a guy with gentian blue eyes and gold-red hair, to whom I had written a love poem. Within three days I'd copied the poem again and dedicated it this time not to Billy but to Stan. I was efficient in recycling the products of passion. Whereas Billy was quite capable of pushing me away with a sad smile and a firm hand, Stan seemed elusive but vulnerable, confused, ultimately biddable.

But I'm jumping ahead. I was so besotted by Stanley (how I disliked that name then, which seemed to me so common, and how I love it now, forty-two years later) that I invited the entire cast of twenty to the big Victorian pile where I lived with five other students, most of them older. I knew we had some ethyl alcohol from a lab that I could mix with orange juice to make a nearly lethal punch. Everyone in the cast came – except Stanley, who, in his Hamlet way, went off to walk through the arboretum till dawn, meditating on his role and Rilke and his own interesting and tragic isolation.

Our whole catty, gossipy but kind and funny gay group in Ann Arbor seemed thrilled that I was pursuing Stanley. I'd spot Stan in the middle room of the Student Union, which was for kids who were neither Beat (an identity that could be established from their black clothes and green book bags and by the chicks' raccoon eyes) nor Greek (frat boys and sorority girls). We arty types, especially the theater queens, were in the middle room, as if we were the intermediate sex. We were neither scrubbed and perky like the Greeks, nor alienated and uncombed like the Beats. We drank but didn't smoke pot, we had nothing resembling a credo beyond a faith in the permanent avant-garde. We revered Brecht, not Marx; Mayakovski, not Lenin; Lotte Lenya, not La Pasionara; both Ingmar *and* Ingrid Bergman; Elizabeth Taylor the actress *and* Elizabeth Taylor the reserved English novelist. Ten years later and the idea of High Culture would begin to crumble, battered by the American cult of success and the distinction-dissolving ironies of Pop Art. But in the late fifties we still believed in honorable poverty. We still thought that beauty should be difficult, that incomprehension was a first necessary step toward initiation and that time would determine irrefutably which of our current artistic developments had been the one, the only, the inevitable next one.

Stanley had been drawn to the world of art not through any desire to be avant-garde but because the theater queens all made such a fuss over him. Back in East Lansing, Michigan, he'd had no idea how beautiful he was. He'd dated a girl who limped and was caustic, bitter and possessive. He was one of four brothers and the son of well-to-do, socially prominent alcoholics. His father owned a printing press and his mother wrote the gossip column for the local paper. She'd drink her way through a four-martini lunch then pull into her driveway with the entire door on the passenger side scraped off. When her husband, himself tipsy, would shout at her she'd shrug and say, 'Take a Miltown.' She'd stagger inside and, still wearing her hat, dictate her column over the phone ('The R. T. Smiths will be joining their grandchildren in Honolulu for Christmas') before collapsing, fully dressed, on the floor.

His parents were selfish and stingy. Stanley had to work a thirty-hour week at the library shelving books in order to make enough to feed himself. I rather liked this necessity since it meant I knew where he was during long stretches of time. Only later did I discover that he had several admirers pursuing him through the stacks.

I was barely a blip on Stanley's screen that first spring. He slept

266

in a room below ground level but with the window placed high, close to the ceiling. One night I was so tormented by love that, unathletic though I might be, I slid in through the window and sat on Stan's bed and awakened him with reverent smoothing gestures through the sheet. He slept nude and sat up, astonished, his broad shoulders and hairless torso exposed for the first time to my gaze. His dark nipples were as stark as raisin eyes on the face of a gingerbread man. Normally he wore very thick, uncomfortable contact lenses; he'd taken them out, of course, to sleep and couldn't quite see me, but didn't want to put on his unflattering horn-rims. Eventually he figured out who I was.

If he'd been the usual man he would have been irritated by my invasion, but Stanley responded to adoration. He wanted to be courted. He was like a princess who can be won only by a knight passing successfully through a hundred arduous trials. Whereas most men like the hunt, Stanley liked being hunted.

Not that he was easily won. Stan resisted Bart, who'd written Malte for him, and Peter Goldfarb, Stan's glamorous New York roommate, and most of the other gay guys chasing after him. What Stan liked were tall, skinny Italians and Jews with kinky hair and the very glasses he eschewed for himself. He liked serious, self-absorbed guys who either stayed silent, smirking, or lectured everyone seriously. Stan was in love with Dick, a young director from New York who was married to Sherry, a redhead and our best actress. Dick looked permanently tired, his eyes circled, his lips blue and bloodless – until suddenly he lit up with a smile, accompanied by hand gestures as eloquent and simple as those in a Giotto painting. He liked to re-create scenes from plays by Ugo Betti and Brecht.

Dick had a lightly satirical look when we spoke (we were younger and had never read Artaud's *The Theater and Its Double*) and an inspired look when he talked. Stanley fell for him partly because he was so intelligent and partly because he was inaccessible and married. Sherry was a warm, cuddly beauty who wore lots of makeup and, when she was with Stan or other minions of the theater department, she would sleepily rest her head on a shoulder, offering her body with all the innocence of a half-awake child. She worried about her weight but we gay boys, struggling with our new identity and trying to stick to it, found her voluptuousness disturbingly sexy.

That spring of my senior year I had only one project: Stanley, seeing Stan, courting him. Love gives us something to do. It ties our days together, as if a composer had linked all the elements of the score with lightly curving *legato* marks, swooping from note to note like telephone wires. I never quite forgot that I'd first seen Stan onstage and for me he remained a brooding figure all in white. Maybe he wasn't a very good actor, but his slow-paced, deeply internal performance suited my fantasies. He was mesmerized, as if he were slowly fermenting his own essence and getting drunk on it. I didn't want him to be someone else, to impersonate a character; I wanted to immerse myself in him, just him, his ideal essence, just as a tomb sculpture in Renaissance France always shows its subject at an ideal age, thirty-three, and whether the subject died much older or younger, he must be presented as he will appear in his perfect form at the Resurrection.

At the end of Stan's junior year (and my senior year), he moved to New York where he sought a role on the Broadway stage. Like thousands and thousands of good-looking Midwesterners before him he got a part-time job, he had his eight-by-ten glossy photos made and copied, he drew up a résumé listing all his acting experiences ('title role in Michigan premiere, Rilke's *The Notebooks of Malte Laurids Brigge*') and offered to supply recommendations on request (Dick, Sherry). He lost ten pounds in New York and became seraphically gaunt.

I was so in love with Stan – and so traumatized by my first sexually transmitted disease – that on his birthday, July 19, 1962, I flew from Chicago to New York and checked into the West Side Y. I'd been accepted into grad school to study Chinese at Harvard, but I decided to skip that. No, I'd go to New York and try my luck as a journalist; after all, I'd edited the U of M literary magazine. My mother and sister liked to say years later that I flew to New York first-class, but I didn't. I had only two hundred dollars to my name. I sat on Stan's stoop all night long, hoping to give him a birthday kiss, but he never came home. In my fantasy he'd been lonely and broke and homesick. I'd forgotten that beautiful twenty-one-year-olds are seldom alone for long.

Stan had moved in with Ty McConnell, an actor from Michigan, who'd in turn moved in with an older Italian-American actor (he was thirty). The Italian was playing the Boy in *The Fantastiks*; this Off-Broadway musical was so long-running that eventually Ty played the role, too, and so did almost everyone else we knew.

New York in July and August 1962 was dowdy, dirty, hot, nearly empty. I picture newspapers and oily wax paper from pizza slices blowing around in the hot updraft above a subway grate. I can see the grime and grit of Forty-second Street with its tattoo parlors and barny stores selling the gay porn of the day – black-and-white photos of boys in G-strings inside translucent glycine envelopes in slippery stacks. Next door would be a movie theater showing old Westerns to an all-male audience with raincoats on their busy laps. There seemed to be lots of lonely people talking to themselves.

I ran through my two hundred dollars and had to borrow money from Peter Goldfarb, Stan's old roommate. At last I landed a job as a writer trainee at Time-Life Books where I earned four hundred dollars a month. With my first paycheck I rented a three-room apartment on MacDougal between Houston and Bleecker. Stanley had decided not to go back to Ann Arbor. He'd never need a college degree. He was going to be a Broadway actor!

Soon I had convinced him to move in with me. We sublet this tiny railroad apartment from a young woman named Sandy. We slept on Sandy's couch bed, which we pulled out every night, and we ate in the kitchen off Sandy's wooden table. In the third room there was just enough space for a single bed.

Stanley knew how to cook spaghetti and lasagna, which I devoured. For the first time in my life I was fat (though it would be far from the last). At the old Whitney Museum I saw a man in the rest room who I had known a few years earlier in Michigan. He said, 'You've become grotesquely fat, and you're not even thirty yet, are you?'

'I'm twenty-three.'

The action of my fat thighs rubbing together wore right through the fabric of my trousers; I complained about the material. Stanley, of course, didn't gain an ounce. He was highly conscious of his 'instrument' (his body). He was studying acting in the evenings at the Herbert Berghof Studio in the Village. By day he did a series of office temp jobs and brought home thirty-five dollars a week. Eventually I got him a job at Time-Life as a copy boy. The company policy was to pay any educational expenses of an employee and Stanley soon finished his degree at New York University and went on to obtain a master's there in English.

We weren't the least jealous of one another or possessive (but then we had no reason to be). Two men living together was still a new thing in those days – at least we knew only one other couple, composed of a tall, dark, funny actor from the South and his lover, Lanford (Lance) Wilson. Lance was writing plays, one after another, which were put on at the Caffe Cino in the Village. I remember *The Madness of Lady Bright*, about a hysterical drag queen, and *Home Free*, a story of brother-sister incest. Stanley appeared in two or three plays there. Lance came to dinner at our place to eat Stan's lasagna.

Lance was always broke because he was determined to earn his living from his pen. New York was so cheap in those days that an actor could support himself by working as a waiter two or three nights a week. There weren't any expensive clubs or discos to go to and just a few bars. We'd sit in coffee shops and eat Salisbury steak with mashed potatoes or hamburgers. Gay boys spent most of their money on powder-blue cashmere sweaters, which they wore with black pegged pants or wheat jeans. No one we knew went to the gym. The ideal was to be boyish and painfully slim. We had our hair straightened so it would hang limply over one eye in the 'surfer' look. All of this in the bland lull before the storm caused by the arrival of the Beatles.

Stan and I thought of ourselves as bohemians, or 'Plastic Hippies,' since we wore coats and ties to the office and only switched to our jeans at night. When the Beatles landed in America we grew our hair long, tied headache bands around our heads, donned puffy-sleeved pirate shirts and red velvet vests inset with bits of mirror.

Stanley seemed mysterious to me in many ways. He was often depressed – poetically, not clinically. He still got up in the morning and shaved and went to work and acting classes, but sometimes he'd refuse to speak for a day or two. I felt responsible for his moods, his welfare, his happiness, and I took his prolonged melancholy as a reproach. Why wasn't I more upbeat, rich, capable? Why couldn't I rearrange the world to make him happy?

In my senior year at Michigan I had written a play, *The Blueboy in Black*, which won a prize. The prize was announced in the *New York Times*, an agent at William Morris named Sylvia Herscher contacted me – and in May 1963 (or was it 1964?) it was put on Off-Broadway starring Cicely Tyson and Billy Dee Williams. Stan was the Blueboy, a cameo I'd written in for him. When the director said that Stan's role only bogged down the action and should be eliminated, I threatened to pull out of the whole project.

The play opened with Stan in it, dressed as Gainsborough's *Blue Boy*, and once again he played in an intense, mesmerized way. Cicely got rave reviews; the play had a few respectful notices – and closed a month later.

In the meantime Ashley Feinstein, the producer and director, had begun an affair with Stan. In fact Stan had already moved out of our dingy little apartment into a boarding house just off lower Fifth Avenue because he didn't want people in 'the business' (show business) to know that we were lovers. Soon Stan had moved into Ashley's Upper East Side building – and I was frantic. If only I were a better writer. If only my play had been a hit.

I visited Stan and Ashley. Ashley chain-smoked and gossiped about people in the business whom I didn't know. Beads of perspiration stood out on Ashley's handsome face. The apartment appeared luxurious and spacious, though I suppose it was only a one-bedroom, but in a pre-war doorman building and furnished with real, grown-up things – matching couches and chairs that had been sent to the upholsterer, heavy curtains the color of the walls. There were flowering plants and accent pillows and brass floor lamps and slick magazines and 'gourmet' hors d'oeuvres for us to eat – all the things that were beyond my means. Stanley looked scared. There were no signs of affection between him and Ashley; maybe Stan was afraid I'd do something awkward.

I didn't. I nodded and joked. Ashley joked about how he'd lost all his money on my play and, though I knew he couldn't exactly blame me for writing a flop and ruining him, I couldn't help but feel guilty. He said he'd have to get a job washing dishes. It occurred to me he was putting Stan on notice that he couldn't support him. Ashley talked a lot about 'therapy.' For him, he said, ironing his chinos was the best therapy. The ironing board was out. Stanley nodded and said, 'Yes, he irons for hours,' happy that he could gently chide his new lover in front of his old lover. It was summer outside and the room was air-conditioned – another luxury. Ashley's cigarette smoke drifted upwards until it was torn to shreds by the updraft. I'd been smoking so much my fingers were yellow and I coughed for half an hour every morning. My cheap shoes looked like stamped and painted cardboard in the sunlight pouring through the spotless windows.

I suppose we were real bohemians, Stan and I, though we worked in the 'straight' world. We were from well-to-do WASP families, a social identity we'd never thought about until we moved to New York, where we were objects of Jewish curiosity, Puerto Rican envy and, once in a while, black contempt. Ashley teased us for our 'naïveté' and innocence, but what we were guilty of was a profound indifference to materialism. Stan's gossip-column mother was impressed by Michigan social credentials, linked to wealth, and his father worked night and day to maintain their standard of living. My mother looked down on 'materialists' who were short on 'idealism.' My father never stopped working, though more out of an abstract theory of success than from any desire to mix socially with other rich people, whom he avoided. Stan's parents and my father were miserable. They'd subscribed to a system that had failed them. We wanted no part of it. But we were still vulnerable to their standards. One day a month, we could be made to feel shabby.

Ashley made me feel that way now. His family had become millionaires in the garment industry. He associated Stan's and my families with heavy drinking and country clubs to which he and his parents wouldn't be admitted. At the same time Stan and I realized that New York legitimate theater was the private province of a few Jewish families. More than once in a chat with a stranger in New York I'd pretended to be a Jew and watched him or her light up – suddenly I was a Nice Jewish Boy. I had a face that potentially enrolled me in several different ethnic identities; in Paris, Rome or London people from those countries, but not those cities, would ask me in their own language for directions. And Jews were ready to believe I was Jewish, especially when I peppered my conversation with some of the new Yiddish words I was learning.

Ashley had been named after his Uncle Asher, though in his case the name had been adapted to this romantic, *Gone with the Wind* version, which made people smile when it was combined with Feinstein. It was an imperfect transformation, a fossil record of an unfinished metamorphosis.

I felt odd leaving Stanley behind. He, too, looked shabby in his badly ironed white shirt and black trousers. Ashley wore spectator shoes and a short-sleeved navy blue knit shirt molded to his powerful body. His hair had been sculpted by a real coiffeur, not by one of the old Italians in the Village who took two bucks for a razor cut.

Ashley was rather self-consciously 'neurotic.' He and Louise Lasser, a TV actress, would hire wheelchairs, sit in them with plaid blankets over their knees, and order in pizza. They'd say to the bewildered delivery boy, 'You can let yourself in. We can't come to the door. We're crippled.' They would look for signs of sympathy in his eyes.

Ashley had been an assistant to Arthur Laurents, who'd written the books for *West Side Story* and *Gypsy*. Laurents invited Ashley and me out to his beach house in Quogue before my play went into rehearsal. I was so impressed by Arthur's quick wit and celebrity that I was prepared to admire and emulate him, but his disparagement of everyone gay ('Oh, *her*! She's nothing, just one more old cocksucker. I had her a hundred years ago when she was still presentable') depressed me. I left his house on Sunday night feeling confused. Of course I wanted to 'develop' a successful 'property' (there was no longer a question of writing a good play) and become rich and famous. If I mentioned Brecht or Artaud or any of our other gods at the U of M, Arthur would scrunch up his face and wave his hand in front of his nose as if one had just made a bad smell. Everything I'd been taught to admire at school – Stanislavsky, Chekhov, Engagé Theater – now seemed stultified. As one of the lyrics in *Gypsy* put it, 'You gotta have a gimmick.' Speed, brassiness, a quick laugh, a novelty act, a bit of bump and grind, tits and ass, a heart-stopping curtain line – these were the elements of a hit. In the theater there was no court of higher appeal. When Arthur attempted something genuinely new (for the prestige of the avant-garde was riding high in the 1960s and even he was seduced by it), his musical *Anyone Can Whistle* was a resounding failure.

Arthur was neurotic, Louise was neurotic, Ashley's friend Woody Allen was neurotic – there was something endearing about so much neurosis. Eating disorders, pill-popping, insomnia, sudden caprices, crying jags, security blankets, expensive Freudians – these were just the outward signs of the inward disposition toward creativity. I remember listening at Ashley's thirtieth birthday party to Woody Allen as he talked about cryogenics, then a brand-new practice. He had a haunted look on his face as he discussed the horrors of dying and death; not too long afterwards he tipped this very unfunny obsession toward humor in his film *Sleeper*, which also seemed to owe something to Mayakovski's play *The Bedbug*. That was how they did it, these New Yorkers. They gave free rein to their worries (no stiff Protestant upper lip for them, no Midwestern stoicism). Then at the last moment the camera pulled back, farther and farther, and looked at the current neurosis with the long shot of humor.

Stan was drawn to this neurotic, creative and celebrated world, the pulsing heart of the city's culture, even if it was afflicted with a troubling dysrhythmia. Stan had grown up with parents engaged in a lifelong and sterile battle with each other. When we saw Edward Albee's *Who's Afraid of Virginia Woolf?* on Broadway, Stan was stunned: Martha and George were just like his parents! Stan's parents were tormented creatures in hell and had produced nothing of value unless it was this beautiful son. Far better were these New Yorkers burnishing their interesting neuroses, stamping them out into one joke after another.

Ashley wouldn't give Stan keys to his apartment. He wouldn't introduce Stan to his friends. When they were scheduled to come by Stan would have to walk around the block. He had to hide his few clothes in the back of the closet. One time Ashley locked Stan into the bathroom when friends came by unexpectedly. Ashley then rushed out, not thinking, and left Stan locked up. Stan didn't know how to contact Ashley even if he'd had access to a phone. He couldn't bang on the door and alarm the neighbors. He had forty-eight hours to endure alone and hungry. He took six of Ashley's super strong sleeping pills and passed out on the floor. When Ashley at last came home he was so freaked out by the sight of this drugged youth on his bathroom floor that he said, 'This isn't working for me. I'm just too neurotic to live with anyone. You're going to have to move out. I know I'm being neurotic, that's the way I am. I feel invaded. I'm just too neurotic.' He made a series of appointments with his shrink.

I took Stanley in. I was so happy to have him back with me. We didn't discuss everything we'd been through except to attempt a few New York-style jokes. Me: 'Hello, Miss Adultery.' Stan: 'Hello, Mr. Cuckold.'

Like any good married couple we no longer had sex but we were very dear to each other. We felt abashed by our misadventure in the theater. I continued to write plays – one after another – but my agent never liked any of them and refused to send them out. I'd stay late at work and mutter to myself as I composed dialogue. I wrote what I deemed a 'comedy' in which two actors and one actress rotated among the three roles, so that at first two men were competing over the woman, but then a man and the woman were fighting over the other man. I suppose I wanted to show that the dynamics of love were always the same, no matter which combination of genders was involved. I spent a few days on Fire Island sleeping with Mart Crowley, who'd just scored a huge hit with *The Boys in the Band*; I read him my play. All he said was, 'Is this supposed to be funny? Do you think it's funny?'

'Wry,' I said, 'amusing. Gently satiric? I should forget it? I should.'

He nodded slowly, his huge eyes trained on mine. He'd written the funniest play of the season, but he never laughed or even smiled. He woke every morning with a giant sigh; he had to come up with another hit to equal his first one. He'd worked for years as Natalie Wood's secretary. Now he was a very big deal. While we were together a top Hollywood producer wanted him to take a meeting. Mart said he'd do so only if a chauffeur came to his door in Fire Island early in the morning, accompanied him to a waiting speedboat and a waiting limo that would get him on a plane to LA, where a limo would convey him to a half-hour meeting – and then the process had to be reversed so he could be back on Fire Island the very same night.

'Doesn't that seem excessive?' I asked.

'They love it,' Mart said. 'That's their idea of how a real writer behaves.'

After my play had its three-week run and its mixed notices I was offered a job writing dialogue for a TV soap, *The Doctors and the Nurses*, at eighty thousand dollars a year – a fortune in those days, especially compared to the six thousand dollars I was earning at Time-Life. But I refused, not because I was afraid of sullying my hands with commerce but because I didn't want to live on Cape Cod next to the head writer. I was too addicted to gay sex, to New York – and to Stan – to move away.

Stan would walk all night through the rain, depressed. He'd spend hours getting dressed and grooming himself, not out of self-love but out of a genuine fear that he was too fat, too short, too hippie. In fact he was so beautiful that older men, complete strangers, would stop him in the street and offer him air tickets to Egypt or beg him to visit in the south of France. Stanley would shrug, slightly offended but not at all surprised by so much enthusiasm. While he was still a copy boy at Time-Life he had sex with two heterosexual men there; he was their unique male adventure. I doubt anyone with an artistic inclination could have resisted so much beauty in one face.

Every year he came to love me more and more because he trusted my devotion. He knew I loved him in spite of his dark moods and inner demons. Yet I could be very stern with him. I'd say, 'You must catch your mood at the very moment it starts to turn and analyze what's bothering you. Sometimes the irritant is so petty that you don't dare admit it. Your pride is wounded at being depressed by something so trivial. Byronic melancholy – vaporous and general – is easier to acknowledge than a spiteful little grudge.' He'd try to combat his moods but they were too strong for him. I was so relentlessly optimistic that I kept reproaching him for being unhappy.

One night he was visiting a friend, Jim Ruddy, in Little Italy, just on the other side of Houston. A gang of teenage boys robbed him – and then kicked him just for good measure. Soon afterwards he came down with an extremely high fever one night, vomited constantly and then fell into a deep sleep. He didn't want to be disturbed and begged me to leave him alone. I called our doctor who came by only much later, toward midnight, after Nureyev's first performance in America, at the old Metropolitan Opera. He made Stan sit up and submit to several neurological tests. He flunked them all.

'He has spinal meningitis,' the doctor said, strangely attractive in his tuxedo, and drove him off to the emergency room at St. Vincent's. I called Stan's parents, who flew in the next day. In the daylight they looked like patients – Virginia under caked white powder, her eyes swimming. She was unable to walk down the corridor unassisted. Stan's father shook like an aspen and he wept when he saw his oldest son in a sleep as deep as that of a Wagnerian heroine. Although I'd never thought of them as religious they went to some local church and prayed for their boy's recovery.

Perhaps because of his white-bread background, Stan was always susceptible to strong, satanic men. He'd met a guy named Joe not long before who now visited him for hours every day in the hospital and even fucked him in his sickbed; Stan was too weak to protest, not that he would have. He was a believer, on his way to a conversion to Catholicism, and his faith included a strong belief in the devil.

Stan survived. He lived a quiet, studious life. He stopped being an actor. No more rehearsals in our kitchen with his friend May for Berghof's scene study class – no more angry exchanges that sounded almost real. He went back to university and took courses in Henry James from Leon Edel. One of his professors, the editor of the seventeenth-century newsletter, fell for him. Stan himself fell in love with Jimmy, a Puerto Rican kid he'd met on Christopher Street.

Stan told me that when he was growing up in East Lansing he'd jerk off late at night looking at the Indians in cowboy movies (the Indians in their loincloths were the only nearly naked men he could study on the little screen); now New York's millions of Puerto Ricans with their black hair, pleated trousers, pale blue shirts over wife beaters and gold medals of the *Virgen del Carmen* seemed like a vast tribe of red Indians brought here to this island just for his pleasure. By the law of opposites Stan interested them with his white skin so sensitive that it rose in red welts wherever it was touched, with his beautiful, plush ass so receptive to male plundering, with his noble face which asleep on the pillow looked like a carved god's head fallen from the statue and nestled on the white beach staring blankly up at the night sky.

We seldom talked to each other about our feelings. We were, after all, these curious creatures, WASPs from the Midwest, and if we turned to demonic or exotic lovers, we did so partly because their intemperance could wring some sentiment out of us. With each other we joked in a good-natured Midwestern way – until an equally Midwestern tragedy would finally strike us down. Stan's father took his wife on an expensive Caribbean cruise. A few days after they returned to East Lansing he sent her out to pick up a prescription for him; he phoned her at the pharmacy and told her to call the cops but under no circumstances to return home. She of course rushed back to the house and found his body on one side of the room and his head on the other, a pistol in his fist. Soon after that Stan's uncle murdered his wife and then committed suicide.

Stan began to do production work first for *Time* and then for *Fortune*.

We didn't really know where to put our feelings. In the beginning I'd loved Stan passionately and for that I did have a language, one I'd learned from books and the movies. I could write him poems about the lover and the beloved, about a gentleman with a cigar (though I smoked only cigarettes) and a beautiful boy. I was inspired by Cavafy. I could sit on his stoop all night, hoping to catch a glimpse of him at dawn. I could write him a part in my play. Even though I lived with him at such close quarters year after year, I never took his beauty for granted, any more than I could have forgotten a friend's patent of nobility. He was a prince with his full, very full lips, his long Grecian nose, his eyes as pale and blue as beach glass that's still underwater, his blond hair and vague smile that betrayed he wasn't really following the conversation. Years later he became genuinely funny, quick on the uptake and 'outrageous' in his shocking statements of the simple truth ('A pedophile is someone whose boys are a year younger than yours'), but during our first years in New York he was still so preoccupied by his alcoholic family, the heavy burden of his beauty, and his anxiety about his career, that he merely smiled his way through life while his eyes, like a blind man's hands in a new room, crept over everything, trying to put it all together, a slight frown on his forehead, his face surrounded by the sand-crunching sound of a thousand ships being launched.

I knew how to express devotion and humility and gratitude, but as we moved into our fourth and fifth years together, and our friendship became more and more nuanced, we no longer said much. We narrated our day to each other, we made observations about other people we knew, but we were secretive about our feelings.

Frances Alexander, one of my many shrinks – this was just before Stonewall and the beginning of gay liberation – convinced me I could never 'grow' unless I broke up with Stan.

Me: 'Even if I leave him that's no guarantee I'll go straight.'

Her: 'Ed, we've been over all this a million times. You're just playing "Yes, but."'

Me: 'I love Stan.'

Her: 'No you don't. You're just dependent on each other.'

Now of course I realize that what she meant by dependence was what anyone else would call love.

I left Stan, who took it very badly. He sat in one of my mother's high-backed, candy-striped chairs and listened over and over to a record, 'Seven Rooms of Gloom.' I'd first told him I was moving out at a diner on Fifty-fifth Street off Sixth; what he'd found most disgusting was that I could still go on eating my supper. I ate all my food and then all of his. He had a hysterical throat condition, triggered by anxiety. Without warning his throat would suddenly clamp shut; if he was eating at the same time he could die.

When we stopped living together something vital between us came to an end. We'd lived together in poverty if not destitution, but we'd scarcely noticed how little money we had. We'd had our first disappointing brushes with the commercial arts scene. Over the years Stan became more and more religious and went frequently on retreats at monasteries, whereas I became more and more a Voltairian atheist. We'd not been jealous or possessive because we'd always been best friends; besides, as two men in the sixties we hadn't known how to be a couple. We'd never observed older, openly gay couples at close range. Anyway, Stan had always seemed so out of my league that the idea of imposing a lover's rights on him struck me as preposterous. I'd always been grateful for his company.

We lived in Greenwich Village and the only milieu where we were welcome as gay men was the bohemian; jealousy – or any niggling form of jealousy that fell short of vengeance and murder – was deemed 'middle-class' by the straight actors, dancers, painters and writers we were living among.

After we broke up Stan lived for fifteen years with a fast-talking Vietnam vet who kept himself and his whole entourage of young men hopped up on blackbirds, yellow jackets, PCP and joints sprayed with Angel Dust. Stan never seemed to have much time for me. When we'd get together he'd talk in circles. Once he tried to escape the vet by barricading himself in with me, but the vet gained access to a neighboring roof where he set up a machine gun trained on my windows. I found the melodrama tiresome, but then again I wasn't sharing in the drugs or the boys. Once I did go with the whole gang up to Killington, Vermont, in a Chrysler station wagon outfitted with quadraphonic sound and ten cute guys. They skied the slopes on acid and then fucked and fisted each other all night on quaaludes; we were occupying the very heart of the 1970s. Another time I went with the whole gang in a hired limo out to Fire Island, drinking jeroboams of champagne in traffic jams we scarcely noticed. Once there we lived in an octagonal house with plate-glass windows taking in every angle of the sea and the neighboring community. The vet gave me a 'cocktail' that turned me first into Bottom and then into an Ass. I was so consumed by desire for a compact little blond wrestler with a brush cut and braces that I crawled across the tatami-matted floor and buried my head with its long ears and bucktoothed muzzle right into his shimmering, diaphanous lap. Never again would I wonder why Stan behaved so strangely on drugs – or why he took them.

I suppose after pushing aside the many men who admired him in his studious twenties, Stan now wanted to enjoy his beauty and its perks in his thirties. Sometimes Stan and the Viet vet would pick me up at midnight in the station wagon and drive me slowly through the empty, illuminated streets of the financial district. I'd get high wedged between laughing, muscular fellows, all exclaiming with childlike awe as we drove over the Brooklyn Bridge while listening to *Ein Heldenleben* or Isaac Hayes from all four speakers. When at last we'd go back to Stan's apartment he'd serve us TV dinners of turkey and gravy right off the tin trays; they tasted sublime.

Most of our friends were other kids we'd known in the Midwest and who'd moved to New York at the same time. We'd turned Manhattan into Ann Arbor East. We never knew what we were missing until suddenly, like a kingdom summoned up by a wand, there it was, glittering before us: immense gay clubs inserted in vast lofts with go-go boys turning slowly under black light and hundreds of men writhing in backrooms, all of us linked by cock, one long cock, like Laocoön and his sons strangled by the serpent.

If Stan was my first lover (and is still one of my closest friends), the great love of my life was Jim Ruddy, the very man Stan was visiting when he was beat up by Italian boys and given the injury that led to his attack of spinal meningitis.

Jim was Polish-American, a dirty blond with straight hair that pushed out of his low brow and big head. He had the flat back of the head typical of Slavic people. He was tall and had developed a low, booming baritone voice. He entered a room with a hail-fellow friendliness stripped of all irony, and perhaps he would have been happy to do nothing the whole time but exchange warm greetings and heartfelt farewells, like a Venetian countess. Unfortunately he was neither an Italian aristocrat nor an American cadet, the two groups who go in for such things. He'd chosen to live among American intellectuals, who used irony as a wall of shields they could leap over at any time in full fatal assault.

He had tiny hips, squirming dark blue eyes, full red lips and skin as cool and small-pored as chamois. His face and neck and chest were alternately pale and rosy. One imagined they were irrigated with a fine spray of blood that could abruptly be switched off. Jim had made a cult of masculinity and rolled his shoulders when he walked and spoke in a slow, deep voice. He had a long penis that curved to one side. When I spoke to him in my high, fast squeak, his eyes would sparkle with hard scrutiny undermined by such deep abysses of self-doubt that I'd be seized by vertigo. He had no sense of humor because he could never achieve a comic distance; his face was pressed so hard up against the present that it flattened his features. He didn't know what he thought about anything. When I would make one of my countless assertions, his eyes would wince and squint as if I had just snapped his picture with a flash. 'Is that right?' he'd ask again and again, his eyes wincing and his head turning as if he were assaulted by a battery of cameras. He was beautiful, if a big Polish nose, fleshy ears and the sweet smell of sperm can be reconciled with the ideal of beauty; he resented any reference to his beauty.

Jim was slightly mad, which took me quite a while to figure out; by then I was thoroughly in love with him and he was lockup crazy.

I was in a trance of love. I thought of him day and night and was as honored to walk with him as if he were a deity. No, really, if he'd been an angel who'd chosen me and hovered beside me, hand on my shoulder, his eerie light surrounding us in a large, glowing nimbus, I couldn't have felt more *elected*: I was one of the elect. I was convinced – I'm still convinced – that if he'd chosen me and kept choosing me again and again, I would have had a better, bigger life. As it is every moment we ever had together remains clear and legible in my memory, forty years later, as if it had been written in bigger, blacker letters, print for failing eyes.

Since I'm writing a chapter about my lovers, I should say what I mean by love. Like all key words in my vocabulary, love puzzles me so much I can scarcely say whether I think it's good or bad. It's good (and bad) because passion-love, unlike esteem-love, is transformative, obsessional, impractical. It can't be fitted in with a job, errands, homework. It pushes friendship aside and upstages family attachments. It crowds out every mild or disinterested pleasure; in fact it has little to do with pleasure of any sort except at the very beginning of its trajectory when the poor lover still imagines he might live happily ever after with the beloved.

Perhaps gay men of my generation were drawn to this peculiar, destructive kind of medieval love precisely because we had so little idea of what domestic happiness between two men would look like. Despair we understood. Desire (especially frustrated, rejected desire) we experienced every day. Regret over lost youth and compromised masculinity was something we'd imagined intensely. Butch-femme role-playing might have approximated traditional male-female interactions but we were too middle-class – too *shy*, I suppose – to try something so extravagant. No, marriage between two men was something as impractical as a male-male *pas de deux*; there was no way to get it off the ground.

I suppose that's why we were attracted to the arts as a career; they made a rags-to-riches scenario seem plausible. If we could become famous overnight, maybe by the same token we could become happy in love with another gritty-jawed, hairy-chested, erection-sporting member of the same sex. A begger and thief like Jean Genet could become a world cultural figure just by writing about his suffering; that was the sort of magic we believed in. We were observers, not participants, given to meditation, not conflict. There was a certain plaintive note, dreamlike and muted, starlit and private, that was sounded by our favorite works of art – Loti's novels of travel, Hawthorne's *The Marble Faun*, Vincent d'Indy's *Symphony on a French Mountain Air*, Ravel's *Mother Goose Suite*, Fantin-Latour's flower paintings, Kiyonaga's prints of tall, pipe-smoking women, all the novels of Kawabata, Anatole France's *The Red Lily*. Years later, when I stayed for several months in Istanbul, I felt I was inhabiting this dream as I sipped tea in a pine forest or as I looked out toward Asia across the Sea of Marmara or when I visited cemeteries of the late Ottoman period and touched the veils carved in stone on the tombs of virgins who'd died young a century earlier. I suppose we were attracted to what was melancholy because even at the beginning of any of our love affairs we could already anticipate the sad ending.

Our problems with gay love were aesthetico-practico. In the 1950s and even afterwards we were attracted only to masculine men or boyish boys; we were turned off by the least hint of effeminacy and we could detect it with inquisitorial zeal. There was always the moment when we'd watch a favorite baseball player leap into a teammate's arms after a home run, wrapping his legs around his waist, or we'd observe the president of the country as he described the course of the latest invasion with a surprisingly limp wrist – and we'd wonder how they could get away with it and we couldn't. Just as an actor who wants to appear drunk concentrates on walking in an absolutely straight line and ends up weaving, in the same way all our efforts to contain our gestures, lower our voices and douse our enthusiasm only made us seem prissier.

I'll never know if Jim Ruddy had deliberately cultivated his masculine mannerisms before I met him, but I suspect not, since his booming voice often embarrassed him and his wooden machismo came off as a form of incomprehension. Maybe his way of pulling his shoulders back and throwing his legs straight out before him was something he reminded himself to do. It certainly seemed deliberate. I don't know. He never confided anything in me and any effort to flush his secrets out only panicked him. Maybe he feared there was nothing in there.

At first, second and third glance he seemed to possess an almost ideal combination of attributes. He was twenty, four years younger than I, and had skin as smooth as a girl's to go with his hairless chest. His lips were as red as candied currants, his eyebrows two blond silk seams that the worrying of an invisible thread could cause to contract. His eyes were small and crazed – full of concentration and incomprehension. He was a scholar and even now, forty years later, I lean with admiring indulgence over a round paperweight which, once the snow settles, reveals Jim in his Pendleton wool shirt unbuttoned over a V-necked T-shirt washed so many times its whiteness has grayed; it has the soft, weaveless feel of a rose petal. He's seated at his desk studying Latin, something dull and easy like *The Gallic Wars* rather than subtle, sophisticated poems by Catullus. Just as well, since Jim shifts about uneasily if a writer can't quite be trusted; playfulness alarms him. He gets up and paces back and forth; even when he's alone he walks with his manly stride, emphasized by the razor-sharp crease of his freshly ironed khakis. The snow is falling outside his two windows – or have I just disturbed the paperweight and roused a swirl of flakes trapped under glass? His bed is made with military neatness, hospital corners and all. In his kitchen, where he's placed his desk under a glaring fluorescent lamp, he's cooking up a big pot of lentils. He's poor and another student has told him you can live for pennies on lentil loaf, lentil burgers, lentil soup. His windows are misted from the heat – or have my glasses clouded over as I stare down into the crystal ball?

I met Jim one evening when he came by our old MacDougal Street apartment. Stan had tricked with him and gone back to his little apartment just a few blocks away. Now Jim knocked on the door, looking for Stan. In fact, he thought I was Stan, which should have made me realize how crazy he was. Stan was short, blond, beautiful, whereas I was none of those things.

If Jim was very masculine he filtered it through an extreme courtliness. He was one of the few people I've ever known who never used contractions in speech; with him it was *cannot* and *should have*. He avoided slang and resorted to formal, even archaic expressions ('albeit' was something he said a lot). 'Perhaps I can tempt you to accompany me during a short walk through the city streets,' he would say.

He smiled and nodded his way into our apartment and to a cup of instant coffee (we didn't know how to prepare real coffee). I soon discovered that he liked ceremonies, or at least actions that were serious, slow, deliberate. He asked me questions about my writing (I told him I wanted to write), but he seemed incapable of taking in what I was saying. 'Is that right?' he'd ask dubiously. It wasn't that he was too egotistical to listen; on the contrary, he had too little ego to be able to prop himself up against the gale force of a strong personality like mine.

I talk so often about my passivity and self-hatred that I might give the misleading impression that I was mousy. But in fact I was a showoff. As a child at school I'd waved my arm constantly, longing to give the correct answer, until I was sick with frustration. I was an intellectual bully; I knew it all.

And yet I was a nice bully, a thoughtful bully interested in the details of other people's lives. I had the ability to encourage timid people to try for something big. Just the other day an old school friend from eighth grade wrote me that because I had encouraged her to direct Ibsen's *Ghosts* back then she grew up to work in the professional theater. I believe in my friends and I have the knack of making my struggles (and by extension theirs) look like a snap. Half a dozen books have been dedicated to me because I encouraged the authors.

But I'm sure I was bad for Jim Ruddy. In spite of his big voice and military bearing, his sure, austere taste in clothes, his classical learning and his powers as an athlete (he swam laps every morning, and when he plunged forward using the butterfly stroke a strong cape of muscle emerged across his back where ordinarily none was visible) – in spite of all his accomplishments he was a mess. He might pull off his round black rubber water goggles with a naturalness I'd never know and shake out his long, straight hair with a lyricism that suspended animation in all observers, he might stride out to the end of the board in his black swimsuit that was one size too big for him and bounce there a second before raising his arms and lifting his ribcage and squeezing his small dark nipples together and turning himself into a cold-seeking missile. But in ordinary life he was lost and confused.

He didn't know what he thought about anything and during the first year we were friends, while he became more anxious and crazy, he would drink in anything I said with a note of authority (or anything anyone said). That invisible string would tug and cause the silk seams of his blond eyebrows to bunch. His small eyes would turn in spirals faster and faster, his red lips would fall open, he'd rake a big pale hand through his straight blond hair and writhe with pain in his chair and say, 'Is that right?' He had no saving prejudices, no necessary blind spots, no subjects he'd put off-limits; no, he was wide open as a receptor to all the energy pulsing around him in every form – he had no filters, no wires to ground him, no band frequencies.

'Is that right?' he'd say, panicked and wincing.

I probably didn't sleep with Stan more than thirty times in seven years, nor with Jim Ruddy more than a dozen times in ten years. I was a specialist in separating sex from love, though all I ever thought about was seduction. I remember Jim had a long, thin cock and very warm balls, as if his sperm had to be maintained at a higher temperature than other men's – as if his sperm was needed for his own survival rather than for reproduction. We'd walk through the warehouse district (not yet known as SoHo) and he'd point out all the various styles of cast-iron Gothic warehouses. I made his interest in architectural history my own; I hung on every word. I struggled to keep up with his long strides. I felt I was back in high school, but this time I was sleeping with my best friend, captain of the swimming team. The first time I ever had sex with Jim I asked him to fuck me. He said, 'Stan asked me to do the same thing. What is it with you guys? I don't really like that.' Not long afterwards, when I tricked with Tom Eyen, another Caffe Cino writer, he said, 'You behave in bed exactly like this kid I had last week – Stan? Was that his name?'

If Jim Ruddy was someone who was losing his bearings, I was destined to confuse him still further. After I'd come to weigh almost two hundred pounds I'd gone to an amphetamine-prescribing diet doctor and had just lost fifty pounds on a regime of orange pills, red steak and green salad. I seldom slept and I licked my lips so much they were chapped. One night I started to look up sources for props for my gender-switching play (I was producing it in someone's loft) and by dawn I had read through the entire yellow pages for New York. Disappointingly, if I sat down to write while speeding only a few lines would come out.

At the same time I went to the gym and started working out ten years before other gay men got the idea. Soon I was slim and muscled – but like an adolescent who's grown five inches in a year I had no idea what was happening to me. Nor was I sanguine about the improvement in my looks. I'd wanted someone to love me first – love me for my hidden sensuality, my pure need – and then and only then would I slim down, like the Beast who becomes the Prince only after Beauty kisses him.

That hadn't happened. No one had wanted me fat; no matter that my heart had burned as ardently as the one that bad polychrome statues show Christ pointing to. I'd been forced to watch my weight, control portions and speed jaw-clenchingly through the night. Suddenly I was wasp-waisted and fox-faced – and Jim Ruddy, meeting me for the first time, didn't consider me beneath him. Later I'd learn that he hadn't the cloudiest what he looked like nor where he placed in any ranking, and I was only a shadow on the wall of the dark cave he was pacing around.

What he needed was a strong, authoritative man, someone focused on his own work and only peripherally conscious of Jim. What he needed was an older man with opinions set in stone, a whole worked-up religion of the self – something as detailed as laws in cuneiform.

When he got me what he got wasn't a male stabile but a shifting, female mobile, every element turning at a different speed on its own micro-axis. I was so focused on him and so eager to please him, so ready to echo every change in his half-formed, half-held opinions that I was designed to drive him even crazier. I was a mirror facing the mirror he'd become, repeating to infinity the slightest trick in the light.

Jim and I went to the same shrink (my idea – a bad one). Of course we were kept apart, but from a girl in Jim's group therapy I learned that he was talking compulsively, striding about and making lewd remarks to the female participants. The shrink had urged him (and me) to go straight.

We were in the late fall of 1968, a little more than six months before the Stonewall Uprising. We were the last victims sacrificed to the old order, as if we were boys in Peking in 1909 being castrated to be eunuchs in a court about to be extinguished by revolution. Perhaps the violence of Jim's reaction to Frances's treatment goals was due to the convulsions of the medium through whom history was struggling to be born. In the 1950s we gay men would not have fought back. We would have buttoned all three buttons of our Brooks Brothers jackets and ordered a fourth martini as we declared with ritualistic despair, 'God, are we sick, Marie! Lay down, Rose. Sick queens. That's what we are, Sister Theresa.'

But now, in 1968, when students were holding hostage the president of Columbia and war protesters were immobilizing the capital, when French kids had torn up the paving stones of Paris and soldiers were marching down the Boulevard St-Germain, when blacks and women everywhere were re-legislating their place in society and the citizens of Prague were struggling to throw out the Russians – amid such worldwide changes our effort to hold the knife to our own balls was failing. The hand shook, doubts assailed us – we were confused and trembling from the inner conflict. In my group I leapt out of my chair when a Russian patient said as I wept over Jim, 'Forgedaboudhim. Whad about da goils? I wanna hear bout da goils!' I wanted to choke him to death but Frances, rising up out of her mint-green Barcalounger, exhaled smoke from her Kool and said, 'Stop. For God's sake, Ed, sit down.'

In his own group, later in the day, Jim was kneeling on the floor in front of a girl and staging a marriage proposal when he leapt up and announced he felt flames coursing up and down his arms – which Frances, exhaling, labeled 'bizarre somatic delusions.' Jim had become so excitable that he couldn't eat and Frances was obliged to feed him rice from a spoon while he grinned and drooled like the village idiot. The puppeteers of history were fighting for control of his strings and he shook and sweated as if in a terrible trance.

The next thing I knew Frances had put him in St. Vincent's Hospital and abandoned the case. A staff psychiatrist was now in charge. Jim was locked up on the fifth floor and heavily sedated. There was talk of shock therapy – 'Which has received very bad press,' Frances said. 'It's no longer the gruesome slash-and-burn practice of the past. Now it's mild and precise – and excellent for erasing obsessive and unwanted thoughts.'

I couldn't sleep at night. I knew something dreadful was happening and no one was noticing. In the waiting room at St. Vincent's I met Steve, the man I realized must be Jim's real lover. Steve was in his mid-thirties, he had gutted and was single-handedly rebuilding an old, dilapidated house at the foot of Christopher Street, and he was about to get married. He was solid and short, he had a deep voice, red hair, an open shirt from which curly bronze hair sprouted and rolled-up sleeves, which exposed golden-haired forearms thick from manual labor. His palm was calloused when we shook hands.

The mathematical horror of gay life (never properly exploited by writers of farce) is that not only do two rivals compete over a third man but they can also sleep with each other. I was instantly attracted to Steve. He seemed to be much more attached to Jim than was reasonable in a man with a fiancée. I never met her nor saw her nor learned her name, though Steve and I spent a lot of time together and talked on the phone sometimes till dawn. We would go over every scrap of information we knew about Jim, details about his parents and sister, his education, his money worries, his growing inability to concentrate and study, his anxiety about ending up homosexual, lonely and childless. Steve appealed to Jim because they wrestled together like dog and puppy and if the dog mounted the puppy for a second it was a kind of canine harmlessness, not a pathology. Steve disliked our shrink and kept muttering, 'Geez . . . a shrink . . .' Sometimes he'd say, 'Fuckin' shrink' or 'Holy Mary, a shrink of all things . . .'

I hated her now because she'd locked Jim up and abandoned

him. He hadn't been this crazy when I brought him to her. 'You don't know what you're talking about,' she'd say, her heavy-lidded eyes drooping shut, her mammoth legs in pale stockings served up massively on the tilted-back leg rest of the fully reclined Barca-lounger.

I'd been allowed to enter the ward. Jim would just sit there and weep without stopping, as if he were a Neapolitan fountain, a water-dripping mask at the dark end of a grotto. One time the nurse told me he'd only been pretending to swallow his antipsychotic pills and then an hour earlier he'd run up and down the halls with his arms spread out, knocking over all obstacles. They'd had to wrestle him into a straitjacket and inject him with something.

Steve and I would each lie in our beds and talk for hours on the phone. Steve's style was to say Jim was just a mixed-up kid; my tack was to say he was the victim of psychiatric incompetence. I suppose if I'd seen Jim wrestling with Steve, both of them bare-chested as they thrashed and flipped each other over, I'd have felt jealous and spurned. But now that Jim was lost to us both I found it consoling to talk to this thoroughly decent man all night every night.

At first we'd debrief on the latest Jim events. Today he was nearly comatose on that fuckin' shit they're feeding him. The nurse said they're scheduling the shock treatment for next Monday – a very mild session, she said, though she did admit they had to put in a rubber dental dam so the patient wouldn't bite out his tongue.

What finally happened was that Jim was shipped off to his grandparents in Minnesota. I didn't see him for a year. Steve and I no longer had a pretext for talking on the phone till dawn and our friendship – so sudden, so intense – came to an abrupt end. I have no idea if he ever got married or lived with his wife in the house he'd restored. Only now does it occur to me that Jim's passion for cast-iron Gothic warehouses was probably something he'd picked up from Steve. His one authentic enthusiasm he had probably bor-rowed from the man he was in love with (Steve was an architect).

For a year I lay on my bed and wept over Jim. I was so stupid, so egotistical, that even though he had had a complete breakdown I took it as a rejection. I felt bereft. For a moment I'd imagined I'd been promoted into a higher order of humanity by this lap-swim-ming, Latin-reading blond giant. Now in a vague allegory I'd been snatched out of the elegant dining room where I'd been toying with a demitasse and hustled back down the stairs into the shouting, stinking kitchen where I was shorn and set to work under dripping pipes – or so I pictured my state in a vivid dream.

Although Jim was weak, confused, even pretty crazy, I was so blind to his problems that I continued to think about him night after night. I didn't try to contact him; I knew I was toxic for him. I felt that he'd snap back and re-enter my life later, in a year or two.

A year and a half later he did move to New Brunswick, New Jersey, where he joined the comparative literature department at Rutgers and worked on his doctorate. His particular campus had been radicalized by 1968; in his comp. lit. program the grad students didn't have to learn other languages. His education didn't seem sound to me; I wanted him to learn German.

But when the *New York Times Book Review* asked me to review the English translation of *Paradiso* by the Cuban novelist José Lezama Lima I called on Jim to help me identify the sources of this compendious modernist masterpiece which recounted a gay boyhood in Havana by recapitulating all of Western literature. It was a bit as if someone would have thrown *Ulysses* at me when it was brand-new and asked me to review it in three weeks. Jim spotted paraphrases of everything from medieval allegories to Renaissance epics and the literature of the Spanish Conquest.

I was so happy to see that his mind was working perfectly once again. He'd found a lover, a Puerto Rican poet, Miguel Algarín, who eventually became celebrated, a portly, handsome man ten or fifteen years older than us who was in possession of the self-assured personality Jim needed as a foil.

Jim had the same lean, lanky body, the same military bearing, the same high coloring. I took the train out to New Brunswick and he made dinner for me and quite unexpectedly led me to bed. He bathed everything we did and said in warm laughter, as if he'd decided a dose of humorous salts was best for his mental hygiene.

Once, over lunch in a New York coffee shop that used to exist on the corner of Hudson and Jane, I asked him to marry me. By now we'd known each other a decade. I felt that if I said, 'Let's be lovers,' he would have bridled and his eyes would have emitted flashes of panic. But I knew of his love of formality. Even to me at that moment this stage in our affair felt very 'late.' We'd moved in our ten years together from dawn to dusk, and night was about to fall. Everything was almost over. And yet for me he remained mysterious, no matter how well I knew him. Love requires incomprehension. We can love only the people who are opaque to us. Or rather opacity is only another aspect of the divine. We don't understand the gods but we can love them, especially when they appear in human form. The proof that I didn't understand Jim is that I'd seen him fall apart before my very eyes and yet, in spite of all ocular evidence, I persisted in believing he was strong. I thought he held all the cards and was just refusing to deal me in. Even now, when I looked at him in the murky light of a rainy March day (we were seated in a glassed-in addition to the restaurant that extended out to the edge of the sidewalk) I couldn't help but see him as the lawgiver and me as the . . . supplicant. As a child my favorite game had been king and slave, I'd never much cared which role I played though I'd had to admit that servant came to me more naturally and as a servant I could think up more cool things to do and say.

And then it was over. Jim smiled graciously, as if I was gently pulling his leg, and with one of his warm but never infectious laughs he said, 'Sure. Of course I'll marry you, kind sir.' This little mock proposal and acceptance, even if it came so late in the day of our love, even if it had no consequences and was undoubtedly something he forgot right away – even so, it satisfied me. I'd asked Jim Ruddy to marry me and he'd said yes.

He and Miguel broke up and then Jim found Ivan, a bearded giant of a man. I had dinner with them once and they laughed heartily, but they seemed unhappy in New York. They opened a ski lodge in California. I lost touch with them. Then in the early nineties, twenty years later, I received a note from Ivan saying that Jim had died of AIDS. They'd had a good life together. Jim had read my portrait of him under the name of 'Sean' in *The Beautiful Room Is Empty* and been touched by it. I wrote back but never heard from Ivan again. I don't even remember his last name.

Blonds make me cry. Maybe women allow themselves to cry, though many feminists resent their own susceptibility to cruelty or rejection or sadness; they'd like to be tougher. Imagine how a man feels. When he cries he's a sissy, and no man, straight or gay, looking at him is touched or persuaded by the lovely sight of his face bathed in tears. He looks ridiculous. That's all. When women cry they sometimes win arguments with their tears; when a man cries he's unbalanced or a pain in the ass and people turn away in disgust.

Even so, I took my own tears very seriously. Maybe that's because I'm used to male privilege, but for me my state of mind was always a subject of great interest. If I was happy I was quick to generalize from my little mood to a major philosophical principle; the humble 'I' immediately became a choral 'we' or an impersonal 'one.' If I was sad I had soon interpreted my melancholy as the next tragic antithesis of the *Weltgeist*. As I went, so went the Western World. Maybe I needed to dignify my moods in order to lift the curse of being a man who cries over blonds.

Why blonds?

Sometimes I felt like a Mayan seeing his first blond Galician mounted on a horse – a centaur with iron hooves and a silver upper body and helmet, which, once removed, revealed a mane of sun-bleached hair the color of gold, a living form of the very gold these Conquistadors sought in its dead, hard form. What to do except drop to both knees and ask this divinity for a blessing?

My shrinks made much of the fact that my father, his mother (Olive Martin) and my sister were all blonds whereas my mother and I and her clan were all dark – except the fair and dark genealogies, like most family myths, were forced. As a child I'd been a towhead. My father was balding but what hair he did have was brown and gray, no one remembered his mother before she turned gray but in some pictures her hair looked dark. My mother, to be sure, had warm brown eyes, but mine were green, which I only noticed recently. I always listed them on documents as brown, in conformity with my mother's theory, but my lover Michael said a couple of years ago, 'They're not brown, they're olive green.'

According to the shrinks' theory I was in awe of my father and intimidated by my sister. As an adult I'd always been attracted to blonds as a way of promoting myself into their superior ranks. Conversely, I despised brunettes, my mother and myself. But I thought everyone in my family was below par, no matter what their coloring was.

More simply, my love of blonds was banal and needed no explanation. Everyone in America liked blonds and wanted to be one. 'If you have but one life to lead, why not live it as a blond?' was a Clairol ad of the day. Blonde women were sexy and dumb; blond men were intelligent and masterful. Blonds had downy hair on their arms, a shock of cotton candy under each arm, skin that was poreless and smooth as old percale and rubbery with youth, cool feet and warm chests, beards that came in late and heads that went bald early. Even their balding was patrician. Blonds were rare, pure; their necks and foreheads burned and their arms became amber brown under a dust of gold shavings. They looked good in pink or pale green linen, faded blue denim, their tanned feet sockless and sinewy in old, highly polished loafers. Blond men were tenors. They had no smell or only the smell of cold lake water. They inspired love, not lust. Their best look was classic, not contemporary. They looked good in camel's hair overcoats, blue blazers, frayed but expensive old Oxford shirts, machine-washed sneakers, an inherited gold signet ring. They should never wear Speedo's, just baggy old swimsuits. Their bellybuttons, optimally, were outies as neat as a child's ear. Their lips should be slightly chapped, sore and pink and unkissable. They should dance badly, self-consciously and seldom. Their bodies should look better in clothes than out of them. During long periods they should not follow the conversation. They are idols and should accept it. An idol doesn't converse.

Of course the whole category is idiotic, reminiscent of Flaubert's *Dictionary of Clichés* in which he writes, under Blondes, 'Hotter than brunettes,' and under Brunettes, 'Hotter than blondes.' These aren't categories but prejudices which correspond not to preferences but to racism. They are even vaguer and finally emptier than ascribed national characteristics.

The following pages are about Keith. He wasn't an ideal blond, not much like the type I've just described. Well, he was mysterious but not bland. He had a sharp personality.

After eight years of working for Time-Life Books in New York, from 1962 to 1970, I moved to Rome for several months. I lived it up during the last spasms of *La Dolce Vita*. I invited ten or twelve people to dinner every other night at the Piazza Navona; everyone drank lots of bad white wine and ate plates of spaghetti with white clam sauce. Mostly we smoked and drank coffee.

By July, six months later, I had spent all my money, written a screenplay no one liked and learned a smattering of Italian. I headed back to New York and found a studio apartment at 88 Horatio Street, not far from the docks, a third-floor walkup with gates on the windows. Almost immediately someone broke in and cleaned me out of my few possessions. In the *Village Voice* I saw the ad of a reformed housebreaker who knew how to burglarproof an apartment. 'I'm going to sink these pegs into the window frame. After a burglar smashes a window he has only two minutes to get in and if he meets up with something complicated he's going to say, "Fuck it." As for the door, I'll cover it on the inside with sheet metal.' He might have wondered what I wanted to safeguard – the two-foot-high fridge with the gas burner on top of it? The soiled single mattress on the floor? The swarms of cockroaches? The kitchen table on which my type-writer was enthroned? The phone? There was nothing else.

At Time-Life Books, thanks to the union, the Writers Guild, I'd had a month's vacation, a decent salary and job security. Now I had nothing – but I was reluctant to find another nine-to-five, coat-and-tie midtown job. I wanted to write fiction.

I began to ghostwrite chapters of university textbooks to pay the rent. My rent was just a hundred dollars a month. I had lots of energy and almost as much free time. I'd come back to New York, where the power of sex had been raised exponentially. Just a few blocks away empty trucks were parked overnight under the West Side Highway. In truck after truck, block after block, spontaneous orgies were taking place. There was nothing more satisfying than jumping up into a truck and inching slowly back into the dark hull and suddenly being grabbed around the waist by a strong pair of invisible hands and then feeling a slippery tongue exploring every filling in one's mouth. Like an Indian god the body would sprout two more hands, then four more, and they each had an assigned task, to tweak a nipple or tug down jeans or spread ass cheeks or liberate an erect penis.

Maybe my greatest pleasure was crouching with other guys under one truck and servicing whoever stood in the narrow space between it and the next truck over. All these drunk teenagers from

Jersey or the Bronx would line up and drop their trousers. For me it was a point of honor to take whoever happened to be standing in front of me. I never looked up to see the boy's face. I took what was offered to me – yet another sign of my saintly vocation.

Larry Kert, the Broadway singer who'd been the first Tony in *West Side Story*, lived across the street from me on the top floor of a nineteenth-century brick house. For him I was a rainy-day fuck. If it was too inclement to go out cruising Larry would call me and I'd come running. He was a native New Yorker; he and his sister had been performers since childhood. He'd always ask me what I was reading and writing; for him it was a natural thing to know artists of all sorts and to keep up. He was a great teaser in conversation. His approach to sex was athletic and callous. He wanted to get right down to it and after it was over he'd talk for the time it took to smoke two cigarettes.

One day I met a young man on a bicycle. His name was Keith and he was living with Larry – 'Just till I find a place of my own,' he said. He looked terribly young, no more than eighteen. But he said that he'd known Larry 'for donkey's years,' an Anglicism that went along with his accent, which was mid-Atlantic, though closer to Britain, despite a few Southern notes detectable here and there. It turned out his mother was Welsh but had married an American soldier. Keith had been brought up in Texas.

Keith was always prone to cures. He'd declare it was youth-and-beauty month and we had to stop smoking and drinking and eat nothing but sprouts and go to the gym every day. He could do it – he had strong self-discipline – but I'd be back to smoking Kents and eating burgers within a week.

One of his self-improvement schemes was the Chastity Club. That organization I gladly joined because Keith was willing to sleep in the same bed with me – chastely. Larry was away, on a tour of *Company*. It was August, the city was hot and deserted – but our state of chastity made everything sparkle. Whereas my little dirty room was filthy and half-alive, Larry's apartment was clean, flooded with light. It looked down on Horatio and, in back, on a garden. He had all the luxuries – air-conditioning, a hi-fi, a full-sized fridge, a vast double bed. Keith and I could fling ourselves across the giant bed, talk till we fell asleep, kiss chastely . . .

Keith had been brought up Catholic but he said he was sick of Catholic horror stories and ex-Catholic refugees. 'I don't want to hear any more about how Sister Mary Catherine beat Tom's palms with a stick or locked Henry in the water closet for three days.' Keith wanted people to be original, not only in their work, but in their lives. His friends assumed his interest in chastity stemmed from his Catholic childhood, but the Chastity Club was more in line with his other hygiene programs. He was chaste only between bouts of pagan excess, whereas I was willing to be chaste forever if it was in his arms. He was a small young man with perfect control over his body. He was good at gymnastics and swimming and his body had a lovely neatness about it. Everything he did seemed a conscious decision; nothing was a habit. He was disengaged and fastidious. Fatally, he'd also picked up Larry's sense of humor, but since Keith was more intelligent his darts were still sharper and he threw them with even more accuracy.

His existence was almost entirely aesthetic. He could see a photograph of a famous philosopher and say, 'I like the way the band around the cuff echoes his black belt' and not mention the distinguished subject. He wore white painter's pants, a T-shirt under a baggy shirt he'd found at Vintage Clothing and sneakers. He spent a fortune having his thick red-gold hair cut and shaped perfectly. He was a waif with expensive hair.

Sometimes his body seemed so young that I felt perverted holding him during our chaste nights. At other times he seemed as manly as Hotspur, especially when he went several days without shaving and his stubble grew in. His torso was thin and boyish but like a dancer's his legs were sturdy and strong. His dick was big, which I could see hard under the sheet in the morning.

At the end of the summer I decided to move to a seven-room apartment on Eighty-sixth and Columbus (for four hundred dollars a month). I asked Keith if he wanted to move with me – I even offered him the master bedroom with an adjoining bathroom. He accepted. He thought we were just friends but I already considered him to be my lover. We'd never made love, but for me our nights of chastity had bewitched me in a way no amount of explicit passion could have done. In the 1970s – in that short decade after gay liberation began and before AIDS arrived – sex was so available it was disappointing. The immediate gratification of desire short-circuited it. Our Chastity Club restored courtship, at least in my eyes. All our excitement was defused with our glances into a burning touch, into a conversation (full of nods and smiles) that lingered late into the night. As a sex partner I would never have felt up to Keith's level, but as a friend I knew I had something to offer. Because we went to sleep horny, sometimes in each other's arms, the fifteen angry minutes of any actual sex act, underscored by insecurity and followed by the sadness all animals experience after coitus, were exchanged for bright, troubling dreams of endless, squirming lap-sitting in gaudy gardens and group gropes in heavenly locker rooms.

Keith was so desirable that even before he turned to chastity he'd had to invent capricious reasons to justify to himself why he didn't have to go home with this one or that, all of them big, strapping specimens used to conquest and deserving of pursuit. Maybe that's one reason his approach to life was aesthetic, if aesthetics begins with the rejection of ordinary norms of beauty. 'That guy is too damn cocky with his big "what me, worry" smile and his tanning salon color and his shirts that look like Italian tablecloths.'

I, who was average in every physical aspect, envied him his choices. Almost any healthy, eager man between twenty and forty who fancied me was entirely to my liking. I didn't care if he grinned all the time or never – and I'd certainly never cared about anyone's fashion sense. When personal ads, which were just beginning to appear in the first alternative newspapers, said that someone was looking for a man in jeans and basketball shoes or a cowboy hat, I was puzzled. Couldn't anyone just buy those clothes for the occasion? And wouldn't they be shed immediately with any luck? Besides, did these uniforms stand for anything real or substantial?

Even a fetish I could understand, but Keith's pickiness didn't conform to any favorite sexual practice. No, he'd just say, 'I couldn't bear to sleep with a man who wore orange Keds,' or, 'You can see how carefully he chose that blue shirt to match his eyes – what a turnoff.'

Given how unsystematic his whims were, I was glad I was not presenting myself as a potential sex partner. I would never have been able to dodge my way across the minefield of his taste.

There were a few constants in his tastes. He liked hairy chests – not a generalized bearish fuzziness or blond down or elderly, disorderly brambles. No, he wanted a man with powerful pectoral muscles that were carpeted with an eagle pattern, perfectly symmetrical, of black, glossy, close-fitting filaments, an eagle opening its great wings over his torso like an Egyptian goddess leaning over an embalmed prince. A trail of black hair seen above white undershorts, heading for the bellybutton, promising a full, shiny bush below, only that piqued his excitement, he who was blond and smooth.

Keith moved in with me and almost immediately dropped the idea of chastity, which for him was no more of a commitment than his weekly singing lessons or his veganism. I was devastated, since like all lovers in a one-sided affair I didn't much mind if my beloved wasn't sleeping with me so long as he wasn't sleeping with anyone else. I was always mooning around our vast, unfurnished apartment looking at Keith reproachfully, and he'd say, 'Stop staring at me, you silly cow!'

He wasn't the least bit attracted to me and never had been. In that case I should never have invited him to move in, since for me familiarity bred adoration and the symbol of living under the same roof was so potent that after a month together I thought we were married.

Keith worked odd jobs – painting apartments, walking dogs, occasionally turning a trick – and he spent everything on food and flowers and books and records. He had a horror of appearing middle-class and today, thirty years later, he remains one of the few pure bohemians I know – no savings, no health plan, few clothes, less furniture. Over the years many rich men have fallen in love with him, but he's always preferred starving artists, bookish nerds with glasses, foreign gymnasts with a speech defect. I never had an aversion to the bourgeoisie. Better a crackling fire than a cold grate. Better a warm coat than chronic bronchitis. On the other hand I was never willing to sacrifice very much time to earning a living. Nevertheless, I was afraid of poverty. I'd grown up with a certain anxiety about having enough money to eat, pay my bills and appear respectable, though I'd never wanted to be a success in my father's unhappy way.

I would buy the basic pieces of furniture for our many rooms –

an ugly dining room table and heavy high-backed chairs that I found at the Salvation Army, a green Chinese carpet with balding patches I discovered in a junk shop, cumbersome floor lamps, a denim-covered couch bed I bought on sale at a neighborhood shop – but Keith wept when he saw them.

One day I came home to find them all out in the hallway. We had our only quarrel.

'I want to invite people over for dinner,' I said. 'I want to sit on the carpet or the couch and watch television with friends and eat popcorn.'

'I don't want people who would do those things in my house,' Keith said. He was stoned. 'Can't you see how ugly it all is?'

'Yes, but I don't want to live like a Zen monk,' I said.

'A Zen – oh!' he exclaimed. 'If only . . .'

I was sad during the years when I lived with Keith, since I was hopelessly in love with him, but all the same it was an exhilarating sadness and one of the most creative periods of my life. He took nothing for granted, and neither could I, and not one of our days resembled another. We're all creatures of habit and every old dog stares reproachfully at whatever disturbs his routine, but inspiration breaks through exactly at those ruptures. Perhaps a schedule is needed to write serious works (if so, then all mine are frivolous because the only thing I'm sure to do every day is stall). But a new idea – let's give it a name, 'originality' – is at least as necessary as what the French call *rédaction*, the writing-out of a book that has already been thoroughly imagined. This original conception springs forth only when we're stoned or having a breakdown or living on the wing or half-asleep or trying to like a new city.

I believe in Rimbaud's *dérèglement des sens* and Keith had an accomplished way of unstringing my lyre. Is there anything more enchanting than coming home late at night, prepared to surrender to a sodden sleep – and to discover that your young lover is wide awake, radiant, and that he absolutely insists that you listen to the avant-garde playlet he and his swarthy friend have just devised? You are seated on the one remaining chair and Keith and Jonathan strike very arch poses with improvised pince-nez and cigarette holder and launch into a scene from Noël Coward's *Private Lives*, except they're reciting all the lines backwards.

If the unexamined life isn't worth living, then ours was exceptionally worthy since there wasn't a radish we ate, a cactus we
talked to, a man we bedded that we didn't study from every angle.

A lot of people entered our lives – my nephew Keith came to live
with us in the mid-1970s. For a while Keith (not my heterosexual
nephew) was having an affair with John Uecker, the Brando
lookalike who was living with Tennessee Williams and was in
the next room when Williams choked to death on a bottle cap.
Then Keith had an idyll with the still-handsome, big virile movie
star of the 1950s, Tab Hunter, and we'd hear Tab shouting, 'Go
on, boy, sit on that big daddy dick!' The rest of the time Tab would
do tatting and talk with my nephew. Keith slept with his idol, the
stage director Robert Wilson, and when Keith moved to Los
Angeles for a while, I had drunken sex with Wilson, too. Once
we even called Keith and had a telephonic three-way with him.

Keith never wanted to sleep with me alone. I rounded up five
guys at the local leather bar and brought them home one night, and
there was Keith spinning around the apartment making art under
bright work lights. He was writing tiny, illegible doodles on big
sheets of paper years before anyone else except Agnes Martin was
doing the same thing. I'd organized my orgy on the off chance that
Keith would be excited (he was) and would join in (he did) and I
could caress him in the mêlée (I could). We even had sex together
after everyone left, as the winter dawn was developing outside, just
the two of us, tender, magical.

We didn't know about Sex Magic in those days. We'd never
heard of the sex act as a ceremony, a spell or exorcism, as a form of
white magic. Too bad, since Keith could have been an ideal
shaman. If at the time I thought it was inexplicably cruel, his
reluctance to make love to me, now I find it inexplicably generous,
the few times he surrendered his perfect, pale body to my clumsy
embraces. Surely he couldn't, from one day to the next, have
changed his mind and ceased to see me as a passionate buffoon,
a pudgy Pagliacci. Which means he really did act out of compassion – he understood how much I was hurting for him.

One night we smoked some powerful dope and stripped to our
underwear. Keith kept me waiting on my knees, blindfolded, in
the interior hallway while he filled our empty living room with

candles. When at last he led me inside, he fed me his beautiful body. If only we'd had words, rites, a pollution and a cleansing, if only we'd had spells to chant and a miracle to perform, but Keith did his best, as if he were a pagan who'd once seen the Catholic Mass and was approximating it now in a child's mud-pie version. I'll never forget that night. Perhaps I'll be lucky enough to think of it on my deathbed. Even now when I'm wheeled into a metal tunnel for a CAT scan and I mustn't panic or even twitch, I medicate myself on memories of T pissing in my mouth or my favorite Scotsman nodding toward me and saying to his lover, 'Not yet, I want to fuck him some more.' While I'm enduring a root canal intervention or an excruciating operation to dig out a deep plantar wart – at these dicey moments the amiable Professor White is so calm and smiling because he's drugged himself on memories of being sodomized at both ends. Sometimes I think I'm just a sex junkie, corrupted through and through by a lost life of vicious habits. But at other times I say to myself that there is nothing but pleasure, moments of pleasure, to redeem the suffering or, worse, the insipidness of this life, and these moments include reading Jean Giono's *The Horseman on the Roof* in a dry, hot house in Provence late at night as a light wind begins to stir the tops of a poplar, which the French more sensibly call a *tremble*. Or walking up a lane between hedgerows in Brontë country in England one July afternoon and swatting at horseflies in the last hot patch of sunlight before steel-gray clouds close in over the moors and time starts up again. Or walking up stairs confected out of stiffly whipped plaster into an empty room in Venice to look at ceiling paintings by Tiepolo which I lean over to contemplate in a mirror I am holding so I won't have to torture my arthritic neck by looking up. Or there is the moment when I realized I'd like to be a grandfather even though I never felt paternal longings; but how I'd love to have a silly, noisy five-year-old, pure as a glass of milk, awakening me from my nap so we could go for a walk through city streets emptied by August – even this unfulfilled longing is a mixed pleasure. But of them all the greatest pleasure is the vision of Keith in the candlelight, his flesh as luminous as the face of one of Blake's sword-wielding angels.

*   *   *

Keith was chosen to play the boy in *Equus* on Broadway opposite Richard Burton, when Burton replaced the original English star, Anthony Hopkins. Keith appeared hundreds of times opposite Burton, then Tony Perkins. Burton was just emerging from years of heavy drinking and it was Keith who fed him his lines when he dried up and Keith who steered him back to Act One when he'd suddenly leapt ahead to an unrelated speech in the second act. When Burton received a special Tony Award for his performance he presented it to Keith onstage during curtain call the next night, telling the audience, 'He deserves this more than I do.'

Keith's role changed our lives. Keith knew that two thousand people would be examining his naked body eight times a week (some of the audience seated on the stage just a few feet away from him) and he feared that every blemish on his butt would be carefully studied for two hours. He had to be in perfect shape, night after night, month after month, and he didn't dare gain or lose a pound because a little belly would be as ludicrous as a gaunt chest would be alarming. He couldn't look tired or pale. No more all-nighters on scraped knees from sessions in the trucks or telltale hickeys from ardent lovers.

If it was my job as temple maiden to keep the vestal intact, there were many recompenses. At least once a day I knew where he would be. Before, when he hadn't been working, he'd introduced disorder, even panic, into our everyday life, but now he sought serenity. He was a worker, even if the work was heroic. Before, he'd turned to sex as his sole form of theater and his many, many partners as his ever-changing audience, but now he had no need to pack the house; he was perceived, he did exist.

I keep being haunted, as I write these pages, by an essay by Susan Sontag in which she criticizes writers for employing a religious vocabulary and borrowing its 'prestige' even though they're not believers. I'm guilty (there I go again!) of that sacrilege in my descriptions of Keith, though I hope to suggest his grail-like glow (oops!), his sacramental generosity (. . .) with his body. I've used the words 'mystical atheist' to describe myself, but that's only a way of saying I like the halo of religion but not the bearded, humorless face the aureole frames or that I want the dividends of grace without making the investment of either faith or good works.

Over the years I've written about Keith frequently – I even made him into a woman, Edwige, in my heterosexual fantasy novel, *Caracole*. He's Kevin in *The Farewell Symphony*, he's the young New York actor living in Los Angeles in my travel book, *States of Desire*. And he made his first appearance as the narrator in *Nocturnes for the King of Naples*, the novel I was writing when I lived with him. In that book he's become an older man looking back on a period when he lived with someone resembling the poet Frank O'Hara or God or me. The older lover, the person he's addressing, has died, as it turns out. I was deep into the Bible when I was writing *Nocturnes* as well as baroque art and poetry, those theatrical works of the Counter-Reformation that attempted to seduce the spirit through the flesh or reach the flesh through heavenly blandishments. In my religion the devil existed (at least I knelt before a fantasy version of him once, when he was dressed in leather on a Tuesday afternoon at three in the hallway of our apartment). There was no rigor in my religion, no bingo games, no commandments. Morality, in fact, had nothing to do with my faith, which was an exalting, not a moderating force. Writing *Nocturnes* was probably driven by my spite toward Keith, the desire to imagine him old and as unattractive as I fervently believed I was then. I hoped that someday his beauty would abandon him, that the Ark would be emptied and the shrine deconsecrated.

Nocturnes was published in 1978. Now, a quarter of a century later, Keith and I have become best of friends. His humor is still so quick he remains the fastest draw in the West, for there is no way to be funny and not mean, but the laughter he provokes neutralizes the sting. He's had the same lover for many years, a gifted Israeli painter, just as I go on and on having the same friends decade after decade. If this book is published as planned I'll undoubtedly have a dinner to celebrate it to which I'll invite Marilyn and Stan and Keith and my lover Michael, maybe T, certainly the ghost of Jim Ruddy.

Keith directs plays now but he's also turned to fiction; his first novel, *Acqua Calda*, has just been published and the writing is as dazzling as his conversation, the moral point as uncompromising and shimmering as his own sweet, sarcastic take on things.

Why did I fall in love hopelessly again and again? I swore when I was in my mid-thirties that I'd never weep over another man – and I never did until my mid-sixties, when T left me. I found all those tears absurd, old-fashioned, even *Catholic*, in the worst, martyred sense.

And yet was there nothing that made all that moisture worthwhile, all that writhing on the bed productive, all that regret fertile? Or was it just a monotonous, prolonged joke in bad taste?

Perhaps I'm only trying to save face belatedly and to elevate something that was essentially humiliating. I have no doubt that my three blonds (four, if one counts T) were muses. They inspired me. Their absence gave me the room to think – even to think about them. I studied them with a focus and an intensity that later I brought only to Jean Genet when I wrote his biography. Just as I speculated every day about whether Genet danced in a woman's pink slip for the Black Panthers and why he would have done something so out of character, in the same way I pondered, week after week in my twenties, why Stanley had left me for Ashley, why Jim Ruddy had gone mad and Keith had consented to make slow, brutal love to me one winter dawn as the hot-water pipes knocked three times like the triple thump that announces the rise of the curtain at the Comédie Française. Proust says that love is the perfect training for a writer since it makes us jealous and alert and suspicious and leads us to submit the beloved to a circular analysis that later we can apply to any literary subject. I was never jealous, or very seldom, and I hatched no stratagems for winning someone back; I can't claim I was perfecting my powers of observation. All I was doing was living – excruciatingly – in the remembered moment, not in the perception of the scene before me (the wet pillowcase, the gauze curtains shifting and swelling in the breeze slipping in through the cracked window) but of the beautiful body that my imagination turned like a vase before setting it out to dry.

At Genet's grave in Larash, Morocco, with John Purcell

My Genet

I had already lived in France four years when my editor Bill Whitehead back in New York asked me if I knew anyone who could write a biography of Jean Genet, the great novelist-thief-homosexual who'd died only the year before, in 1986. I was astonished that there was no proper biography of him already.

Of course there was Jean-Paul Sartre's *Saint Genet*, which was termed an 'existential psychoanalysis.' Eventually I realized that the hard biographical facts in this book could be reduced to a thirty-page summary. All of its hundreds of other pages were filled with speculation, brilliant but controvertible.

I proposed myself as Genet's biographer and Bill accepted me instantly. What I didn't know was that Bill was already ill with AIDS and would be dead within two years. He certainly seemed at the height of health and fitness; he stayed with me in Paris and when I tried to keep up with his daily aerobics exercises I was left crippled.

I'd known that I was HIV-positive since 1985 and I kept imagining that in another year or two I'd be dead. Doing the Genet biography was my way of shaking my fist at fate. I figured it would take at least three years to research and write. And it wasn't the sort of personal elegy readers might expect, but an objective study of someone I had never known.

I decided that Genet deserved a scrupulous, highly detailed, strictly chronological biography in which the biographer himself would never intrude as a voice or character. Maybe because I was an autobiographical novelist and tired of the word 'I,' I longed for the 'otherness' of traditional biography. Nor did I believe '*Monsieur Genet, c'est moi,*' since I knew that Genet had despised fellow homosexuals, most whites, all white Americans, fellow writers, all middle-class people – on five counts I was out. Whereas I'd been sent to private schools and psychiatrists and had never gone to bed cold or hungry, Genet had been '*un enfant abandonné*' and had entered into a life of crime (petty thefts in order to eat) in his early adolescence and had known years of deprivation and imprisonment. But I remembered that once I'd intended to run away to New York, dye my hair and become a whore.

In the end the biography took seven years of my life and like George Eliot, who said when she finished *Romola*, 'I started it as a young woman and finished it as an old one,' I, too, felt that the book divided my youth from old age. Bill Whitehead died early on but my own health remained stable. Throughout the seven years of researching and writing *Genet*, however, the possibility of not dying soon had not yet been envisioned.

As I toiled on the book one vociferous gay American critic attacked me for wasting my time and shirking my responsibilities by not tackling AIDS, the one and only subject demanding our attention. Of course I recognized the need to write about AIDS, which eventually I did in my stories, *Skinned Alive*, and in two novels, *The Farewell Symphony* and *The Married Man*. But for the moment, all through the worst years, before an effective treatment was invented, I pecked away at the immense Genet project. Perhaps I believed the gods would preserve me until it was finished. More likely I thought that if I lived I'd write about AIDS later, after it had cooled off as a topic. I saw my fiction as something like stitching quilts which are made out of used and faded materials. I'd lived through the 1950s when homosexuality had been treated as a disease; in the 1980s I saw it being 'medicalized' again and I wanted to remind gay readers of at least one cultural giant, Genet, whose life had had nothing to do with AIDS.

The only hitch was that I didn't know how to write a biography. Certainly not this one. Most literary biographies are about middle-class men and women who have spent their lives in an intellectual and artistic milieu. Their juvenilia are carefully preserved by a doting mother. Their success is often early, their friends are fellowscribblers who generate and put into archives their journals and letters, whose movements are documented by cultural journalists and whose manuscripts are sold to libraries.

Genet was the opposite. His first thirty years were spent as a foster child, runaway, delinquent, soldier, prostitute and thief, and only his extraordinary intelligence and imagination saved him – and especially his ability to transcend himself. He was brought up by peasants in the Morvan (the equivalent to Tennessee in the States) in a narrow-minded world, but he ended up as a friend to the Palestinians and Black Panthers. He established a reputation by writing five autobiographical novels in five years, books that reversed all the conventional views of homosexuality and did so in an eloquent, sometimes arch literary manner, and then he moved on to write three of the key plays of the twentieth century (*The Balcony*, *The Blacks* and *The Screens*) which in no way touched on the homosexual experience but dealt with the inner workings of political power, colonialism, race and the fate of those who remain marginal and excluded even after a popular revolution. If I'd changed as a writer and person over the years my development had been much more modest. I began as more privileged and I ended up as less radical than Genet.

His life was difficult to document. Over the years he'd dropped most of his friends and whenever I met one I first had to soothe wounded feelings. And then some of his friends had been jailbirds who didn't live long, who if they survived were hard to find, who if found wouldn't talk, or if they talked had to be paid and weren't to be believed. During a period of just seven years Genet had mixed with Parisian artistic folk, everyone from Simone de Beauvoir to the sculptor Giacometti. Of his artistic friends only Leonor Fini was still alive (she has since died) when I began my research and she wouldn't see me until the last few minutes before the book went to press. Then she talked to me briefly on the phone. All those who had remained loyal to Genet didn't want to give me an interview; Genet had never wanted a biography written about him, possibly because he didn't want a set of facts that would compete with what he called, in medieval tones, his 'golden legend.'

And I should mention that though Genet rejected France and exulted when Hitler's armies marched into Paris, he remained thoroughly French. When I began my research I still spoke French with some difficulty and my comprehension of speech was full of holes. I'd 'only' been in France four years at that time; it would take another six before I'd feel at ease in the language. Learning a language is hard after age forty and I'd never been gifted for the task. Thank heavens I could tape interviews and listen to them later with native French speakers.

Genet had provided a record, real or invented, of his life in four of his five novels and most people referred to *The Thief's Journal*, the last one, as his 'autobiography.' Moreover he'd been friendly with Sartre at the time *Saint Genet* had been written; Genet was constantly feeding Sartre either correct or fallacious or careless information. Genet loved to invent poetic lies. For instance, in *Miracle of the Rose* he claimed he'd been imprisoned at Fontevrault, but later I discovered that he'd only visited the prison as a tourist. What he liked about Fontevrault was that it had been a royal abbey before the Revolution and it housed the tombs of Richard the Lion-Heart and Eleanor of Aquitaine – Plantagenets who he thought were somehow related to him, Genet.

I'd hired two young Americans in Paris, not because they were trained researchers but because I liked them. One of them, Gregory Rowe, interviewed half a dozen people for me – and chanced upon a crucial discovery, the name of the village where Genet had grown up. A friend of Gregory's saw an article by a certain Joseph Bruley, a classmate of Genet's, in a newspaper published in Paris for readers who'd once lived in the Morvan. The article was full of false cheer and an unreliable, upbeat portrait of the little Genet, but discovering the name of the village was a breakthrough. We learned that there were thirteen people from the village who'd known Genet and were still alive and not all of them bought Bruley's sunny version of things. Genet's foster parents' house was still standing, though it had been restructured, and the school next door – even the school library – was virtually unchanged. We learned that Genet had been sent to this place, the village of Alligny-en-Morvan, when he was seven months old, not seven years (as Sartre had stated), and that the terrible scene Sartre reported of the villagers driving Genet away because he'd been accused of theft – that this scene had never taken place. Many people knew that Genet filched little things, like erasers and pencils, but he left the village at age twelve in triumph as the best scholar in the region, assigned to a trade school in Paris for typography, which was the best assignment possible for a ward of the state.

The other young American I hired, Roberta Fineberg, helped me crack a very hard nut. Genet had worked for years with a woman, Paule Thévenin, on preparing the final text of his most difficult and ambitious play, *The Screens*. On the phone she refused to see me, citing Genet's dislike of biography – in particular one about him.

It turned out that Roberta knew Paule, who felt a motherly tenderness for the young and attractive American. Although Roberta's French was excellent, I encouraged her to take language lessons from Paule, which I would secretly pay for. My idea was that if the two became sufficiently intimate Roberta might be able to vouch for me.

Paule lived in a ramshackle but spacious and modern apartment in a complex that had been bought and converted into housing by a group of friends. When she at last agreed to see me she was surly and suspicious. Her mother was Algerian, her father a French soldier; she'd been trained as a psychiatrist, and now she was in her late sixties. Years before she'd been adopted as a 'daughter' by the mad visionary painter and writer and man of the theater, Antonin Artaud. She was in the process of editing every last scrap of Artaud's writings in more than twenty volumes published by Gallimard. Though her edition was scholarly and beautifully annotated, her critics said that all of Artaud that was worth reading could have been issued in three cheap paperbacks, easily accessible and tempting to the wider public, and that Paule's edition had succeeded only in reducing the number of his readers. In the same way Gallimard, which was also Genet's publisher, had been slow to publish Genet's works in affordable editions; a whole generation of students in France had not been able to buy them.

Paule offered me nothing, not even a glass of water; the French don't like to confuse business meetings with friendly gatherings. But she liked me. She could see I was serious and humble and appreciative. She could also tell that I had no desire to sit in judgment on Genet. She called a mutual friend, who repeated her words: 'Monsieur White came by and I opened the top drawer of information for him; maybe I'll open other drawers in later encounters.'

Paule's husband was dead but when he'd been alive he'd written prescriptions for Genet of the high doses of sleeping pills, Nembutal, that he'd taken every night. He'd also X-rayed Genet's diseased kidneys and soon Paule was gaily pulling the huge, flimsy X-rays out of their yellowing envelopes and showing me pictures of my subject's vital organs.

Paule looked like a big, sleepy toad, her eyes devoured by puffy sacs, her mouth turned down and inscrutable, but at some unpredictable moment her tongue would unscroll and stun her victim. There was also something of the crafty eunuch about her, bored and evil. And yet she was motherly, even (under all the layers of Gallic disdain and North African haughtiness) . . . (dare I say it?) – even *twinkly*.

I had her to dinner. If the other guests chattered about things irrelevant to her, the toad settled more heavily into her folds, the filmed-over eyes betrayed no curiosity. But if the conversation came back to Genet, she'd hop about excitedly.

Most of the time she was dismissive. She had a practiced way of turning her mouth down and saying, 'But no, no, it's not that' ('*Mais non, non, c'est pas ça*'), which in her vocabulary was extremely damning (after we listened to a Benjamin Britten CD she said, '*La musique, c'est pas ça,*' as in 'That's not music') – an expression so definitive it was not debatable.

Once she took an interest in someone she fussed and scolded like a mother. I introduced Stephen Barber to her, a young Englishman from Leeds who eventually wrote my biography but who at that time was writing a life of Artaud. He started off with an article about Artaud's drawings based on Paule's show at the Centre Georges Pompidou. Paule professed to be scandalized by Stephen's sketchy French (which was improving dramatically day by day) and his *embonpoint* (a fault he shared with me). Her preferred mode was at once put-upon and indulgent, exactly like a mother who bails her spendthrift son out one more time, frowning and smiling at the same moment.

Her huge duplex was comfortable, with skylights, polished cedar and black leather couches, the walls covered with Artaud's draw-ings. Despite her calm domestic surface, she'd harbored terrorists in her day, especially Klaus Croissant, the lawyer who represented (and sympathized with) the most extreme German group, the Baader-Meinhof. Croissant had gone from legally representing these murdering terrorists to illegally collaborating with them. Paule was careful to point out that she never approved of the violence committed by the Baader-Meinhof, but she was equally against the prison conditions to which they were subjected. She had hidden Croissant, a fugitive from justice, in her apartment for a month.

Many of France's most brilliant people respected Paule; she introduced Genet to the philosopher Jacques Derrida (who wrote a curious meditation on Genet and Hegel named *Glas*, the French word for 'knell') and through her Genet became reacquainted and friendly with the composer Pierre Boulez. Boulez and Genet planned to write an opera together in the late 1970s, but nothing came of it; at that time Genet had no confidence in his own work.

If the French aristocracy has little left but its exquisite manners, the French intelligentsia prides itself on its rudeness, its all-too-painful honesty. Of all the rude people I've known, Paule was the most disagreeable. As Hubert Sorin, my lover, said in a formula that only a Frenchman could have pronounced, 'She has a nasty nature which is very appealing' (*'Elle a un sale caractère, très attachant'*).

After two years of research I'd made almost no progress on the biography. I had no strategy, no goals, no procedures. I had no skills for dismissing hearsay and evaluating competing versions of an event. I lied and told my English and American editors that I was a third of the way done, though I'd written nothing yet. I'd been given sizable advances in England and America. If I didn't turn the book in I'd have to repay all that money – which was totally impossible. I'd spent it. In New York I saw a bus hurtling toward me and I thought, if I just step in front of it I won't have to write my biography.

Meanwhile, in 1988 a brief biography of Genet, based on a mosaic of newspaper clippings, was published in France, written by Jean-Bernard Moraly, a Frenchman who had recently moved to Israel and become an Israeli patriot, perhaps not the ideal person to

313

write about someone ardently pro-Palestinian (even less ideal than a bourgeois American). A more useful work that also came out in 1988 was an *Essai de chronologie* of the first thirty-five years of Genet's life, worked out in meticulous detail by Albert Dichy and Pascal Fouché. These two brilliant and resourceful scholars had reconstructed Genet's entire police record from tiny items in provincial newspapers (Genet, for instance, had 'doctored' a train ticket, changing the destination from one city to another farther along, and he'd been caught for it – or he'd stolen a fabric sample or even the signature of King François I; these were his most serious crimes). I thought that if I could fill in this masterful chronology with the relationship between his life and his work and give the social background (the world of the foster-child system, the reform school, the army) that I'd have the first half of Genet's life done. But what about the second half?

At the time, 1988–89, Albert Dichy was working part-time in a minuscule research library housed in one room in a ghastly modern tower, lined with asbestos, at Paris III, a branch of the city university on the Left Bank. He was the sole guardian of the burgeoning archives of IMEC (l'Institut Mémoires de l'édition contemporaine), a library devoted to the papers of key French writers of the twentieth century – and of their editors. Previously no one had been much interested in the contracts, correspondence and proofs generated by a publishing house, but IMEC inaugurated a new era of studying the editorial apparatus surrounding a few great novelists and poets.

Albert was then in his mid-thirties, I suppose. He'd been born and brought up in Beirut and educated in French Jesuit schools (though his father was an Egyptian Jew and his mother a Ladino-speaking Turkish Jew). His parents talked to each other in French and indeed each generation of his mother's family had been registered at the local French consulate as French citizens. It had all started when a great-grandfather had benefited from a decision the French made to grant Algerian Jews citizenship, though neither that great-grandfather nor any of his descendants had ever visited France.

When Beirut collapsed in civil war in the mid-1970s, Albert and his mother and brother, as French citizens, fled to Brittany (Albert's wife, Danielle, was French and Breton). Albert's father had lost his Egyptian citizenship when King Farouk was deposed. Later Monsieur Dichy had finagled an Iranian passport (which became invalid when the Shah was overthrown). As a stateless individual he had a considerable problem getting into France, but eventually he managed it.

Albert worked as a door-to-door salesman in Rennes. Eventually he found a job in Paris in advertising. But his real love was literature and by the time I met him he was devoting a few hours a day to IMEC.

I was always trying to wheedle information about Genet out of Albert – until one day it occurred to me I could hire him. He went to work part-time for me, he quit advertising, and suddenly I began to receive neatly typed sheets of blue paper on which Albert summarized everything known to date about Genet's lovers or his foster mother or his stay as an adolescent as a French soldier in Damascus. Albert showed me that the most important framework for a biography was a chronology, which with any luck metastasized into ever more elaborate (and accurate) detail.

My life as a biographer changed. Albert made appointments for me with all the difficult, aging people Genet had known. He taught me to be skeptical about people's versions of events and to speculate why they might see things one way rather than another. Since the people I was meeting would end up as 'characters' in my book, I needed to know something about them, remember what they looked like, place them in the subtle but highly articulated French social structure. Like me Albert was an outsider but he was a heterosexual man with wide sympathies, a survivor's powers of observation, a deep, international culture and a richly paradoxical mind. He was also extremely diplomatic.

With Albert at my side many previously closed doors sprang open. We went to Genet's village and interviewed his godmother, Lucie Wirtz, who was one hundred and spoke in the dialect of the Morvan; her granddaughter had to translate her words into French for us. Little things came clear. We were curious about what Genet was describing when he said the boys at his reform school, Mettray, tattooed themselves; Albert located an old jailbird who'd been at Mettray and he showed us his 'tattoos,' i.e. designs dug into the flesh with the graphite from ordinary pencils. The Minister of the Interior himself told us he didn't have the power to open Genet's dossier at the Assistance Publique. It seemed Genet might have a living brother, who insisted that the dossier remain closed. We bribed someone at the Assistance to read passages from the dossier over the phone.

Together Albert and I visited Jacques Guérin in 1990 at his magnificent country house outside Paris, a mansion that had been designed by Gabriel, the architect who'd built the Place de la Concorde. Guérin had been born illegitimate in 1902 and raised by a rich mother in a vast apartment on the Parc Monceau filled with gory paintings of suspended meat by Soutine. Erik Satie was a frequent visitor – as was Gaston Monteux, the wealthy shoe manufacturer (and Jacques's father and Madame Guérin's lover).

At age eighty-eight Jacques Guérin was a *grand seigneur* in the most unpleasant sense of the term. A young live-in Italian scholar, Carlo Jansiti, who was writing a biography of Violette Leduc, another great Guérin protégée, danced constant attendance on the rich old man. Guérin made nasty cracks about black people while two black servants from the Antilles served the four of us at table with impassive good manners. He was extremely vain about the books and manuscripts he'd been collecting all his life; when they were finally auctioned off the sales lasted three days and made headlines.

As Albert Dichy explained to me, an art collector who possesses a unique object (a painting or sculpture) likes to show off his possession, but a book and manuscript collector is much more cagey. If he reveals the content of a previously unpublished item and if it's reprinted by someone else, it loses its uniqueness. A collector is happy to show you his Monet – what can you do but admire it and envy him? But Guérin was reluctant to show me the pages Genet had cut from *The Thief's Journal*. On the other hand, if I had no idea whatsoever of the nature of his treasure I'd not be filled with the right covetous longings. So, as a compromise, Guérin decided to read out loud selected passages from the dropped pages.

What Guérin didn't know (because his eyes weren't very good) was that I was taping him. The Italian assistant, however, later told Guérin that I'd recorded him – and Guérin was furious. He called me that same evening and told me that I wasn't a gentleman. He demanded I mail him the tape immediately – which I did only after I'd copied from it everything of use to me. Fortunately, Guérin liked my book when it eventually came out and forgot about my caddishness. Albert pointed out to me that Genet had made an amateur movie (now lost) at Guérin's estate. The film was about a baptism and Genet played the baby, Violette Leduc the mother and Guérin's brother the priest. 'Considering that all three characters were born illegitimate,' Albert said, 'it was inevitable that the subject of the film would be a baptism.'

Guérin was an extraordinary collector – of Renaissance manuscripts, of Rimbaud's manuscript of *A Season in Hell*, of the copy of *Les Fleurs du Mal* that Baudelaire inscribed to his mother, of the copy of his first poems that Genet inscribed to Sartre and Beauvoir. Guérin also owned several important Genet manuscripts.

And Proust's bedroom! Guérin owned all the contents of the bedroom in which Proust had died, including thirteen notebooks, the bed and other furniture, printer's proofs and letters. In the 1980s Guérin gave the shabby room and its priceless contents to the Musée Carnavalet, a seventeenth-century mansion in which the great letter writer Madame de Sévigné had lived – a fitting setting, since Sévigné had been one of Proust's favorite writers.

Genet sometimes said that he'd begun writing after he read Proust in his prison cell – in particular the passage about Françoise cooking a *boeuf en gelée* with carrots for the elegant and hypocritical diplomat Monsieur de Norpois. One of the people I interviewed was Claude Mauriac, who was not only the son of the great Catholic, François Mauriac, but also the husband of Proust's great-niece. Claude told me that once Genet met Claude's mother-in-law, Proust's niece, Madame Mantes-Proust, and ever afterwards Genet would ask to be remembered to '*Madame votre belle-mère.*' If Genet was a thug and normally derisive, he had the manners of a prince when he was addressing someone connected to one of the very few people in his personal pantheon.

One day Albert and I visited Lydie Dattas, a poet published by Gallimard and the estranged wife of Alexandre Bouglione, a scion of the great circus family. Lydie had held the revolver pointed at the lion when her husband had entered the lion's cage.

Genet had met Alexandre in 1976 and had fallen in love with him. Genet had moved into the building where Alexandre and Lydie lived in Pigalle – a building on which was emblazoned the Bouglione family name. But in 1984 Genet quarreled with Alexandre – and was thrown out of the building. Genet left behind a suitcase full of unpublished manuscripts. When I met Lydie in 1992 she was living in poverty and selling off the manuscripts page by page, for one thousand francs a page (about a hundred fifty dollars). I tried to convince Yale to buy the manuscripts intact, but no one was interested.

One of the most striking people I interviewed was the actress Chantal Darget, a beautiful blonde of a certain age who'd played Madame Irma in a celebrated production of *The Balcony*. She chitchatted with me for a while and then took my hand with tears in her eyes. She said, 'Monsieur White, I have lung cancer and I'll be dead in a month. I want you to have these letters from Genet to me. What good will they do me where I'm going?'

The phone rang. She picked it up and began to baby talk, then she hung up.

'Grandchild?' I asked.

'No, Ionesco. He's lost his mind but it comforts him to call me every once in a while and hear me gurgle . . .'

Soon afterwards I read her obituary with sadness since I'd so admired her straightforwardness and simplicity (and generosity). Though she was ill she'd maintained her platinum-blonde hair and Chinese red nails. She spoke in an 'effective' deep voice, yet strangely enough I couldn't help but feel that all her theatrical discipline was precisely what was helping her now.

A young English friend of mine, Jane Giles (at that time Stephen Barber's lover), wanted to interview Lucien Sénémaud, the star of Genet's 1950 twenty-five-minute long, black-and-white silent movie, *The Song of Love*. Genet had helped Lucien build a house outside Cannes and bankrolled a garage for him, which Lucien named the Garage Saint Genet. In 1989 Jane and I took a train to Cannes, and a taxi to the garage. We spotted the slender, still handsome Lucien, now a man close to sixty. When we told him we'd like to interview him about Genet he just slid back under a car he was repairing. His plain-talking wife, Ginette, was sitting in a dark little office and she spoke to us at length. Considering that *The Song of Love* was long considered to be gay pornography, it was startling to hear her say, 'Oh, yes, I'm sure the movie was shot in the spring of 1950 because when Lucien was in Paris making it I was here having our daughter Nelly and Lucien was sorry not to be with me.'

Irritated that Ginette was talking so freely about his homosexual past, Lucien began to gun the motor he was working on louder and louder until the garage was filled with noise and fumes. Ginette told us, once the roar died down, that Genet had approved of her when he first met her because he liked beautiful things and she was, in her own words, 'thin, beautiful, with frank manners.' She told us how Genet had been one of only four people to attend her wedding. He had always sided with her in her arguments with Lucien. Money for their house came from Genet's play *The Maids*.

Genet, I realized, had a pattern of marrying off his lovers and then building or planning to build houses for the new couple in which there would always be a room for him, though he seldom visited. It was as if the abandoned child were creating parents and a hearth to which he'd never be completely welcome.

Ginette Sénémaud had had two children by an earlier husband. One of them, Jacky Maglia, had been just seven when Lucien married his mother. Genet had taken an instant liking to the boy, who eventually became a car racer to please him (and briefly a car thief). Genet had taught Jacky to write, and their handwriting was exactly alike. Genet and Jacky had been lovers (in that sense Genet had loved both father and stepson), though another lover of that period we interviewed, Java, told us that Genet's sexuality was mainly in his head. Java and his wife, incidentally, became great friends of the Sénémauds. Genet himself once said that he'd never lived out his sexuality 'in a pure form,' meaning he'd always mixed affection in with sex (presumably a weakness in Genet's estimation).

I began to see that in the old Mediterranean world an established man of means who took a long-term interest in a poor young man was simply considered a benefactor – and no one questioned what they did when the lights were off. Parents were happy that the son suddenly had a few opportunities; the man of means was happy to have a protégé (and eventually an heir). The combination of devoted older man and beautiful ephebe, after all, went back to ancient Greece, though the Greek ideal had excluded a disparity in wealth.

Both the ancient and the modern models entailed a pedagogical relationship. Genet thought he was an expert in every field except the one in which he truly excelled, writing. He pushed his lover Abdellah, a high-wire artist, to attempt ever riskier feats – until the young man fell not once but twice, shattered his body and finally committed suicide, using some of Genet's own Nembutals. Genet coached Jacky Maglia to drive the Lotus he bought him – and then Jacky crashed and his right arm was left permanently paralyzed. When Jacky was operated on, Genet donned a white mask and tried to direct the surgery. And later Genet would coach Alexandre Bouglione as he practiced the lute six or seven hours a day. Genet was the expert.

Genet brought more grief than wisdom to his protégés. Often he instructed them to disobey the law or, unwittingly, he encouraged them in their vices and weaknesses. His last lover, Mohammed El Katrani, drank to excess in despair over Genet's death. A year after Genet died the drunken Moroccan drove the fast car Genet had given him into a tree and died.

Jacky Maglia never agreed to meet with me. He was living with his second wife, Isako, a Japanese, in Greece, but he made frequent lightning visits to Paris after Genet's death to handle his affairs and to see old friends. The Gallimard lawyer, Laurent Boyer, tried to approach Jacky on my behalf, but to no avail.

And then one day in 1991 I was having lunch with Albert Dichy at a large table on the sidewalk, outside a Lebanese cafeteria. A Japanese woman asked if she could sit at our table and we said yes. Then her husband emerged with a tray and was forced to sit with us. It was Jacky Maglia. Since we were united in our obsession for Jean Genet, soon we were talking volubly. I asked Jacky about certain details regarding Genet's visit to Japan that I'd never been able to pin down. After Jacky and Isako left, Albert and I took many notes of everything that had been said.

An old friend of mine, the poet and translator Edouard Roditi, who was close to eighty, filled me in on the gay and criminal slang of the past. Edouard made his living as a conference interpreter and could translate into and out of half a dozen languages, including Turkish (his father was a Turk, his mother English, and Edouard had been born in France).

It was Edouard who told me that when Genet refers in a poem to *'une biche dorée'* he doesn't mean 'a gilded doe' but a virginal boy (*'une biche'*) screwed for the first time (*'dorée'*). Edouard also advised Genet's official translator, Bernard Frechtman, a straight man, on period gay slang, though unfortunately Frechtman didn't always follow Edouard's advice and some passages don't make much sense in English. Edouard knew some of Genet's tricks. He also filled me in on a boy whorehouse in Montmartre run by an Arab that Genet frequented, just as Proust, thirty years earlier, had visited his male brothel on the rue de l'Arcade.

Frechtman's girlfriend (or *'maîtresse,'* as the French would have it) was Annette Michelson, an American film scholar and critic whom I interviewed in New York. She told me that she had inadvertently provided the *déclic*, or inspiration, for Genet's play *The Blacks*. She'd invited Genet in 1955 to see a documentary, at a Paris cinema. The film, *Les Maîtres Fous* (*The Master Madmen*) by Jean Rouch, pictured a group of black workers in Accra, Ghana, on their day off. They go to a sort of compound outside the city, get high, enter a trance and impersonate the Governor, the General, the wife of the Doctor – all the white authorities who oppress them. One even impersonates the Locomotive, symbol of white power. The frenzy and the stunned, drooling faces are frightening, as is the sacrifice of a dog – a sacrilegious act, since the dog is sacred to this tribe.

Genet was directly inspired by this film in writing *The Blacks*. In his play black characters assume the roles of the white queen, cardinal, judge and so on – and a sacrifice of a woman is performed (though in fact the coffin turns out to be empty and the murder a hoax).

Annette Michelson gave me a good sense of how Genet the theatrical genius thought. She made me understand how imperious Genet could be with his friends, treating them in an off-with-their-heads manner. When he and Frechtman quarreled over money, Genet excluded Frechtman from his life and ended their collaboration of many years. Frechtman and Annette Michelson had already split up. His new girlfriend institutionalized him when he became dangerously depressed. Upon release he headed directly to the new girlfriend's house. She made clear to him that their affair was over – and Frechtman hanged himself from a nearby tree.

Albert Dichy and I unearthed innumerable stories, but because they weren't directly relevant to Genet's life, I was unable to include them in my biography. For instance, Albert interviewed someone from Genet's village who was also a foster child. This man's mother had abandoned him but just before doing so she'd stipulated that he should be raised as a Jew. The boy, of course, knew no other Jews, nor did the peasants and craftsmen and shopkeepers in Alligny know what to do with a Jew except mock him and torment him. He wasn't allowed to attend catechism class; he was treated as a stand-in for the devil. Only Genet was nice to him. They came in number one (Genet) and number two in the school exams at age twelve for the entire *département*. Once the Jewish kid, Marc, left the village he lived his life as a normal, nonpracticing French Catholic. No one knew of his Jewishness – until two decades later with the arrival of the Nazis. Marc told Albert that in the last days of the German occupation someone denounced him as a Jew and he was summoned to the notorious Gestapo headquarters off the Champs-Elysées. When the German officer left the room for a moment Marc glanced at the document on the desk to see who had informed on him. It was his own wife.

In recent years Genet has been accused of anti-Semitism – just as critics have sneeringly suggested that his real interest in the Palestinians was sexual. In fact, Genet was a writer first and foremost. He was careful to keep all references to anti-Semitism out of his published work, not because he was playing it cautious, since he was, on the contrary, a transgressive writer who courted public opprobrium. For instance, Genet wrote an essay, 'Violence and Brutality,' defending the murders committed by the Baader-Meinhof. When it was cut and reprinted in *Le Monde*, it drew so many letters of outrage that the editor of the newspaper was forced to insert a disclaimer. Obviously Genet was a fearless controversialist and would not have hesitated to publish anti-Semitic opinions if he had truly held them. An examination we made of his manuscripts from the 1970s reveals that he crossed out every anti-Semitic slur from his writings before they were published. He cut an anti-Semitic passage from *The Thief's Journal* and when, years later, he delivered a speech at Yale University defending the Black Panthers, he deleted an anti-Semitic reference to a *New York Times* reporter. In 1982, after observing the dead bodies in a Palestinian camp in Beirut, slaughtered with Ariel Sharon's complicity, Genet indulged in anti-Israeli rhetoric – and then carefully edited it out. In our culture of gossip we make no distinction between remarks and published texts, between first impulses and revised statements, but for a real writer this is an important difference, especially for a writer of Genet's generation. Moreover, Genet was more anti-Zionist than anti-Jewish, though he could drive his French Jewish friends crazy by quizzing them about what it meant to be Jewish. And in *Prisoner of Love* Genet is careful to point out that the biggest enemies of the Palestinians are the reactionary Arab regimes, followed by America and only then Israel. Surely as a peasant raised in the Morvan, he shared in a general rural French fund of anti-Semitism. Later, as a provocateur, he enjoyed probing the delicate tissue of Jewish identity in Europe. His constant association in the 1970s and early 1980s with the anti-Semitic Black Panthers and Palestinians meant that his own anti-Semitism was exacerbated. But I still insist that a more reasonable spirit caused him to censor these thoughts from his writing, which he hoped would be his permanent contribution to art and culture.

As to his sexual attraction to the Palestinians, Genet once pointed out that his erotic interests usually confirmed his political sympathies, not vice versa. If he found the Palestinian soldiers sexy it was partly because he embraced their cause. Palestinian soldiers looked almost exactly like Israeli soldiers.

When I was asked to speak about Jean Genet at the Institute of the Arab World in Paris I was apprehensive. After all, there would be several key witnesses to Genet's life in the audience who, I imagined, would be suspicious of me as an American. But I acquitted myself well and was careful not to turn Genet into a political apologist. In no way did I court what I thought would be the Palestinian investment in Genet. As it turned out, the Palestinians whom I was addressing were all intellectuals, many of them sensitive to the restraints of art. Elias Sanbar, the editor of the *Palestinian Review*, even told me that Genet did not want his last book, *Prisoner of Love*, to be read as a political tract.

One of the people I met that afternoon was Leila Shahid, the representative of the PLO in Paris. She and Genet had been extremely close. In September 1982 they traveled together to Beirut and were there during the Israeli siege of the city. While the Israeli armed forces, directed by General Sharon, stood guard, the local Christian Phalangist forces entered the Palestinian refugee camp of Shatila and killed between eight hundred and a thousand women and children. The recent effort to have Sharon condemned as an international war criminal by the European High Court was based on this massacre.

Genet was the first European to visit the camp after the slaughter and to describe what he had seen in his best literary work in nearly two decades, 'Four Hours at Shatila.' Paule Thévenin noticed the joyfulness in this tragic essay about death – perhaps the joy expressed Genet's thrill at returning to writing after years of silence or literary groping (all those half-baked film scenarios he'd abandoned in the suitcase he left behind at Lydie Dattas's apartment and had never wanted to reclaim). The skill of 'Four Hours at Shatila' pointed the way to *Prisoner of Love*, which was published one month after Genet's death in 1986.

Leila accompanied Genet on his path toward death as he grew weaker and weaker from cancer. She and I had lunch in Paris in 1989 at a busy restaurant that had been installed in a beautiful old telegraph office from the beginning of the twentieth century. After the other diners had gone she spoke to me at length about Shatila, about Genet's rebirth as a writer and about his feverish composition of *Prisoner of Love*. In those last busy months he was living in the Hôtel Rubens near the Gobelins. He was reading Nietzsche and Claudel, both vigorous stylists; the Frenchman was the last eloquent defender of a god the German had pronounced dead. Genet was also listening to a tape of Mozart's Requiem, which *Prisoner of Love* refers to frequently. Like Mozart, Genet did his last great work in the shadow of imminent death.

When Leila told Genet that she had just lost a baby she was carrying, he barely registered the news and certainly didn't express any sympathy, though in fact her loss was due partly to the energy she'd expended in taking care of Genet. In general, Genet's women friends were superior to the cold, egotistical men he courted. Perhaps because he was gay he was more clear-eyed in his choice of women friends. Certainly Leila impressed me when she said that upon reflection she understood that for Genet his last lover's son, Azzedine, the child of Mohammed El Katrani, was more important to him than her miscarriage was even to her. I was puzzled until she said that for him it was more important to *choose* a son than 'merely' to become pregnant and bear a child (or lose him).

As I worked on Genet I sometimes felt I could triangulate one of his opinions by speculating from two fixed points I'd already pinned down – and sometimes my suppositions were right and sometimes they were wrong. For instance, I knew that Genet had had long hair when he was in his early twenties and had sold his body in prostitution by wearing makeup and bits of female finery. A friend of Genet's from the forties, François Sentein, told me he'd once seen a photo of Genet in drag. In those days, especially in the criminal world, a boy who was '*femme*' was desirable but an old queen was a figure of fun. Genet had gone through a painful transition in his early thirties as he deliberately turned himself into a butch man (at the same time he was going bald).

When I attempted to interview a French photographer (hetero-sexual and leftist) who'd accompanied Genet to America in March and April 1970, when Genet was living with the Panthers, the photographer said he didn't want to talk about that period, that he'd been cruelly disappointed by Genet the man. When I pressed him to tell me why, he muttered that Genet had danced for the Panthers in a pink negligee.

I knew that this had to be a lie or a misrepresentation. Genet was sixty at the time and not a youthful sixty; his years as a beggar, prisoner and fugitive from justice, his neglect of his health, his heavy consumption every night of nine Nembutals, his bad teeth and perennial malnutrition had aged and weakened him. Besides, he was careless about his clothes – there wasn't a trace of coquetry in him. The Panthers, who were sharp dressers, had even been ashamed of his shabbiness and had one of their members in Oakland dress him for free out of his men's clothes store. I was so sure the story of the pink negligee was false that I started to speculate in my mind about the mean motives behind the lie.

And then I met Angela Davis in 1991, who said spontaneously and unbidden, 'Genet was the original gender-bender. He'd get high on Nembutal and dance for the Panthers in a pink negligee. It was good for them – it loosened them up a bit.' She laughed.

If I struck out on that one I had a lucky hit on another occasion. Someone asked me why Genet never put homosexuals onstage in any of his three major full-length plays. 'Because he thought gays onstage were embarrassing,' I blurted out, though later I realized I had made that up. And yet only a day or two afterwards I read in a Spanish theatrical magazine an interview of Genet in which he'd said that homosexuals onstage embarrassed him.

I was writing about someone who I may never have met but who was filmed extensively in long television interviews. I could see from these interviews how restless his mind was, how funny he could be, how mercurial his moods. At moments he'd speak seriously about death or politics or art or the Palestinians – and the next he'd be scoffing. During a BBC television interview in 1985 the English presenter, Nigel Williams, asked Genet about love. But because of his accent Genet thought Williams was saying 'death' (*la mort*), not 'love' (*l'amour*). When he realized that a serious question about the annihilation he was facing was actually a more trivial one about an emotion that no longer interested him, he laughed and revealed his contempt.

At the end of the shoot, on the second day, Genet insisted that he wanted to interview the technical crew. Genet rejected the idea of genius (except when he spoke of Giacometti, who he claimed was the only exceptional person he'd ever known). Certainly he disliked being grilled by an Englishman in an interior that reminded him of Miss Marple (the show was filmed in Williams's house). But he was a skillful enough man of the theater to know that once one submitted to a format (the television interview in this case) one had already lost. The only radical statement an interviewee can make is to change the formula. To this day anyone who saw the show in which Genet interviewed the technicians remembers it, usually with fury. People can ignore radical statements if they are made by a man in a chair under spotlights drinking tea. What they can't ignore is a camera jerkily turned around to disrupt everyone's expectations. Genet criticized the radical students in Paris in 1968 when they took over the Odéon Theater and put the leaders onstage and the followers in the audience. Genet pointed out they were already aping the conventional hierarchy, even if they'd replaced the personnel – and they had already lost the battle. Similarly, when Castro asked Genet to visit Cuba, Genet said he would do so if Castro would get rid of the national flag and all marching songs; Genet knew that the trappings of power perpetuate it.

The many years I devoted to Genet changed me. Before my research I'd known something about Paris – the Paris of foreigners and cultural events and fashion (I worked for *Vogue*) and home décor (I also freelanced for *House & Garden*). But because of Genet I met Palestinian women doctors and one of the founders of Club Med and an Ethiopian-born film producer and the lawyer who'd defended the Nazi butcher Klaus Barbie and the heir to a Lyons pharmaceuticals fortune and several ex-cons. I met Marianne de Pury, who'd translated for Genet when he was in America and who'd lived with the Panthers. She'd started out as the pretty blonde daughter of a prominent Lausanne family (her cousin was head of Sotheby's). In the sixties she'd gone to America and fallen in love with Big Man, the Panthers' Minister of Information. She'd worked with the experimental New York theater director and actor Joe Chaikin. After the violent and tragic collapse of the Panthers movement, Marianne had married a white man, moved to Santa Fe and found a job as a legal secretary. When I met her she was divorced, her children were heading off for college – and she was moving back to Switzerland to resume belatedly a career in the theater; one of the first plays she directed was a German production of *The Maids*.

She told me many funny stories. When American journalists asked Genet why he, a white man, had written *The Blacks*, he lied and said, according to Marianne, 'I was living in Switzerland and was tired of everything being white – the people, the snow.' Marianne also told me that Genet had met Jane Fonda at a Hollywood fund-raising party for the Panthers in 1970. He'd taken to her, since she could speak good French, and had asked her for her number. Early the next morning when he awakened in a strange mansion he called Fonda. She said, 'But where are you?' He said he had no idea. 'Listen,' she said, 'go outside and look at the swimming pool, then come back to me and describe it.' Genet did and Fonda said, 'Oh, you're at Donald Sutherland's. I'll be right over.' Fonda's daughter, Vanessa Vadim, studied creative writing with me at Brown in 1990; she set up the interview with her mother for me. By this time Fonda was married to Ted Turner and seemed embarrassed by recollections of her radical past.

Because of Genet I spent days at the military library at the Château de Vincennes on the edge of Paris tracking down the biographies of the officers he'd served under. Because of Genet I consulted rare dictionaries of criminal slang, read a dozen French homosexual novels of the period in order to grasp the extent of his originality. Because of Genet I traveled to Damascus, where he had worked on the construction of a French fort.

One of Genet's friends from the 1940s, Boris Kochno, who had been Diaghilev's last assistant in the 1920s and later the lover of Christian Bérard (Bérard designed the sets for the 1947 premiere of *The Maids*), refused to speak to me. He was very old (he'd been born in 1904) and told me he preferred spending his remaining days among members of his 'milieu.' As it turned out, I knew several members of his milieu. I insisted they invite Kochno and me to dinner and quiz him the whole time about Genet. Kochno, with his Slavic good looks and Boris Karloff accent, spoke happily all evening about Genet as I taped him covertly. By the time my book came out he'd forgotten the whole incident and soon enough he was dead. I felt I was recording all of this information that would soon be lost. Sometimes, quite unprofessionally, I was relieved when someone died before I could interview him; at least no one else will interview him, either, I thought in my petty way.

I welcomed the few times when I had to interview Americans, who were always accessible, honest and voluble. The only exception was David Hilliard, the heterosexual Panther with whom Genet had been hopelessly in love. Hilliard wanted to save his stories for his own memoirs. Yet when his book came out it contained only one dull mention of Genet's name. Perhaps Hilliard had been embarrassed by Genet's devotion.

Most Americans, however, are sunny and open, unlike most French intellectuals, who think of information as property and guard it jealously.

Thanks to Genet I met French-born Arabs, circus performers, criminal lawyers and prominent statesmen. I spent many hours with Spain's leading avant-garde novelist, Juan Goytisolo, who had been a great friend of Genet's and a sort of disciple. His wife, Monique Lange, had known Genet since the forties. Once when she wanted to understand what it would be like to be a whore (she was a nice Jewish girl who worked as an editor at Gallimard and wrote small, perfect novels), Genet dressed her, put her out on the sidewalk and acted as her pimp. Only after he'd negotiated a deal with a john did Monique and Genet run off laughing. When she wanted to know what sex in a dark room among men would look like, Genet dressed her as a man and took her to a gay bar in Montmartre. They emerged from the bar and Monique said, 'That was totally disgusting – not at all beautiful as in your books.' 'I have talent, don't I?' Genet asked ('*J'ai du talent, n'est-ce pas?*'), very pleased with himself.

For the last five years of my work on Genet I was living with Hubert Sorin. He lived long enough to see me win the National Book Critics Circle Award for the biography. Hubert explained many French words and customs to me for the book. Wherever we went we had to travel with huge heavy boxes of books and the hundreds of files Albert had put together on every subject – and our pudgy basset, Fred. We were living half the time in a farmhouse near Tours (and Genet's reform school Mettray) that our American friends Harlan and Frank had lent us. The rest of the time we were in a walkup apartment in Paris. To convey the books back and forth I bought, at age fifty, the first car of my life, a used Renault 5. I'd sit at one desk in the farmhouse looking out a window onto the golden wheat fields beyond and at an old barn that master tilers were patiently roofing. Just outside the door was a patch of nettles that Hubert always wanted to pick and make into a soup. An old hayrick outside was slowly filling up with reeds. In the other room Hubert was ensconced at another desk before another window. He was working with patient application on his satirical illustrations. Often our friend Christine was also there, doing her drawings for children's books. A radio tuned to France Musique was proving once again the French preference for didactic chat to actual musical performance. I found the announcer's scarcely audible, well-modulated voice reassuring.

The afternoon would settle breathlessly on us. The wheat would blaze with a radiance that reached into the darkest corners of the old farmhouse. The winter smell of the blackened, walk-in fireplace would remind us of the cold and darkness that lay in store for the world. Dragonflies hovered in the air. Fred, who was dozing on the cool lintel stone, raised one heavy-lidded eye like a London clubman napping in the safety of a leather armchair.

Like an idiot I wrote my whole biography longhand (as I'm writing this book now). Dictating hundreds and hundreds of handwritten pages was tedious for me, but the real disaster came when I tried to reconstruct the notes ('Now I'm sure I put that reference on the flyleaf of a book – but which one?'). It took me nearly three months to do the annotations.

My real delight came from the French publication of the book by Gallimard. Antoine Gallimard took a special interest in Genet, since when he was a child Genet was the only house author who'd been kind to him (Genet always got along with children, surprisingly). Antoine told me that Genet would often seat him on his lap. Isabelle Gallimard, Antoine's sister, told me that was strange, since Antoine was sixteen when he met Genet, but Isabelle loves a joke.

When the book was published the leading cultural review, *Le Monde des Livres*, devoted four pages to Genet. The biography coincided with a renewed French interest in him. His plays were often revived, sometimes in bizarre productions. An opera based on *The Balcony* was successfully presented at Aix-en-Provence. Dozens and dozens of scholarly books about Genet were published. Albert Dichy, who by now was generally recognized as the world's foremost expert on Genet, was invited to colloquia as far away as Ankara (where he spoke to an unassuming elderly Frenchman, who turned out to be the hapless dupe married off unsuspectingly to a Chinese man – the basis of *M. Butterfly*).

Albert had edited and annotated the definitive Pléiade edition of Genet's *Complete Theater* and a volume of his political writings called *The Declared Enemy*. IMEC was no longer housed in a room in a faulty tower at Paris III but in a vast former abbey outside Caen. In a few years under the direction of Olivier Corpet it had become the chief rival to the Bibliothèque National as an archive for writers' manuscripts. The perennially avant-garde novelist Alain Robbe-Grillet (who invented the New Novel and wrote the script for the influential film *Last Year at Marienbad*) promised IMEC all his archives and home movies, if the library would build a greenhouse for his precious cactuses (or *cacte*, as he prefers) – and IMEC has agreed. Robbe-Grillet's wife, Catherine, though close to eighty, is still a famous sadist who tortures chic literary couples in the dungeon of her Norman castle; perhaps IMEC will someday house the book in which she writes down which punishments she has meted out to which victims – as a good hostess writes down which dishes she's served to which guests, with the matching wine labels pasted in beside the menu.

I made a trip to Morocco to see Genet's grave. He had died during the night of April 14–15, 1986 in a small hotel room in Paris. He had stumbled on his way to the bathroom and suffered a concussion. His body had been transported to Morocco in a coffin wrapped in burlap. When the coffin was unloaded from the plane it was marked 'immigrant worker.' Since Genet was not a Muslim he had to be buried in the old Spanish Catholic cemetery at Larache, once a Spanish possession; no one had been buried there since the 1930s, when the Spanish gave up the city. But a Muslim woman looked after the cemetery and lived in a cottage amidst the tumbledown gravestones. She kept a few goats. A line of wash was hung out to dry. Toward the end of his life and after his death Genet came to be considered a sort of Muslim saint or holy man; his grave was visited by the pious – and many tourists. A charming, voluble French cultural attaché, Georges, drove me and a friend to Larache. At the time Georges was living in Tangier with a handsome young man, Azit, and Azit's mother (the cook) and Azit's retarded brother (the gatekeeper). Georges knew the widow and son, Azzedine, of Genet's last lover, Mohammed El Katrani. We met the little Azzedine, a bright, sweet child who had been the joy of Genet's old age (the two of them liked to box with each other). Azzedine attended a good boarding school and spoke French. He also studied Latin and Greek – at Genet's insistence.

Azzedine was one of the three heirs to Genet's estate, along with Jacky Maglia (the executor) and Ahmed, a circus performer who'd been a friend of Abdellah, the high-wire artist who'd killed himself on March 12, 1964 in a little maid's room in Paris. Genet had buried Abdellah in Paris in a Muslim cemetery, but had forgotten years later to renew the lease on the grave. As a result Genet's grave was being dug in Morocco at the same time as Abdellah's bones were being disinterred in Paris. Nevertheless, in his last few days of life in 1986, Genet had still been haunted by Abdellah's suicide. Genet had said to Leila Shahid, 'I really destroy these people, don't I?' He also felt responsible for Jacky's paralyzed arm.

Genet's tomb at Larache looks out on three of the main subjects of his fiction and theater – the sea, the bordello and the local prison. When a visitor stole the carved headstone, Jacky Maglia wrote Genet's name and dates on the stone. Their handwriting was so similar that it looks as if Genet signed his own grave, as the last tome in his collected works.

The French often say that a trip to an exotic place leads to a certain *dépaysement*, a removal from one's usual element or country (*pays*). I suppose writing a biography can bring on a similar disorientation or sense of exile. Albert and I would become so excited over some new bit of information about Genet that his wife would have to remind us that no one would want to know a similar fact even about Shakespeare. Certainly we wouldn't have cared to uncover a comparable fact about ourselves (that the soldier Genet had sex with in Morocco in the 1920s was the son of La Goulue, the cabaret artist in Toulouse-Lautrec's posters).

I forgot myself for long stretches of time. Once, when I was speaking about Genet to a group in London someone in the audience said, 'And what about your work? You've said nothing about your own writing and that's why we're here.' I was astonished. For a moment I had forgotten that I, too, had once been a novelist. Of course I could be as self-absorbed as any other writer, but I was so fascinated by Genet I'd lost sight of my own work.

Was it worth it?

Genet had been an icon for American gay men of my generation –

and for rebels in general. He was widely read and even more widely produced, someone who belonged to readers everywhere – satanic, but no more so than Sade, Bataille, Céline. He was a writer for everyone, despite his indifference to marriage, the family, the battle of the sexes, adultery and all the other great bourgeois topics. What he did write about in his fiction was prison rape, transvestite prostitution, theft and betrayal, and he wrote about those subjects in gorgeous language that transformed degradation into saintliness.

No gay writer of his period had affirmed homosexuality except through some Nietzschean legerdemain, by reversing all normal values. Even Proust was obliged to come up with unflattering botanical arguments that acknowledged how repulsive homosexuality is – except Proust invented so many different theories that they ended up canceling each other out.

Proust, Gide, Genet – three writers who not only were homosexual but who made 'inversion' central to their art – convince me that homosexuality was crucial to the development of the modern novel because it led to a reinvention of love, a profound skepticism about the naturalness of gender roles and a revival of the classical tradition of same-sex love that had dominated Western poetry and prose until the birth of Christianity. There was no way that the golden tranquillity of Greek man-boy love could be recovered now, to be sure. In fact Proust and Genet depended on the monstrous perversity of modern homosexual love to animate their moral universes. But if they were sovereign minds, great stylists and bewilderingly philosophical, their idiosyncratic take on the human trajectory came from having a big, fresh, genuine subject. Unlike heterosexual male writers, they weren't simply fine-tuning an examination of adultery or proving their masculinity; on the contrary, Proust and Genet were dismantling all received ideas about the couple, manhood, love and sexual roles. Proust elaborated the rules that governed jealousy, straight or gay; Gide looked at the romance between young and old men in *The Counterfeiters*, one of the handful of great books of the last century; and Genet made pariahs into saints and wallowed in the poetry of abjection.

To me this tradition was inspirational. It suggested that the mythmaking, transformative power of art was still functioning. It showed that fiction was not only mimetic but also prophetic.

With Truman Capote, 1981

With Michel Foucault
in Paris, 1981

With Marie-Claude de Brunhoff,
La Rochelle, France, 1995

My Friends

I think of so many other ways I could have written this book. I could have described my years of teaching literature and creative writing – starting at Yale in the mid-1970s and going on to Johns Hopkins, Columbia, New York University and ending up at Brown and finally Princeton, where I'm director of my department and my colleagues include Joyce Carol Oates, Toni Morrison, Chang-rae Lee, Paul Muldoon, C.K. Williams, Yusef Komunyakaa and, as I write, the Man Booker Prize-winning novelist, Alan Hollinghurst.

I've taught courses in Proust and in contemporary world fiction, covering everything from the novels of Günther Grass to those of Kawabata and Tanizaki, passing by way of Pynchon and García Márquez. Over the years I've taught students such as Mona Simpson, Louise Erdrich and Andrew Greer. I've seen some of my favorite students die of AIDS (the novelist John Fox, the playwright John Russell) and I've seen some of the most gifted not blossom at all (did I overpraise them and frighten them?) and others bloom late (like the great nature essayist, Trudi Dittmar).

Or I could have written about my participation in the beginning of gay liberation at the Stonewall Uprising; a letter I wrote at the time describing the event has often been reprinted. In 1981 I was one of the founders of the GMHC (Gay Men's Health Crisis), the first AIDS organization in the world. Four years later I attended the first few meetings of AIDES, the French equivalent to GMHC. After I was diagnosed as positive in 1985, I was one of the first people in the world to 'come out' voluntarily while still healthy as an HIV-positive person. I wrote several of the first essays (in a

335

special issue of *Life* and in *Artforum*) on AIDS as a worldwide phenomenon and, more specifically, as a destroyer of artistic talent. A few years back I edited an anthology, *Loss Within Loss*, of essays by other writers about individuals in the arts who had died from AIDS. I was the keynote speaker at a conference on AIDS and Literature in Key West.

Or I could have gone to the opposite extreme, toward frivolity, and written a chapter called 'My Celebrities.' Over the years I've met everyone from Christopher Isherwood to Iris Murdoch, from Joan Didion to John Updike, from José Saramago to Joseph Brodsky and Derek Walcott to Nadine Gordimer (just to stay with the Nobel Prize winners). I have met the Queen of England and the King and Queen of Sweden. When the Swedish Queen led me from her private quarters at Drottningholm to the public, museum half of the building, she said, 'Here we go. It's show business time!' – which struck me as a realistic way of looking at her exalted effect. I have met Elton John and attended his fiftieth birthday party. I have been to spectacular parties such as a masked ball in Paris given after Pavarotti's performance in *A Masked Ball* at the Palais Garnier. The ball, a fund-raiser, was hosted in the 1980s by Madame Chirac *and* Madame Mitterrand. My date was the editor of French *Vogue*. I have slept over at Jasper Johns's country house in Connecticut and run into Cy Twombly in Crete and at Luxor. In the sixties I went to three New Year's Eve parties at the Fifth Avenue apartment of Charles Mingus. I have eaten a box lunch with Andy Warhol at the Factory and I've had a formal lunch featuring truffles with the Baron Redé in the most beautiful house in Paris, the Rothschilds' Hôtel Lambert on the Île Saint-Louis. I've had a private tour of the library at Eton and held one of its two Gutenberg Bibles in my hands. I've eaten dinner between Garrison Keillor and Arthur Schlesinger. I was once Alice Tully's dinner partner. I interviewed Truman Capote while Robert Mapplethorpe took our picture.

But perhaps because I don't keep a journal and because I met most of these people after I was forty and was less impressionable, I don't have much to say about them beyond dropping their names. Like everyone I'm impressed by names (even the Dalai Lama seems impressed by Richard Gere's name), but I prefer my names to be legendary; I once introduced Frank Stella's daughter to Picasso's son and I had an amorous friendship with Hemingway's grandson. I taught Diane von Furstenburg's daughter and the daughter of Jane Fonda. I wept on Gloria Vanderbilt's shoulder as I talked about a broken heart.

I suppose a 'real' celebrity is someone famous who doesn't become a personal friend. By that definition most of the writers I know, from Richard Ford to Peter Carey, from Diane Johnson to Alison Lurie, must count as friends and not as celebrities. They are the people whose advice I ask, whose jokes I laugh at, whose sorrows I share, who write blurbs for my books.

Friendship has been one of the great pursuits of my life. I think I have some of the qualities necessary in a friend – tenacity, a large capacity for acceptance, curiosity, a genuine pleasure in other people's happiness. I'm not competitive; I owe my lack of competitiveness to the 'progressive' grade school I attended in Evanston, in which grades were not handed out, only individual evaluations, and a student was not allowed to compare his work to another's. No distinction was ever made between work and play and the student's 'contribution' to the subject at hand (a bit of extra research, private ruminations, a report of a relevant trip) was eagerly solicited and warmly praised. All of us who went to the Miller School have no stage fright (thanks to endless creative dramatics classes), no shyness, no sense of rivalry nor the conviction that another person's gain is our loss. I was fortunate to have lived before Sputnik made Americans lose confidence in progressive education.

A Midwestern egalitarianism, a Deweyite freedom from rivalry, a Christian Scientist blindness to evil – these forces on my development have left me with a sunny but perilously unsuspicious nature.

As a child I lived with my parents and my sister at the end of a lane on which there were just three houses and no other children. My sister, three and a half years older than I, was a cold, beautiful princess out of a fairy tale with blue eyes, long platinum-blonde hair and small, precise features. She attended Miss Dougherty's School for Girls but forbade her classmates to play with me when they came to visit. They might have been ready to pat me on the head or say 'Goochy goo,' as if I were an infant, but eight-year-old girls like intense, conspiratorial games within their clan and have little use for five-year-old boys.

During long stretches of time I was alone. The maids – Blanche and Anna – ignored me; they weren't babysitters. We had a friendly, always eager collie the color of butterscoth and whipped cream. He was named Timmy and the instant I put aside my coloring book and stood up, he woke and stood too, sliding back and forth on his long-nailed tawny feet on the linoleum floor, peering at me down the length of his aristocratic nose to see what was up.

I had three imaginary friends – Georgie-Porgie, Cottage Cheese (a bossy girl) and Tom Thumb Thumb (a bad boy whom the rest of us were always trying to reform). Cottage Cheese went with me everywhere. A place was set for her at table and she sat beside me in Daddy's big Chrysler.

We moved so much that I never had enough time to make friends. I was in Cincinnati in first grade, Evanston in second, Dallas in third, Rockford, Illinois, in fourth and Evanston again in fifth and sixth. I spent those three Evanston years at the Miller School, and there I made a few friends – Anne, Cathleen, Julie. Not that I knew what friends were exactly. I liked people (mainly I liked those who seemed to like me), and I was drawn sleepily toward them as a baby snuggles unconsciously against something soft and warm.

I played no games and was probably too nearsighted to see the ball rushing toward me; I only discovered I was myopic when I was eight and my mother bought balcony seats to Jean Arthur in *Peter Pan*; I saw nothing but the general radiance of the glowing proscenium arch. I was quickly outfitted with glasses in thick black frames. I was permanently marked as a nerd. When I look at photos of me in my early and middle teens I see someone tall for his age but slumping, his hair shorn not in a military buzz cut but as a sheep is shorn. My head was lowered. Across my features played a sour smile, a compromise between resentment and a feeble desire to please or at least not to be noticed.

I mumbled when I wasn't, on rare occasions, shrieking. My father was always telling me to enunciate or to keep my voice down. He forbade me to say 'You know' at ends of phrases or to say 'like' whenever it could be omitted (as in 'The Empire State is, like, the tallest building in the world'); he knew that a man never hedges his linguistic bets but makes clear statements, unless they're impolite. Ideally a man speaks seldom but when he does say something it is clear and modest and positive. Not too extravagant. When I said I loved Mexico my father said, 'A man likes things, he doesn't love them.' My father's lessons evidently didn't take. When I entered boarding school at fifteen a classmate told me I was the first person he'd ever met who used the word *charming* in conversation. My whole vocabulary was lightly tinged with words such as 'divine,' 'maddening,' 'intoxicating,' 'tawdry' and 'frivolous,' all intended positively. I'd pick them up from the dialogue in Evelyn Waugh's novels and from old movies, but I used these words only very occasionally, mainly as a way of testing my interlocutor for a sympathetic response. I'd move my 'divine' and if he'd counter with a 'delightful' I'd give him a 'maddening' or a 'delicious' (said of a woman, not dinner).

My father had also taught me not to be a know-it-all, which was unbecoming when a kid was talking to an adult. 'If you disagree with an older man,' he said, 'soften it by adding "I may be wrong" or "Someone told me the opposite but I'm sure you're right."' Though my father was a dogmatic bore at home, when he was with other businessmen he put on a shit-eating grin and attempted feeble, long-winded jokes which lent his face a sly, shifty look. He was masculine enough but too egotistical and insensitive, and fundamentally too misanthropic, to woo other people.

Until I was fourteen it never occurred to me to woo anyone except my mother; I was as responsive as a Pavlovian dog to every stimulus she emitted, and I was indifferent to everyone else to the same degree. I had no toys, I played no sports, my only card game was the imbecilic Crazy Eights. I wasn't sufficiently musical to keep up with the famous choir I tried out for as a boy soprano. I wasn't quick-witted or Machiavellian enough to succeed in the debating club and I felt too desperately needy to be a do-gooder in the community. Why should I help other people when I myself was neglected and deprived? I was a good student in English and history and social studies and eventually Latin and French, but I was bored and frightened by math and science and never got beyond plane geometry and introductory biology and two or three introductory science courses. Actual frogs, reeking of formaldehyde, seemed like so much cold, gristly incoherence under my dissecting knife and never resembled the neat diagrams of organs we were working from. Life – or rather this repulsive dead reality – was too messy and arbitrary to illustrate these schematic drawings. Maybe, in fact, these drawings were wrong. Or perhaps my frogs were freaks.

A challenge was something that made me shut down. My mother based her praise of me – at once extravagant and provisional – on the condition that I was a genius. If I was shown laboring at something, striving to perfect a skill or memorize a formula, then obviously I wasn't a genius after all, just a dull crammer. I longed for instant gratification. Even learning a musical instrument took too much time. I tried my hand at painting and did an imaginary portrait of a Roman soldier in a helmet under a half moon, but neither my mother nor my sister could tell what it was meant to be and I gave up.

I was always acting and singing and dancing in school musicals. My greatest role was dancing in boarding school as Harry Beaton in *Brigadoon*. Disappointed in love, Harry decides to run away from the village, which has gone on existing one day a year for centuries. If Harry succeeds in leaving the village, it will vanish forever. The escape through the woods and my eventual capture dramatized for me my dislike of other people, raised to the level of lethal despair and theatrical fantasy. All the other men in the village (other prep school boys) were pursuing me. I liked being caught and killed by them; nothing seemed more interesting and, somehow, right than ending up a tragic victim at male hands. The same runs and leaps I was incapable of performing on the playing field came naturally to me when I danced; what had been competitive became artistic and expressive. I was used to dancing. Since the age of nine or ten I'd been dancing interpretively to classical music at home, fluttering my great swan wings while mincing on tiptoe or opening my arms and leaping forward, bare-chested and crowned with my mother's turban, a lunatic grin on my lips, the Favorite Slave. For *Brigadoon* I added the Scottish sword dance to my repertoire.

Although I felt intensely lonely as a teenager keeping the terrible secret of my homosexuality, in fact I was beginning to have some friends. People who knew me back then remember me as an amusing and likable 'brain.' I suppose if I'd lived in the typical Midwestern town I might never have cracked the popularity code; I wasn't from a solid family, my mother worked too hard to join the United Way or the PTA. Instead of sports I liked dramatics. In class I was a compulsive showoff and always waving my arm.

But Evanston was an old, prosperous city, racially integrated, a small city of Unitarians and Congregationalists, home to North-western University. The other kids had a vague respect for egg-heads.

I became the gay sidekick to handsome straight guys in blue sweaters and red windbreakers, just as the dusky Sal Mineo in *Rebel Without a Cause* dances fond attendance on the light-haired, small-featured James Dean and his paramour Natalie Wood. I saw that movie when I was fifteen and it was the first time it ever occurred to me that a work of art could be about *me*, about the way we live now.

My sister had taught me how to clean up my act and to make friends. Maybe she was afraid to be associated with a geek like me whose clothes were dirty, whose glasses were crooked and fogged with thumbprints, who didn't know how to alternate between perky insolence and unblinking sincerity in the usual desirable way. My sister said that you must figure out which boys and girls belong to the 'in' group, the 'crowd', and then phone them systematically every two or three days in the evening. I made my list and tracked down phone numbers but there was a greater obstacle: small talk. I suppose there really were kids who thought in small-talk units but I saw it as a perverse, nearly aristocratic code deliberately designed to exclude anyone incapable of the necessary Mozartian lightness, anyone guilty of allowing a real thought or a real feeling to flavor the meringue of contentless chatter. Perhaps this very art is the one perfected by talk-show hosts today and their starlet guests: 'cute' anecdotes, my most embarrassing moment, the announcement of an engagement to be married, uttered with a calm, smiling face straight out to the audience, which provokes sustained and ob-ligatory applause. Back then we announced we were going steady and exchanged ID bracelets, only to break up two weeks later. Boys whispered innuendos and girls blushed and pretended to be vexed before dissolving in giggles. We disapproved ('Ew . . .') or approved ('Neat') of nearly everything brought to our attention; sometimes we intensified these responses to 'yuck' and 'cool.' Elvis had yet to happen, doo-wop music was about to crest and splash into rock-and-roll, drugs didn't exist and hoods did nothing worse than wear leather jackets and drink beer and refuse to go out for sports and skip classes. We still lived in a Republican world. At the Y we joined the Eisenhower Club. When General MacArthur was brought home from Korea we cheered his motorcade. We came out in favor of free trade.

Politics, especially in its blandest, most unquestioning form, didn't interested me. My new obsession was being popular. For the gossamer subtleties of small talk I substituted eager, interested questioning. I asked my friends endless questions but never pressed too hard. I never led them toward uncomfortable revelations. I praised whatever decision they'd made and sympathized over any indignity they'd suffered. I never offered unwelcome advice. I never reproached them for anything but for being too kind and too generous. I never grew impatient with an unhappy lover's circular lack of reasoning. Fortunately at that age everything moved very quickly. Enemies turned into lovers a week later and became indifferent ten days after that.

The thrill of being popular is fragile and pales so quickly that few people are willing to acknowledge how exhilarating it can be to walk down the school hallway between classes and garner ten 'hi's,' eight of them from leaders of the crowd. To know the same jokes, dance the same steps, and grow flushed from the radiance of so much recognition and simple acceptance – that was the highest pleasure a lonely gay guy could know. There were no other gay people around, at least none I knew. All of my friends were these couples who let me entertain them, admire them. At the sock hop there were slow dances and I, too, could link my hands behind a girl's back while she wrapped her arms around my neck. I, too, could inch her across the darkened floor while I ground my boner into her pelvis and watched other boys' skinny hips shift inside their low-slung jeans and smear their desire against so much perfumed receptivity. I was half participant and half voyeur, and I felt excited and guilty about both roles.

In order to become popular I made friends with Steve Turner, a tennis player who lived in a big Spanish-style house with tile floors and a grand staircase lined with oil portraits of the four kids. I was in love with Steve. I didn't want to be him but have him – if not as a lover then as a friend. A best friend. Maybe only he had the confidence to befriend someone already suspected of being a 'queer.' The first time I slept over in Steve's room (we were in twin beds, each of us propped up on elbows and wearing underpants and unironed T-shirts and discussing everything from God to grades), I made it a rule not to let my eyes linger on his crotch or to reach across and touch him. I was so convincing that the next morning Steve even said something: 'Some guy said you were kinda queer, but I can see there ain't nothin' to it.'

And he loved me too in a tender, brotherly way – proud of my accomplishments, protective of my geekiness in sports, accepting of my shyness around girls. Eventually he knew I was gay but he thought it was just a phase, a lack of experience, lack of confidence. He tried to fix me up on dates once or twice, but he was too clever to make a big deal out of it. After I went away to boarding school at the end of every vacation he'd come down to the train station to see me off. He'd have tears in his eyes and on his lips a joke and then words of great seriousness: 'Hey, Eddie, take good care of yourself.'

He liked almost everyone, as Prince Hal does, knowing someday he'll be king and have to give up the riffraff. He never doubted his superiority but at the same time he had a common touch. Because I loved him, but couldn't sleep with him, I ended up studying him – his antics by day, his unconscious body by night. In his messy bedroom the smell of underpants and T-shirts, of cigarettes (we smoked Parliaments) and wet towels, of week-old sheets and the sweet odor of adolescent sperminess, of Clearasil and fruity chewing gum, of Canoe or Mennan Aftershave on date night – for me all of this was the perfume of desire, distilled and melancholy. We didn't drink much, just a stolen beer now and then, but we smoked and got drunk on talk. I was attentive and devoted and required nothing beyond the occasional handshake or lopsided smile. I wanted to be indispensable.

Twenty-five years later when I wrote a novel, *A Boy's Own Story*, and based the character Tommy on Steve, it put his nose out of joint. He said, 'Now I know what it's like to feel like a sex object. Now I know what women are complaining about.' He laughed but it was a bit sour, what the French call a 'yellow laugh.' He was still irritated years after that, until his daughter Molly said, 'Dad, it's a famous novel and you should be proud to be in it. You only read the part about you – you should read the rest.' He did and stopped complaining, pleased to be reprimanded by his brilliant daughter. Now he's a patriarch with children and grandchildren, a whole tribe of thirty, whom he invites to Hawaii for family vacations. He, who was always flaky in school and ended up attending the University of South Dakota, the only place that would let him in, has made lots of money over the years with that same charm that back in high school turned him into the leader of the crowd. He's been married forty years to Anny, a smiling, dynamic beauty who has strong opinions on all subjects, who's kept her tiny waist by eating only once a day and seems thoroughly liberated, except she calls Steve 'Daddy' and has never earned a salary. She's radiant and interested and excitable, a loyal, loving friend and a superb mother. She and Steve swoop in to New York or Princeton or Paris or wherever I'm living and take me out to expensive restaurants. Steve has grown a bit sly with age; maybe he was always like that and I just didn't notice it when he was young and beautiful, the high school tennis champ, the famous surgeon's son.

Now we both look like old duffers with heart problems and cataracts and only Anny stays eternally youthful except for her exquisite silver hair. Steve and I are a bit isolated, though he's surrounded by his tribe and his employees and I by students and fellow writers. But we're both sort of alone in the way everyone over sixty is alone, as if preparing for the ultimate solitude. Our loyalty to each other is intense, almost overwhelming, though we can let a year go by between visits. I still love his sense of humor, his curiosity, his lack of pretension. I started out coveting his body, which led me to appreciate his qualities; now it's his qualities I prize. Unpretentious. Curious. Goofy. Cunning. If I hadn't been so in love with him would we be such friends now? It's interesting to grow old and to see how stories turn out.

Later, in boarding school, I had three or four friends who appealed to my mind and sense of humor and even more important my sense of conspiracy. Jack McQuaid had read as much as I had, plus he had a hobby, the Nazi Party. Though he was nearsighted and soft-spoken and fat-cheeked, he'd lock his door and pull out his SS uniform from a suitcase kept under the bed. Soon he'd be strutting around in jack boots, a swastika glittering on his chest, his small, weak eyes blinking under the visor of his military hat. When he'd bark out *Sieg heil!* and thrust his right hand upward I could see the retainer glinting on his lower teeth. I argued all the time with him about his ideology but he was quite inflexible. He'd read his Nietzsche, he was convinced there was a master race and that he belonged to it (he said I didn't because of my homo-Marxo-Judeo leanings). He ordered as much Nazi paraphernalia as he could afford and had it shipped directly to our door in plain brown wrappers. The secrecy thrilled him; the more I warned him about the practical consequences if he was apprehended, the more he grinned his silver-lined, evil smile. I reminded him that Kant considered everyone to be a Universal Legislator and that therefore every moral choice Jack made he was making for all of humanity. Did he really want to impose fascism on all of humanity?

'First of all,' he said haughtily, 'that's Kant's idea, not mine. And second of all, why not? I'm going to establish a Fourth Reich. Anyway, I'm sure the Führer is alive and well in Paraguay and will soon regain power. Sometimes it's necessary to take one step back in order to take two steps forward.'

Jack was the first brainy friend I ever had whom I couldn't bully. His stubborn resistance to my liberalism shocked me, but also irritated me. Why wasn't he convinced by my idealism, my humanity?

We'd both entered Cranbrook in the middle of our sophomore year and we were thrown together for that reason. Although he read Mallarmé's poetry and loved translating Catullus in Latin class and was even writing a short story about an unhappy esthete, he nevertheless liked pop music and was completely ignorant about classical music. That was the Detroit side of him (his father was a Ford executive).

We went home for the summer and when he came back in the fall he'd changed entirely. He'd become a Woody Guthrie populist. He'd grown two inches and slimmed down. He had a sweet little mustache. He was now in jeans and cowboy boots, contact lenses and gentle smiles. He'd thrown out his copy of *Mein Kampf*. Whereas before I'd felt he would some day be gay, now he had one crush after another on girls. He sometimes talked about dying young. I laughed at the idea, as if it were a sorrowful Werther pose, but by the time we were in our second year of university he was dead of nephritis, a kidney disease that soon afterwards became curable. His was the first funeral of someone my age I attended. There was a whiny electric organ at the funeral home, curtains on the stage that opened to reveal the shiny coffin and a clueless minister who dealt in inapplicable generalities. The parents looked small and young and lost in their smart dark clothes.

A second friend was Thomas McGuane, who later became a successful novelist, who married one movie star and lived with another, whose daughter married an eminent literary critic. He lived on a big ranch out West and went hunting and fishing with Raymond Carver and Richard Ford.

In those days, however, he was a hellion who drove us all to a black whorehouse and then back to his parents' house for the weekend. They were away somewhere and we had their big lake-side place to ourselves. For us boarders a weekend off campus was a thrilling treat. We were so used to rising and eating and studying by a system of bells, of living frugally and tucking into bad food, of almost never enjoying a free moment, that we wallowed in the luxury of turning night into day, drinking dozens of beers and smoking hundreds of cigarettes, of listening to Big Bill Broonzy records and eating hot dogs and hamburgers – and talking. In his *Paris Review* interview thirty years later Tom said I was the first person who'd encouraged him to be a writer.

I wasn't in love with him though he had a raw-boned, hell-raising streak (he was almost suspended several times from Cran-brook) joined to a real artistic courtesy, a knee-buckling sense of humor and a lovelornness evidenced in two superb early novels, *Ninety-two in the Shade* and *Panama*. In a note to him I compared *Panama* to the early novels of Knut Hamsun, a favorite author whom we'd each discovered independently.

I'd loved or lusted after so many of my early friends that sex and romance seemed a necessary concomitant of friendship. Even in fifth grade I'd become friendly with a pretty boy named Camille with whom I would wrestle for hours and hours. I didn't even like wrestling but I longed for his knees to burn into my biceps and for his blue-jeaned crotch to be shoved triumphantly into my face. Once I convinced him to strip down to his underpants in his mother's bedroom (she was at work) but I think we were both a bit discouraged when we looked at our tiny, hairless, erect pre-pubic penises, no bigger than white snails emerging from white shells. Concealed within jeans that smelled of piss they'd seemed, at least potentially, so much bigger.

So many of the boys I liked later when I was in eighth grade wrestled with me. Evanston, city of churches, was full of big lawns and rambling, comfortable wood houses; we'd dive into piles of raked leaves and play squirrel ('grab the nuts and run'); I thought I was the only one who imagined that the pleasure in such a painful game was sexual. When all the other boys, their sweating faces red from the cold and the exertion, drifted away for supper in the faltering twilight, and the air was streaked with the smell of burning leaves, I was still out there shouting, 'What's the matter with you guys? Chicken? Hey, Jerry – your mother!' Sometimes they'd get really mad and in the fallen dark Jerry would chase after me, trip me, pull down my pants and grab my balls and twist. The hand on his own hard-on through the buttoned jeans felt good in a weird, scarcely acknowledged way.

So many of the guys I liked in high school – and who became friends – I first lusted after. The guys with whom I played strip poker. The guys I showered with after swim class. The guy whose ankles I sat on while he did sit-ups. The dark freckled redhead who always sat opposite me during library reading period just after he'd roughhoused with someone. He was sweating profusely with his burnt-hay smell and he pressed my legs between his during the whole hour, three times a week for the entire year, but he never wanted to do more, see me later, alone, behind closed doors. He would clamp his legs like a vice around one of mine while both he and I mimed reading, turning the pages at the regular rhythm and even leaning forward as if to squint at a meaningful passage (but

347

only so that he could nudge his knee a bit farther into my crotch). He'd never catch my eye or smile to himself or lift an eyebrow and above the table we were relaxed, even slightly bored though certainly attentive to our books, whereas out of sight, under the table, our legs clamped, harder and harder, then relaxed, then closed again, and our knees nudged closer and closer to their goal, I by scooting down in my chair until I was virtually supine and he by sitting more and more forward.

Outside the library we were good friends, mainly through Steve, and when I saw the dark redhead with his girlfriend, I wondered if he made out with her all the more passionately on the afternoons following our intense library sessions.

Not that I made the distinction between sexual and amorous or amicable feelings. I may have had strong sexual desires but I didn't long to get laid so much as to love and be loved. I floated on a shining cloud of longing that now turned gray with melancholy and now flushed pink with hope. Every stirring of longing within me was soulful; later, when I would hear older men and women cackle about horny teens I knew how wrong they were. Teenagers do everything out of love.

For a gay youngster in the fifties this amorousness was directed – well, in my case toward couples. I fell in love with a guy and his girl, one couple after another. I gave them advice when they quarreled and acted as the peace broker. I wanted a reconciliation between them so much that sometimes I had tears in my eyes. I also entertained them in the long lulls between bouts of fighting or heavy petting. The girls liked me less than the boys did, but the boys were crazy about me. I was a riot, a laugh a minute and a good egg, not to mention a great guy and smart as a whip. I had learned how to win them over and, if the girls were only mildly amused and longed to be alone again with Butch or Howie or Buster, the guys themselves laughed and stretched their muscled arms above their heads and stroked their own pure necks or chewed attractively on a leaf of grass and shook their curly heads in amazement over so much flattering energy and ingenuity: mine.

Now I'm a bit more reserved and would sooner be at home reading or watching TV, but if I can make young beautiful couples laugh or regale old, famous men with my anecdotes and dotty way of talking (all ellipses and insinuations, childlike piping or matronly swooping) then I will catch fire just as I once did. With this difference: now I can put all of myself into a quip and my painful honesty is the main source of my humor, whereas back then, half a century ago, I could never let on that I was attracted to boys not girls. Now I can be just as funny in French as in English and I have more friends in London than in New York. I'm no longer a kid in a checked shirt doing my soft-shoe routine for high school buddies. Now I'm a massive Edwardian gentleman joking with Martin Amis and Salman Rushdie – but the impulse, or at least the skill, is the same and the state an evening with friends leaves me in is still exhilarating almost to the point of hysteria.

I have had so much time to be me by now that I forget when and from whom I borrowed this laugh or that gasp, this bit of clownishness or that wicked routine, but once – say, twenty years ago – I could still have traced every tic to its origin. Just as my manner is a patchwork of borrowings, in the same way my opinions and ideas have come from my friends as well. Surely there are certain constants that are innate, but they are so abstract and omnipresent, like universals in philosophy, as to be almost unnameable. One of my friends, Adam Mars-Jones, once remarked that he thought I was the least camp person he'd ever known, and he had certainly identified a constant in me: a very American earnestness. I've always read to improve myself, never to kill time, and like our Puritan ancestors I don't drink, smoke, dance or play games of chance, though I came to this sobriety only after I was forty. I don't think in paradoxes, which limber up a system of meanings and make it supple, but rather by questioning the very reality of the subject at hand.

I thrive on complexity and my novels are ambiguous in tone and plot and form and mix genres freely. I suppose what I'm talking about is taste, which in my case is constructed as much out of negations and omissions as it is from assertions. I know what I don't like and work on a novel begins by rejecting a lot of appealing bad ideas.

My taste, probably like everyone's, was assembled out of a hundred chance remarks made by friends who possessed the authority of glamour or conviction or strong personal style or experience.

I met Charles Burch when I was twenty and he thirty; I picked him up in Chicago on the Oak Street Beach. He was reading Alexander Trocchi's *Cain's Book* and I was reading *Lolita*. Charles didn't like Humbert's civilized way of talking, nor his high-culture references, but he did think Lolita as a girl was pretty cool though wasn't it a lapse to have an American girl call an elevator a 'lift'? Charles loved Ezra Pound's 'ear' and swooned over many of his lines; when people brought up his politics Charles just shrugged. Charles liked Pound's repetitions ('drums and kettledrums') and suave eroticisms:

> *Me happy, night, night full of brightness;*
> *Oh couch made happy by my long delectations;*
> *How many words talked out with abundant candles;*
> *Struggles when the lights were taken away;*
> *Now with bared breasts she wrestled against me,*
>   *Tunic spread in delay;*
> *And she then opening my eyelids fallen in sleep,*
> *Her lips upon them; and it was her mouth saying: Sluggard!*

Charles laughed himself sick over William Burroughs's vaudeville routines, Dr. Benway performing an abortion with a toilet plunger. He liked Sarah Vaughn and Miles Davis and Charlie Parker. He disliked what he called 'scrambled egg' jazz. He liked Italian tailoring, disliked overly clever advertising, and intermittently looked up to the Catholic Church, not because it was right but because it was old. He liked the way Catholics expressed their beliefs in beautiful language about the eternal verities – the sacredness of a human life, the indissoluble bond between a man and a woman. He liked whatever was beautiful. He lived for art and love, and so would I.

When we're young we imitate our older friends and adopt wholesale their beliefs and quirks and wisecracks. If our friends are very different from each other – as my friends Marilyn and Charles were – then we synthesize their values. One of the great debates of the sixties was between politics and art and Marilyn argued various positions with passion and acuity over the years. There were moments when she felt art – what it meant to the artist, what it could do for its audience – was trivial compared to the smallest political advance. She was willing to abolish art altogether if women could receive equal pay for equal work. She placed crafts on the same level as the high arts, but this 'democratization of the arts' was a cause quickly embraced by philistines and we all fled it.

I suppose every young artist is trying to hammer out an aesthetic, as well as a justification for his activity, and Marilyn and Charles and I struggled over every aspect of the question. Finally I kept returning to those painters who brought me pleasure (Matisse and Bonnard) and those writers who made me swoon (Colette and Chekhov and Nabokov) and to Balanchine in dance and Ravel and Stravinsky in music. This list took precedence over any theoretical pose I might strike. It reminded me that what I really liked in art was entertainment, if what was being entertained was the mind as well as the parts of the spirit and body that register pleasure.

One of the things we treasure in a friend is that he should get us and see us in the proportions that truly exist. I'm ironic but never uniformly or exclusively so, and people who see me as an ironist make me nervous. I can be bawdy but I detest vulgarity – anything that suggests sex is not a mystery but rather a cozy, funny pastime. My true friends share my feeling of being a tourist on earth, a visitor dropping in on life, whereas vulgar people use dirty jokes to suggest they're on intimate, even dismissive terms with the great mysteries. That must be a goal: to be worldly without being blasé, to be innocent without being naïve – to know everything and to take nothing for granted, to know the value of everything and the price of nothing.

In my middle years my great friend was David Kalstone, a professor of English who fell in love with me. I wasn't attracted to him and much as I tried to unbend nothing worked. I was impotent with him; I placed my unresponsive body at his disposal, handed over to him, the dearest person in the world, my unco-operative penis. I wanted him to see that my failure to be his lover had nothing to do with a lack of willingness.

It took two years to get past this painful imbalance of sentiments, but once we did our friendship flourished. I'd never paid much attention to poetry but when I met him David was writing a book about five 'temperaments' including James Merrill and John

Ashbery, who both became touchstones of value and exaltation for me. (The others were Robert Lowell, Adrienne Rich and Elizabeth Bishop.) Merrill was alive and well in Stonington, Connecticut, and after 1980 in Key West. David and I visited Merrill in Stonington, a whole intensely observed world, and as full as Mt. Olympus with mortals whom Merrill had deified by writing about them.

In New York David and I would drink wine and lethal stingers and then read Merrill's poems out loud to each other and comment upon them. He found so much in each poem! I had no idea what close reading could be until I met David. Once as a joke he taped our conversation and played it back the next day – when I heard my drunken braying, my slurred pretentiousness, I was mortified. It was only a few years later that I decided to stop drinking forever; I had to silence all that empty alcoholic opining.

David was a great Venetian. He lived moderately in New York during the year, taking the cheap bus rather than the expensive train out to Rutgers where he taught, serving pasta rather than a roast, but in June he'd migrate to Venice and rent the top floor of the Palazzo Barbaro and I'd join him in July. I was always poor in those years, but David would arrange for me to interview Peggy Guggenheim for a glossy magazine or he'd convince James Merrill's foundation, a front for Merrill's personal generosity, to award me a six-thousand-dollar grant. David and I were always on a diet and in Venice we'd eat a salad and slices of prosciutto and bits of fontina for lunch before he'd head out for the Cipriani pool.

I met a big-featured, sandy-haired Venetian servant named Giuliano who slept with me in my room until I felt David growing jealous. I suggested to Giuliano that he might spend the next night with the *Professore*, and they emerged from their room the following morning as lovers. David always called Giuliano *il tesoro*, 'the treasure,' and saw him for many years to come. As a servant and cook for an old man in the Veneto, Giuliano had strong ideas about what's done and not done in the kitchen. If we'd invite Peggy for dinner Giuliano would add so many old-fashioned flourishes to the food that 'Davide' would howl with rage. The '*Principessa*' had to be served a proper veal roast and not a pasta *arrabbiata* and the *macedonia di frutta* had to be floated in a frothy local champagne.

David, who worried about culinary overkill, would be grumbling the whole time.

Although David and Giuliano had a final falling out, for years they saw each other every summer – and David could eat his fill sexually. He no longer felt deprived. Nor did Giuliano hustle him. He was happy to have such a distinguished lover and a home base on the Grand Canal and someone he could twitter with in the kitchen and dominate in the pink bedroom hung with ancient, discolored mirrors. Giuliano was happy to take all of David's castoffs and once, when we visited Giuliano's mother's house on the mainland, we found it furnished with all that flotsam; her house was our Sargasso Sea.

David could barely see, another reason he loved Venice, since there were no cars to fear. The steps were outlined in white stones and he could ricochet through the intestinal tract of that very serene city. He was so shortsighted he was always doffing his hat to imaginary countesses – in truth nothing but a flurry of laundry blowing on a line or a swarm of white cats circling a bowl on a ledge behind a blue convolvulus.

For us Venice was a Proustian world of titles and tales, of vacuous society chatter and half-erased anecdotes. If we received the Franchins we wouldn't be admitted to the Franchettis. David and I would dissolve into laughter with our parodies of proper Venetian housewives. He would accompany Peggy in the gondola (the last private gondola in Venice) and read *The Wings of the Dove* to her for the third time. He spent a small fortune on a tailor-made black linen suit lined in red silk ('Priest without, cardinal within,' Giuliano said).

David was superb at maneuvering his way in the world. He always got the highest raises, the best addresses, the choicest seat at the opera. He gave me expert advice on how to advance my career as a novelist. He even helped me as a public speaker by teaching me that if someone asks a trick question, all you need to do is to rephrase it into something you can answer. In private he was a ditherer but in public unflappable.

I loved David for his mind – so delicate and subtle – but his whole way of life I loved even more. We talked to each other twice a day and saw each other once a week. A friend is someone who shares your life, who cares about the results of your dental examinations and detests the ex-lover who rejected you so cruelly. David and I went to the ballet constantly; whereas I cared only about Balanchine's choreography, he was, characteristically, besotted by the dancers. Eventually the sheer warmth of his ardor led him into a friendship with Suzanne Farrell, the greatest ballerina of the day. David used to say that a race as contentious as New Yorkers could only have agreed to admire a nonverbal art form.

A clear glass bowl of yellow freesias, a pot of Hu-Kwa tea, a rustling silk dressing gown, the *New York Review* plundered and scattered on a yellow couch under a cool blue William Bailey painting of three perfect eggs, the sound of Maria Callas in a mad scene and of the phone ringing constantly – this was the feel of a morning at David's. Insecure and distractable, he wrote with glacial slowness – a book about Sir Philip Sidney and *Five Temperaments*. But everything he wrote set the standard and his posthumous work on Elizabeth Bishop was the first of hundreds of subsequent books; he helped to establish her as the greatest American poet after Wallace Stevens.

He was such fun! He'd call up and pretend to be a fourteen-year-old Chinese who had just read *The Joy of Gay Sex* and wanted to meet the author to try out some of the more strenuous positions with him. He'd play four-hand piano with a friend, performing Fauré's *Dolly Suite*, or show me the photos he'd just developed of our evening at La Fenice. He was as warm and hypochondriacal as the father in a Victorian novel, as observant as Proust; his guffawing mime and description of the gloomy Romanian aphorist Cioran eating periwinkles with a straight pin in a Paris café was a classic.

Of course I could never corner the market on a great charmer like David. If he was my best friend he was also the best friend of half a dozen other people; when David died in 1986 from AIDS his memorial ceremony in the Trustees Room at the 42nd Street Library was virtually a state occasion and each eulogy, painfully eloquent in a room full of writers, was also an act of possessiveness: I knew him better than you did. With me he was funnier and even more civilized than with you.

To be sure, friends also fight and disputes have thinned out the ranks of people I see. After sixty you feel you are recounting the nine hundredth of the thousand and one tales you have been allotted to tell and a new friend will never catch up. Better to meet some breezy kid who has no idea who you are; Tennessee Williams used to say, 'My type has never heard of me.' And yet for me friends still mark the rhythm of my days and convince me it's still worthwhile to stoke the mechanism and produce certain lifelike gestures. A few of my friends, such as the man to whom I have dedicated this book, constitute my audience. Joyce Carol Oates and I teach together at Princeton and we talk on the phone two or three times a week and try to see each other every ten days or so. Recently she told an audience, 'My friend and colleague Edmund White told everyone he was gay in the 1950s when even straight people were still in the closet.' Inspired by her example I've become a more prolific writer and a more various one, willing to try on different genres, though unlike her I haven't yet attempted children's books or books about boxing or mysteries. Of course her productivity is phenomenal, but what I prize in her is her world-class intelligence, her wryness and her clear-eyed but forgiving vision into the hearts of other people. She has too much energy; she's always jogging up and down the halls at Princeton or in between buildings while I trudge exhausted and breathless up a single flight of stairs. As quick as a dragonfly, Joyce neglects nothing – she's an ambitious hostess, a devoted teacher, an observant friend and a towering writer. Nor can she resist a single invitation; she's always off to give a reading in Normal, Illinois.

One friend is so dear to me I've never been able to write about her – Marie-Claude de Brunhoff. I met her in 1974 in New York but we didn't become close until 1983 when I moved to Paris. Soon after that her husband left her for a younger American woman and Marie-Claude was so devastated that I pitched in as her *chevalier servant*, hand-holder and resident writer, for she's always had writers in her salon (Georges Perec, Julio Cortázar). I was able to cheer her up and she introduced me to the whole Left Bank – editors, writers, translators, an entire intellectual métier. She reads three books a day and remembers them all. Sometimes I'll call and she'll say, 'I'm in Peru' or 'The Medicis are murdering each other. Last week the Swedes and the Russians were at each other's throats.'

But most of all we have become family members and we care about each other as siblings do. We call each other from one continent to another and talk each other through terrible doubts and dark days. When my French lover Hubert died Marie-Claude met me at my apartment with her nightgown and toothbrush in her bag. She was there. She will always be there, as I will be for her. Sometimes I must get on her nerves (that happens in families) but we are witnesses to each other's life. Even so, I imagine this odd memoir will contain several surprises for her. At least I hope so. Being predictable is the one unforgivable sin in a friend.

ACKNOWLEDGMENTS

I would like to acknowledge the sympathy and understanding (and expert help) I received from my editors in England and the States, Rosemary Davidson and Dan Halpern. I would specially like to thank Liz Calder for believing in this project when no one else did.

My American agent, Amanda Urban, has had a wonderfully generous hands-on approach to this book, which is entirely a matter of tone and voice; she has often intervened at the right moment, though mistakes of taste or judgment should not be blamed on her (I didn't always follow her advice, just most of the time). In England Deborah Rogers, my agent, has showered me with affection and attention as she has for so many years.

Parts of this book have appeared in magazines and reviews and I'd like to thank the editors for working on the manuscript, including Deborah Triesman of *The New Yorker*, Ian Jack of *Granta*, Richard Burgin of *Boulevard* and Ray Smith of *Ontario Review*.

Finally I want to thank friends who heard bits of this book as I worked on it, especially Joyce Carol Oates, my muse. As always, I owe everything to Michael Carroll, my partner for the last ten years, who hears every word I write almost as soon as I've written it.

Edmund White

Michael Carroll, my partner since 1995.